Getting Started with LibreOffice 6.0

by
LibreOffice Documentation Team

Copyright

Contributors

This book is adapted and updated from *Getting Started with OpenOffice.org 3.3*.

To this edition

Andrew Jensen	Amanda Labby	Cathy Crumbley
Dan Lewis	Dave Barton	Jean Hollis Weber
Jorge Rodriguez	Olivier Hallot	Paul Figueiredo

To previous editions

Agnes Belzunce	Alan Madden	Alex Thurgood
Alexander Noël Dunne	Andrew Jensen	Andrew Pitonyak
Barbara M. Tobias	Carol Roberts	Chris Bonde
Claire Wood	Dan Lewis	Daniel Carrera
Dave Koelmeyer	David Michel	Gary Schnabl
Hazel Russman	Iain Roberts	Ian Laurenson
Janet M. Swisher	Jean Hollis Weber	Jared Kobos
Jeremy Cartwright	JiHui Choi	Jim Taylor
Joe Sellman	John A Smith	John Kane
Kevin O'Brien	Laurent Duperval	Leo Moons
Linda Worthington	Magnus Adielsson	Martin Fox
Martin Saffron	Michael Kotsarinis	Michel Pinquier
Michele Zarri	Miklos Vajna	Nicole Cairns
Olivier Hallot	Peter Hillier-Brook	Peter Kupfer
Peter Schofield	Rachel Kartch	Regina Henschel
Richard Barnes	Richard Detwiler	Richard Holt
Robert Scott	Ron Faile Jr.	Simon Quigley
Spencer E. Harpe	Stefan A. Keel	Steve Schwettman
Thomas Astleitner	TJ Frazier	Valerii Goncharuk

Feedback

Please direct any comments or suggestions about this document to the Documentation Team's mailing list: documentation@global.libreoffice.org

 Note

> Everything you send to a mailing list, including your email address and any other personal information that is written in the message, is publicly archived and cannot be deleted.

Publication date and software version

Published September 17, 2018. Based on LibreOffice 6.0.

Publisher

Friends of OpenDocument, Inc.
544/60 Beck Drive North, Condon, QLD 4815, Australia
ISBN 978-1-921320-54-5

Documentation for LibreOffice is available at https://documentation.libreoffice.org/en/english-documentation/

Contents

Getting Started Guide

Preface

Who is this book for?

Anyone who wants to get up to speed quickly with LibreOffice will find this Getting Started Guide valuable. You may be new to office software, or you may be familiar with another office suite.

What's in this book?

This book introduces the main components of LibreOffice:

- Writer (word processing)
- Calc (spreadsheets)
- Impress (presentations)
- Draw (vector graphics)
- Base (database)
- Math (equation editor)

It also covers some of the features common to all components, including setup and customization, styles and templates, macro recording, and printing. For more detail, see the user guides for the individual components.

Where to get more help

This book, the other LibreOffice user guides, the built-in Help system, and user support systems assume that you are familiar with your computer and basic functions such as starting a program, opening and saving files.

Help system

LibreOffice comes with an extensive Help system. This is the first line of support for using LibreOffice. Windows and Linux users can choose to download and install the offline Help for use when not connected to the Internet; the offline Help is installed with the program on macOS.

To display the Help system, press *F1* or select **LibreOffice Help > LibreOffice Help** from the Help menu. If you do not have the offline help installed on your computer and you are connected to the Internet, your default browser will open the online Help pages on the LibreOffice website.

The Help menu includes links to other LibreOffice information and support facilities.

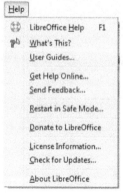

Figure 1: The Help Menu

Note

The following options shown here prefixed by a ‡ sign are only accessible if your computer is connected to the Internet.

- **What's This?** For quick tips when a toolbar is visible, place the mouse pointer over any of the icons to see a small box ("tooltip") with a brief explanation of the icon's function. For a more detailed explanation, select **Help > What's This?** and hold the pointer over the icon. In addition, you can choose whether to activate Extended Tips using **Tools > Options > LibreOffice > General**.

- **User Guides** ‡ Opens your default browser at the Documentation page of the LibreOffice website https://documentation.libreoffice.org/en/english-documentation/. There you will find copies of User Guides and other useful information.

- **Get Help Online** ‡ Opens your default browser at the Ask LibreOffice forum of questions and answers from the LibreOffice community https://ask.libreoffice.org/en/questions/.

- **Send Feedback** ‡ Opens your default browser at the Feedback page of the LibreOffice website https://www.libreoffice.org/get-help/feedback/. From there you can report bugs, suggest new features and communicate with others in the LibreOffice community.

- **Restart in Safe Mode** Opens a dialog window where you will have the option to restart LibreOffice and reset the software to it's default settings.

- **Donate to LibreOffice** ‡ Opens your default browser at the Donation page of the LibreOffice website https://donate.libreoffice.org/. There you can choose to make a donation to support LibreOffice.

- **License Information** outlining the licenses under which LibreOffice is made available.

- **Check for Updates** ‡ Opens a dialog window and checks the LibreOffice website for updates to your version of the software.

- **About LibreOffice** Opens a dialog window and displays information about the version of LibreOffice and the operating system you are using. This information will often be requested if you ask the community for help or assistance with the software.

Other free online support

The LibreOffice community not only develops software, but provides free, volunteer-based support. In addition to the Help menu links above, there are other online community support options available, see the table below.

Free LibreOffice support	
FAQs	Answers to frequently asked questions https://wiki.documentfoundation.org/Faq
Mailing lists	Free community support is provided by a network of experienced users https://www.libreoffice.org/get-help/mailing-lists/
Native language support	The LibreOffice website in various languages https://www.libreoffice.org/community/nlc/ Mailing lists for native languages https://wiki.documentfoundation.org/Local_Mailing_Lists Information about social networking https://wiki.documentfoundation.org/Website/Web_Sites_services
Accessibility options	Information about available accessibility options https://www.libreoffice.org/get-help/accessibility/
OpenOffice Forum	Another forum that provides support for LibreOffice, among other open source office suites http://forum.openoffice.org/en/forum/

Paid support and training

You can also pay for support through service contracts from a vendor or consulting firm specializing in LibreOffice. For information about certified professional support, see The Document Foundation's website: https://www.documentfoundation.org/gethelp/support/

What you see may be different

Illustrations

LibreOffice runs on Windows, Linux, and macOS operating systems, each of which has several versions and can be customized by users (fonts, colors, themes, window managers). The illustrations in this guide were taken from a variety of computers and operating systems. Therefore, some illustrations will not look exactly like what you see on your computer display.

Also, some of the dialogs may be different because of the settings selected in LibreOffice. You can either use dialogs from your computer's operating system or from LibreOffice. The differences affect mainly Open, Save, and Print dialogs. To change which dialogs are used, go to **Tools > Options > LibreOffice > General** and select or deselect the option **Use LibreOffice dialogs**.

Icons

The LibreOffice community has created icons for several icon sets: Breeze, Galaxy, High Contrast, Oxygen, Sifr, and Tango. Each user can select a preferred set. The icons in this guide have been taken from a variety of LibreOffice installations that use different sets of icons. The icons for some of the many tools available in LibreOffice may then differ from the ones used in this guide.

To change the icon set used, go to **Tools > Options > LibreOffice > View**. In the **User Interface** section, choose from the drop-down lists under **Icon size and style**.

 Note

> Some Linux distributions include **LibreOffice** as part of the installation and may not include all the icon sets mentioned above. You should be able to download other icon sets from the software repository for your Linux distribution if you wish to use them.

Using LibreOffice on macOS

Some keystrokes and menu items are different on macOS from those used in Windows and Linux. The table below gives some common substitutions for the instructions in this book. For a more detailed list, see the application Help.

Windows or Linux	macOS equivalent	Effect
Tools > Options menu selection	LibreOffice > Preferences	Access setup options
Right-click	Control+click and/or right-click depending on computer setup	Open a context menu
Ctrl (Control)	⌘ (Command)	Used with other keys
F5	Shift+⌘+F5	Open the Navigator
F11	⌘+T	Open the sidebar Styles and Formatting deck

What are all these things called?

The terms used in LibreOffice for most parts of the user interface (the parts of the program you see and use, in contrast to the behind-the-scenes code that actually makes it work) are the same as for most other programs.

A dialog is a special type of window. Its purpose is to inform you of something, or request input from you, or both. It provides controls to use to specify how to carry out an action. The technical names for common controls are shown in Figure 2. In most cases the technical terms are not used in this book, but it is useful to know them because the Help and other sources of information often use them.

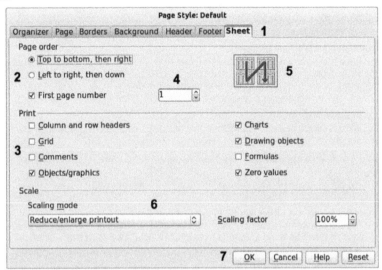

Figure 2: Dialog showing common controls

1) Tabbed page (not strictly speaking a control).
2) Radio buttons (only one can be selected at a time).
3) Checkbox (more than one can be selected at a time).
4) Spin box (click the up and down arrows to change the number shown in the text box next to it, or type in the text box).
5) Thumbnail or preview.
6) Drop-down list from which to select an item.
7) Push buttons.

In most cases, you can interact only with the dialog (not the document itself) as long as the dialog remains open. When you close the dialog after use (usually, clicking **OK** or another button saves your changes and closes the dialog), then you can again work with your document.

Some dialogs can be left open as you work, so you can switching back and forth between the dialog and the document. An example of this type is the Find & Replace dialog.

Frequently asked questions

How is LibreOffice licensed?

LibreOffice is distributed under the Open Source Initiative (OSI) approved Mozilla Public License (MPL). See https://www.libreoffice.org/about-us/licenses/

It is based on code from Apache OpenOffice made available under the Apache License 2.0 but also includes software that differs from version to version under a variety of other Open Source licenses. New code is available under LGPL 3.0 and MPL 2.0.

May I distribute LibreOffice to anyone? May I sell it? May I use it in my business?

Yes.

How many computers may I install it on?

As many as you like.

Is LibreOffice available in my language?

LibreOffice has been translated (localized) into over 40 languages, so your language probably is supported. Additionally, there are over 70 spelling, hyphenation, and thesaurus dictionaries available for languages, and dialects that do not have a localized program interface. The dictionaries are available from the LibreOffice website at: www.libreoffice.org.

How can you make it for free?

LibreOffice is developed and maintained by volunteers and has the backing of several organizations.

I am writing a software application. May I use programming code from LibreOffice in my program?

You may, within the parameters set in the MPL and/or LGPL. Read the licenses: http://www.mozilla.org/MPL/2.0/.

Why do I need Java to run LibreOffice? Is it written in Java?

LibreOffice is not written in Java; it is written in the C++ language. Java is one of several languages that can be used to extend the software. The Java JDK/JRE is only required for some features. The most notable one is the HSQLDB relational database engine.

Java is available at no cost. More information and download links to the appropriate edition for your operating system can be found at: https://java.com/en/download/manual.jsp

 Note

> If you want to use LibreOffice features that require Java it is important that the correct 32 bit or 64 bit edition matches the installed version of LibreOffice. See the Advanced Options in Chapter 2 of this guide. If you do not want to use Java, you can still use nearly all of the LibreOffice features.

How can I contribute to LibreOffice?

You can help with the development and user support of LibreOffice in many ways, and you do not need to be a programmer. To start, check out this webpage: https://www.libreoffice.org/community/get-involved/

May I distribute the PDF of this book, or print and sell copies?

Yes, as long as you meet the requirements of one of the licenses in the copyright statement at the beginning of this book. You do not have to request special permission. We request that you share with the project some of the profits you make from sales of books, in consideration of all the work we have put into producing them.

Donate to LibreOffice: https://www.libreoffice.org/donate/

What's new in LibreOffice 6.0?

The LibreOffice 6.0 Release Notes are here:
https://wiki.documentfoundation.org/ReleaseNotes/6.0

Getting Started Guide

Chapter 1
Introducing LibreOffice

What is LibreOffice?

LibreOffice is a freely available, fully-featured office productivity suite. Its native file format is Open Document Format (ODF), an open standard format that is being adopted by governments worldwide as a required file format for publishing and accepting documents. LibreOffice can also open and save documents in many other formats, including those used by several versions of Microsoft Office.

LibreOffice includes the following components.

Writer (word processor)

Writer is a feature-rich tool for creating letters, books, reports, newsletters, brochures, and other documents. You can insert graphics and objects from other components into Writer documents. Writer can export files to HTML, XHTML, XML, Adobe Portable Document Format (PDF), and several versions of Microsoft Word files. It also connects to your email client.

Calc (spreadsheet)

Calc has all of the advanced analysis, charting, and decision making features expected from a high-end spreadsheet. It includes over 300 functions for financial, statistical, and mathematical operations, among others. The Scenario Manager provides "what if" analysis. Calc generates 2D and 3D charts, which can be integrated into other LibreOffice documents. You can also open and work with Microsoft Excel workbooks and save them in Excel format. Calc can also export spreadsheets in several formats, including for example Comma Separated Value (CSV), Adobe PDF and HTML formats.

Impress (presentations)

Impress provides all the common multimedia presentation tools, such as special effects, animation, and drawing tools. It is integrated with the advanced graphics capabilities of LibreOffice Draw and Math components. Slideshows can be further enhanced using Fontwork special effects text, as well as sound and video clips. Impress is compatible with Microsoft PowerPoint file format and can also save your work in numerous graphics formats.

Draw (vector graphics)

Draw is a vector drawing tool that can produce everything from simple diagrams or flowcharts to 3D artwork. Its Smart Connectors feature allows you to define your own connection points. You can use Draw to create drawings for use in any of the LibreOffice components, and you can create your own clip art and then add it to the Gallery. Draw can import graphics from many common formats and save them in over 20 formats, including PNG, HTML and PDF.

Base (database)

Base provides tools for day-to-day database work within a simple interface. It can create and edit forms, reports, queries, tables, views, and relations, so that managing a relational database is much the same as in other popular database applications. Base provides many new features, such as the ability to analyze and edit relationships from a diagram view. Base incorporates two relational database engines, HSQLDB and PostgreSQL. It can also use dBASE, Microsoft Access, MySQL, or Oracle, or any ODBC compliant or JDBC compliant database. Base also provides support for a subset of ANSI-92 SQL.

Math (formula editor)

Math is the LibreOffice formula or equation editor. You can use it to create complex equations that include symbols or characters not available in standard font sets. While it is most commonly used to create formulas in other documents, such as Writer and Impress files, Math can also work as a standalone tool. You can save formulas in the standard Mathematical Markup Language (MathML) format for inclusion in web pages and other documents not created by LibreOffice.

Advantages of LibreOffice

Here are some of the advantages of LibreOffice over other office suites:

- **No licensing fees**. LibreOffice is free for anyone to use and distribute at no cost. Many features that are available as extra cost add-ins in other office suites (like PDF export) are free with LibreOffice. There are no hidden charges now or in the future.
- **Open source.** You can distribute, copy, and modify the software as much as you wish, in accordance with the LibreOffice Open Source licenses.
- **Cross-platform.** LibreOffice runs on several hardware architectures and under multiple operating systems, such as Microsoft Windows, Mac OS X and Linux.
- **Extensive language support**. The LibreOffice user interface, including spelling, hyphenation, and thesaurus dictionaries, is available in over 100 languages and dialects. LibreOffice also provides support for both Complex Text Layout (CTL) and Right to Left (RTL) layout languages (such as Urdu, Hebrew, and Arabic).
- **Consistent user interface.** All the components have a similar "look and feel," making them easy to use and master.
- **Integration.** The components of LibreOffice are well integrated with one another.
  - All the components share a common spelling checker and other tools, which are used consistently across the suite. For example, the drawing tools available in Writer are also found in Calc, with similar but enhanced versions in Impress and Draw.
  - You do not need to know which application was used to create a particular file. For example, you can open a Draw file from Writer.
- **Granularity.** Usually, if you change an option, it affects all components. However, LibreOffice options can be set at a component level or even at document level.
- **File compatibility.** In addition to its native OpenDocument formats, LibreOffice includes support for opening and saving files in many common formats including Microsoft Office, HTML, XML, WordPerfect, Lotus 1-2-3, and PDF.
- **No vendor lock-in.** LibreOffice uses OpenDocument, an XML (eXtensible Markup Language) file format developed as an industry standard by OASIS (Organization for the Advancement of Structured Information Standards). These files can easily be unzipped and read by any text editor, and their framework is open and published.
- **You have a voice.** Enhancements, software fixes, and release dates are community-driven. You can join the community and affect the course of the product you use.

You can read more about LibreOffice and The Document Foundation on their websites at http://www.libreoffice.org/ and http://www.documentfoundation.org/.

Minimum requirements

LibreOffice 6.0 requires one of the following operating systems:

- **Microsoft Windows:** Windows Server 2008, Windows 7, Windows 8/8.1, Windows Server 2012, or Windows 10.
- **GNU/Linux** Kernel version 2.6.18, glibc2 v2.5 or higher, and gtk v2.10.4 or higher
- **Mac OS X** 10.8 (Mountain Lion) or higher

Administrator rights are needed for the installation process.

Some LibreOffice features (wizards and the HSQLDB database engine) require that the Java Runtime Environment (JRE) is installed on your computer. Although LibreOffice will work without Java support, some features will not be available.

Java is available at no cost. More information and download links to the appropriate edition for your operating system can be found at: https://java.com/en/download/manual.jsp

 Note

> If you want to use LibreOffice features that require Java it is important that the correct 32 bit or 64 bit edition matches the installed version of LibreOffice. See the Advanced Options in Chapter 2 of this guide.

For a more detailed listing of requirements, see the LibreOffice website, http://www.libreoffice.org/get-help/system-requirements/.

How to get the software

Versions of LibreOffice for Windows, Linux, and Mac OS X can be downloaded free from http://www.libreoffice.org/download. You can also download the software by using a Peer-to-Peer client, such as BitTorrent, at the same address.

Linux users will also find LibreOffice included in many of the latest Linux distributions; Ubuntu is just one example.

macOS users can also get two versions of LibreOffice from the App Store: LibreOffice Vanilla (small fee) and LibreOffice-from-Collabora (an enterprise-ready version; small fee).

How to install the software

Information on installing and setting up LibreOffice on the various supported operating systems is given here: http://www.libreoffice.org/get-help/install-howto/.

Extensions and add-ons

Extensions and add-ons are available to enhance LibreOffice. Several extensions are installed with the program and you can get others from the official extensions repository, http://extensions.libreoffice.org/. See *Chapter 14, Customizing LibreOffice* for more information on installing extensions and add-ons.

Starting LibreOffice

In general, you start LibreOffice the same way you start any other program on your computer.

On computers with Windows or Linux operating systems, a menu entry for LibreOffice and each LibreOffice component appears in the system menu of your computer. On computers operating macOS, only a menu entry for LibreOffice is added to the Applications menu.

Clicking on the LibreOffice menu entry, desktop icon, or tile opens the LibreOffice Start Center (Figure 3) from where you can select the individual components of LibreOffice. You can also select to open an existing file or use a template.

Opening an existing document before starting LibreOffice

You can start LibreOffice by double-clicking the filename of an ODF document on the desktop, or in a file manager such as Windows Explorer or the Mac's Finder. The appropriate component of LibreOffice will start and the document will be loaded.

You can also open files stored in remote servers running Content Management Interoperability Services (CMIS). CMIS, like OpenDocument Format, is an OASIS standard. When using CMIS servers, the service will ask you for the necessary credentials for file access.

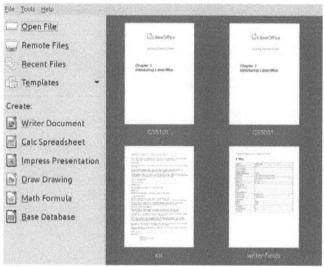

Figure 3: LibreOffice Start Center

If you do not have Microsoft Office installed on your computer, or if Microsoft Office is installed but you have associated Microsoft Office file types with LibreOffice, then when you double-click on the following files, they open in LibreOffice:

- A Word file (*.doc or *.docx) opens in Writer.
- An Excel file (*.xls or *.xlsx) opens in Calc.
- A PowerPoint file (*.ppt or *.pptx) opens in Impress.

If you did not associate the file types and Microsoft Office is installed on your computer, then when you double-click on a Microsoft Office file, it opens using the appropriate Microsoft Office component.

For more information on opening files, see "Opening existing documents" on page 28.

Quickstarter

When LibreOffice is installed on computers running Windows or Linux, a Quickstarter feature may also be installed. When Quickstarter is activated, the necessary library files are loaded when the computer system is started, resulting in a shorter startup time for LibreOffice components.

Computers with macOS do not have a Quickstarter.

Activating Quickstarter

On a computer using Linux or Windows operating systems, the default installation of LibreOffice does not set the Quickstarter to load automatically. To activate it:

1) Open LibreOffice.
2) Go to **Tools > Options > LibreOffice > General** on the Menu bar and select *Load LibreOffice during system start-up (if using Windows) or select Enable systray Quickstarter (if using Linux)*.
3) Close and restart LibreOffice to have Quickstarter appear.

Using Quickstarter on Linux or Windows

After Quickstarter has been activated, an icon 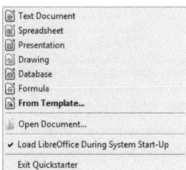 is installed into the system tray at the bottom of the display. Quickstarter is then available at all times, whether LibreOffice is open or not.

To start a LibreOffice component directly by using Quickstarter:

1) Right-click the **Quickstarter** icon in the system tray to open a pop-up menu (Figure 4).
2) Select the LibreOffice component you want to open to create a new document, or select **From Template** to open the Template Manager, or select **Open Document** to open an existing document.

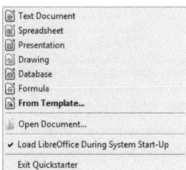

Figure 4: Quickstarter menu in Windows

Disabling Quickstarter

To temporarily close Quickstarter on a computer using a Windows operating system, right-click on the **Quickstarter** icon in the system tray and select **Exit Quickstarter** in the pop-up menu. However, when the computer is restarted, Quickstarter will be loaded again.

To prevent the Quickstarter from loading during system startup, do one of the following:

- Right-click on the **Quickstarter** icon and deselect **Load LibreOffice during system start-up** on the pop-up menu (on Windows) or select **Disable systray Quickstarter** (on Linux).
- Go to **Tools > Options > LibreOffice > General** on the Menu bar and deselect **Load LibreOffice during system start-up** (on Windows) or deselect **Enable systray Quickstarter** on Linux.

Reactivating Quickstarter

If Quickstarter has been disabled, you can reactivate it by using the instructions given in "Activating Quickstarter" above.

Parts of the main window

The main window is similar for each component of LibreOffice, although some details vary. See the relevant chapters in this guide about Writer, Calc, Draw, and Impress for descriptions of those details.

Common features include the Menu bar, standard toolbar, and formatting toolbar at the top of the window and the status bar at the bottom.

Menu bar

The *Menu bar* is located across the top of the LibreOffice window, just below the title bar. When you select one of the menus listed below, a sub-menu drops down to show commands. Below is the case for Writer:

- **File** – contains commands that apply to the entire document such as Open, Save, and Export as PDF.
- **Edit** – contains commands for editing the document such as Undo, Find & Replace, Cut, Copy, and Paste.
- **View** – contains commands for controlling the display of the document such as Zoom and Web Layout.
- **Insert** – contains commands for inserting elements into your document such as Header, Footer, and Image.
- **Format** – contains commands for formatting the layout of your document.
- **Styles** – contains commands for quickly applying common styles; for editing, loading, and creating new styles; and for accessing the Styles and Formatting section of the Sidebar.
- **Table** – contains commands to insert and edit a table in a text document.
- **Tools** – contains functions such as Spelling and Grammar, AutoCorrect, Customize, and Options.
- **Window** – contains commands for the display window.
- **Help** – contains links to the LibreOffice Help file, What's This?, and information about the program.

Toolbars

LibreOffice has two types of toolbars: docked (fixed in place) and floating. Docked toolbars can be moved to different locations or made to float, and floating toolbars can be docked.

In a default LibreOffice installation, the top docked toolbar, just under the Menu bar, is called the *Standard* toolbar. It is consistent across the LibreOffice applications.

The second toolbar at the top, in a default LibreOffice installation, is the *Formatting* bar. It is context-sensitive; that is, it shows the tools relevant to the current position of the cursor or the object selected. For example, when the cursor is on a graphic, the Formatting bar provides tools for formatting graphics; when the cursor is in text, the tools are for formatting text.

In some cases it is convenient to reduce the number of toolbars displayed and get more space for the document. LibreOffice provides a single-toolbar alternative to the default double-toolbar setup. It contains the most-used commands. To activate it, enable **View > Toolbars > Standard (Single Mode)** and disable **View > Toolbars > Standard** and **View > Toolbars > Formatting**.

Displaying or hiding toolbars

To display or hide toolbars, go to **View > Toolbars** on the Menu bar, then click on the name of a toolbar from the drop-down list. An active toolbar shows a check-mark beside its name. Toolbars created from tool palettes are not listed in the View menu.

To close a toolbar go to **View > Toolbars** on the Menu bar and deselect the toolbar, or right-click in an empty space between the icons on a toolbar and select **Close toolbar** from the context menu.

Sub-menus and tool palettes

Toolbar icons with a small triangle to the right will display *sub-menus*, *tool palettes*, and alternative methods of selecting items, depending on the icon.

Tool palettes can be made into a floating toolbar. Figure 5 shows an example of a tool palette from the Drawing toolbar made into a floating toolbar. See "Moving toolbars" and "Floating toolbars" below for more information on moving and floating these toolbars created from tool palettes.

Figure 5: Example of tearing off a tool palette

Moving toolbars

Docked toolbars can be undocked and moved to a new docked position or left as a floating toolbar.

1) Move the mouse cursor over the toolbar handle, which is the small vertical bar to the left of a docked toolbar and highlighted in Figure 6.

2) Hold down the left mouse button and drag the toolbar to the new location. The toolbar can be docked in a new position at the top, sides or bottom of the main window, or left as a floating toolbar.

3) Release the mouse button.

To move a floating toolbar, click on its title bar and drag it to a new floating location or dock the toolbar at the top or bottom of the main window.

Figure 6: Toolbar handles

Floating toolbars

LibreOffice includes several additional toolbars, whose default setting appear as floating toolbars in response to the current position of the cursor or selection. You can dock these toolbars to the top or bottom of the main window, or reposition them on your computer display (see "Moving toolbars" above).

Some of these additional toolbars are context sensitive and will automatically appear depending on the position of the cursor. For example, when the cursor is in a table, a *Table* toolbar appears, and when the cursor is in a numbered or bullet list, the *Bullets and Numbering* toolbar appears.

Customizing toolbars

You can customize toolbars in several ways, including choosing which icons are visible and locking the position of a docked toolbar. You can also add icons and create new toolbars, as described in *Chapter 14 Customizing LibreOffice*. To access the customization options for a toolbar, right-click in an empty space between the icons on a toolbar to open a context menu as follows:

- To show or hide icons defined for the selected toolbar, click **Visible Buttons**. Visible icons on a toolbar are indicated by an outline around the icon (Figure 7) or by a check mark beside the icon, depending on your operating system. Select or deselect icons to hide or show them on the toolbar.

Figure 7: Selection of visible toolbar icons

- Click **Customize Toolbar** to open the Customize dialog; See *Chapter 14 Customizing LibreOffice* for more information.
- Click **Dock Toolbar** to dock the selected floating toolbar. By default, a toolbar will dock at the top of the workspace. You can reposition the toolbar to a different docked position. See "Moving toolbars" on page 23.
- Click **Dock All Toolbars** to dock all floating toolbars. By default, toolbars will dock at the top of the workspace. You can reposition the toolbars to different docked positions. See "Moving toolbars" on page 23.
- Click **Lock Toolbar Position** to lock a docked toolbar into its docked position.
- Click **Close Toolbar** to close the selected toolbar.

Context menus

Context menus provide quick access to many menu functions. They are opened by right-clicking on a paragraph, graphic, or other object. When a context menu opens, the functions or options available will depend on the object that has been selected. A context menu can be the easiest way to reach a function, especially if you are not sure where the function is located in the menus or toolbars. By default, context menus will display an applicable keyboard shortcut if one has been set. If you wish, you can toggle this visibility off or on in **Tools > Options > View > Menu**.

Figure 8: Keyboard shortcuts in context menus

Status bar

The status bar is located at the bottom of the workspace. It provides information about the document and convenient ways to change some features quickly. It is similar in Writer, Calc, Impress, and Draw, but each LibreOffice component includes some component-specific items. An example of the Writer status bar is shown in Figure 9.

Figure 9: Example status bar from Writer

Page, sheet, or slide number and page count
Shows the current page, sheet, or slide number and the total number of pages, sheets, or slides in the document. Click on this field to open the Go to Page dialog. Other uses of this field depend on the LibreOffice component.

Words and characters
Shows the total number of words and characters in the document or in the selection.

Page style or slide design
Shows the current page style or slide design. To edit the current page style or slide design, double-click on this field. To choose a different page style or slide design, right-click on this field and select from the list that pops up.

Language
Shows the current language of the text at the current cursor position.

Insert mode
Shows the type of insert mode the program is in. This field is blank if the program is in Insert mode. Each time the *Ins* key is pressed, or this field is clicked, the mode toggles between Insert and Overwrite.

Selection mode
> Click to choose different selection modes. The icon does not change, but when you hover the mouse pointer over this field, a tooltip indicates which mode is active.

Unsaved changes
> The icon shown here is different when changes to the document have not been saved.

Digital signature
> If the document has been digitally signed, an icon shows here. You can click the icon to sign the document, or to view the existing certificate.

Object information
> Displays information relevant to the position of the cursor or the selected element of the document.

View layout
> Select between Single-page view, Multiple-page view, and Book view to change how your document is displayed.

Zoom slider
> Drag the Zoom slider, or click on the + and − signs to change the view magnification of your document.

Zoom percentage
> Indicates the magnification level of the document. Right-click on the percentage figure to open a list of magnification values from which to choose. Cicking on this percentage figure opens the **Zoom & View Layout** dialog.

Sidebar

To activate the Sidebar, select **View > Sidebar** from the Menu bar. The Sidebar (Figure 10) is located on the right side of the edit views of Writer, Calc, Impress, and Draw. It contains one or more panels, based on the current document context. Panels are organized into decks. A tab bar on the right side of the sidebar allows you to switch between different decks.

All components contain the Properties, Styles and Formatting, Pages , Gallery, and Navigator decks. Some components have additional decks, such as Master Pages, Custom Animation, and Slide Transition for Impress; Manage Changes for Writer; and Functions for Calc.

A panel is like a combination of a toolbar and a dialog. For example, you can freely mix working in the main edit window to enter text and use the Properties panel in the sidebar to change text attributes.

Tool bars and Sidebar panels share many functions. For example, the buttons for making text bold or italic exist in both the Formatting toolbar and the Properties panel.

For more detail, see the Sidebar explanation in the relevant LibreOffice component's user guide.

To hide the Sidebar, click on the gray **Hide** button on the left. Click on the same button to show the Sidebar again.

To undock the Sidebar and make it floating, and to dock a floating Sidebar, use the **Sidebar settings** drop-down list at the top of the tab bar (see Figure 11). From the same list you can choose which items to show in the Sidebar.

Figure 10: Properties panel of Sidebar in Writer

Figure 11: Floating (undocking) or docking the Sidebar

Starting new documents

You can start a new, blank document in LibreOffice in several ways.

When LibreOffice is running but no document is open, the Start Center (Figure 3 on page 20) is shown. Click one of the icons to open a new document of that type, or click the **Templates** icon to start a new document using a template.

You can also start a new document in one of the following ways:

- Use **File > New** on the Menu bar and select the type of document from the context menu.
- Use the keyboard shortcut *Ctrl+N* to create a new document. The type of document created depends on which LibreOffice component is open and active. For example, if Calc is open and active, a new spreadsheet is created.

- Use **File > Wizards** on the Menu bar and select the type of document from the context menu.
- If a document is already open in LibreOffice, click the **New** icon on the Standard toolbar and a new document of the same type is created in a new window. For example, if Calc is open and active, a new spreadsheet is created. The New icon changes depending on which component of LibreOffice is open.
- If a document is already open in LibreOffice, click on the small triangle to the right of the **New** icon on the Standard toolbar and select the type of document from the context menu that opens.
- On Windows or Linux, use the Quickstarter feature included with LibreOffice. See "Using Quickstarter on Linux or Windows" on page 21 for more information.

 Note

If all documents are closed without closing the last LibreOffice window, then the Start Center will be displayed.

Opening existing documents

You can also open an existing document in one of the following ways:
- When no document is open, click **Open File** or **Remote files** in the Start Center to reach the Open dialog.
- Go to **File > Open** or **File > Open Remote...** on the Menu bar to reach the Open dialog.
- Use the keyboard shortcut *Ctrl+O* to reach the Open dialog.
- If a document is already open, click the **Open** icon on the Standard toolbar and select from a list of available documents from the Open dialog, or click **Open Template...** to select a template.
- Click the small triangle to the right of the **Open** icon and select from a list of recently opened documents.
- When no document is open, double-click on a thumbnail of recently opened documents displayed in the Start Center. You can scroll up or down in the Start Center to locate a recently opened document.

When using the Open dialog, navigate to the folder you want and select the file you want, and then click **Open**. If a document is already open in LibreOffice, the second document opens in a new window.

In the Open dialog, you can reduce the list of files by selecting the type of file you are looking for. For example, if you choose **Text documents** as the file type, you will only see documents Writer can open (including .odt, .doc, .txt); if you choose **Spreadsheets**, you will see .ods, .xls, and other files that Calc opens.

You can also open an existing document that is in a format that LibreOffice recognizes by double-clicking on the file icon on the desktop or in a file manager such as Windows Explorer. LibreOffice has to be associated with file types that are not ODF files for the appropriate LibreOffice component to open.

 Note

When opening files stored in a remote server, you may be asked to enter your user name and password to log in the server.

Saving documents

You can save documents as follows:

- **Save** command – use if you are keeping the document, its current filename and location.
- **Save Remote** - use if your document is already stored in a remote server or will be stored in a remote server.
- **Save As** – use if you want to create a new document, or change the filename and/or file format, or save the file in a different location on your computer.
- **Save a copy** - use if you want to save a copy of your current document and keep it open for more editing.
- **Save All** - use to save all the files open in your current session.

Save command

To save a document if you are keeping the document's current filename and location, do one of the following:

- Use the menu option **File > Save**
- Use the keyboard shortcut *Ctrl+S*.
- Click the **Save** icon on the Standard toolbar.
- Use the menu option **File > Save All**
- Use the menu option **File > Save Remote**
- Use the menu option **File > Save a Copy (Similar to the** Save As command**)**

Using the Save command will immediately overwrite the last saved version of the file.

Save As command

Figure 12: Example of LibreOffice Save As dialog

If you want to create a new document file, change the filename and/or file format, or save the file in a different location on your computer:

- Use the keyboard shortcut *Ctrl+Shift+S*.
- Use the menu option **File > Save As**.

When the **Save As** dialog (Figure 12) or **Save** dialog opens, enter the file name, change the file type (if applicable), navigate to a new location (if applicable), and click **Save**.

Password protection

To restrict who can open and read a document, or open and edit the document, use password protection.

1) Using the Save As command command above, select the **Save with password** option in the Save As dialog or Save dialog.

2) Click **Save** and the **Set Password** dialog opens (Figure 13).

3) In *File Encryption Password*, enter a password to open the document and then enter the same password as confirmation.

4) To restrict who can edit the document, click **Options**.

5) In *File Sharing Password*, select **Open file read-only**, enter a password to allow editing, and then enter the same password as confirmation.

6) Click **OK** and the dialog closes. If the passwords match, the document is saved password-protected. If the passwords do not match, you receive an error message.

Figure 13: Set Password dialog

 Caution

> LibreOffice uses a very strong encryption mechanism that makes it almost impossible to recover the contents of a document if you lose or forget the password.

Changing the password

When a document is password-protected, you can change the password while the document is open. Go to **File > Properties > General** on the Menu bar and click the **Change Password** button. This opens the Set Password dialog where you can enter a new password.

Saving documents automatically

LibreOffice can save files automatically as part of the **AutoRecovery** feature. Automatic saving, like manual saving, overwrites the last saved state of the file.

To set up automatic file saving:

1) Go to **Tools > Options > Load/Save > General** on the Menu bar.
2) Select **Save AutoRecovery information every** and set the time interval.
3) Click **OK**.

Opening and saving files on remote servers

LibreOffice can open and save files stored on remote servers. Keeping files on remote servers allows you to work with the documents using different computers. For example, you can work on a document in the office during the day and edit it at home for last-minute changes. Storing files on a remote server also backs up documents from computer loss or hard disk failure. Some servers are also able to check-in and check-out files, thus controlling their usage and access.

LibreOffice supports many document servers that use well known network protocols such as FTP, WebDav, Windows share, and SSH. It also supports popular services like Google Drive and Microsoft OneNote, as well as commercial and open source servers that implement the OASIS CMIS standard.

To enable a remote server connection, use one of these methods:

- Click on the **Remote Files** button in the Start Center
- Select **File > Open Remote**
- Select **File > Save Remote**

On the Remote Files dialog (Figure 15), click on the **Add Service** button in the upper right to open the File Services dialog (Figure 14).

Depending on the type of file service you choose in the **Type** listbox, different parameters are necessary to fully qualify the connection to the remote server.

Figure 14: Remote server configuration

Once the connection is defined, click **OK** to connect. The dialog will dim until the connection is established with the server. A dialog asking for the user name and the password may pop up to let you log in the server. Proceed entering your credentials.

The Remote Files dialog (Figure 15) which then appears has many parts. The upper list box contains the list of remote servers you have previously defined. The line below the list box shows the path to access the folder. On the left is the folder structure of the user space in the server. The main pane displays the files in the remote folder. Click the **Open** or **Save** button to proceed.

Figure 15: Remote Files dialog when connected to a server

Renaming and deleting files

You can rename or delete files within the LibreOffice dialogs, just as you can in a file manager. Select a file and then right click to open a context menu. Select either **Delete** or **Rename**, as appropriate. However, you cannot copy or paste files within the dialogs.

Using the Navigator

The LibreOffice Navigator lists objects contained within a document, collected into categories. For example, in Writer it shows Headings, Tables, Text frames, Comments, Graphics, Bookmarks, and other items, as shown in Figure 16. In Calc it shows Sheets, Range Names, Database Ranges, Graphics, Drawing Objects, and other items. In Impress and Draw it shows Slides, Pictures, and other items.

To open the Navigator, click the **Navigator** icon on the Standard toolbar, or press the *F5* key, or go to **View > Navigator** on the Menu bar,, or click on the Page Number/Count area of the Status Bar, or click the Navigator icon in the Sidebar.

Click the marker (+ or triangle) by any of the categories to display the list of objects in that category.

The Navigator provides several convenient ways to move around a document and find items in it:

- When a category is showing the list of objects in it, double-click on an object to jump directly to that object's location in the document.
- Objects are much easier to find if you have given them recognizable names when creating them, instead of keeping the default names such as Sheet1, Table1, or Table2. The default names may not correspond to the actual position of the object in the document.
- Navigator also provides the facility to move, promote, demote items within a document.
- Each Navigator in the individual LibreOffice components has a different range of functions. These functions are further explained in the user guide for each LibreOffice component.

Figure 16: Navigator in Writer

Undoing and redoing changes

To undo the most recent unsaved change in a document, use the keyboard shortcut *Ctrl+Z*, or click the **Undo** icon on the Standard toolbar, or go to **Edit > Undo** on the Menu bar. Click the small triangle to the right of the **Undo** icon to get a list of all the changes that can be undone. You can select multiple changes and undo them at the same time.

After changes have been undone, you can redo changes. To redo a change use the keyboard shortcut *Ctrl+Y*, or click the **Redo** icon, or go to **Edit > Redo** on the Menu bar. As with Undo, click on the triangle to the right of the arrow to get a list of the changes that can be reapplied.

To repeat the last command applied to your document, use the shortcut *Ctrl+Shift+Y*. This can save several repetitive menu navigation clicks or keyboard shortcuts, especially when the command is taken from a secondary menu.

Reloading a document

You may want to discard all the changes made in an editing session after the last document save. But undoing each change or remembering where the changes took place can be a difficult task. If you are sure you do not want to keep the changes from the last save operation, you can reload your document. A copy of the document that is currently stored in the file system is loaded. The document returns to the state where it was last saved.

To reload a document, go to **File > Reload** on the menu bar. If you have made changes to a file since the last save, a confirmation dialog will warn you that Reloading will discard your last changes. On reloading your document, the File dialog will not open, because the file is already selected.

Closing a document

If only one document is open and you want to close that document, go to **File > Close** on the Menu bar or click on the X on the right or left end of the Menu bar. On Windows and Linux, the document closes and the LibreOffice Start Center opens. On macOS, the document closes and only the Menu bar remains at the top of the screen.

If more than one document is open and you want to close one of them, go to **File > Close** on the Menu bar or click on the X on the title bar of that document's window. The X may be located on either the right or left end of the title bar.

If the document has not been saved since the last change, a message box is displayed. Choose whether to save or discard your changes.

 Caution

> Not saving your document could result in the loss of recently made changes, or worse still, the entire file.

Closing LibreOffice

To close LibreOffice completely, go to **File > Exit** on the Menu bar in Windows and Linux operating systems. In a Mac operating system, go to **LibreOffice > Quit LibreOffice** on the Menu bar.

When you close the last document using the X on the title bar of the window, then LibreOffice will close completely. A Mac operating system does not have this function; instead, you need to use to **LibreOffice > Quit LibreOffice**.

You can also use a keyboard shortcut as follows:

- In Windows and Linux – *Ctrl+Q*
- In macOS – *Command ⌘+Q*

If any documents have not been saved since the last change, a message box is displayed. Choose whether to save or discard your changes.

Getting Started Guide

Chapter 2
Setting up LibreOffice

Choosing Options to Suit the Way You Work

Using LibreOffice on macOS

Some keystrokes and menu items are different on macOS from those used in Windows and Linux. The table below gives some common substitutions for the instructions in this book. For a more detailed list, see the application Help.

Windows or Linux	macOS equivalent	Effect
Tools > Options menu selection	**LibreOffice > Preferences**	Access setup options
Right-click	Control+click and/or right-click depending on computer setup	Open a context menu
Ctrl (Control)	⌘ (*Command*)	Used with other keys
F5	*Shift+⌘+F5*	Open the Navigator
F11	*⌘+T*	Open the sidebar Styles and Formatting deck

Choosing options for all of LibreOffice

This section covers some of the settings that apply to all the components of LibreOffice. For information on settings not discussed here, see the Help.

Click **Tools > Options**. The list in the left-hand box of the Options – LibreOffice dialog varies depending on which component of LibreOffice is open. The illustrations in this chapter show the list as it appears when a Writer document is open.

Click the marker (+ or triangle) by LibreOffice on the left-hand side. A list of pages drops down. Selecting an item in the list causes the right-hand side of the dialog to display the relevant page.

Figure 17: LibreOffice options

Note

> The **Reset** button, located in the lower right of the full Options dialog, has the same effect on all pages of the dialog. It resets the options to the values that were in place when you opened the dialog.

If you are using a version of LibreOffice other than US English, some field labels may be different from those shown in the illustrations.

User Data options

Because LibreOffice can use the name or initials stored in the *LibreOffice – User Data* page for several things – including document properties ('created by' and 'last edited by' information), the name of the author of comments and changes, and the sender address in mailing lists – you will want to ensure that the correct information appears here.

Fill in the form (not shown here), or amend or delete any existing information. If you do not want user data to be part of the document's properties, clear the box at the bottom.

General options

The options on the *LibreOffice – General* page (Figure 18) are described below.

Help – Extended tips
    When *Extended tips* is active, a brief description of the function of a particular icon or menu command or a field on a dialog appears when you hold the mouse pointer over that item.

Figure 18: Setting general options for LibreOffice

Print Dialogs – Use LibreOffice dialogs
    Same as above, but for the Print dialogs. Available only in some operating systems and desktop managers. (Not shown in illustration.)

Document status – Printing sets "document modified" status
    If this option is selected, then the next time you close the document after printing, the print date is recorded in the document properties as a change and you will be prompted to save the document again, even if you did not make any other changes.

Year (two digits)

Specifies how two-digit years are interpreted. For example, if the two-digit year is set to 1930, and you enter a date of 1/1/30 or later into your document, the date is interpreted as 1/1/1930 or later. An "earlier" date is interpreted as being in the following century; that is, 1/1/20 is interpreted as 1/1/2020.

Help Improve LibreOffice – Collect usage data and send it to The Document Foundation

Send usage data to help The Document Foundation improve usability of the software. Data about usage patterns helps with identifying the most frequently used sequences of commands while performing common tasks; the developers can then design a user interface that is easier to use and more productive. The usage data is sent anonymously and carries no document contents, only the commands used.

View options

The options on the *LibreOffice – View* page affect the way the document window looks and behaves. Some of these options are described below Figure 19. Set them to suit your personal preferences.

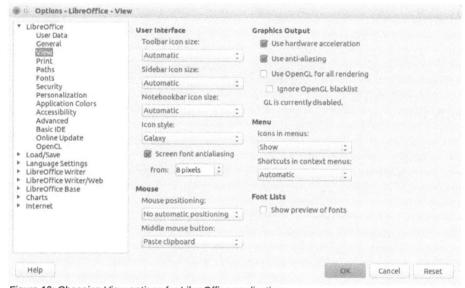

Figure 19: Choosing View options for LibreOffice applications

User Interface – Scaling

If the text in the help files or on the menus of the LibreOffice user interface is too small or too large, you can change it by specifying a scaling factor. Sometimes a change here can have unexpected results, depending on the screen fonts available on your system. However, it does not affect the actual font size of the text in your documents.

User Interface – Icon size

This box specifies the display size of toolbar icons (Automatic, Small, or Large). The Automatic icon size option uses the setting for your operating system.

User Interface - Icon style

This box specifies the icon style (theme). Here the Automatic option uses an icon set compatible with your operating system and choice of desktop: for example, KDE or Gnome on Linux.

User interface – Screen font anti-aliasing
(Not available in Windows.) Select this option to smooth the screen appearance of text. Enter the smallest font size to apply anti-aliasing.

Mouse positioning
Specifies if and how the mouse pointer will be positioned in newly opened dialogs.

Middle mouse button
Defines the function of the middle mouse button.

- **Automatic scrolling** – dragging while pressing the middle mouse button shifts the view.

- **Paste clipboard** – pressing the middle mouse button inserts the contents of the "Selection clipboard" at the cursor position.

The "Selection clipboard" is independent of the normal clipboard that you use by **Edit > Copy/Cut/Paste** or their respective keyboard shortcuts. Clipboard and "Selection clipboard" can contain different contents at the same time.

Function	Clipboard	Selection clipboard
Copy content	**Edit > Copy** *Ctrl+C*	Select text, table, or object.
Paste content	**Edit > Paste** *Ctrl+V* pastes at the cursor position.	Clicking the middle mouse button pastes at the mouse pointer position.
Pasting into another document	No effect on the clipboard contents.	The last marked selection is the content of the selection clipboard.

Graphics output – Use hardware acceleration
Directly accesses hardware features of the graphical display adapter to improve the screen display. Not supported on all operating systems and LibreOffice distributions.

Graphics output – Use anti-aliasing
Enables and disables anti-aliasing, which makes the display of most graphical objects look smoother and with fewer artifacts. Not supported on all operating systems and LibreOffice distributions.

 Tip

Press *Shift+Ctrl+R* to restore or refresh the view of the current document after changing the anti-aliasing settings, to see the effect.

Graphics output – Use OpenGL for all rendering (on restart)
Enables and disables the use of the 3D graphics language OpenGL. Not supported on all operating systems and LibreOffice distributions.

Graphics output – Force OpenGL even if blacklisted (on restart)
Forces the use of OpenGL even if the graphics device is blacklisted. A device is blacklisted when it is buggy or may render graphics with poor quality. Not supported on all operating systems and LibreOffice distributions.

Menu – icons in menus
Causes icons as well as words to be visible in menus.

Font Lists – Show preview of fonts
Causes the font list to look like Figure 20, Left, with the font names shown as an example of the font; with the option deselected, the font list shows only the font names, not their formatting (Figure 20, Right). The fonts you will see listed are those that are installed on your system.

Fonts which are tuned for use with a specific script, such as Arabic, Hebrew, Malayalam, and so on, now show an additional preview of some sample text in the target script.

Figure 20: Font list (Left) with preview; (Right) without preview

Print options

On the *LibreOffice – Print* page, set the print options to suit your default printer and your most common printing method. Most of these options should be self-explanatory.

The option **PDF as Standard Print Job Format** is not available on Windows. Select this option to change the internal print job format from a Postscript document description to a PDF description. This format has a number of advantages over Postscript. For more information, see http://www.linuxfoundation.org/collaborate/workgroups/openprinting/ pdf_as_standard_print_job_format

Deselecting this option reverts to the Postscript document workflow system.

In the *Printer warnings* section near the bottom of the page, you can choose whether to be warned if the paper size or orientation specified in your document does not match the paper size or orientation available for your printer. Having these warnings turned on can be quite helpful, particularly if you work with documents produced by people in other countries where the standard paper size is different from yours.

 Tip

If your printouts are incorrectly placed on the page or chopped off at the top, bottom, or sides, or the printer is refusing to print, the most likely cause is page size incompatibility.

Figure 21: Choosing general printing options to apply to all LibreOffice components

Paths options

On the *LibreOffice – Paths* page, you can change the location of files associated with, or used by, LibreOffice to suit your working situation. In a Windows system, for example, you might want to store documents by default somewhere other than My Documents.

To make changes, select an item in the list shown in Figure 22 and click **Edit**. On the Select Path dialog (not shown; may also be titled Edit Paths), add or delete folders as required, and then click **OK** to return to the Options dialog. Note that some items can have at least two paths listed: one to a shared folder (which might be on a network) and one to a user-specific folder (normally on the user's personal computer).

 Tip

You can use the entries on the *LibreOffice – Paths* page to compile a list of files, such as those containing AutoText, that you need to back up or copy to another computer.

Paths used by LibreOfficeDev

Type ▲	Path
AutoCorrect	/home/olivier/.config/libreofficedev/4/user/autocorr
AutoText	/home/olivier/.config/libreofficedev/4/user/autotext
Backups	/home/olivier/.config/libreofficedev/4/user/backup
Classification	/opt/libreofficedev6.0/program/../share/classification/example.xml
Dictionaries	/home/olivier/.config/libreofficedev/4/user/wordbook
Gallery	/home/olivier/.config/libreofficedev/4/user/gallery
Images	/home/olivier/.config/libreofficedev/4/user/gallery
My Documents	/home/olivier/Documents
Templates	/home/olivier/.config/libreofficedev/4/user/template;/home/olivier/Templa
Temporary files	/tmp

Figure 22: Viewing the paths of files used by LibreOffice

Fonts options

You can define replacements for any fonts that might appear in your documents. If you receive from someone else a document containing fonts that you do not have on your system, LibreOffice will substitute fonts for those it does not find. You might prefer to specify a different font from the one that the program chooses.

 Note

> These choices do **not** affect the default font for your documents. To do that, you need to change the default template for documents, as described in Chapter 3.

On the *LibreOffice – Fonts* page:

1) Select the **Apply replacement table** option.

2) Select or type the name of the font to be replaced in the **Font** box. (If you do not have this font on your system, it will not appear in the drop-down list in this box, so you need to type it in.)

3) In the **Replace with** box, select a suitable font from the drop-down list of fonts installed on your computer.

4) The check mark to the right of the **Replace with** box turns green. Click on this check mark. A row of information now appears in the larger box below the input boxes. Select **Always** to replace the font, even if the original font is installed on your system. Select **Screen only** to replace the screen font only and never replace the font for printing. The results of combining these selections are given in Table 18.

5) In the bottom section of the page, you can change the typeface and size of the font used to display source code such as HTML and Basic (in macros).

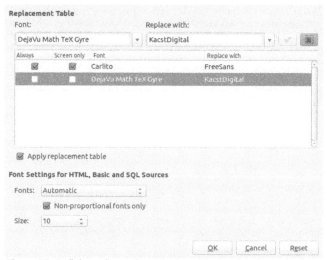

Figure 23: Defining a font to be substituted for another font

Table 1. Font substitution replacement actions

Always checkbox	Screen only checkbox	Replacement action
checked	blank	Font replacement on screen and when printing, whether the font is installed or not.
checked	checked	Font replacement only on screen, whether the font is installed or not.
blank	checked	Font replacement only on screen, but only if font is not available.
blank	blank	Font replacement on screen and when printing, but only if font is not available.

Security options

Use the *LibreOffice – Security* page to choose security options for saving documents and for opening documents that contain macros.

Security options and warnings

If you record changes, save multiple versions, or include hidden information or notes in your documents, and you do not want some of the recipients to see that information, you can set warnings to remind you to remove it, or you can have LibreOffice remove some of it automatically. Note that (unless removed) much of this information is retained in a file whether the file is in LibreOffice's default OpenDocument format, or has been saved to other formats, including PDF.

Click the **Options** button to open a separate dialog with specific choices (Figure 26). See "Security options and warnings" on page 45.

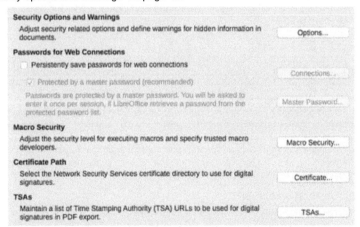

Figure 24: Choosing security options for opening and saving documents

Passwords for web connections

You can enter a master password to enable easy access to websites that require a user name and password. If you select the **Persistently save passwords for web connections** option, the Set Master Password dialog opens (Figure 25). LibreOffice will securely store all passwords that you use to access files from web servers. You can retrieve the passwords from the list after you enter the master password.

Figure 25: Set Master Password dialog for web connections

Macro security

Click the **Macro Security** button to open the Macro Security dialog (not shown here), where you can adjust the security level for executing macros and specify trusted sources.

Certificate Path

Users can digitally sign documents using LibreOffice. A digital signature requires a personal signing certificate. Most operating systems can generate a self-signed certificate. However, a personal certificate issued by an outside agency (after verifying an individual's identity) has a higher degree of trust associated with it than does a self-signed certificate. LibreOffice does not provide a secure method of storing these certificates, but it can access certificates that have been saved using other programs. Click the **Certificate** button and select which certificate store to use.

 Note

> The Certificate Path option appears only on Linux and Mac systems. On Windows, LibreOffice uses the default Windows location for storing and retrieving certificates.

TSAs –Time Stamping Authorities

Allows you to optionally select a Time Stamping Authority (TSA) URL for PDF documents created by LibreOffice. Adding a trusted timestamp to an electronic signature on a PDF provides a digital seal of data integrity and a trusted date and time of when the file was signed. Recipients of PDF documents with a trusted timestamp can verify when the document was digitally or electronically signed, as well as verify that the document was not altered after the date the timestamp vouches for.

Security options and warnings

The following options are on the Security options and warnings dialog (Figure 26).

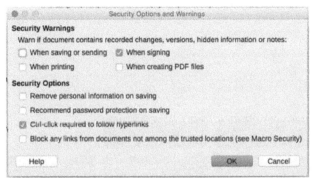

Figure 26: Security options and warnings dialog

Remove personal information on saving

Select this option to always remove user data from the file properties when saving the file. To manually remove personal information from specific documents, deselect this option.

Ctrl-click required to follow hyperlinks

The default behavior in LibreOffice is to *Ctrl+click* on a hyperlink to open the linked document. Many people find creation and editing of documents easier when accidental clicks on links do not activate the links. To set LibreOffice to activate hyperlinks using an ordinary click, deselect this option.

The other options on this dialog should be self-explanatory.

Personalization

You can customize the overall appearance of LibreOffice with themes designed for Mozilla Firefox.

On the *LibreOffice – Personalization* page, select **Own Theme** and then click **Select Theme.** Another dialog opens. Type a search term, click **Search**, and wait while theme thumbnails load. Select one and click **OK** to apply the theme. After a brief pause the appearance of LibreOffice will refresh and reflect the selected theme. An example is shown in Figure 29. For full details about themes, visit the Mozilla website: https://www.https://addons.mozilla.org/en-US/firefox/themes/

Figure 27: Personalization dialogs

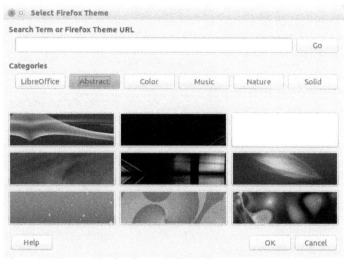

Figure 28: Theme selection from Mozilla Firefox

Figure 29: Sample personalized theme

Application colors

Writing, editing, and (especially) page layout are often easier when you can see the page margins (text boundaries), the boundaries of tables and sections (in Writer documents), page breaks in Calc, grid lines in Draw or Writer, and other features. In addition, you might prefer to use colors that are different from LibreOffice's defaults for such items as comment indicators or field shadings.

On the *LibreOffice – Application colors* page (Figure 30), you can specify which items are visible and the colors used to display various items.

- To show or hide items such as text boundaries, select or deselect the options next to the names of the items.

- To change the default colors for items, click the down-arrow in the *Color Setting* column by the name of the item and select a color from the list box. Note that you can change the list of available colors selecting other available palettes

- To save your color changes as a color scheme, click **Save**, type a name in the *Scheme* box, and then click **OK**.

Figure 30: Showing or hiding text, object, and table boundaries

Accessibility options

Accessibility options include whether to allow animated graphics or text, how long help tips remain visible, some options for high contrast display, and a way to change the font for the LibreOffice user interface.

Accessibility support relies on the Java Runtime Environment for communication with assistive technology tools. The *Support assistive technology tools* option is not shown on all LibreOffice installations. See *Assistive Tools in LibreOffice* in the Help for other requirements and information.

Select or deselect the options as required.

Figure 31: Choosing accessibility options

Advanced options

Java options
If you install or update a Java Runtime Environment (JRE) after you install LibreOffice, or if you have more than one JRE installed on your computer, you can use the *LibreOffice – Advanced options* page to choose the JRE for LibreOffice to use.

Note

LibreOffice needs Java to run several wizards (such as **File > Wizards > Letter**) and to run databases with the internal HSQLDB engine.

Figure 32: Choosing a Java runtime environment

If you are a system administrator, programmer, or other person who customizes JRE installations, you can use the Parameters and Class Path pages (reached from the Java page) to specify this information.

If you do not see anything listed in the middle of the page, wait a few minutes while LibreOffice searches for JREs on the hard disk.

If LibreOffice finds one or more JREs, it will display them there. You can then select the **Use a Java runtime environment** option and (if necessary) choose one of the JREs listed.

Optional (unstable) options

Enable experimental features

Selecting this option enables features that are not yet complete or contain known bugs. The list of these features is different version by version.

Enable macro recording (limited)

This option enables macro recording, with some limitations. Opening a window, switching between windows, and recording in a different window to that in which the recording began, are not supported. Only actions relating to document contents are recordable, so changes in Options or customizing menus are not supported. For more about macro recording, see Chapter 13, Getting Started with Macros.

Expert Configuration

Most users will have no need to use this. Click the **Expert Configuration** button to open a new window in which you can fine-tune the LibreOffice installation. The page offers detailed configuration options for many aspects of LibreOffice's appearance and performance. Double-click on a listed preference to enter a value to configure the preference.

Caution

The Expert Configuration dialog lets you access, edit, and save configuration preferences that can turn the user profile of LibreOffice unstable, inconsistent, or even unusable.

Basic IDE options

The Basic IDE Options are available after **Enable experimental features** has been selected on the Advanced page of the Options dialog and the options have been saved. These options are for macro programmers and are not discussed here.

Figure 33: Basic IDE Options dialog

Online update options

On the *LibreOffice – Online Update* page (Figure 34), you can choose whether and how often to have the program check the LibreOffice website for program updates. If the **Check for updates automatically** option is selected, an icon appears at the right-hand end of the menu bar when an update is available. Click this icon to open a dialog where you can choose to download the update.

If the **Download updates automatically** option is selected, the download starts when you click the icon. To change the download destination, click the **Change** button and select the required folder in the file browser window.

If the **Send OS version & simple hardware info** option is selected, the information of the computer architecture and operating system will be sent to the server for statistics collection.

Figure 34: Online update options

OpenCL options

OpenCL (Open Computing Language) is a software architecture used to write programs that run in different processors of the computer, such as the CPU and GPU (graphics processing unit) of the video card. With OpenCL enabled, LibreOffice can benefit from the very fast numerical calculations performed in the GPU, which is especially useful in very large spreadsheets with extensive calculations. The computer video card driver must have support for OpenCL to use this feature.

OpenCL Options –Allow use of Software Interpreter (even when OpenCL is not available)
Mark this box to emulate OpenCL if your computer video card driver does not support OpenCL.

Allow use of OpenCL
Let LibreOffice use the video card GPU to perform numerical calculation with great speed gain. The two boxes below list the OpenCL drivers whitelist and blacklist. Click the **Edit**, **Add...** and **Delete** buttons to modify the lists entries.

Figure 35: OpenCL options

Choosing options for loading and saving documents

You can set the options for loading and saving documents to suit the way you work.

If the Options dialog is not already open, click **Tools > Options**. Click the expansion symbol (+ or triangle) to the left of **Load/Save**.

General

Most of the choices on the *Load/Save – General* page are familiar to users of other office suites. Some items of interest are described below.

Load user-specific settings with the document
A LibreOffice document contains certain settings that are read from the user's system. When you save a document, these settings are saved with it.

Select this option so that when a document loads, it ignores the stored settings in favor of the settings on your computer.

Even if you do not select this option, some settings are taken from your LibreOffice installation:

- Settings available in **File > Print > Options**
- Name of Fax
- Spacing options for paragraphs before text tables
- Information about automatic updating for links, field functions and charts
- Information about working with Asian character formats.

Figure 36: Choosing Load and Save options

The following setting is **always** loaded with a document, whether or not this option is marked:

- Data source linked to the document and its view.

If you deselect this option, the user's personal settings do not overrule the settings in the document. For example, your choice (in the options for LibreOffice Writer) of how to update links is affected by the Load user-specific settings option.

Load printer settings with the document

If enabled, the printer settings will be loaded with the document. This can cause a document to be printed on a distant printer (perhaps in an office setting), if you do not change the printer manually in the Print dialog. If disabled, your standard printer will be used to print this document. The current printer settings will be stored with the document whether or not this option is selected.

Save AutoRecovery information every __ Minutes

Choose whether to enable AutoRecovery and how often to save the information used by the AutoRecovery process. AutoRecovery in LibreOffice saves the information needed to restore all open documents in case of a crash. If you have this option set, recovering your document after a system crash will be easier.

Edit document properties before saving

If you select this option, the Document Properties dialog pops up to prompt you to enter relevant information the first time you save a new document (or whenever you use **Save As**).

Always create backup copy

Saves the previous version of a document as a backup copy whenever you save a document. Every time LibreOffice creates a backup copy, the previous backup copy is replaced. The backup copy gets the extension BAK. Authors whose work may be very lengthy should always consider using this option.

Save URLs relative to file system / internet

Use this option to select the default for relative addressing of URLs in the file system and on the Internet. Relative addressing is only possible if the source document and the referenced document are both on the same drive.

A relative address always starts from the directory in which the current document is located. In contrast, absolute addressing always starts from a root directory. The following table demonstrates the difference in syntax between relative and absolute referencing.

Examples	File system	Internet
relative	../images/img.jpg	../images/img.jpg
absolute	file:///c|/work/images/img.jpg	http://myserver.com/work/images/img.jpg

If you choose to save relatively, the references to embedded graphics or other objects in your document will be saved relative to the location in the file system. In this case, it does not matter where the referenced directory structure is recorded. The files will be found regardless of location, as long as the reference remains on the same drive or volume. This is important if you want to make the document available to other computers that may have a completely different directory structure, drive or volume names. It is also recommended to save relatively if you want to create a directory structure on an Internet server.

If you prefer absolute saving, all references to other files will also be defined as absolute, based on the respective drive, volume or root directory. The advantage is that the document containing the references can be moved to other directories or folders, and the references remain valid.

Default file format and ODF settings

ODF format version. LibreOffice by default saves documents in OpenDocument Format (ODF) version 1.2 Extended. While this allows for improved functionality, there may be backwards compatibility issues. When a file saved in ODF 1.2 Extended is opened in an editor that uses earlier versions of ODF (1.0/1.1), some of the advanced features may be lost. Two notable examples are cross-references to headings and the formatting of numbered lists. If you plan to share documents with people who use editors that use older versions of ODF, you may wish to save the document using ODF version 1.0/1.1.

Document type. If you routinely share documents with users of Microsoft Office, you might want to change the **Always save as** attribute for documents to the Microsoft Office formats. Current versions of Microsoft Word can open ODT files, so this may no longer be needed.

VBA Properties

On the *VBA Properties* page, you can choose whether to keep any macros in Microsoft Office documents that are opened in LibreOffice.

If you choose **Load Basic code**, you can edit the macros in LibreOffice. The changed code is saved in an ODF document but is not retained if you save into a Microsoft Office format.

If you choose **Save original Basic code**, the macros will not work in LibreOffice but are retained unchanged if you save the file into Microsoft Office format.

If you are importing a Microsoft Word or Excel file containing VBA code, you can select the option **Executable code**. Whereas normally the code is preserved but rendered inactive (if you inspect it with the StarBasic IDE you will notice that it is all commented), with this option the code is ready to be executed.

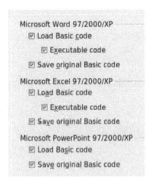

Figure 37: Choosing Load/Save VBA Properties

Save original Basic code takes precedence over **Load Basic code**. If both options are selected and you edit the disabled code in LibreOffice, the original Microsoft Basic code will be saved when saving in a Microsoft Office format.

To remove any possible macro viruses from the Microsoft Office document, deselect **Save original Basic code**. The document will be saved without the Microsoft Basic code.

Microsoft Office

On the *Load/Save – Microsoft Office* page (Figure 38), you can choose what to do when importing and exporting Microsoft Office OLE objects (linked or embedded objects or documents such as spreadsheets or equations).

Select the [L] options to convert Microsoft OLE objects into the corresponding LibreOffice OLE objects when a Microsoft document is loaded into LibreOffice (mnemonic: "L" for "load").

Select the [S] options to convert LibreOffice OLE objects into the corresponding Microsoft OLE objects when a document is saved in a Microsoft format (mnemonic: "S" for "save").

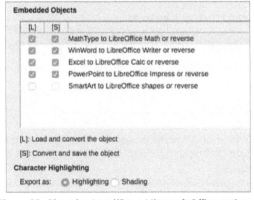

Figure 38: Choosing Load/Save Microsoft Office options

HTML compatibility

Choices made on the *Load/Save – HTML Compatibility* page (Figure 39) affect HTML pages imported into LibreOffice and those exported from LibreOffice. See *HTML documents; importing/exporting* in the Help for more information.

Figure 39: Choosing HTML compatibility options

Font sizes
> Use these fields to define the respective font sizes for the HTML <font size="1"> to <font size="7"> tags, if they are used in the HTML pages. (Many pages no longer use these tags.)

Import – Use 'English (USA)' locale for numbers
> When importing numbers from an HTML page, the decimal and thousands separator characters differ according to the locale of the HTML page. The clipboard, however, contains no information about the locale. If this option is **not** selected, numbers will be interpreted according to the **Locale setting** in **Tools > Options > Language Settings > Languages** (see page 55). If this option is selected, numbers will be interpreted as for the English (USA) locale.

Import – Import unknown HTML tags as fields
> Select this option if you want tags that are not recognized by LibreOffice to be imported as fields. For an opening tag, an HTML_ON field will be created with the value of the tag name. For a closing tag, an HTML_OFF will be created. These fields will be converted to tags in the HTML export.

Import – Ignore font settings
> Select this option to have LibreOffice ignore all font settings when importing. The fonts that were defined in the HTML Page Style will be used.

Export
> To optimize the HTML export, select a browser or HTML standard from the **Export** box. If LibreOffice Writer is selected, specific LibreOffice Writer instructions are exported.

Export – LibreOffice Basic
> Select this option to include LibreOffice Basic macros (scripts) when exporting to HTML format. You must activate this option *before* you create the LibreOffice Basic macro; otherwise the script will not be inserted. LibreOffice Basic macros must be located in the header of the HTML document. Once you have created the macro in the LibreOffice Basic IDE, it appears in the source text of the HTML document in the header.

> If you want the macro to run automatically when the HTML document is opened, choose **Tools > Customize > Events**. See Chapter 13, Getting Started with Macros, for more information.

Export – Display warning
When the **LibreOffice Basic** option (see above) is *not* selected, the **Display warning** option becomes available. If the **Display warning** option is selected, then when exporting to HTML a warning is shown that LibreOffice Basic macros will be lost.

Export – Print layout
Select this option to export the print layout of the current document as well. The HTML filter supports CSS2 (Cascading Style Sheets Level 2) for printing documents. These capabilities are only effective if print layout export is activated.

Export – Copy local graphics to Internet
Select this option to automatically upload the embedded pictures to the Internet server when uploading using FTP.

Export – Character set
Select the appropriate character set for the export.

Choosing language settings

To customize the language settings in LibreOffice, you can do any of the following:

- Install the required dictionaries
- Change some locale and language settings
- Choose spelling options

Install the required dictionaries

LibreOffice automatically installs many dictionaries with the program. To add other dictionaries, be sure you are connected to the Internet, and then choose **Tools > Language > More Dictionaries Online**. LibreOffice will open your default web browser to a page containing links to additional dictionaries that you can install. Follow the prompts to select and install the ones you want.

Change some locale and language settings

You can change some details of the locale and language settings that LibreOffice uses for all documents, or for specific documents.

In the Options dialog, click the expansion symbol (+ sign or triangle) by **Language Settings > Languages**. The exact list shown depends on the *Enhanced language support* settings (see Figure 41).

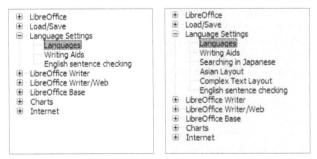

Figure 40: LibreOffice language options, without and with Asian and CTL options enabled

On the right-hand side of the *Language Settings – Languages* page, change the *User interface*, *Locale setting*, *Default currency*, and *Default languages for documents* as required. In the example, English (USA) has been chosen for all the appropriate settings.

gs - Languages

Language Of

User interface:	Default - English (USA)
Locale setting:	English (USA)
Decimal separator key:	☑ Same as locale setting (,)
Default currency:	Default - USD
Date acceptance patterns:	M/D/Y;M/D

Default Languages for Documents

Western:	🔤 English (USA)
☐ Asian:	Default - Chinese (simplified)
☐ Complex text layout:	Default - Hindi
	☐ For the current document only

Enhanced Language Support

☐ Ignore system input language

Figure 41: Choosing language options

User interface

The language of the user interface is usually set at the time LibreOffice is installed to match the language of the operating system. If more than one language has been installed for LibreOffice, you can select which language will be used for menus, dialogs, and help files.

Locale setting

The local setting is the basis for many other settings within LibreOffice, for example defaults for numbering, currency, and units of measure. Unless you select something else here, the locale of the operating system will be set as default.

Decimal separator key

If the *Decimal separator key* option is selected, LibreOffice uses the character defined by the default locale. If this option is not selected, the keyboard driver defines the character used.

Default currency

The *Default currency* is that used in the country entered as *Locale*. The default currency determines the proper formatting of fields formatted as currency. If the locale setting is changed, the default currency changes automatically. If the *default currency* is changed, all dialogs involving currency and all currency icons will be changed in all open documents. Documents that were saved with one currency as the default will open using the new currency defaults.

Date acceptance patterns

Date acceptance patterns define how LibreOffice recognizes input as dates. *Locale* also defines the default expression of dates. You can define additional date patterns, separated by semicolons, using Y, M, & D for Year, Month, and Day. LibreOffice will always correctly interpret dates entered in ISO 8601 format as Y-M-D and YYYY-MM-DD.

Caution

Data entered into a Calc spreadsheet or a Writer table must be entered in a format defined by *Locale* in order to be recognized as dates.

Default languages for documents

Select the languages used for the spelling checker, thesaurus, and hyphenation features of LibreOffice. If these options are only for the current document, select *For the current document only.*

If necessary, select the options to enable support for Asian languages (Chinese, Japanese, Korean) and support for CTL (complex text layout) languages such as Urdu, Thai, Hebrew, and Arabic. If you choose either of these options, the next time you open this dialog, you will see some extra choices under Language Settings, as shown in Figure 40. These choices (*Searching in Japanese, Asian Layout,* and *Complex Text Layout*) are not discussed here.

Enhanced language support – Ignore system input language

Default language settings depend on the *Locale* setting. The default locale is based on that of the computer's operating system. A keyboard layout is normally based on the language used by the operating system but can be changed by the user. If this option is not selected, and there is a change in keyboard layout, input from the keyboard will be different from what is expected.

Choose spelling options

To choose the options for checking spelling, click **Language Settings > Writing Aids**. In the *Options* section of the page (Figure 42), choose the settings that are useful for you.

Some considerations:

- If you do not want spelling checked while you type, deselect **Check spelling as you type**. This option can also be deselected using the **Automatic Spell Checking** button on the Standard toolbar.

- If you want grammar to be checked as you type, you must have **Check spelling as you type** enabled too.

- If you use a custom dictionary that includes words in all uppercase and words with numbers (for example, AS/400), select **Check uppercase words** and **Check words with numbers**.

- **Check special regions** includes headers, footers, frames, and tables when checking spelling.

Here you can also select which user-defined (custom) dictionaries are active by default, and add or remove user-installed dictionaries, by clicking the **New** or **Delete** buttons. Dictionaries installed by the system cannot be deleted.

Figure 42: Choosing languages, dictionaries, and options for checking spelling

English sentence checking

On the **Language Settings > English sentence checking** page, you can choose which items are checked for, reported to you, or converted automatically. This menu is also found in the English dictionaries extension installed by default by LibreOffice. Select **Tools > Extension Manager**, select the English spelling dictionaries and click the **Options** button to reveal the menu. Select which of the optional features you wish to check.

After selecting the additional grammar checks, you must restart LibreOffice, or reload the document, for them to take effect.

Figure 43: Choosing options for checking sentences in English

Grammar checking

Possible mistakes
> Checks for things such as; *with it's, he don't, this things* and so on.

Capitalization
> Checks for the capitalization of sentences. The sentence boundary detection depends on abbreviations.

Word duplication
> Checks for all word duplication, rather than just the default words 'and', 'or', 'for', and 'the'.

Parentheses
> Checks for pairs of parentheses and quotation marks.

Punctuation

Word spacing
> This option is selected by default. It checks for single spaces between words, indicating instances of double or triple spaces, but not of more spaces than that.

Sentence spacing
> Checks for a single space between sentences, indicating when one or two extra spaces are found.

More spaces
> Checks word and sentence spacing for more than two extra spaces.

Em dash; En dash
> These options force a non-spaced em dash to replace a spaced en dash, or force a spaced en dash to replace a non-spaced em dash.

Quotation marks
> Checks for correct typographical double quotation marks.

Multiplication sign
> This option is selected by default. It replaces an 'x' used as a multiplication symbol with the correct typographical symbol.

Apostrophe
> Replaces an apostrophe with the correct typographical character.

Ellipsis
> Replaces three consecutive periods (full stops) with the correct typographical symbol.

Minus sign
> Replaces a hyphen with the correct minus typographical character.

Others

Convert to metric; Convert to non-metric
> Converts quantities in a given type of unit to quantities in the other type of unit: metric to imperial or imperial to metric.

Thousands separation of large numbers
> Converts a number with five or more significant digits to a common format, that is one which uses the comma as a thousands separator, or to the ISO format which uses a narrow space as a separator, depending on the locale setting for the document.

Other languages sentence checking

LibreOffice can also check sentences in other languages, notably Hungarian, Russian, and Brazilian Portuguese. These checkers are enabled by default if the language is the computer's default language. The set of rules available for these sentence checkers depends on the language.

Choosing Internet options

The Internet options available depend on your operating system.

Use the Proxy page (if available) to save proxy settings for use with LibreOffice.

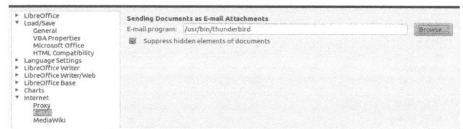

Figure 44: Internet options, showing E-mail page available to Linux users

If you are using a Unix- or Linux-based operating system (including Mac OS X), an additional page of E-mail options is available, where you can specify the e-mail program to use when you send the current document as e-mail. Under Windows the operating system's default e-mail program is always used.

A MediaWiki publisher is included on Windows and Linux. To enable it, select MediaWiki in the Internet options, then click the **Add** button to open the dialog shown in Figure 45. Here you can specify the address (URL) and log-in information for a wiki. You can add several wikis to the list.

Figure 45: Specifying a MediaWiki server account

Controlling LibreOffice's AutoCorrect functions

Some people find some or all of the items in LibreOffice's AutoCorrect function annoying because they change what you type when you do not want it changed. Many people find some of the AutoCorrect functions quite helpful; if you do, then select the relevant options. But if you find unexplained changes appearing in your document, this is a good place to look to find the cause.

To open the AutoCorrect dialog, click **Tools > AutoCorrect > AutoCorrect Options**. (You need to have a document open for this menu item to appear.) In Writer, this dialog has five tabs. In other components of LibreOffice, the dialog has only four tabs. More details are given in the component guides.

Troubleshooting LibreOffice in Safe Mode

Safe Mode offers various options to help restore an instance of LibreOffice that has become corrupted and stopped working or fails to launch for a variety of reasons.

To access Safe Mode:

- Choose Help > Restart in Safe Mode... from the menu bar
- Start LibreOffice from the command line with the --safe-mode option
- In Windows Only, choose LibreOffice (Safe Mode) from the Start Menu

Figure 46: LibreOffice Safe Mode

In Safe Mode, you can find options for repairing or restoring your copy of LibreOffice. The following options get more extreme from the top down, so it is recommended that you try them successively.

- Restore from Backup – LibreOffice keeps backups of previous configurations and activated extensions. Use this option to restore the user configuration, installed extensions or both, to a previous known working state if you suspect that your problems were caused by recent changes to either.
- Configure – This option allows you to disable all user extensions, hardware acceleration, or both. This is a good option if you are experiencing crashes on start up or visual glitches that are often related to hardware acceleration.
- Extensions – If you suspect that a corrupted extension is blocking or causing LibreOffice to crash, this option allows you to uninstall all user extensions, as well as resetting the state of any shared or bundled extensions. In the case of shared or bundled extensions, the option will only work if the user has the proper system access rights and should be exercised with caution.
- Reset to Factory Settings – If all of the above fails, you can reset your settings and your user interface modifications, or your entire profile back to factory defaults.
  - Reset Settings and User Interface Modifications – this will reset your User Interface and configuration changes, but keep things like your personal dictionary, templates, etc...
  - Reset Entire User Profile – this will erase all customized options and return your user profile to the factory default state.

- Apply Changes and Restart - Choose this option to apply any of the above changes and restart LibreOffice.

- Continue in Safe Mode – Continuing in Safe Mode will allow you to work in LibreOffice as you are used to, but using a temporary profile that was created on start up. Any extensions or configuration options you had set up previously will have to be reconfigured in order to be used, bearing in mind that any changes made to the temporary user profile will be lost after any restart.

- Restart in Normal Mode – If you arrived in Safe Mode accidentally, this option will discard any changes, terminate Safe Mode and restart LibreOffice normally.

 Note

If you are unable to solve your problem using Safe Mode, the advanced tab will provide instructions on receiving further aid.

In the advanced tab you also have the option to create a zip file of your corrupted user profile which can then be uploaded to the bug tracking system where it can be further investigated by the developers.

However, be aware that your uploaded user profile may contain sensitive information such as installed extensions, personal dictionaries and settings.

Getting Started Guide

Chapter 3
Using Styles and Templates

Using Consistent Formatting in Your Documents

Direct formatting

The key idea to use computers in document production is to split a document in the combination of contents and formatting. While contents is originated in human intellectual activity, formatting is a task computers can perform easily and is often repetitive.

Formatting a document can be manual or automated. The manual formatting or direct formatting is performed when user format each element of the document individually, as it was done at times when typewriters were used in offices, page by page. Direct formatting is a repetitive activity where, for example, you apply bold characters to several words, set individual margins for each paragraph, or change font size of a heading.

In contrast, style formatting is a modern way to let computers format documents much more efficiently and reduce the time spent in direct formatting.

What are styles?

Style are a set of formats that you can apply to selected pages, text, frames, and other elements in your document to quickly change their appearance. Applying a style often means applying a whole group of formats at the same time.

Many people manually format paragraphs, words, tables, page layouts, and other parts of their documents without paying any attention to styles. They are accustomed to writing documents according to *physical* attributes. For example, you might specify the font family, font size, and any formatting such as bold or italic, like a typewriter described above.

Styles are *logical* attributes. Using styles means that you stop saying "font size 14pt, Times New Roman, bold, centered" and you start saying "Title" because you have defined the "Title" style to have those characteristics. In other words, using styles means that you shift the emphasis from what the text (or page, or other element) looks like, to what the text *is*.

Styles help improve consistency in a document. They also make major formatting changes easy. For example, you may decide to change the indentation of all paragraphs, or change the font of all titles. Doing this manually for a long document may require making individual changes in dozens of places. By contrast, when you use styles, you only need to make a single change.

In addition, styles are used by LibreOffice for many processes, even if you are not aware of them. For example, Writer relies on heading styles (or other styles you specify) when it compiles a table of contents. Some common examples of style use are given in "Examples of style use" on page 80.

LibreOffice supports the following types of styles:

- *Page styles* include margins, headers and footers, borders and backgrounds. In Calc, page styles also include the sequence for printing sheets.
- *Paragraph styles* control all aspects of a paragraph's appearance, such as text alignment, tab stops, line spacing, and borders, and can include character formatting.
- *Character styles* affect selected text within a paragraph, such as the font and size of text, or bold and italic formats.
- *Table Styles* applies predefined formats to tables and tables elements in a text document.
- *Frame styles* are used to format graphic and text frames, including text wrap, borders, backgrounds, and columns.
- *List styles* allow you to select, format, and position numbers or bullets in lists.
- *Cell styles* include fonts, alignment, borders, background, number formats (for example, currency, date, number), and cell protection.
- *Graphics styles* in drawings and presentations include line, area, shadowing, transparency, font, connectors, dimensioning, and other attributes.

- *Presentation styles* include attributes for font, indents, spacing, alignment, and tabs.

Different styles are available in the various components of LibreOffice, as listed in Table 47.

LibreOffice comes with many predefined styles. You can use the styles as provided, modify them, or create new styles, as described in this chapter.

Table 2. Styles available in LibreOffice components

Style Type	Writer	Calc	Draw	Impress
Page	X	X		
Paragraph	X			
Character	X			
Frame	X			
Numbering	X			
Table	X			
Cell		X		
Presentation			X	X
Graphics	(included in Frame styles)		X	X

Applying styles

LibreOffice provides several ways for you to select styles to apply:

- The Styles menu in Writer
- The Styles deck in the Sidebar
- Fill Format Mode
- Apply Style List in the Formatting toolbar
- Keyboard shortcuts

Using the Styles menu in Writer

The Styles menu has the most important paragraph, character, and list styles for almost every text document, with an extra entry for custom style management options listed in the bottom of the menu. The Styles menu does not have styles for frames, pages, or tables.

To apply a paragraph style, position the cursor anywhere in the paragraph, and then select one of the paragraph styles in the **Styles** menu. To apply a character style to several characters or more than one word, select the characters first and apply the character style from the menu.

 Note

You cannot add custom styles to the Styles menu.

Using the sidebar Styles deck

The Styles deck (called Styles and Formatting in some installations) includes the most complete set of tools for styles. To use it for applying styles:

1) Select **View > Styles** or **Styles > Manage Styles** from the Menu bar, or press *F11* (⌘+*T* on a Mac), or click the Styles tab in the Sidebar (**View > Sidebar** to open it).

    The Styles deck shows previews of the styles available. Figure 47 shows the panel for Writer, with Paragraph Styles visible.

2) Select one of the buttons at the top left of the Styles deck to display a list of styles in that category.

3) To apply an existing style, position the insertion point in the paragraph, frame, page, or word, and then double-click the name of the style in one of these lists. To apply a character style to more than one word, select the characters first.

Tip

At the bottom of the Styles deck is a drop-down list. In Figure 47 the panel might show *Applied Styles*, meaning the list includes only the styles used in the document. You can choose to show all styles or other groups of styles, for example only custom styles.

Figure 47: The Styles deck for Writer, showing paragraph styles

Using Fill Format Mode

Use Fill Format to apply a style to many different areas quickly without having to go back to the Styles deck and double-click every time. This method is quite useful when you need to format many scattered paragraphs, cells, or other items with the same style:

1) Open the Styles deck and select the style you want to apply.

2) Select the **Fill Format Mode** button.

3) To apply a paragraph, page, or frame style, hover the mouse over the paragraph, page, or frame and click. To apply a character style, hold down the mouse button while selecting the characters. Clicking a word applies the character style for that word.

4) Repeat step 3 until you have made all the changes for that style.

5) To quit Fill Format mode, click the **Fill Format Mode** button again or press the *Esc* key.

 Caution

When this mode is active, a right-click anywhere in the document undoes the last Fill Format action. Be careful not to accidentally right-click and undo actions you want to keep.

Using the Set Paragraph Style list

After you have used a paragraph style at least once in a document, the style name appears in the Set Paragraph Style list at the left-hand end of the Formatting toolbar.

You can open this list and click the style you want, or you can use the up and down arrow keys to move through the list and then press *Enter* to apply the highlighted style.

Figure 48: The Set Paragraph Style list on the Formatting toolbar

Using keyboard shortcuts

Some keyboard shortcuts for applying styles are predefined. For example, in Writer *Ctrl+0* applies the *Text body* style, *Ctrl+1* applies the *Heading 1* style, and *Ctrl+2* applies the *Heading 2* style. You can modify these shortcuts and create your own; see Chapter 14, Customizing LibreOffice, for instructions.

Direct formatting and Style formatting

Direct formatting (also called *manual formatting*) overrides styles, and you cannot remove the direct formatting by applying a style to it.

To remove manual formatting, select the text, right-click, and choose **Styles > Clear Direct Formatting** from the context menu, or select the text and press *Ctrl+M*.

Creating and modifying styles

LibreOffice includes some predefined styles, but you can also create custom styles. You can modify both in several ways:

- Change a style using the Styles deck
- Update a style from a selection
- Use AutoUpdate (paragraph and frame styles only)
- Load styles from another document or template

 Note

Any changes you make to a style are effective only in the current document. To change styles in more than one document, you need to change the template or copy the styles into the other documents as described on page 69.

Changing a style using the Styles deck

To change an existing style using the Styles deck, open the Sidebar Styles deck, then right-click on the required style and select **Modify** from the pop-up menu.

The Style dialog displayed depends on the type of style selected. Each Style dialog has several tabs. See the chapters on styles in the user guides for details.

Updating a style from a selection

To update a style from a selection:

1) Open the Styles deck in the Sidebar.

2) In the document, select an item that has the format you want to adopt as a style.

 Caution

> When updating a paragraph style, make sure that the selected paragraph contains unique properties. If it mixes font sizes or font styles, those mixed properties will remain the same as before.

3) In the Styles deck, select the style to update, then click on the arrow next to the **New Style from Selection** icon and click **Update Style**.

Figure 49: Updating a style from a selection

 Tip

> You can also modify styles using the submenu on each style in the Set Paragraph Style list on the Formatting toolbar (see Figure 50).

Figure 50: Modifying a style from the Set Paragraph Style list

Using AutoUpdate

AutoUpdate applies to paragraph and frame styles only. If the AutoUpdate option is selected on the Organizer page of the Paragraph Style or Frame Style dialog, applying direct formatting to a paragraph or frame using this style in your document automatically updates the style itself.

 Tip

> If you are in the habit of manually overriding styles in your document, be sure that AutoUpdate is **not** enabled.

Updating styles from a document or template

You can update styles by copying (loading) them from a template or another document. See "Copying styles from a template or document" on page 71.

Creating new (custom) styles

You may want to add some new styles. You can do this by using either the New Style dialog or the New Style from Selection tool.

Creating a new style using the New Style dialog

To create a new style using the New Style dialog, open the sidebar Styles deck and select the category of style (eg. paragraph, character, etc.) wish to create by clicking one of the icons at the top of the deck, then click the arrowhead on the right hand icon and select **New** from the pop-up menu.

If you want your new style to be linked with an existing style, first select that style from the list of styles shown in the deck, then right-click on the selected style and select **New**.

If you link styles and you later change the base style (for example, by changing the font from Times to Helvetica), all the linked styles will change as well. Sometimes this is exactly what you want; other times you do not want the changes to apply to all the linked styles. It pays to plan ahead.

The dialogs and choices are the same for defining new styles and for modifying existing styles. See the chapters on styles in the user guides for details.

Tip

If a document needs custom styles derived from base styles, consider prefixing the name of the custom styles with a few characters to highlight them among other styles in the list. For example, you might name a modified Heading 1 style for an annual report *AR Heading 1*.

Creating a new style from a selection

You can create a new style by copying an existing manual format. This new style applies only to this document; it will not be saved in the template.

1) Open the Styles deck and choose the category of style you want to create.

2) In the document, select the item you want to save as a style.

3) In the Styles deck, select on the **New Style from Selection** icon.

4) In the Create Style dialog, type a name for the new style. The list shows the names of existing custom styles of the selected category. Click **OK** to save the new style.

Figure 51: Naming a new style created from a selection

Dragging and dropping to create a style

You can drag and drop a selection into the Styles deck to create a new style. The element to drag depends upon the LibreOffice application.

Writer

Select some text and drag it to the Styles deck. If Paragraph Styles are active, the paragraph style will be added to the list. If Character Styles are active, the character style will be added to the list.

Calc

Drag a cell selection to the Styles deck to create a cell style.

Draw/Impress

Select and drag a drawing object to the Styles deck to create a graphic style.

Adding table styles in Writer

Table styles are stored in the LibreOffice user profile, and are available to all Writer documents. You can define new table styles following these steps:

1) Create a table and apply formatting for cells, backgrounds, borders and more.

2) Select the whole table.

3) Drag the table and drop in the Table Styles category of the Styles deck in the sidebar.

Alternatively,

1) Open menu **Table > AutoFormat Styles** and click the **Add** button (Figure 52).

2) Enter a name for the new table style, click **OK**

3) The new table style is listed in the left pane of the dialog. Click **OK** again to close the AutoFormat dialog.

Figure 52: Table autoformat styles

The new table style can be applied to tables as described in Applying styles on page 65.

Copying styles from a template or document

You can copy styles into a document by loading them from a template or from another document:

1) Open the document you want to copy styles into.

2) In the Styles deck, click the arrow next to the **New Style from Selection** icon, and then select **Load Styles** (see Figure 49).

3) On the Load Styles dialog (Figure 53), find either a template or an ordinary document from which to copy styles. Click the **From File** button to open a window from which to select the required document.

4) Select the categories of styles to copy from the checkboxes at the bottom of the dialog.

5) Select **Overwrite** if you want to replace styles in the original document that have the same name as styles in the document from which you are importing styles. If this box is not selected, you will only copy styles whose names are not used in the original document.

6) Click **OK** to copy the styles.

Figure 53: Copying styles from a template into the open document

Caution

If your document has a table of contents, and if you have used custom styles for headings, the heading levels associated with outline levels in **Tools > Outline Numbering** will revert to the defaults of Heading 1, Heading 2, and so on when you load Text Styles from a file that does not use the same custom styles. You will need to change these back to your custom heading styles.

Note:

You cannot copy character style into a document. Table styles, including custom table styles are stored in your computer and are available to all Writer documents.

Deleting styles

You cannot remove (delete) any of LibreOffice's predefined styles from a document or template, even if they are not in use.

You can remove any user-defined (custom) styles; but before you do, you should make sure the styles are not in use in the current document.

To delete any unwanted styles, in the Styles deck select each one to be deleted (hold *Ctrl* while selecting multiple styles), and then right-click on a selected style and select **Delete** on the context menu.

If the style is not in use, it is deleted immediately without confirmation. If the style is in use, you receive a warning message asking you to confirm deletion.

Caution

If you delete a style that is in use, all objects with that style will return to the default style.

What is a template?

A *template* is a model document that you use to create other documents. For example, you can create a template for business reports that has your company's logo on the first page. New documents created from this template will always have your company's logo on the first page.

Templates can contain anything that regular documents can contain, such as text, graphics, a set of styles, and user-specific setup information such as measurement units, language, the default printer, and toolbar and menu customization.

All documents in LibreOffice are based on templates. You can create a specific template for any document type (text, spreadsheet, drawing, presentation). If you do not specify a template when you start a new document, then the document is based on the default template for that type of document. If you have not specified a default template, LibreOffice uses the blank template for that type of document that is installed with LibreOffice. See "Setting a default template" on page 77 for more information.

You can create templates for Master Documents as well as for ordinary documents.

Using a template to create a document

Creating a document from the Templates dialog

To use a template to create a document:

1) From the Menu bar, choose **File > New > Templates**. You can also click on the small arrow next to the **New** icon and select **Templates**. The Templates dialog opens.

2) From the listbox at the top of the dialog, select the category of template you want to use. All the templates contained in that folder are listed on the page (as shown in Figure 54).

3) Select the required template and click **OK**, or double-click on the selected template. A new document based on the template opens in LibreOffice.

The template the document is based upon is listed in **File > Properties > General**. The connection between the template and the document remains until the template is modified and, the next time that the document is opened, you choose not to update it to match the template.

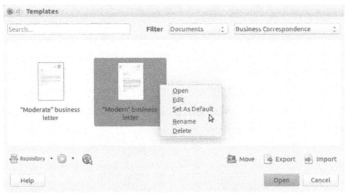

Figure 54: Templates dialog, showing a selected template

Creating a document from a template in the Start Center

You can create a document from the template view of the Start Center. The Start Center is visible when no other document is open.

To open the Templates dialog from the Start Center, click on the **Templates** button in the left pane. The button is also a drop-down list to select the templates of a given type of document. The **Manage Templates** option on the list opens the Templates dialog (Figure 54).

Creating a template

You can create templates in two ways: by saving a document as a template or by using a wizard.

Creating a template from a document

In addition to formatting, any settings that can be added to or modified in a document can be saved within a template. For example, you can also save printer settings, and general behaviors set from **Tools > Options**, such as **Paths** and **Colors**.

Templates can also contain predefined text, saving you from having to type it every time you create a new document. For example, a letter template may contain your name, address, and salutation.

You can also save menu and toolbar customization in templates; see *Chapter 14, Customizing LibreOffice*, for more information.

To create a template from a document and save it to My Templates:

1) Open a new or existing document of the type you want to make into a template (text document, spreadsheet, drawing, or presentation).

2) Add any content that you want to appear in any document you create from the new template, for example company logo, copyright statement, and so on.

3) Create or modify any styles that you want to use in the new template.

4) From the Menu bar, choose **File > Templates > Save as Template**. The Save as Template dialog (Figure 55) opens, displaying the existing categories and a textbox to enter a name for the new template.

5) Select the My Templates folder.

6) Click **Save**. The template is saved and the dialog closes.

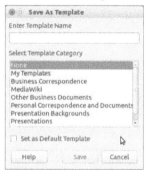

Figure 55: Save as Template dialog

 Note

> Although the Save as Template dialog shows no document type when saving a new template of any type, the template will appear on the correct tab (Documents, Spreadsheets, Presentations, Drawings) when you return to the Templates dialog.

Creating a template using a wizard

You can use wizards to create templates for letters, faxes, and agendas.

For example, the Fax Wizard guides you through the following choices:

- Type of fax (business or personal)
- Document elements like the date, subject line (business fax), salutation, and complimentary close
- Options for sender and recipient information (business fax)
- Text to include in the footer (business fax)

To create a template using a wizard:

1) From the Menu bar, choose **File > Wizards > [type of template required]** (see Figure 56).

2) Follow the instructions on the pages of the wizard. This process is slightly different for each type of template, but the format is very similar.

3) In the last section of the wizard, you can specify the template name which will show in the Templates dialog, and also the name and location for saving the template. The two names can be different but this may later cause confusion. The default location is your user templates directory, but you can choose a different location.

4) To set the file name or change the directory, select the **Path** button (the three dots to the right of the location). The **Save As** dialog opens. Make your selections and click **Save** to close the dialog.

Figure 56: Creating a template using a wizard

5) Finally, you can choose whether to create a new document from the template immediately, or manually change the template, and then click **Finish** to save the template. For future documents, you can re-use the template created by the wizard, just like any other template.

You may need to open the Templates dialog and click **Refresh** on the **Settings** menu to have any new templates appear in the listings.

Editing a template

You can edit a template's styles and content, and then, if you wish, you can reapply the template's styles to documents that were created from that template. You cannot reapply content.

To edit a template:

1) From the Menu bar, choose **File > Templates > Manage Templates** or press *Ctrl+Shift+N*. The Templates dialog opens. You can also open the Templates dialog from the Start Center.

2) Navigate to the template that you want to edit. Click once on it to activate the file handling controls (see Figure 54). Right-click to open the context menu click **Edit**. The template opens in LibreOffice.

3) Edit the template as you would edit any other document. To save your changes, choose **File > Save** from the Menu bar.

Updating a document from a changed template

If you make any changes to a template and its styles, the next time you open a document that was created from the template before the changes, a confirmation message is displayed.

To update the document:

1) Click **Update Styles** to apply the changed styles in the template to the document.

2) Select **Keep Old Styles** if you do not want to apply the changed styles in the template to the document (but see the Caution notice below).

Caution

If you choose **Keep Old Styles**, the document is no longer connected to the template, even though the template is still listed under **File > Properties > General.** You can still import styles manually from the template, but to reconnect it to the template, you will have to copy it into an empty document based on the template.

Adding templates obtained from other sources

LibreOffice refers to sources for templates as repositories. A repository can be local (a directory on your computer to which you have downloaded templates) or remote (a URL from which you can download templates).

You can get to the official template repository by using the **Browse Online Templates** button at the lower left-hand end of the Templates dialog, as shown in Figure 57, or by typing https://extensions.libreoffice.org/templates in your browser's address bar.

On other websites you may find collections of templates that have been packaged into extension (OXT) files. These are installed a little differently, as described below.

Figure 57: Getting more templates for LibreOffice

Installing individual templates

To install individual templates:

1) Download the template and save it anywhere on your computer.

2) Import the template into a template folder by following the instructions in "Importing a template" on page 79.

 Tip

You can manually copy new templates into the template folders. The location varies with your computer's operating system. To learn where the template folders are stored on your computer, go to **Tools > Options > LibreOffice > Paths**.

Installing collections of templates

The Extension Manager provides an easy way to install collections of templates that have been packaged as extensions. Follow these steps:

1) Download the extension package (OXT file) and save it anywhere on your computer.

2) In LibreOffice, select **Tools > Extension Manager** from the Menu bar. In the Extension Manager dialog, click **Add** to open a file browser window.

3) Find and select the package of templates you want to install and click **Open**. The package begins installing. You may be asked to accept a license agreement.

4) When the package installation is complete, restart LibreOffice. The templates are available for use through **File > Templates > Manage Templates** and **File > New > Templates** and the extension is listed in the Extension Manager.

See Chapter 14, Customizing LibreOffice, for more about the Extension Manager.

Setting a default template

If you create a document by choosing **File > New > Text Document** (or **Spreadsheet**, **Presentation**, or **Drawing**) from the Menu bar, LibreOffice creates the document from the default template for that type of document. You can, however, change the default whenever you choose.

 Note for Microsoft Word users

> You may know that Microsoft Word employs a `normal.dot` or `normal.dotx` file for its default template and how to regenerate it.
>
> LibreOffice does not have a similar default template file; the "factory defaults" are embedded within the software.

Setting a template as the default

Most default settings, such as page size and page margins, can be changed in **Tools > Options**, but those changes apply only to the document you are working on. To make those changes the default settings for that document type, you need to replace the default template with a new one.

You can set any template displayed in the Templates dialog to be the default for that document type:

1) From the Menu bar, choose **File > Templates > Manage Templates**.

2) In the Templates dialog, open the category containing the template that you want to set as the default, then select the template.

3) Right-click on the selected template and click the **Set as default** button (see Figure 54).

The next time that you create a document of that type by choosing **File > New,** the document will be created from this template.

Resetting the default template

To re-enable LibreOffice's original default template for a document type as the default for that type:

1) In the Templates dialog, click the **Action Menu** icon on the bottom left (Figure 58).

2) Point to **Reset Default Template** on the drop-down menu, and click **Text Document** (or other template type).

These choices do not appear unless a custom template has been set as the default, as described in the previous section.

The next time that you create a document by choosing **File > New**, the document will be created from the original default template for the document type.

Figure 58: Resetting the default template for text documents

Organizing templates

LibreOffice can manage only those templates that are in its template folders or categories. You can create new template categories and use them to organize your templates. For example, you might have one template category for report templates and another for letter templates. You can also import and export templates.

To begin, choose **File > Templates > Manage Templates** to open the Templates dialog.

Creating a template category

To create a template category:

1) Click the **Action** button of the Templates dialog.

2) Click **New category** on the context menu (see Figure 59).

3) In the pop-up dialog, type a name for the new category and click **OK**.

Figure 59: Creating a new category

 Note

You cannot create a sub-category inside a template category in LibreOffice.

Deleting a template category

You cannot delete template categories supplied with LibreOffice. Nor can you delete any categories added by the Extension Manager unless you first remove the extension that installed them.

However, you can delete a category that you created. Open the Templates dialog, choose the category from the **Filters** drop-down lists at the top of the dialog. Then click the **Settings** button and select **Delete** from the pop-up menu (See Figure 59). When a message box appears asking you to confirm the deletion, click **Yes**.

Moving a template

To move a template from one template category to another, select it in the Templates dialog, and click the **Move** button in the bottom center of the dialog. In the popup dialog (Figure 60), select the destination category and click **OK**.

Figure 60: Moving templates to another category

Deleting a template

You cannot delete templates supplied with LibreOffice. Nor can you delete any templates installed by the Extension Manager except by removing the extension that installed them.

However, you can delete templates that you have created or imported:

1) From the **Filters** drop-down lists at the top of the Templates dialog, select the category that contains the template you want to delete.

2) Select the template to delete.

3) Right-click on the template to open the context menu and click **Delete** (Figure 54).

4) A message box appears and asks you to confirm the deletion. Click **Yes**.

Importing a template

While it not essential to store templates in one of the folders listed for the Template path in **Tools > Options > LibreOffice > Paths** before you can use a template in LibreOffice, but it is the easiest and most convenient way of managing templates. To import a template:

1) In the Templates dialog, click the **Import** button on the bottom right. The Select Category dialog appears.

2) Find and select the category where you want to import the template and click **OK**. A standard file browser window opens.

3) Find and select the template that you want to import and click **Open**. The file browser window closes and the template appears in the selected category.

Exporting a template

To export a template from a template category to another location in your computer or network:

1) In the Templates dialog, locate the category that contains the template to export.

2) Select the template that you want to export.

3) Click the **Export** button in the bottom right of the dialog. The Save As window opens.

4) Find the folder into which you want to export the template and select **Save**.

Examples of style use

The following examples of common use of page and paragraph styles are taken from Writer. There are many other ways to use styles; see the guides for the various components for details.

Defining a different first page for a document

Many documents, such as letters and reports, have a first page that is different from the other pages in the document. For example, the first page of a letterhead typically has a different header, or the first page of a report might have no header or footer, while the other pages do. With LibreOffice, you can define the *page style* for the first page and specify the style for the following pages to be applied automatically.

As an example, we can use the *First Page* and *Default* page styles that come with LibreOffice. Figure 61 shows what we want to happen: the first page is to be followed by the default page, and all the following pages are to be in the *Default* page style. Details are in Chapter 4, Formatting Pages, in the *Writer Guide*.

Figure 61: Flow of page styles

Dividing a document into chapters

In a similar way, you can divide a document into chapters. Each chapter might start with the *First Page* style, with the following pages using the *Default* page style, as above. At the end of the chapter, insert a manual page break and specify the next page to have the *First Page* style to start the next chapter, as shown in Figure 62.

Figure 62: Dividing a document into chapters using page styles

Changing page orientation within a document

A Writer document can contain pages in more than one orientation. A common scenario is to have a landscape page in the middle of a document, whereas the other pages are in a portrait orientation. This setup can also be created with page breaks and page styles.

To insert a landscape page in the middle of your document, insert a page break and select a page style with the landscape orientation on. LibreOffice default landscape page style is Landscape. You may have to adjust the other page properties such as headers, footers, and page numbering of the landscape style. To go back to the portrait page style, insert another page break and select the default portrait page style of your document.

Displaying different headers on right and left pages

Page styles can be set up to have the facing left and right pages *mirrored* or only right (first pages of chapters are often defined to be right-page only) or only left. When you insert a header on a page style set up for mirrored pages or right-and-left pages, you can have the contents of the header be the same on all pages or be different on the right and left pages. For example, you can put the page number on the left-hand edge of the left pages and on the right-hand edge of the right pages, put the document title on the right-hand page only, or make other changes.

Controlling page breaks automatically

Writer automatically flows text from one page to the next. If you do not like the default settings, you can change them. For example, you can require a paragraph to start on a new page or column and specify the style of the new page. A typical use is for chapter titles to always start on a new right-hand (odd-numbered) page.

Compiling an automatic table of contents

To compile an automatic table of contents, first apply styles to the headings you want to appear in the contents list, then use **Tools > Outline Numbering** to tell Writer which styles go with which level in the table of contents. By default, tables of contents use Heading styles, but you can use whatever combination of styles you prefer. See Chapter 4 for more information.

Defining a sequence of paragraph styles

You can set up one paragraph style so that when you press *Enter* at the end of that paragraph, the following paragraph automatically has the style you wish applied to it. For example, you could define a *Heading 1* paragraph to be followed by a *Text Body* paragraph. A more complex example would be: *Title* followed by *Author* followed by *Abstract* followed by *Heading 1* followed by *Text Body*. By setting up these sequences, you can usually avoid having to apply styles manually.

Formatting a table in Writer

Tables in a Writer document can have a predefined set of formatting attributes applied, including cell background, font, emphasis, and number formatting (Figure 63). To apply table styles, position the cursor in the table to be formatted and choose **Table > AutoFormat Styles** in the main menu and select a style from the dialog that appears. Or, alternatively, position the cursor in the table to be formatted and double click on a style listed in the **Table Styles** tab of the **Styles** menu or the sidebar.

Box List Blue

James	Colin	Angela	Victoria	Aline	Thomas
100	200	300	400	500	600
1000	1500	2000	2500	3000	3500
1100	1700	2300	2900	3600	4100

Box List Green

James	Colin	Angela	Victoria	Aline	Thomas
100	200	300	400	500	600
1000	1500	2000	2500	3000	3500
1100	1700	2300	2900	3500	4100

Figure 63: Some table styles in LibreOffice

For more information refer to the *LibreOffice Writer guide, Chapter 13: Tables of Data.*

Getting Started Guide

Chapter 4
Getting Started with Writer

Word Processing with LibreOffice

What is Writer?

Writer is the word processor component of LibreOffice. In addition to the usual features of a word processor (spelling check, thesaurus, hyphenation, autocorrect, find and replace, automatic generation of tables of contents and indexes, mail merge and others), Writer provides these important features:

- Templates and styles (see Chapter 3)
- Page layout methods, including frames, columns, and tables
- Automated tables of contents and indexes
- Embedding or linking of graphics, spreadsheets, and other objects
- Built-in drawing tools
- Master documents—to group a collection of documents into a single document
- Change tracking during revisions
- Database integration, including a bibliography database
- Mail merge
- Export to PDF, including bookmarks (see Chapter 10)
- Document digital signature
- Form design and filling
- And many more

These features are covered in detail in the *Writer Guide*.

The Writer interface

The main Writer workspace is shown in Figure 64. The menus and toolbars are described in Chapter 1, Introducing LibreOffice. Some other features of the Writer interface are covered in this chapter.

Figure 64: The main Writer workspace

Status Bar

The Writer Status Bar provides information about the document and convenient ways to change some document features quickly.

Figure 65: Status bar components

Page number

Shows the current page number, the sequence number of the current page (if different), and the total number of pages in the document. For example, if you restarted page numbering at 1 on the third page, its page number is 1 and its sequence number is 3.

If any bookmarks have been defined in the document, a right-click on this field pops up a list of bookmarks; click on one to go to that location.

To jump to a specific page in the document, double-click on this field. The Navigator opens. Click in the Page Number field and type the *sequence* number of the required page and press *Enter*.

Word and character count

The word and character count of the document is shown in the Status Bar, and is kept up to date as you edit. When text is selected, the word and character counts for the selection will appear here.

To display extended statistics such as character counts that exclude spaces, double-click the word count in the Status Bar, or choose **Tools > Word Count**.

You can also see the number of words and characters (and other information including the number of pages, tables, and graphics) in the entire document in **File > Properties > Statistics**.

Page style

Shows the style of the current page. To change the page style, right-click on this field. A list of page styles pops up; choose a different style by clicking on it.

To edit the current page style, double-click on this field. The Page Style dialog opens.

Language

Shows the language at the cursor position, or for the selected text, that is used for checking spelling and grammar as well as for hyphenation and thesaurus dictionaries.

Click to open a menu where you can choose another language for the selected text or for the paragraph where the cursor is located. You can also choose **None (Do not check spelling)** to exclude the text from a spelling check or choose **More** to open the Character dialog. Any directly formatted language settings can be reset to the default language from this menu.

Insert mode

This area is blank when in Insert mode. Click to change to *Overwrite* mode; click again to return to Insert mode. In Insert mode, any text after the cursor position moves forward to make room for the text you type; in Overwrite mode, text after the cursor position is replaced by the text you type. This feature is disabled when in **Record Changes** mode.

Selection mode

Click to choose different selection modes. A context menu displays the available options. Howevering the mouse pointer over this field, also displays a tooltip that shows which mode is active. Note that the icon does not change.

Mode	Effect
Standard selection	Click in the text where you want to position the cursor; click in a cell to make it the active cell. Any other selection is deselected.
Extending selection (*F8*)	Clicking in the text extends or crops the current selection.
Adding selection (*Shift+F8*)	A new, separate selection is added to an existing selection. The result is a multiple selection.
Block selection (*Ctrl+Shift+F8*)	A block of text can be selected.

On Windows systems, you can hold down the *Alt* key while dragging to select a block of text. You do not need to enter the block selection mode.

Document changes status

The icon that is displayed here changes from this one (🖺) if the document has no unsaved changes, to this one (🖺*) if it has been edited and the changes have not been saved. Click on the unsaved changes icon to save the document.

Digital signature

If the document has been digitally signed, this icon (🖺) is displayed here; otherwise, it is blank. To sign the document, or to view the certificate, click the icon.

Section or object information

When the cursor is on a section, heading, or list item, or when an object (such as a picture or table) is selected, information about that item appears in this field. Double-clicking in this area opens a relevant dialog. For details, consult the Help or the *Writer Guide*.

View layout

Click an icon to change between single page, side-by-side, and book layout views. The effect varies with the combination of window width and zoom factor in use. You can edit the document in any view. See Figure 66.

Zoom

To change the view magnification, drag the Zoom slider, or click on the + and − signs, or right-click on the zoom level percent to pop up a list of magnification values from which to choose. Zoom interacts with the selected view layout to determine how many pages are visible in the document window.

Figure 66: View layouts: single, side-by-side, book.

Sidebar

The Sidebar (Figure 67) is normally open by default on the right side of the Writer window. If necessary, select **View > Sidebar** from the Menu bar to display it. The Sidebar also has a Hide/Show button.

Figure 67: Default Properties panel of Sidebar in Writer

The Writer Sidebar contains five decks by default: *Properties, Page, Styles, Gallery, and Navigator*. If you have selected *Enable experimental features* in **Tools > Options > LibreOffice > Advanced**, a sixth deck (*Manage Changes*) will appear, and a seventh (*Design*) can be selected in **Sidebar Settings > Customization**. Each deck has a corresponding icon on the Tab bar on the right of the sidebar, allowing you to switch between them.

Each deck consists of a title bar and one or more content panels. Toolbars and sidebar panels share many functions. For example, the buttons for making text bold or italic exist in both the Formatting toolbar and the Character panel of the Properties deck.

Some panels contain a small **More Options** button (⋯), which opens a dialog to give greater choice of editing controls. When a dialog is open, the document is locked for editing until the dialog is closed.

The decks are described below.

Properties Deck

Contains tools for direct formatting within the document.

For **text editing,** the default view shows tools organized into three panels:

- *Styles:* Apply a paragraph style at the cursor position. Create or update a style.
- *Character*: Modify text by the font type, size, color, weight, style and spacing.
- *Paragraph*: Style the paragraph by alignment, lists or bullets, background color, indent, and spacing.

Additional panels appear when specific types of items are selected:

If a graphic is selected, then the following panels open:

- *Area:* Modify the graphic background area fill mode and transparency. Further colors, gradients, hatching, patterns, and bitmap selection and importing are available in **More Options**.
- *Image:* Modify the graphic's brightness, contrast, color mode and transparency.
- *Wrap: Modify wrap and spacing where these are available.*
- *Position and Size:* Modify width and height.

If a drawing object is selected, then the following panels are available:

- *Area:* Modify fill and transparency.
- *Wrap:* Modify wrap and spacing.
- *Position and Size:* Edit width, height, rotation, and flip attributes.

If a frame is selected, then the wrap panel opens but may be grayed-out if frame wrap is not available.

If a video or audio clip is inserted by selecting Insert > Media > Audio or Visual, the following panel opens when the clip is selected:

- Media Playback: Control for play, pause, stop, seek, loop, and volume
- Position and Size: Modify width and height.

Page Deck

Modifies the page style to change the most commonly used page properties. It is organized in four panels:

- Format modifies the size, width, height, orientation, and page margins;

- Styles modifies the numbering scheme, background, page layout (specifies whether the page style should apply to odd or even pages or to both), and columns;
- Header and Footer modify the respective margins, spacing, and content across pages.

 Caution

Be aware that by changing the options on the Page deck, you will change the page style in use, modifying not only the current page but all pages in the document using the same page style.

Styles Deck

Manages the styles used in the document. This includes applying existing styles, modifying them, or creating new ones. You can preview the changes by checking **Show Previews** at the bottom.

Gallery Deck

Contains images and diagrams included in the Gallery themes. The Gallery has two sections. The first lists the themes by name (Arrows, Background, Diagrams, etc.) and the second displays the images in the selected category. Select the **New Theme** button to create new categories. To insert an image into a file, or add a new image to the new category, drag and drop the selected image.

Navigator Deck

Makes it easy to navigate to specific types of content and to reorganize contents based on categories, such as headings, tables, frames, graphics, etc. This deck is similar to the floating toolbar that can be opened from **View > Navigator** on the Menu bar or the **Navigator** button on the Standard Toolbar, or by pressing *F5*. However, the Sidebar Navigator does not contain a **List Box On/Off** button that reduces the size of the window.

Manage Changes Deck

Lists all changes made to the document since the Track Changes mode was activated. This deck is an alternative view of the Manage Changes dialog that can be opened from **Edit > Track Changes > Manage Changes** on the Menu bar. This tab is available only when **Enable experimental features** has been selected in **Tools > Options > LibreOffice > Advanced**.

Design Deck

Provides quick access to themes (fonts and colors) and style presets. This deck is available only when Experimental Features is enabled in **Tools > Options > LibreOffice > Advanced** and when the deck is selected in **Sidebar Settings > Customization**.

Changing document views

Writer has three ways to view a document: Normal, Web, and Full Screen. To change the view, go to the **View** menu and click on the desired view.

Normal view

Previously called Print Layout, Normal is the default view in Writer. In this view, you can use the View Layout icons and the Zoom slider on the Status bar to change the magnification. You can set these same options by choosing **View > Zoom > Zoom** from the menu bar to display the Zoom & View Layout dialog.

Normal view also allows you to hide or show the headers and footers and the gap between pages. To do this, choose **View > Hide Whitespace** from the Menu bar. When activated, a check mark appears next to the option. This also hides headers, footers, and white space in Full Screen view. Note that this only works when single-page view is activated in the Status Bar.

Web Layout view

In Web Layout view, you can use only the Zoom slider; the View Layout buttons on the Status bar are disabled, and most of the choices on the Zoom & View Layout dialog are not available. In Web layout there is no visual indication of page boundaries.

Full Screen view

In Full Screen view, the document is displayed using the zoom and layout settings previously selected in the other views. To exit Full Screen view and return to Normal view, press the *Esc* key or toggle the Full Screen button on the floating toolbar in the top left-hand corner. You can also use *Ctrl+Shift+J* to toggle between Full Screen and Normal views.

Moving quickly through a document

Using the Navigator

In addition to the navigation features of the Status Bar (described above), you can use the Navigator window and the Navigation toolbar, from either the Standard toolbar or from the Sidebar, as described in Chapter 1, Introducing LibreOffice.

The Navigation toolbar (Figure 68), created from the down arrow of the Navigator window, shows buttons for all the object types shown in the Navigator.

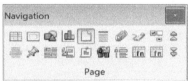

Figure 68: Navigation toolbar

When the button is selected for a specific object type, clicking the **Previous** and **Next** buttons will jump to the previous or next occurrence of the object. This is particularly helpful for finding items like index entries, which can be difficult to see in the text. The names of the buttons (shown in the tooltips) change to match the selected category, such as **Next Graphic**, **Next Bookmark**, or **Continue search forward**.

For more uses of the Navigator in Writer, see the *Writer Guide*.

Using Go to Page Option

To move to a page in the document use the menu: **Edit > Go to Page** or the keyboard shortcut *CTRL + G* to open the Go To Page dialog (Figure 69). It initially shows the number of the current page and the number of pages in the document. Then type the number of the required destination page into the text box and click the **OK** button.

Figure 69: Go to Page dialog

Working with documents

Chapter 1, Introducing LibreOffice, includes instructions on creating new documents, opening existing documents, saving documents, accessing remote servers, and password-protecting documents. Chapter 3, Using Styles and Templates, covers how to create a document from a template.

By default, LibreOffice creates and saves files in the OpenDocument file format (ODF), a standardized file format (ISO-IEC 26300) used by many software applications. Writer documents have the extension .ODT.

 Tip

> Whenever possible to choose the document file format, choose the default ODF format. This reduces the possibility of errors.

Saving as a Microsoft Word file

If you need to exchange documents with users of Microsoft Word who are unwilling or unable to receive .ODT files, you can open, edit, and save documents in Microsoft Word formats.

You can also create and edit .ODT files and then save them as .DOC or .DOCX files. To do this:

1) **Important**—First save your document in the file format used by LibreOffice Writer (.ODT). If you do not, any changes you made since the last time you saved will appear only in the Microsoft Word version of the document. Also, saving in ODF format enables you to re-save or modify the document if the recipient of your document experiences trouble with the Microsoft format.

2) Then choose **File > Save As**.

3) On the Save As dialog, in the **File type** (or **Save as type**) drop-down menu, select the type of Word format you need. You may also choose to change the file name.

4) Click **Save.**

This creates a separate document with a different file extension (such as .DOCX). From this point on, *all changes you make to the document will occur only in the new document.* If you want to go back to working with the ODT version of your document, you must open it again.

 Tip

> To have Writer save documents by default in a Microsoft Word file format, go to **Tools > Options > Load/Save > General**. In the section named *Default file format and ODF settings*, under **Document type**, select **Text document,** then under *Always save as*, select your preferred file format.

Using built-in language tools

Writer provides some tools that make work easier if you use more than one language in the same document or if you write documents in various languages. Changing the language for specific text enables you to use the correct dictionaries and rules to check spelling, grammar, and hyphenation. It also applies the localized versions of Autocorrect replacement options and uses the appropriate thesaurus.

Options for applying languages

 Tip

The language used at the location of the cursor is shown in the Status Bar, next to the page style in use.

Using styles
Languages can be set on the Font tab of the Paragraph Styles dialog or of the Character Styles dialog.

See the *Writer Guide* for information on how to manage the language settings of a style.

 Note

Be careful when changing a language in character or paragraph styles, as this will change the language for all characters or paragraphs using that style. It may be useful to include the language in the name of the style.

Also, note that languages set with direct formatting will override languages set using styles.

Using direct formatting
The language of a whole document can be set by using **Tools > Options > Language Settings > Languages**. In the *Default languages for documents* section, you can choose the language for all the text that is not explicitly marked as a different language.

Set the language for the whole document, for individual paragraphs, or even for individual words and characters, from **Tools > Language** on the Menu bar.

Alternatively, you can set the language for individual paragraphs and characters by selecting text or putting the cursor in a paragraph and changing the language on the Status Bar.

 Note

Although these methods are a type of direct formatting, they cannot be cleared by using "Clear Direct Formatting" on the Format menu or by using Ctrl+M.

Preventing text from being checked for spelling

You can set the language for a paragraph or a group of characters as **None (Do not check spelling)** using any of the methods described above. This option is especially useful for text such as web addresses or programming language snippets that you do not want to check for spelling.

Obtaining resources for additional languages

The spelling checker works only for those languages in the Spelling dialog list (described on page 97) that have the symbol (ABC) next to them. If you do not see the symbol next to your preferred language, you can install the additional dictionary using **Tools > Language > More Dictionaries Online**.

Working with text

Selecting, copying, pasting, or moving text in Writer is similar to working with text in other programs. LibreOffice also has some convenient ways to select items that are not next to each other, select a vertical block of text, and paste unformatted text.

Selecting items that are not consecutive

To select nonconsecutive items (as shown in Figure 70) using the mouse:

1) Select the first piece of text.
2) Hold down the *Ctrl* key and use the mouse to select the next piece of text.
3) Repeat as often as needed.

To select nonconsecutive items using the keyboard:

1) Select the first piece of text.
2) Press *Shift+F8*. This puts Writer in "Adding selection" mode.
3) Use the arrow keys to move to the start of the next piece of text to be selected. Hold down the *Shift* key and select the next piece of text.
4) Repeat as often as required.

Now you can work with the selected text (copy it, delete it, change the style, and so on).

Press *Esc* to exit from this mode.

> **Around the World in 80 Days - Jules Verne**
>
> A puzzled grin overspread Passepartout's round face; clearly he had not comprehended his master.
>
> "Monsieur is going to leave home?"
>
> "Yes," returned Phileas Fogg. "We are going round the world."
>
> Passepartout opened wide his eyes, raised his eyebrows, held up his hands, and seemed about to collapse, so overcome was he with stupefied astonishment.
>
> "Round the world!" he murmured.
>
> "In eighty days," responded Mr. Fogg. "So we haven't a moment to lose."
>
> "But the trunks?" gasped Passepartout, unconsciously swaying his head from right to left.
>
> "We'll have no trunks; only a carpet-bag, with two shirts and three pairs of stockings for me, and the same for you. We'll buy our clothes on the way. Bring down my mackintosh and traveling-cloak, and some stout shoes, though we shall do little walking. Make haste!"

Figure 70: Selecting items that are not next to each other

For more information about keyboard selection of text, see the topic "Navigating and selecting with the keyboard" in LibreOffice Help (*F1*).

Selecting a vertical block of text

You can select a vertical block or "column" of text that is separated by spaces or tabs (as you might see in text pasted from e-mails, program listings, or other sources), using LibreOffice's block selection mode. To change to block selection mode, use **Edit > Selection Mode > Block Area**, or press *Ctrl+F8*, or click on the **Selection** icon in the Status Bar and select **Block selection** from the list.

Figure 71: Selection icon

Now highlight the selection, using mouse or keyboard, as shown below.

January	February	March
April	May	June
July	August	September
October	November	December

Figure 72: Selecting a vertical block of text

Cutting, copying, and moving text

Cutting and copying text in Writer is similar to cutting and copying text in other applications. You can use the mouse or the keyboard for these operations. You can copy or move text within a document, or between documents, by dragging or by using menu selections, toolbar buttons, or keyboard shortcuts. You can also copy text from other sources such as Web pages and paste it into a Writer document.

To *move* (drag and drop) selected text using the mouse, drag it to the new location and release it. To *copy* selected text, hold down the *Ctrl* key while dragging. The text retains the formatting it had before dragging.

To *move* (cut and paste) selected text, use *Ctrl+X* to cut the text, insert the cursor at the paste-in point and use *Ctrl+V* to paste. Alternatively, use the buttons on the **Standard** toolbar.

Pasting text

When you paste text, the result depends on the source of the text and how you paste it. If you click on the **Paste** button on the Standard toolbar or *Ctrl+V*, any formatting the text has (such as bold or italics) is retained. Text pasted from Web sites and other sources may also be placed into frames or tables. If you do not like the results, click the **Undo** button or press *Ctrl+Z*.

To make the pasted text inherit the paragraph style at the insertion point:

* Choose **Edit > Paste Special**, or
* Click the arrow button of the combination **Paste** button, or
* Click the **Paste** button without releasing the left mouse button.

Then select **Unformatted text** from the resulting menu. Unformatted text can also be pasted with *Shift+Ctrl+Alt+V.*

The range of choices on the Paste Special menu or *Ctrl+Shift+V* varies depending on the origin and formatting of the text (or other object) to be pasted. See Figure 73 for an example when text is on the clipboard.

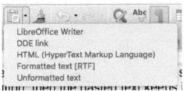

Figure 73: Paste Special menu

Finding and replacing text and formatting

Writer has two ways to find text and formatting within a document: the Find toolbar for fast searching and the Find & Replace dialog. In the dialog, you can:

* Find and replace words and phrases
* Use wildcards and regular expressions to fine-tune a search
* Find and replace specific attributes or formatting

- Find and replace paragraph styles

Using the Find toolbar

By default, the Find toolbar is shown docked at the bottom of the LibreOffice window (just above the Status Bar) as shown in Figure 74, but you can float it or dock it in another location. If the Find toolbar is not visible, you can display it by choosing **View > Toolbars > Find** from the Menu bar or by pressing *Ctrl+F*. For more information on floating and docking toolbars, see Chapter 1, Introducing LibreOffice.

Figure 74: Docked position of Find toolbar

To use the Find toolbar, click in the box and type your search text, then press *Enter* to find the next occurrence of that term. Click the **Find Next** or **Find Previous** buttons as needed.

Click the **Find All** button to select all instances of the search term within the document. Select **Match Case** to find only the instances that also match the case. To open the Find & Replace dialog, select the button ( ) to the right of Match Case.

To search in only specific types of content, click the **Page** option in the Find toolbar and choose from the pop-up menu. For example, to search for something inside the document headings, select the *Headings* entry in the menu.

Figure 75: Selective Search List.

To close the Find toolbar, click the X button on the left, or press *Esc* on the keyboard when the cursor is in the search box. *Ctrl+F* toggles the Find toolbar off and on.

⌾ Tip

'Regular expressions' offer powerful ways to search and replace text. For example, they can find all instances where any number is followed by specific letters. However, they can be challenging to understand. Refer to the Help files for guidance.

Using the Find & Replace dialog

To display the Find & Replace dialog, use the keyboard shortcut *Ctrl+H* or choose **Edit > Find & Replace** from the Menu bar. If the Find toolbar is open, click the Find & Replace button ( ) to the right of it. When the dialog is open, optionally click **Other Options** to expand it. Click the button again to reduce the dialog options.

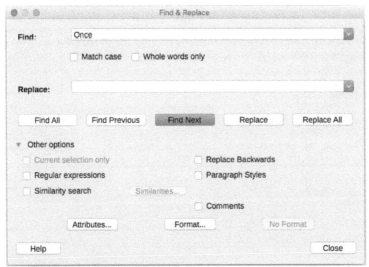

Figure 76: Expanded Find & Replace dialog

To use the Find & Replace dialog:

1) Type the text you want to find in the **Find** box.

2) To replace the text with different text, type the new text in the **Replace** box.

3) You can select various options such as matching the case, matching whole words only, or doing a search for similar words.

   The other options include searching only in selected text, searching from the current cursor position backwards toward the beginning of the file, searching for similar words, and searching in comments.

4) When you have set up your search, click **Find Next**. To replace the found text, click **Replace.**

If you click **Find All**, LibreOffice selects all instances of the search text in the document. Similarly, if you click **Replace All**, LibreOffice replaces all matches, without stopping for you to accept each instance.

For more information on using Find & Replace, see the *Writer Guide*.

Caution

Use **Replace All** with caution; otherwise, you may end up with some highly embarrassing (and often hilarious) mistakes. A mistake with **Replace All** might require a manual, word-by-word, search to fix.

Inserting special characters

A *special character* is one not found on a standard user's keyboard. For example, © ¾ æ ç ñ ö ø ¢ are all special characters not available on an English keyboard. To insert a special character:

1) Place the cursor where you want the character to appear.

2) Choose **Insert > Special Character** or click on the Special Character icon in the main toolbar to open the Special Characters dialog.

3) Select the characters (from any font or mixture of fonts) you wish to insert, in order, then click **OK**. Characters previously selected for insertion are shown in the lower left of the dialog. As you select a character, it is shown on the right, along with its numerical code.

The Special Characters dialog (Figure 77) includes areas to select *Recent* and *Favorite Characters*. To add a new character to the Favorite Characters, click on a character and click the **Add to Favorites** button.

 Tip

> Different fonts have their own distinct special characters. If you do not find a particular special character, try changing the *Font* selection.

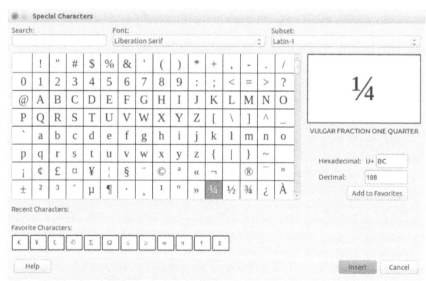

Figure 77: The Special Characters insert dialog

Inserting dashes and non-breaking spaces and hyphens

Inserting non-breaking spaces

To prevent two words from being separated at the end of a line, press *Ctrl+Shift* when you type the space between the two words. This inserts a non-breaking space.

Inserting non-breaking hyphens

In cases where you do not want the hyphen to appear at the end of a line, for example in a number such as 123-4567, you can press *Shift+Ctrl+minus sign* to insert a non-breaking hyphen.

Inserting en and em dashes

To enter en and em dashes, you can use the *Replace dashes* option on the Options tab under **Tools > AutoCorrect >AutoCorrect Options**. This option replaces two hyphens, under certain conditions, with the corresponding dash.

– is an en-dash; that is, a dash the width of the letter "n" in the font you are using. Type at least one character, a space, one or two hyphens, another space, and at least one more letter. The one or two hyphens will be replaced by an en-dash.

— is an em-dash; that is, a dash the width of the letter "m" in the font you are using. Type at least one character, two hyphens, and at least one more character. The two hyphens will be replaced by an em-dash. Exception: if the characters are numbers, as in a date or time range, the two hyphens are replaced by an en-dash.

See the Help for more details. For other methods of inserting dashes, see the *Writer Guide*.

Checking spelling and grammar

By default, four dictionaries are installed for each language: a spelling checker, a grammar checker, a hyphenation dictionary, and a thesaurus (assuming it is available for that language). The spelling checker determines if each word in the document is in the installed dictionary. The grammar checker in combination with the spelling checker.

Checking spelling automatically

When highlighted, the Automatic Spell Checking option on the Tools menu checks each word as it is typed and displays a wavy red line under any unrecognized words. Right-click on an unrecognized word to open a context menu. You can click on one of the suggested words to replace the underlined word with the one selected. If the list does not contain the word you want, click **Spelling** to open a dialog. When the word is corrected, the line disappears.

Checking spelling and grammar

To perform a combined spelling and grammar check on the document (or a text selection), click the Check **Spelling bu**tton on the Standard toolbar, or choose **Tools > Spelling.** This checks the document or selection and opens the Spelling dialog if any unrecognized words are found. To also identify potential grammar problems, check the **Check grammar** box. .

Here are some more features of the spelling checker:

Change dictionary language
Change the dictionary language (for example, Spanish, French or German) in the Spelling dialog by selecting the appropriate language in the Text language drop-down list.

Add a word to the dictionary
Add a word to the dictionary by clicking **Add to Dictionary** in the Spelling dialog or in the context menu. The word will be added to the Standard dictionary, unless you have created another dictionary in the same language. If you have created a new dictionary, you will be given a choice of dictionaries to add the word to.

Choose text for spell checking
Choose whether to check uppercase words or words that contain numbers, by clicking the **Options** button on the Spelling and Grammar dialog to open a Writing Aids dialog similar to the one in **Tools > Options > Language Settings > Writing Aids**, described in Chapter 2.

Manage custom dictionaries
Create, edit, or delete dictionaries and edit words in the dictionary in the same Writing Aids dialog.

Specify language for specific paragraphs

Set paragraphs to be checked in a language (different from the rest of the document) using several methods—for example, by clicking on the Text Language field on the Status Bar or by creating paragraph styles for specific languages. See "Using built-in language tools" on Page 90 or refer to the *Writer Guide* for more information.

Set additional grammar checking rules

Select additional grammar checking rules through **Tools > Options > Language Settings > English sentence checking**, or through **Tools > Extension Manager > English spelling dictionaries > Options**.

"Grammar by" spell checking

A new feature in LibreOffice 6.0 is "Grammar by" spelling checking. It enables the dictionary to recognize different forms of the same word. It is particularly helpful for new words or specialized words that are unlikely to have all variations in the dictionary. As an example, variations of the word "motorcycle"—motorcycles, motorcycled, motorcycling, motorcyclist, etc.— would all be accepted, without having to enter each of them individually.

To use the Grammar by feature, first create a new dictionary in the Options window of the Spelling dialog. Select the dictionary and click **Edit**. Then enter the base word in the **Word** field and enter a word in the **Grammar by** field that that has the same variations as the base word. In the motorcycle example, the word could be cyclist.

See the *Writer Guide* for more information about the spelling and grammar checking options.

Using synonyms and the thesaurus

To access a short list of synonyms, right-click on a word and point to **Synonyms** on the context menu. A submenu of alternative words and phrases is displayed. Click on a word or phrase in the submenu to have it replace the highlighted word or phrase in the document.

The thesaurus gives a more extensive list of alternative words and phrases. To use the thesaurus, click on **Thesaurus** from the Synonyms submenu. If the current language does not have a thesaurus installed, this feature is disabled.

 Note

> The thesaurus and synonyms are writing aids provided by language communities. If these aids are not available for your language, consider joining the LibreOffice project to help your language community develop them.

Using AutoCorrect

Writer's AutoCorrect function has a long list of common misspellings and typing errors, which it corrects automatically. For example, "hte" will be changed to "the". It also includes codes for inserting special characters, emoji, and other symbols.

AutoCorrect is turned on by default. You may wish to disable some of its features, modify others, or turn it off completely.

You can add your own corrections or special characters or change those supplied with LibreOffice. Choose **Tools > AutoCorrect > AutoCorrect Options** to open the AutoCorrect dialog. On the Replace tab, you can define which strings of text are corrected and how. In most cases, the defaults are fine.

To stop Writer replacing a specific spelling, go to the **Replace** tab, highlight the word pair, and click **Delete**. To add a new spelling to the list, type it into the *Replace* and *With* boxes on the Replace tab, and click **New**.

See the different tabs of the dialog for the wide variety of other options available to fine-tune AutoCorrect.

To turn AutoCorrect off, uncheck **Tools > AutoCorrect > While Typing**.

 Tip

LibreOffice has an extensive list of special characters accessible with AutoCorrect. For example, type *:smiling:* and AutoCorrect will replace it with ☺. Or, (c) will be changed to ©. You can add your own special characters.

Using Word Completion

If Word Completion is enabled, Writer tries to guess which word you are typing and offers to complete the word for you. To accept the suggestion, press *Enter*. Otherwise, continue typing.

To turn off Word Completion, select **Tools > AutoCorrect > AutoCorrect Options > Word Completion** and deselect **Enable word completion**.

Figure 78: Word completion tab in AutoCorrect dialog

Options for customizing word completion from the *Word Completion* page of the AutoCorrect dialog include:

- Add (append) a space automatically after an accepted word.
- Show the suggested word as a tip (hovering over the word) rather than completing the text as you type.
- As you add words when working on documents, you can either save them for later use in other documents or select the option to remove them from the list when closing documents.
- Change the maximum number of words remembered for word completion and the length of the smallest words to be remembered.
- Delete specific entries from the word completion list.

- Change the key that accepts a suggested entry—the options are *right arrow*, *End* key, *Return* (*Enter*), *Space bar*, and *Tab*.

 Note

Automatic word completion only occurs after you type a word for the second time in a document.

Using AutoText

Use AutoText to store text, tables, fields, and other items for reuse and assign them to a key combination for easy retrieval. For example, rather than typing "Senior Management" every time you use that phrase, you can set up an AutoText entry to insert those words when you type "sm" and press *F3*.

To store some text as AutoText:

1) Type the text into your document.
2) Select the text.
3) Choose **Tools > AutoText** (or press *Ctrl+F3*).
4) In the AutoText dialog, type a name for the AutoText in the *Name* box. Writer will suggest a one-letter shortcut, which you can change.
5) Choose the category for the AutoText entry, for example *My AutoText*.
6) Click the **AutoText** button at the bottom of the dialog and select from the menu either **New,** to have the AutoText retain specific formatting, no matter where it is inserted, or **New (text only),** to have the AutoText take on the existing formatting around the insertion point.
7) Click **Close** to return to your document.
8) To insert AutoText, type the shortcut and press *F3*.

 Tip

If the only option under the **AutoText** button is **Import**, either you have not entered a name for your AutoText or there is no text selected in the document.

AutoText is especially powerful when assigned to fields. See the *Writer Guide* for more information.

Formatting text

There are two basic ways to format text. Understanding these two alternatives is essential for unlocking the power of LibreOffice:

Direct (or Manual) formatting

Applies formatting directly to specific paragraphs, characters, pages, frames, lists, or tables. For example, you can select a word, then click on a button on the Formatting toolbar to format the text as bold or italics.

Styles

Bundles formatting options under one name. For example, a paragraph style defines numerous settings for options such as font type and size, whether paragraphs should be indented, the space between lines, how paragraphs should be aligned on the page, and many others.

Using styles is highly recommended

Writer is designed to be a style-based program. This means that it may work somewhat differently from other word processing programs you are familiar with. It requires some planning but the time spent in planning can save time and frustration over the longer term.

Because styles apply whole groups of formats at the same time, they enable you to easily format a document consistently and to change the formatting of an entire document with minimal effort. In addition, styles are used by LibreOffice for many processes, even if you are not aware of them. For example, Writer relies on heading styles (or other styles you specify) when it compiles a table of contents.

Writer defines six types of styles: paragraph, character, page, frame, list, and table. See Chapter 3, Using Styles and Templates, in this book and also refer to the *Writer Guide*.

Formatting paragraphs using styles

Styles can be applied to paragraphs using the Styles drop-down selection list at the left end of the Format toolbar, by using the **Styles** deck of the Sidebar and by using the Styles menu in the Menu Bar.

 Tip

> You can use keyboard shortcuts *Ctrl+1* to *Ctrl+5* to apply paragraph styles Heading 1 to Heading 5.

There is also an option to open a styles toolbar under the **View Menu > Toolbars > Formatting (Styles)** (Figure 79).

Figure 79: Formatting (Styles) toolbar

 Tip

> For important information about using paragraph styles to format documents, see Chapter 3 of this book and the *Writer Guide*.

Formatting paragraphs directly

You can manually apply many direct formats to paragraphs using the buttons on the Formatting toolbar and by using the Paragraph panel of the Sidebar's Properties deck. Not all buttons are visible in a standard installation, but you can customize the toolbar to include those you use regularly. These buttons and formats include:

- Set Paragraph Style
- Bullets On/Off (with a palette of bullet styles)
- Numbering On/Off (with a palette of numbering styles)
- Align Left, Center Horizontally, Align Right, or Justified
- Align Top, Center Vertically, Align Bottom
- Line Spacing (choose from 1, 1.15, 1.5, 2, or custom spacing
- Increase Paragraph Spacing, Decrease Paragraph Spacing
- Increase Indent, Decrease Indent
- Paragraph (to open the Paragraph dialog)

Note

Direct formatting (also called *manual formatting*) overrides styles. This means that when a new style is applied, direct formatting is not removed and still determines the displayed format.

Removing direct formatting

To remove direct formatting, select the text and choose **Format > Clear Direct Formatting** from the Menu bar, or right-click and choose **Styles > Clear Direct Formatting** from the context menu, or click the **Clear Direct Formatting** button on the Formatting toolbar, or press *Ctrl+M* on the keyboard.

 Note

When clearing direct formatting, the text formatting will return to the applied paragraph and character style and not the Default paragraph style or Default character style (unless these styles are actually applied to the text).

Formatting characters using styles

To apply a character style, highlight the characters or words and apply the selected character style from the **Styles** menu on the *Main Menu bar,* from the **Character Styles** tab of the Sidebar *Styles* deck, or from the right-click *context menu.*

Formatting characters directly

It is recommended that you use *styles* to format characters as much as possible rather than formatting characters directly, as described in this section.

You can directly apply many formats to characters using the buttons on the Formatting toolbar and by using the Character panel of the Sidebar's Properties deck. Not all buttons are visible in a standard installation, but you can customize the toolbar to include those you use regularly. These buttons and formats include:

- Font Name, Font Size
- Bold, Italic, Underline, Overline, Double Underline, Strikethrough, Outline
- Superscript, Subscript
- Uppercase, Lowercase
- Increase Font Size, Decrease Font Size
- Font Color (with a palette of colors)
- Background Color (with a palette of colors)
- Highlighting (with a palette of colors)

 Note

Just as direct paragraph formatting overrides the current paragraph style, applying direct character formatting to characters overrides the current character style formatting.

Formatting tables

Tables in a Writer document share the same sets of formatting elements as the spreadsheets in LibreOffice Calc.

To apply table styles, place your cursor in the table to be formatted and choose **Table >
Autoformat Styles** in the main menu and select a style from the dialog that appears. Or,
alternatively, place your cursor in the table to be formatted and double click on a style listed in the
Table Styles tab of the sidebar *Styles* deck. For more information refer to the *LibreOffice Writer
Guide.*

AutoCorrection

You can set Writer to format or correct parts of a document automatically as you type, according to
the choices made on the Options page of the AutoCorrect dialog (**Tools > AutoCorrect >
AutoCorrect Options**).

Some common unwanted or unexpected formatting changes include:

- Horizontal lines. If you type three or more hyphens (---), underscores (___) or equal signs
  (===) on a line and then press *Enter*, the paragraph is replaced by a horizontal line as wide
  as the column in the page. Note that the line is actually the lower border of the preceding
  paragraph.
- Bulleted and numbered lists. A bulleted list is created when you type a hyphen (-), star (*),
  or plus sign (+), followed by a space or tab at the beginning of a paragraph. A numbered list
  is created when you type a number followed by a period (.), followed by a space or tab at
  the beginning of a paragraph. Automatic numbering is only applied to paragraphs formatted
  with the *Default, Text body* or *Text body indent* paragraph styles.

 Tip

> If you notice unexpected formatting changes occurring in your document, this is the
> first place to look for the cause. In most cases Undo (*Ctrl+Z*) fixes the issue.

To turn AutoCorrect on or off, choose **Format > AutoCorrect** and select or deselect the items on
the list. The Help describes each of these choices.

Creating lists with styles

Creating bulleted and numbered lists

Whenever possible, use paragraph styles for creating bulleted and numbered lists. Writer comes
with two sets of paragraph styles for this purpose. However, these styles do not include options for
settings such as the type of bullet or position of numbers. Those settings come from list styles,
which are a different type of style than paragraph styles. It is recommended to use them together
in these ways:

- Use paragraph styles List 1, List 2, List 3, etc. for creating bulleted lists. These styles use
  list styles List 1, List 2, List 3, etc.
- Use paragraph styles Numbering 1, Numbering 2, Numbering 3, etc, for creating numbered
  lists. These styles use the list styles called Numbering 1, Numbering 2, etc.

To associate one of these paragraph styles to a list style, go to **Styles < Manage Styles** or click
F11 to open the list of styles. Right click on the paragraph style you want to use, then **Modify <
Outline & Numbering**. In the Numbering drop-down list, choose the appropriate list style.

Paragraph styles such as List 1 Start and List 1 End enable you to adjust specific properties (such
as the space between paragraphs) for items at the beginning or end of the list.

 Note

> List styles are not meant to be used on their own. Rather, they are designed to be
> attached to paragraph styles.

Creating nested lists

With paragraph styles, you can easily create nested lists, in which where list items have subpoints under them, as in an outline. This requires specifying the settings for the additional levels. To do this, right click on the list style (not the paragraph style) and specify how each layer will be labeled, using the Numbering Style page. Also specify the position and spacing for each level on the Position page. Refer to the *Writer Guide* for details.

Once you have set up nested lists, you can readily change the hierarchy of an item. To demote an item one level, position the cursor at the beginning of the line (after the bullet or number) and press *Tab*. To promote an item one level, press *Shift + Tab*.

Creating lists with direct formatting

Creating bulleted and numbered lists

Bullets and numbers can be manually applied in three basic ways:

- Use AutoCorrect to autoformat text, as described above.
- Use the Bullets and Numbering buttons on the Formatting bar
- Use the Paragraph panel of the Sidebar's Properties deck

Bullets and numbering can be applied to already selected text or they can be applied as you type.

 Tip

> Bullets and numbering applied in these ways cannot be removed with the command "clear direct formatting" on the Format menu or by using *Ctrl + M*. Rather, they are turned off or removed from selected text by toggling the Bullets and Numbering buttons on the Formatting bar or on the Sidebar's Properties deck.

Creating nested lists

Use the buttons on the Bullets and Numbering toolbar (Figure 80) to move items up or down the list, create sub-points, change the style of bullets, and access the Bullets and Numbering dialog, which contains more detailed controls. Use **View > Toolbars > Bullets and Numbering** to see the toolbar.

 Note

> If numbering or bullets are being applied automatically in a way that you find inappropriate, you can switch them off temporarily by unchecking **Format > AutoCorrect > While Typing**.

1 Promote One Level	**5** Insert Unnumbered Entry	**8** Move Up with Subpoints
2 Demote One Level		**9** Move Down with Subpoints
3 Promote One Level with Subpoints	**6** Move Up	**10** Restart Numbering
4 Demote One Level with Subpoints	**7** Move Down	**11** Bullets and Numbering dialog

Figure 80: Bullets and Numbering toolbar

The Bullets and Numbering buttons on the Sidebar's Properties deck can also be used to create nested lists. Click the down arrow next to the Bulleted List or Numbered List button, then **More Bullets/Numbering to** access the Bullets and Numbering dialog. However, the Sidebar does not include tools for promoting and demoting items in the list, as found on the Bullets and Numbering toolbar.

Setting tab stops and indents

The horizontal ruler shows the tab stops. Any tab stops that you have defined will overwrite the default tab stops. Tab settings affect indentation of full paragraphs (using the **Increase Indent** and **Decrease Indent** buttons on the Formatting toolbar) as well as indentation of parts of a paragraph (by pressing the *Tab* key on the keyboard).

Using the default tab spacing can cause formatting problems if you share documents with other people. If you use the default tab spacing and then send the document to someone else who has chosen a different default tab spacing, tabbed material will change to use the other person's settings. Instead of using the defaults, define your own tab settings, as described in this section.

To define indents and tab settings for one or more selected paragraphs, double-click on a part of the ruler that is not between the left and right indent icons to open the *Indents & Spacing* page of the Paragraph dialog. You can also double-click anywhere between the left and right indent icons on the ruler to open the *Tabs* page of the Paragraph dialog.

A better strategy is to define tabs for the paragraph *style*. This is done on the Tab page of the Paragraph Style dialog. Press *F11*, then right click on the style to open the dialog. See the *Writer Guide* for more information.

 Tip

Using tabs to space out material on a page is not recommended. Depending on what you are trying to accomplish, a table or frame might be a better choice.

Changing the default tab stop interval

 Caution

Any changes to the default tab setting will affect the existing default tab stops in any document you open afterward, as well as tab stops you insert after making the change.

To set the spacing of default tab stop intervals, go to **Tools > Options > LibreOffice Writer > General**.

Figure 81: Selecting a default tab stop interval

Changing measurement units for tab stops and rulers

Change the measurement unit for rulers in the current document by right-clicking on the ruler to open a list of units. Click on one of them to change the ruler to that unit. The selected setting applies only to that ruler.

Figure 82: Changing the measurement unit for a ruler

Hyphenating words

Hyphenate words at the end of a line in two ways: let Writer do it automatically (using its hyphenation dictionaries), or insert conditional hyphens manually for specific words.

Automatic hyphenation using styles

To turn automatic hyphenation of words on or off:

1) Click on the **Styles** tab in the Sidebar to open the Styles deck.

2) On the Paragraph Styles page (Figure 83), right-click on **Default Style** (or another style you want to use) and select **Modify**.

3) On the Paragraph Style dialog (Figure 84), go to the *Text Flow* page.

4) Under Hyphenation, select or deselect the **Automatically** option. When automatic hyphenation is on, you can also set the criteria for when it should occur. Click **OK** to save.

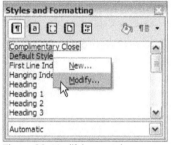

Figure 83: Modifying a style

 Note

Turning on hyphenation for the paragraph Default Style affects all other paragraph styles that are based on Default Style. You can individually change other styles so that hyphenation is not active; for example, you might not want headings to be hyphenated.

Any styles not based on Default Style are not affected. See Chapter 3, Using Styles and Templates, for more about styles based on styles other than Default Style.

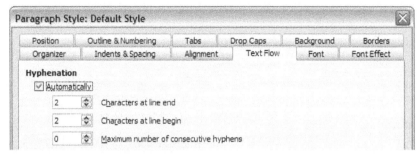

Figure 84: Turning on automatic hyphenation

Setting Hyphenation with Writing Aids

You can also set hyphenation choices through **Tools > Options > Language Settings > Writing Aids**. In Options, near the bottom of the dialog, scroll down to find the hyphenation settings.

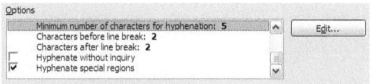

Figure 85: Setting hyphenation options

To change the minimum number of characters for hyphenation, or the minimum number of characters before or after a line break, select the item, and then click the **Edit** button in the Options section.

 Note

> Hyphenation options set on the Writing Aids dialog are effective only if hyphenation is turned on through paragraph styles.

Manual hyphenation

Manually hyphenate words when you want only a specific word hyphenated at the end of a line. Do not use a normal hyphen, which will remain visible even if the word is no longer at the end of a line (when you add or delete text or change margins or font size). Instead, use a conditional hyphen, which is visible only when required.

To insert a conditional hyphen inside a word, click where you want the hyphen to appear (when needed) and press *Ctrl+hyphen* or use **Insert > Formatting Mark > Soft hyphen**. When the word is at the end of the line it will be hyphenated at this position, even if automatic hyphenation for this paragraph is switched off.

Formatting pages

Every page in Writer is based on a page style. Pages styles define basic layout, including page size, margins, headers and footers, borders, backgrounds, etc. Changes to these settings automatically change the page style. This means that, in contrast to paragraph styles, these settings cannot be used to directly format individual pages.

As with other styles, Writer comes with a number of page styles. You can modify these styles or create new ones. The Default page style is used when no other page style has been specified.

In addition to page styles, several features enable you to further control page layouts, including columns, frames, tables, and sections. For more information, see the *Writer Guide*.

 Tip

> Page layout is usually easier if you show text, object, table, and section boundaries in **Tools > Options > LibreOffice > Application Colors,** and paragraph ends, tabs, breaks, and other items in **Tools > Options > LibreOffice Writer > Formatting Aids**.

Creating headers and footers

A header is an area that appears at the top of a page above the margin. A footer appears at the bottom of the page below the margin. Information such as page number is inserted into the header or footer of a page style. That information is then displayed on every page with the same page style (unless the page style enables separate settings for the first page or for left and right pages).

Inserting a header or footer

You can insert a header in several ways. Here is the easiest:

- Click above the top margin (or below the bottom margin) to make the Header or Footer marker appear (Figure 86), and then click on the **+**.

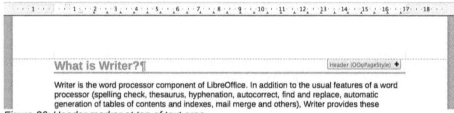

Figure 86: Header marker at top of text area

After a header/footer has been created, a down-arrow appears on the marker. Click on this arrow to drop down a menu of choices for working with the header (Figure 87).

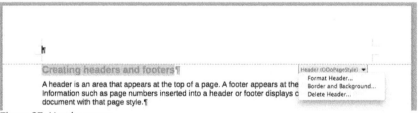

Figure 87: Header menu

Alternatively, you can choose **Insert > Header and Footer > Header > Default Style** (or some other page style, if not Default Style).

Determining header and footer appearance

To format a header (use similar settings for a footer), you can either click on **Format Header** in the menu shown in Figure 87 or go to **Format > Page > Header**. Both methods take you to the same tab on the Page Style dialog.

Here you can specify if headings on the left and right pages should be the same or different. You can also specify whether the first page will have no header or a different header than other pages.

In this dialog, you can also turn the header on or off, set the margins, and set the spacing between the header and document text.

Figure 88: Page header dialog

Inserting document title in headers and footers

Information such as a document title is often put into the header or footer. These items are best added as fields. That way, if something (such as the name) changes, the headers and footers are updated automatically. Here is one common way to use fields to insert the document title into the header:

1) Choose **File > Properties > Description** and type a title for your document.

2) Add a header with **Insert > Header and Footer > Header > Default Style** (or appropriate page style).

3) Place the cursor in the header area at the top of the page. If needed, click on the **+ to be able to click in the header.**

4) Choose **Insert > Fields > Title**. The title should appear on a gray background. The background does not show when printed and can be turned off in **Tools > Options > LibreOffice > Application Colors**.

5) To change the title for the whole document, go back to **File > Properties > Description**.

For more about headers, footers, and fields, see the *Writer Guide*.

Numbering pages

Displaying the page number

To display page numbers automatically:

1) Insert a header or footer, as described in "Creating headers and footers" above.

2) Place the cursor in the header or footer where you want the page number to appear and choose **Insert > Page Number**.

Including the total number of pages

To include the total number of pages (as in "page 1 of 12"):

1) Type the word "page" and a space, then insert the page number as above.

2) Press the space bar once, type the word "of" and a space, then choose **Insert > Field > Page Count**.

Note

The Page Count field inserts the total number of pages in the document, as shown on the Statistics tab of the document's Properties window (**File > Properties**). If you restart page numbering anywhere in the document, then the total page count may not be what you want. See the *Writer Guide* for more information.

Restarting page numbering

Often you will want to restart the page numbering at 1, for example on the page following a title page or a table of contents. In addition, many documents have the "front matter" (such as the table of contents) numbered with Roman numerals and the main body of the document numbered in Arabic numerals, starting with 1. To restart page numbering:

Place the cursor in the first paragraph of the new page.

1) Choose **Format > Paragraph.**
2) On the Text Flow tab of the Paragraph dialog (Figure 84 on page 107), select **Breaks**.
3) Select **Insert** and then **With Page Style** and specify the page style to use.
4) Specify the page number to start from, and then click **OK**.

 Tip

This is also useful for numbering the first page of a document with a page number greater than 1. For example, you may be writing a book, with each chapter in a separate file. Chapter 1 may start with page 1, but Chapter 2 could begin with page 25 and Chapter 3 with page 51.

Changing page margins

You can change page margins in three ways:

- Using the page rulers—quick and easy, but does not allow fine control
- Using the Page Style dialog—can specify margins to two decimal places
- Using the Page deck of the Sidebar

 Caution

When you change the margins, the page style is also changed and the changed margins apply to **all** pages using that style.

To change margins using the rulers:

1) The gray sections of the rulers are the margins. Put the mouse cursor over the line between the gray and white sections. The pointer turns into a double-headed arrow and displays the current setting in a tool-tip.
2) Hold down the left mouse button and drag the mouse to move the margin.

 Caution

The two small gray triangles on the ruler are used for indenting paragraphs. The double-headed arrows shown in Figure 89 are mouse cursors shown in the correct position for moving the margin markers. Because the triangles and arrows are often in the same place, when changing page margins you need to be careful to move the arrows, not the gray triangles.

Figure 89: Moving the margins

To change margins using the Page Style dialog:

1) Right-click anywhere in the text area on the page and select **Page** from the context menu.

2) On the **Page** tab of the dialog, type the required distances in the Margins boxes.

To change margins using the Page deck of the Sidebar:

1) On the Sidebar (**View > Sidebar**) open the **Page** tab.

2) In the Format panel, use the Margins drop-down list to select the desired margins. Click the **More Options** button to open the Page Style dialog where you can enter exact margin distances.

Adding a custom watermark to the page background

To add a watermark to a page background:

1) Choose **Format > Watermark**.

2) In the Watermark dialog, type the text and select the font, angle, transparency and color of the watermark. Then click the **OK** button.

Figure 90: The Watermark dialog

 Note

The watermark will automatically become part of the page style where it is inserted and all other pages of the same style will have the watermark. Pages with different or no watermarks need different Page Styles for those pages.

Adding comments to a document

Authors and reviewers often use comments to exchange ideas, ask for suggestions, or mark items needing attention.

You can connect a comment to multiple paragraphs or a single point. To insert a comment, select the text, or place the cursor in the place the comment refers to, and choose **Insert > Comment** or press *Ctrl+Alt+C*. The anchor point of the comment is connected by a dotted line to a box on the right-hand side of the page where you can type the text of the comment. A Comments button is also added to the right of the horizontal ruler at the top of the page; you can click this button to toggle the display of the comments.

Formatting comments

At the bottom of the comment, Writer automatically adds the author's name and a time stamp indicating when the comment was created. If more than one person edits the document, each author is automatically allocated a different background color. Figure 91 shows an example of text with comments from two different authors.

Figure 91: Example of comments

Choose **Tools > Options > LibreOffice > User Data** to configure the name you want to appear in the Author field of the comment, or to change it.

Right-click on a comment to open a context menu where you can delete the current comment, all the comments from the same author, or all the comments in the document. From this menu, you can also reply to a comment and open a dialog to apply some basic formatting to the text.

Navigating through comments

To navigate from one comment to another, open the Navigator (*F5*), expand the Comments section, and click on the comment text to move the cursor to the anchor point of the comment in the document. Click the comment directly to edit it and right-click on the comment to delete it.

You can also navigate through the comments using the keyboard. Use *Ctrl+Alt+Page Down* to move to the next comment and *Ctrl+Alt+Page Up* to move to the previous comment.

Printing comments

When a document contains comments, the print dialog has an option for comments to be printed next to the text in the right margin, as they appear on the screen. In that case, the text on each page is scaled down to make space for the comments. The Print dialog also has options for placing comments at the end of the page or at the end of the document, or for printing only the comments.

Creating a table of contents

Writer can generate a table of contents from the headings in your document. Before you start, make sure that the headings are styled consistently. For example, you can use the *Heading 1* style for chapter titles and the *Heading 2* and *Heading 3* styles for chapter subheadings.

Although tables of contents can be customized extensively in Writer, often the default settings are all you need. Creating a quick table of contents is simple:

1) When you create your document, use the following paragraph styles for hierarchical heading levels (such as chapter and section headings): *Heading 1*, *Heading 2*, *Heading 3*, and so on. These headings are what will appear in your table of contents.

2) Place the cursor where you want the table of contents to appear.

3) Choose **Insert > Table of Contents and Index > Table of Contents, Index or Bibliography**.

4) Change nothing in the Insert Index/Table dialog (unless you want to change the number of levels shown). Click **OK**.

If you add or delete text (so that headings move to different pages) or you add, delete, or change headings, you need to update the table of contents.

To do this:

1) Place the cursor within the table of contents.

2) Right-click and choose **Update index** from the context menu.

 Note

> If you cannot place the cursor in the table of contents, choose **Tools > Options > LibreOffice Writer > Formatting Aids**, and then select **Enable Cursor** in the **Protected areas** section.

You can customize an existing table of contents at any time. Right-click anywhere in it and choose **Edit Index** from the context menu. The *Writer Guide* describes in detail all the customizations you can choose.

Creating indexes and bibliographies

Indexes and bibliographies work in a similar way to tables of contents. In addition to alphabetical indexes, other types of indexes supplied with Writer include those for illustrations, tables, and objects, and you can even create a user-defined index.

For example, you might want an index containing only the scientific names of species mentioned in the text, and a separate index containing only the common names of species. Before creating some types of indexes, you first need to create index entries in your Writer document. The *Writer Guide* describes the process in detail.

Working with graphics

Graphics in Writer are of three basic types:

• Image files, including photos, drawings, scanned images, and others
• Diagrams created using LibreOffice's drawing tools
• Charts created using LibreOffice's Chart component

See Chapter 11, Graphics, the Gallery, and Fontwork, in this book and the *Writer Guide*.

Printing

See Chapter 10, Printing, Exporting, and Emailing, in this book and the *Writer Guide* for details on previewing pages before printing, selecting print options, printing in black and white on a color printer, printing brochures, and other printing features.

Using mail merge

Writer provides very useful features to create and print:

- Multiple copies of a document to send to a list of different recipients (form letters)
- Mailing labels
- Envelopes

All these features use data from a Writer table or another registered data source (a spreadsheet or database containing name and address records or other information). The *Writer Guide* describes the merge processes.

Tracking changes to a document

You can use several methods to keep track of changes made to a document.

1) Make your changes to a copy of the document (stored in a different folder, or under a different name, or both), then use Writer to combine the two files and show the differences. Choose **Edit > Track Changes > Compare Document**.

2) Save versions that are stored as part of the original file. However, this method can cause problems with documents of non-trivial size or complexity, especially if you save a lot of versions. Avoid this method if you can.

3) Use Writer's change marks (often called "redlines" or "revision marks") to show where you have added or deleted material, or changed formatting. Choose **Edit > Track Changes > Record Changes** before starting to edit. Later, you or another person can review and accept or reject each change. Choose **Edit > Track Changes > Show Changes**. Right-click on an individual change and choose **Accept Change** or **Reject Change** from the context menu, or choose **Edit > Track Changes > Manage Changes** to view the list of changes and accept or reject them. Details are in the *Writer Guide*.

 Tip

Not all changes are recorded. For example, changing a tab stop from align left to align right, and changes in formulas (equations) or linked graphics are not recorded.

 Caution

A document with track changes activated but with the changes not shown carries an invisible history of document editing that the current user may not be aware of. Contents deleted or modified can be recovered. While this is a feature, it is also a potential privacy risk.

Using fields

Fields are extremely useful features of Writer. They are used for data that changes (such as the current date or the total number of pages) and for inserting document properties such as name, author, and date of last update. Fields are the basis of cross-referencing (see below); automatic numbering of figures, tables, headings, and other elements; and a wide range of other functions—far too many to describe here. See the *Writer Guide* for details.

Linking and cross-referencing within a document

If you manually type in cross-references to other parts of a document, those references can easily get out of date if you reorganize the order of topics, add or remove material, or reword a heading. Writer provides two ways to ensure that your references are up to date: hyperlinks and cross-references.

Both methods insert links to other parts of the same document or to an external source, taking you directly to the cross-referenced item. However, they have major differences:

- The text in a hyperlink does **not** automatically update if you change the text of the linked item (although you can change it manually), but changed text does automatically update in a cross-reference.
- When using a hyperlink, you do not have a choice about the type of content linked to (such as text or page number), but when using a cross-reference, you have several choices, including bookmarks.
- To hyperlink to an object such as a graphic, and have the hyperlink show useful text such as *Figure 6*, you need to give such an object a useful name (instead of a default name like *Graphics6*), or use the Hyperlink dialog to modify the visible text. In contrast, cross-references to figures with captions automatically show useful text, and you have a choice of several variations of the name.
- If you save a Writer document to HTML, hyperlinks remain active but cross-references do not. Both remain active when the document is exported to PDF.

Using hyperlinks

See Chapter 12, Creating HTML Files, for details on creating hyperlinks within a document and to other documents and websites.

Creating and using cross-references

After a cross-reference has been created, use *F9* to update all references so that the current wording or page numbers are displayed. The *Cross-references* tab of the Fields dialog lists some items, such as headings, bookmarks, figures, tables, or numbered items such as steps in a procedure. You can also create your own reference items; see "Setting References" in the *Writer Guide* for instructions.

To insert a cross-reference:

1) In your document, place the cursor where you want the cross-reference to appear.
2) If the Fields dialog is not open, click **Insert > Cross-reference**. On the *Cross-references* tab (Figure 92), in the *Type* list, select the type of item to be referenced (for example, *Headings* or *Figure*). You can leave this page open while you insert many cross-references.
3) Click on the required item in the *Selection* list, which shows all the items of the selected type. You can type some characters in the top box under *Selection* to filter the list in the selection box.

4) In the *Insert reference to* list, select the option needed. The options determine the text inserted for the hyperlink and how it is formatted. The list varies according to the Type chosen. The most commonly used options are **Reference** (to insert the full text of a heading or caption), **Category and Number** (to insert a figure number preceded by the word *Figure* or *Table*, but without the caption text), **Numbering** (to insert only the figure or table number, without the word "Figure" or "Table"), or **Page** (to insert the number of the page the referenced text is on). Click **Insert**.

Figure 92: The Cross-references tab of the Fields dialog

Using bookmarks

Use bookmarks to rapidly navigate or link to specific locations in a document. They are listed in the Navigator and can be accessed directly from there with a single mouse click. You can cross-reference to bookmarks and create hyperlinks to bookmarks, as described above. To create a bookmark:

1) Select the text you want to bookmark. Click **Insert > Bookmark**.

2) On the Insert Bookmark dialog, the larger box lists any previously defined bookmarks. Type a name for this new bookmark in the top box, and then click **Insert**.

Using master documents

A master document joins separate text documents into one larger document, and unifies the formatting, table of contents, bibliography, index, and other tables or lists. Master documents are typically used for producing long documents such as a book, thesis, or long report. They are especially handy when different people are writing different sections of a document, eliminating the need to continually share the full document. For details on using master documents, see the *Writer Guide*.

You can add master document templates to LibreOffice in the same way as ordinary document templates. Creating a new document based on a master document template creates a master document with the same initial content as the template it is based upon. See Chapter 3, Styles and Templates, for more about creating and using templates.

Classifying document contents

Document classification and security are important for businesses and governments. Where sensitive information is exchanged between users and organizations, the parties agree how such information will be identified and handled. LibreOffice provides standardized means for sensitive information to be identified and protected, using a set of standard fields that can be used to hold sensitive information.

LibreOffice implemented the open standards produced by TSCP (Transglobal Secure Collaboration Participation, Inc.). It contains three BAF (Business Authentication Framework) categories: Intellectual Property, National Security and Export Control. Each category has four BAILS (Business Authorization Identification and Labeling Scheme) levels: Non-Business, General Business, Confidential, and Internal Only.

To enable document classification, open the TSCP bar (**View > Toolbars > TSCP**). This toolbar contains list boxes to help in selecting the security of the document. LibreOffice then adds custom fields in the document properties (**File > Properties**, **Custom fields** tab) to store the classification policy as document metadata.

To prevent a breach in security policy, contents with a higher classification level cannot be pasted into documents with a lower classification level.

For more information, refer to the *Writer Guide*.

Creating fill-in forms

In a standard text document, such as a report, any text can be edited. By contrast, a form has sections that are not to be edited, and other sections that are designed for the reader to fill in information. For example, a questionnaire has an introduction and questions (which do not change) and spaces for the reader to enter answers.

Forms are used in three ways:

- To create a simple document for the recipient to complete, such as a questionnaire sent out to a group of people who fill it in and return it.
- To enter information directly into a database or data source. Someone taking orders might enter the information for each order into a database using a form.
- To view information held in a database or data source. A librarian might call up information about books.

Writer offers several ways to organize information fields in a form, including check boxes, option buttons, text boxes, pull-down lists, and spinners. Options for creating forms are available in the Forms menu of the Standard toolbar. See the *Writer Guide for more information*.

Getting Started Guide

Chapter 5
Getting Started with Calc

Using Spreadsheets in LibreOffice

What is Calc?

Calc is the spreadsheet component of LibreOffice. You can enter data (usually numerical) in a spreadsheet and then manipulate this data to produce certain results.

Alternatively, you can enter data and then use Calc in a "What if..." manner by changing some of the data and observing the results without having to retype the entire spreadsheet or sheet.

Other features provided by Calc include:

- Functions, which can be used to create formulas to perform complex calculations on data.
- Database functions, to arrange, store, and filter data.
- Dynamic charts; a wide range of 2D and 3D charts.
- Macros, for recording and executing repetitive tasks; scripting languages supported include LibreOffice Basic, Python, BeanShell, and JavaScript.
- Ability to open, edit, and save Microsoft Excel spreadsheets.
- Import and export of spreadsheets in multiple formats, including HTML, CSV, PDF, and PostScript.

Compatibility with other spreadsheet applications

Wildcards

Simple wildcards such as the *asterisk (*), question mark (?),* and *tilde (~)* from other spreadsheet applications are recognized by LibreOffice. Wildcards are more widespread in other spreadsheet applications and adopting a similar option in LibreOffice allows for better compatibility and a better experience for users who may not be familiar with the use of regular expressions.

Formula syntax

By default, LibreOffice Calc uses its own formula syntax, referred to as *Calc R1* rather than the *Excel R1* syntax that is used by Microsoft Excel. LibreOffice will translate seamlessly between the two. However, if you are familiar with Excel you may wish to change the default syntax in Calc by going to **Tools > Options > LibreOffice Calc > Formula > Formula Syntax** and choosing *Excel R1* from the drop-down menu provided.

For more information on formula syntax, see the *Calc Guide Chapter 7 Formulas and Functions*.

Macros

Microsoft Office uses *Visual Basic for applications* (VBA) code, and LibreOffice uses *Basic* code based on the LibreOffice API. Although the programming languages are the same, the objects and methods are different and therefore not entirely compatible.

LibreOffice can however run *some* Excel Visual Basic Scripts if you enable this feature at **Tools > Options > Load/Save > VBA Properties.**

For more information on macros, refer to the Calc Guide Chapter 12 Calc Macros.

Spreadsheets, sheets, and cells

Calc works with documents called *spreadsheets*. Spreadsheets consist of a number of individual *sheets*, each sheet containing cells arranged in rows and columns. A particular cell is identified by its row number and column letter.

Cells hold the individual elements – text, numbers, formulas, and so on – that make up the data to display and manipulate.

Each spreadsheet can have several sheets, and each sheet can have many individual cells. In Calc, each sheet can have a maximum of 1,048,576 rows and a maximum of 1024 columns. LibreOffice Calc can hold up to 32,000 sheets.

Calc main window

When Calc is started, the main window opens (Figure 93). The parts of this window are described below.

Title bar

The Title bar, located at the top, shows the name of the current spreadsheet. When a spreadsheet is newly created from a template or a blank document, its name is *Untitled X*, where *X* is a number. When you save a spreadsheet for the first time, you are prompted to enter a name of your choice.

Figure 93: Calc main window

Menu bar

When you select an item on the Menu bar, a sub-menu drops down to show commands. You can also customize the Menu bar; see *Chapter 14 Customizing LibreOffice* for more information.

- **File** – contains commands that apply to the entire document; for example, *Open, Save, Wizards, Export as PDF, Print, Digital Signatures, and Templates.*
- **Edit** – contains commands for editing the document; for example, *Undo, Copy, Paste, Track Changes, Find and Replace, Compare and Merge Documents.*
- **View** – contains commands for modifying how the Calc user interface looks; for example, *Toolbars, Grids, Column & Row Headers, Full Screen, Zoom.*
- **Insert** – contains commands for inserting elements into a spreadsheet; for example, *Pictures, Media, Objects, Formula Design, Frames, Special Characters, Charts, Functions,*

Shapes, Pivot Tables, Named Ranges, Comments, Hyperlinks, Headers and Footers, Form Controls.

- **Format** – contains commands for modifying the layout of a spreadsheet; for example, *Cells, Page, Styles, Alignment, Merge Cells, Print Range, Conditional Formatting, Spreadsheet Themes, Image, Chart, Object.*
- **Styles** – contains commands to apply standard styles to cell, group of cells or sheets contents.
- **Sheet** – contains the most often used commands for handling sheets, such as *Insert* and *Delete Cells, Columns, Rows and Sheets, Sheets from File, Cell Reference Type, Link to External Data,* as well as *Comments* and *Fill cells.*
- **Data** – contains commands for manipulating data in the spreadsheet; for example, *Define Database Range, Sort,* Filters, *Statistics, Pivot Tables, Consolidate, Forms, Groups and Outlines.*
- **Tools** – contains various functions to help you check and customize the spreadsheet; for example, *Spelling, Share Document, Gallery, Macros, Goal Seek, Solver, Detective, Protect Sheet, XML Filter Settings, Extension Manager.*
- **Window** – contains commands to open a *New* window or *Close* an open window.
- **Help** – contains links to the LibreOffice help system and other miscellaneous functions; for example, *Help, License Information, User Guides, Check for Updates, Send Feedback,* and *Donate.*

Toolbars

The default setting when Calc opens is for the Standard and Formatting toolbars to be docked at the top of the workspace (Figure 93).

Calc toolbars can be either docked and fixed in place, or floating; you can move a toolbar into a more convenient position on the workspace. Docked toolbars can be undocked and either moved to different docked position on the workspace, or left as a floating toolbar. Toolbars that are floating when opened can be docked into a fixed position on the workspace.

You can choose the single-toolbar alternative to the default double toolbar arrangement. It contains the most-used commands. To activate it, enable **View > Toolbars > Standard (Single Mode)** and disable **View > Toolbars > Standard** and **View > Toolbars > Formatting**.

The default set of icons (sometimes called buttons) on toolbars provides a wide range of common commands and functions. You can also remove or add icons to toolbars; see *Chapter 14 Customizing LibreOffice* for more information. When hovering the toolbar with the mouse, a tool tip shows the action performed by each icon in the toolbar.

Formula bar

The Formula Bar (Figure 94) is located at the top of the sheet in the Calc workspace. The Formula Bar is permanently docked in this position and cannot be used as a floating toolbar. If the Formula Bar is not visible, go to **View** on the Menu bar and select **Formula Bar**.

Figure 94: Formula bar

From left to right, the Formula Bar consists of the following:

- **Name Box** – gives the current active cell reference using a combination of a letter and number, for example A1. The letter indicates the column and the number indicates the row of the selected cell. If you have selected a range of cells that is also a named range, the name of the range is shown in this box. You can also type a cell reference in the Name Box to jump to the referenced cell. If you type the name of a named range and press the *Enter* key, the named range is selected and displayed.

- **Function Wizard** – opens a dialog from which you can search through a list of available functions. This can be very useful because it also shows how the functions are formatted.

- **Sum** Σ – clicking on the Sum icon totals the numbers in the cells above the selected cell and then places the total in the selected cell. If there are no numbers above the selected cell, then the cells to the left are totaled. When the **Sum** icon is used, Calc suggest the range to sum with a colored box, but does not insert the formula. You need to confirm the suggested range by typing *Enter*, or reject pressing *Esc*. You can also adjust the range with the mouse by dragging the colored box or its edges to adjust the range. The icons ✖ ✔ in the formula bar are equivalent to the *Enter* and *Esc* commands.

- **Function** = – clicking on the Function icon inserts an equals (=) sign into the selected cell and the **Input line**, allowing a formula to be entered. The Name box now displays the most frequently used functions, for a quick access to the function name and syntax.

- **Input line** – displays the contents of the selected cell (data, formula, or function) and allows you to edit the cell contents. To turn the Input line into a multiline input area for very long formulas, click the drop down button on the right.

You can also edit the contents of a cell directly in the cell itself by double-clicking on the cell. When you enter new data into a cell, the Sum and Function icons change to **Cancel** and **Accept** ✖ ✔ icons.

> **Note**
>
> In a spreadsheet the term "function" covers much more than just mathematical functions. See the *Calc Guide Chapter 7 Using Formulas and Functions* for more information.

Status bar

The Calc status bar (Figure 95) provides information about the spreadsheet as well as quick and convenient ways to change some of its features. Most of the fields are similar to those in other components of LibreOffice; see *Chapter 1 Introducing LibreOffice* in this guide and the *Calc Guide Chapter 1 Introducing Calc* for more information.

Figure 95: Calc status bar

The status bar has a quick way to do some math operations on selected cells in the spreadsheet. You can calculate average and sum, count elements, and more on the selection by right-clicking over the cell information area of the status bar and selecting the operations you want to display in the status bar (Figure 122).

Sidebar

The Calc Sidebar (**View > Sidebar**) is located on the right side of the window. It is a mixture of toolbar and dialog. It is similar to the sidebar in Writer (shown in Chapter 1 and Chapter 4 of this book) and consists of five decks: Properties, Styles, Gallery, Navigator, and Functions. Each deck has a corresponding icon on the Tab panel to the right of the sidebar, allowing you to switch between them. The decks are described below.

- **Properties**: This deck includes five content panels.
  - **Styles:** Access to the available cell styles, update cell styles, and new cell styles.
  - **Character**: Controls for formatting the text, such as font family, size, and color. Some controls, such as superscript, only become active when the text cursor is active in the Input line of the Formula bar or the cell.
  - **Number Format:** Quickly change the format of numbers including decimals, currency, dates, or numeric text. Numerical and label field controls for Forms are also available.
  - **Alignment**: Controls to align the text in various ways, including horizontal and vertical alignment, wrapping, indenting, merging, text orientation, and vertical stacking.
  - **Cell Appearance:** Controls to set the appearance options, including cell background color, cell border formats including line color and style, and grid lines.

  Each of these panels has a **More Options** button, which opens a dialog giving a greater number of options. These dialogs lock the document for editing until they are closed.
- **Styles:** This deck contains a single panel, which is the same as that opened by selecting the **Styles** button (*F11*) from the Text Formatting toolbar.
- **Gallery**: This deck contains a single panel, which is the same as that opened by selecting **Gallery** from the Standard toolbar or **Tools > Gallery** from the Menu bar.
- **Navigator**: This deck contains a single panel, which is essentially the same as the Navigator window opened by clicking the **Navigator** button on the Standard toolbar or selecting **View > Navigator** (*F5*) from the Menu bar. Only the **Contents** button is absent in the Sidebar's Navigator panel.
- **Functions**: This deck contains a single panel, which is the same as the window opened by selecting **Insert > Function...** from the Menu bar.

To the right side of the title bar of each open deck is a **Close** button (**X**), which closes the deck to leave only the Tab bar open. Clicking on any Tab button reopens the deck.

To hide the Sidebar, or reveal it if already hidden, click on the edge Hide/Show button. To adjust the deck width, drag on the left edge of the sidebar.

Spreadsheet layout

Individual cells

The main section of the workspace in Calc displays the cells in the form of a grid. Each cell is formed by the intersection of one column and one row in the spreadsheet.

At the top of the columns and the left end of the rows are a series of header boxes containing letters and numbers. The column headers use an alpha character starting at A and go on to the right. The row headers use a numerical character starting at 1 and go down.

These column and row headers form the cell references that appear in the Name Box on the Formula Bar (Figure 94). If the headers are not visible on the spreadsheet, go to **View** on the Menu bar and select **Column & Row Headers**.

Sheet tabs

In Calc, you can have more than one sheet in a spreadsheet. At the bottom of the grid of cells in a spreadsheet are sheet tabs indicating how many sheets there are in the spreadsheet. Clicking on a tab enables access to each individual sheet and displays that sheet. An active sheet is indicated with a white tab (default Calc setup). You can also select multiple sheets by holding down the *Ctrl* key while clicking on the sheet tabs.

To change the default name for a sheet (Sheet1, Sheet2, and so on), right-click on a sheet tab and select **Rename Sheet** from the context menu or double click on the sheet tab to open a dialog to let you type a new name for the sheet. Click **OK** when finished to close the dialog.

To change the color of a sheet tab, right-click on the tab and select **Tab Color** from the context menu to open the **Tab Color** dialog. Select a color and click **OK** when finished to close the dialog. To add new colors to this color palette, see *Chapter 14 Customizing LibreOffice*.

Opening a CSV file

Comma-separated-values (CSV) files are spreadsheet files in a text format where cell contents are separated by a character, for example a comma or semicolon. Each line in a CSV text file represents a row in a spreadsheet. Text is entered between quotation marks; numbers are entered without quotation marks.

 Note

> Most CSV files come from databases tables, queries, or reports, where further calculations and charting are required. On Microsoft Windows, CSV files often have the XLS file name extension to look like an Excel file, but they are still CSV files internally.

To open a CSV file in Calc:

1) Choose **File > Open** on the Menu bar and locate the CSV file that you want to open.

2) Select the file and click **Open**. By default, a CSV file has the extension .csv. However, some CSV files may have a .txt extension.

3) The **Text Import** dialog (Figure 97) opens. Here you can select the various options available when importing a CSV file into a Calc spreadsheet.

4) Click **OK** to open and import the file.

Figure 96: Text Import dialog

The options for importing CSV files into a Calc spreadsheet are as follows:

- **Import**
  - *Character Set* – specifies the character set to be used in the imported file.
  - *Language* – determines how the number strings are imported.

    If Language is set to Default for CSV import, Calc will use the globally set language. If Language is set to a specific language, that language will be used when importing numbers.
  - *From Row* – specifies the row where you want to start the import. The rows are visible in the preview window at the bottom of the dialog.
- **Separator Options** – specifies whether the data uses separators or fixed widths as delimiters.
  - *Fixed width* – separates fixed-width data (equal number of characters) into columns. Click on the ruler in the preview window to set the width.
  - *Separated by* – select the separator used in the data to delimit the data into columns. If you select *Other*, specify the character used to separate data into columns. This custom separator must also be contained in the data.
  - *Merge delimiters* – combines consecutive delimiters and removes blank data fields.
  - *Text delimiter* – select a character to delimit text data.
- **Other Options**
  - *Quoted fields as text* – when this option is enabled, fields or cells whose values are quoted in their entirety (the first and last characters of the value equal the text delimiter) are imported as text.
  - *Detect special numbers* – when this option is enabled, Calc will automatically detect all number formats, including special number formats such as dates, time, and scientific notation. The selected language also influences how such special numbers are detected, since different languages and regions many have different conventions for such special numbers.

    When this option is disabled, Calc will detect and convert only decimal numbers. The rest, including numbers formatted in scientific notation, will be imported as text. A decimal number string can have digits 0-9, thousands separators, and a decimal separator. Thousands separators and decimal separators may vary with the selected language and region.
- **Fields** – shows how the data will look when it is separated into columns.
  - *Column type* – select a column in the preview window and select the data type to be applied the imported data.
  - *Standard* – Calc determines the type of data.
  - *Text* – imported data are treated as text.
  - *US English* – numbers formatted in US English are searched for and included regardless of the system language. A number format is not applied. If there are no US English entries, the *Standard* format is applied.
  - *Hide* – the data in the column are not imported.

Saving spreadsheets

To save a spreadsheet, see *Chapter 1 Introducing LibreOffice* for more details on how to save files manually or automatically. Calc can also save spreadsheets in a range of formats and also export spreadsheets to PDF, HTML, XHTML file formats and JPEG and PNG images formats; see the *Calc Guide Chapter 6 Printing, Exporting, and E-mailing* for more information.

Saving in other spreadsheet formats

If you need to exchange files with users who are unable to receive spreadsheet files in Open Document Format (ODF) (*.ods), which Calc uses as default format, you can save a spreadsheet in another format.

1) Save the spreadsheet in Calc spreadsheet file format (*.ods).

2) Select **File > Save As** on the Menu bar to open the **Save As** dialog (Figure 97).

3) In **File name**, you can enter a new file name for the spreadsheet.

4) In the **File type** drop-down menu, select the type of spreadsheet format you want to use.

5) If **Automatic file name extension** is selected, the correct file extension for the spreadsheet format you have selected will be added to the file name.

6) Click **Save**.

Figure 97: Save As dialog

7) When saving in a non default file format, the **Confirm File Format** dialog opens (Figure 98). Click **Use [xxx] Format** to continue saving in your selected spreadsheet format or click **Use ODF Format** to save the spreadsheet in Calc ODS format.

Figure 98: File Format dialog

8) If you select **Text CSV** format (`*.csv`) for your spreadsheet, the **Export Text File** dialog (Figure 99) may open. Here you can select the character set, field delimiter, text delimiter, and so on to be used for the CSV file.

Figure 99: Export Text File dialog for CSV files

 Tip

To have Calc save documents by default in a file format other than the default ODF format, go to **Tools > Options > Load/Save > General**. In **Default file format** and **ODF settings > Document type**, select **Spreadsheet,** then in **Always save as**, select your preferred file format.

Exporting contents as image

If you want to send a fragment of your spreadsheet to a colleague, business partner or publish it in the internet, Calc can export a range selection or a selected group of shapes (images) to a PNG or JPG graphics format:

1) Select the range or the group of shapes in your spreadsheet.
2) Select **File – Export...** to open the Export dialog.
3) Enter a name for your image in the **File name** box.
4) Select the graphics file format in the **Type** list
5) Mark the **Selection** checkbox in the **Export** dialog.
6) Click **Export...**

Navigating within spreadsheets

Calc provides many ways to navigate within a spreadsheet from cell to cell and sheet to sheet. You can generally use the method you prefer.

Cell navigation

When a cell is selected or in focus, the cell borders are emphasized. When a group of cells is selected, the cell area is colored. The color of the cell border emphasis and the color of a group of selected cells depends on the operating system being used and how you have set up LibreOffice.

- **Using the mouse** – place the mouse pointer over the cell and click the left mouse button. To move the focus to another cell using the mouse, simply move the mouse pointer to the cell where you want the focus to be and click the left mouse button.
- **Using a cell reference** – highlight or delete the existing cell reference in the Name Box on the Formula Bar (Figure 94 on page 121). Type the new cell reference of the cell you want

to move to and press *Enter* key. Cell references are case-insensitive: for example, typing either a3 or A3 will move the focus to cell A3.

- **Using the Navigator** – press the *F5* key to open the Navigator dialog (Figure 103) or click the **Navigator** button in the open Sidebar. Type the cell reference into the Column and Row fields and press the *Enter* key.

Figure 100: Navigator in Calc

- **Using the Enter key** – pressing *Enter* moves the cell focus down in a column to the next row. Pressing *Shift+Enter* moves the focus up in a column to the previous row.
- **Using the Tab key** – pressing Tab moves the cell focus right in a row to the next column. Pressing *Shift+Tab* moves the focus to the left in a row to the previous column.
- **Using the arrow keys** – pressing the arrow keys on the keyboard moves the cell focus in the direction of the arrow pressed.
- **Using Home**, **End**, **Page Up** and **Page Down**
  - *Home* moves the cell focus to the start of a row.
  - *End* moves the cell focus to the last cell on the right in the row in the right-most column that contains data.
  - *Page Down* moves the cell focus down one complete screen display.
  - *Page Up* moves the cell focus up one complete screen display.

Sheet navigation

Each sheet in a spreadsheet is independent of the other sheets, though references can be linked from one sheet to another. There are three ways to navigate between sheets in a spreadsheet:

- **Using the Navigator** – when the Navigator is open (Figure 103), double-click on any of the listed sheets to select the sheet.
- **Using the keyboard** – use key combinations *Ctrl+Page Down* to move one sheet to the right and *Ctrl+Page Up* to move one sheet to the left.
- **Using the mouse** – click on one of the sheet tabs at the bottom of the spreadsheet to select that sheet.

If your spreadsheet contains a lot of sheets, then some of the sheet tabs may be hidden. If this is the case:

- Using the four buttons to the left of the sheet tabs can move the tabs into view (Figure 101).
- Right-clicking on any of the arrows opens a context menu where you can select a sheet (see Figure 102).

Note

When you insert a new sheet into a spreadsheet, Calc automatically uses the next number in the numeric sequence as a name. Depending on which sheet is open when you insert a new sheet, and the insertion method you use, the new sheet may not be in its correct numerical position. It is recommended to rename sheets in a spreadsheet to make them more recognizable.

Move to the first sheet
Move to the next sheet on the left
Move to the next sheet on the right
Move to the last sheet
Insert a new sheet after the last sheet

Sheet tabs

Figure 101: Navigating sheet tabs

Figure 102: Right-click any arrow button

Keyboard navigation

To navigate a spreadsheet using the keyboard, pressing a key or a combination of keys. For a key combination, press more than one key at the same time. Table 93 lists the keys and key combinations you can use for spreadsheet navigation in Calc.

Table 3. Keyboard cell navigation

Keyboard shortcut	Cell navigation
→	Moves cell focus right one cell.
←	Moves cell focus left one cell.
↑	Moves cell focus up one cell.
↓	Moves cell focus down one cell
Ctrl+→	Moves cell focus to the first column on the right containing data in that row if cell focus is on a blank cell.
	Moves cell focus to the last column on the right in the same range of occupied cells in that row if cell focus is on a cell containing data.
	Moves cell focus to the last column on the right in the spreadsheet if there are no more cells containing data.

Ctrl+←	Moves cell focus to the last column on the left containing data in that row if cell focus is on a blank cell.
	Moves cell focus to the first column on the left in the same range of occupied cells in that row if cell focus is on a cell containing data.
	Moves cell focus to the first column in that row if there are no more cells containing data.
Ctrl+↑	Moves cell focus from a blank cell to the first cell above containing data in the same column.
	Moves cell focus to the first row in the same range of occupied cells if cell focus is on a cell containing data.
	Moves cell focus from the last cell containing data to the cell in the same column in the first row of the spreadsheet.
Ctrl+↓	Moves cell focus from a blank cell to the first cell below containing data in the same column.
	Moves cell focus to the last row in the same range of occupied cells in that column if cell focus is on a cell containing data.
	Moves cell focus from the last cell containing data to the cell in the same column in the last row of the spreadsheet.
Ctrl+Home	Moves cell focus from anywhere on the spreadsheet to Cell A1 on the same sheet.
Ctrl+End	Moves cell focus from anywhere on the spreadsheet to the last cell in the lower right-hand corner of the rectangular area of cells containing data on the same sheet.
Alt+Page Down	Moves cell focus one screen to the right (if possible).
Alt+Page Up	Moves cell focus one screen to the left (if possible).
Ctrl+Page Down	Moves cell focus to the cell on the next sheet to the right in sheet tabs where the focus was there before; if the spreadsheet has more than one sheet.
Ctrl+Page Up	Moves cell focus to the cell on the next sheet to the left in sheet tabs where the focus was there before; if the spreadsheet has more than on sheet.
Tab	Moves cell focus to the next cell on the right.
Shift+Tab	Moves cell focus to the next cell on the left.
Enter	Moves cell focus down one cell (unless changed by user). See the next topic.
Shift+Enter	Moves cell focus up one cell (unless changed by user).

Customizing the Enter key

You can customize the direction in which the *Enter* key moves the cell focus by going to **Tools > Options > LibreOffice Calc > General**. Select the direction cell focus moves from the drop-down list. Depending on the file being used or the type of data being entered, setting a different direction can be useful. The *Enter* key can also be used to switch into and out of editing mode. Use the first two options under *Input settings* in Figure 103 to change the *Enter* key settings.

Figure 103: Customizing the Enter key

Selecting items in a spreadsheet

Selecting cells

Single cell

Left-click in the cell. You can verify your selection by looking in the Name Box on the Formula Bar (Figure 94 on page 121).

Range of contiguous cells

A range of cells can be selected using the keyboard or the mouse.

To select a range of cells by dragging the mouse cursor:

1) Click in a cell.
2) Press and hold down the left mouse button.
3) Move the mouse around the screen.
4) Once the desired block of cells is highlighted, release the left mouse button.

To select a range of cells without dragging the mouse:

1) Click in the cell which is to be one corner of the range of cells.
2) Move the mouse to the opposite corner of the range of cells.
3) Hold down the *Shift* key and click.

> **Tip**
>
> You can also select a contiguous range of cells by first clicking in the **Selection mode** field on the Status Bar (Figure 95 on page 122) and selecting **Extending selection** before clicking in the opposite corner of the range of cells. Make sure to change back to **Standard selection** or you may extend a cell selection unintentionally.

To select a range of cells without using the mouse:

1) Select the cell that will be one of the corners in the range of cells.
2) While holding down the *Shift* key, use the cursor arrows to select the rest of the range.

> **Tip**
>
> You can also directly select a range of cells using the Name Box. Click into the Name Box on the Formula Bar (Figure 94 on page 121). To select a range of cells, enter the cell reference for the upper left-hand cell, followed by a colon (:), and then the lower right-hand cell reference. For example, to select the range that would go from A3 to C6, you would enter *A3:C6*.

Range of non-contiguous cells

1) Select the cell or range of cells using one of the methods above.
2) Move the mouse pointer to the start of the next range or single cell.
3) Hold down the *Ctrl* key and click or click-and-drag to select another range of cells to add to the first range.
4) Repeat as necessary.

Note:

Some Calc operations cannot be used with non-contiguous cells. For example, you cannot copy a non-contiguous range.

Selecting columns and rows

Single column or row

To select a single column, click on the column header (Figure 93 on page 120).

To select a single row, click on the row header.

Multiple columns or rows

To select multiple columns or rows that are contiguous:

1) Click on the first column or row in the group.
2) Hold down the *Shift* key.
3) Click the last column or row in the group.

To select multiple columns or rows that are not contiguous:

1) Click on the first column or row in the group.
2) Hold down the *Ctrl* key.
3) Click on all of the subsequent columns or rows while holding down the *Ctrl* key.

Entire sheet

To select the entire sheet, click on the corner box between the column header A and the row header 1 (Figure 104), or use the key combination *Ctrl+A* to select the entire sheet, or go to **Edit** on the Menu bar and select **Select All**.

Figure 104: Select All box

Selecting sheets

You can select one or multiple sheets in Calc. It can be advantageous to select multiple sheets, especially when you want to make changes to many sheets at once.

Single sheet

Click on the sheet tab for the sheet you want to select. The tab for the selected sheet becomes white (default Calc setup).

Multiple contiguous sheets

To select multiple contiguous sheets:

1) Click on the sheet tab for the first desired sheet.
2) Move the mouse pointer over the sheet tab for the last desired sheet.
3) Hold down the *Shift* key and click on the sheet tab.
4) All tabs between these two selections will turn white (default Calc setup). Any actions that you perform will now affect all highlighted sheets.

Multiple non-contiguous sheets

To select multiple non-contiguous sheets:

1) Click on the sheet tab for the first desired sheet.
2) Move the mouse pointer over the sheet tab for the second desired sheet.
3) Hold down the *Ctrl* key and click on the sheet tab.
4) Repeat as necessary.
5) The selected tabs will turn white (default Calc setup). Any actions that you perform will now affect all highlighted sheets.

All sheets

Right-click a sheet tab and choose **Select All Sheets** from the context menu.

Hiding and showing sheets

Sometimes you may want to hide the contents of a sheet to preserve data from accidental editing or because its contents are not important to display. To hide a sheet or many sheets, select the sheet or sheets as above, right-click to open the context menu, and select **Hide Sheet**. To show hidden sheets, right-click any sheet tab and select **Show Sheet** on the context menu. A dialog will appear with all hidden sheets listed. Click on the desired sheet and then click **OK**.

 Tip

LibreOffice Calc does not let you hide the last visible sheet.

Working with columns and rows

Inserting columns and rows

Single column or row

Using the **Sheet** menu:

1) Select a cell, column, or row where you want the new column or row inserted.
2) Go to **Sheet** on the Menu bar and select either **Insert > Columns > Columns Left** or > **Columns Right** or **Insert > Rows > Rows Above** or > **Rows Below**.

Using the mouse:

1) Select a column or row where you want the new column or row inserted.
2) Right-click the column or row header.
3) Select **Insert Columns Left**, **Insert Columns Right**, **Insert Rows Above**, or **Insert Rows Below** from the context menu.

Multiple columns or rows

Multiple columns or rows can be inserted at once rather than inserting them one at a time.

1) Highlight the required number of columns or rows by holding down the left mouse button on the first one and then dragging across the required number of identifiers.
2) Proceed as for inserting a single column or row above.

Deleting columns and rows

Single column or row

To delete a single column or row:

1) Select a cell in the column or row you want to delete.
2) Go to **Sheet** on the Menu bar and select **Delete Cells** or right-click and select **Delete** from the context menu.
3) Select the option you require from the Delete Cells dialog (Figure 105).

Figure 105: Delete Cells dialog

Alternatively:

1) Click in the column or header to select the column or row.
2) Go to **Sheet** on the Menu bar and select **Delete Cells** or right-click and select **Delete Columns** or **Delete Rows** from the context menu.

Multiple columns or rows

To delete multiple columns or rows:

1) Select the columns or rows, see "Multiple columns or rows" on page 132 for more information.
2) Go to **Sheet** on the Menu bar and select **Delete Cells**, or right-click and select **Delete Columns** or **Delete Rows** from the context menu.

Working with sheets

Inserting new sheets

Click on the **Add Sheet** icon ![icon] on the bottom of the screen to insert a new sheet after the last sheet in the spreadsheet without opening the **Insert Sheet** dialog. The following methods open the **Insert Sheet** dialog (Figure 106), where you can position the new sheet, create more than one sheet, name the new sheet, or select a sheet from a file.

1) Select the sheet where you want to insert a new sheet, then go to **Sheet > Insert Sheet...** on the Menu bar.
2) Right-click on the sheet tab where you want to insert a new sheet and select **Insert Sheet** from the context menu.
3) Click in the empty space at the end of the sheet tabs.
4) Right-click in the empty space at the end of the sheet tabs and select **Insert Sheet** from the context menu.

You can insert several sheets by specifying the number of sheets to insert.

Figure 106: Insert Sheet dialog

Moving and copying sheets

You can move or copy sheets within the same spreadsheet by dragging and dropping, or by using the **Move/Copy Sheet** dialog. To move or copy a sheet into a different spreadsheet, you have to use the **Move/Copy Sheet** dialog.

Dragging and dropping

To move a sheet to a different position within the same spreadsheet, click and hold on the sheet tab and drag it to its new position before releasing the mouse button.

To *copy* a sheet within the same spreadsheet, hold down the *Ctrl* key (*Option* key on Mac) then click on the sheet tab and drag it to its new position before releasing the mouse button. The mouse pointer may change to include a plus sign depending on the setup of your operating system.

Using a dialog

Use the **Move/Copy Sheet** dialog (Figure 107) to specify exactly whether you want the sheet in the same or a different spreadsheet, its position within the spreadsheet, and the sheet name when you move or copy the sheet.

1) In the current document, right-click on the sheet tab you wish to move or copy and select **Move/Copy Sheet** from the context menu or go to **Sheet > Move or Copy Sheet...** on the Menu bar.

2) Select **Move** to move the sheet or **Copy** to copy the sheet in the Action area.

3) Select the spreadsheet where you want the sheet to be placed from the drop-down list in **To document**. This can be the same spreadsheet, another spreadsheet already open, or a new spreadsheet.

4) Select the position in **Insert before** where you want to place the sheet.

5) Type a name in the **New name** text box if you want to rename the sheet when it is moved or copied. If you do not enter a name, Calc creates a default name (Sheet 2, Sheet 3, and so on).

6) Click **OK** to confirm the move or copy and close the dialog.

 Caution

When you move or copy to another spreadsheet or a new spreadsheet, a conflict may occur with formulas linked to other sheets in the previous location.

Figure 107: Move/Copy Sheet dialog

Deleting sheets

To delete a single sheet, right-click on the sheet tab you want to delete and select **Delete Sheet** from the context menu, or go to **Sheet > Delete Sheet...** on the Menu bar. Click **Yes** to confirm the deletion.

To delete multiple sheets, select the sheets (see "Selecting sheets" on page 132), then right-click one of the sheet tabs and select **Delete Sheet** from the context menu, or go to **Sheet > Delete Sheet...** from on the Menu bar. Click **Yes** to confirm the deletion.

Renaming sheets

By default, the name for each new sheet added is *Sheet*X, where X is the number of the next sheet to be added. While this works for a small spreadsheet with only a few sheets, it can become difficult to identify sheets when a spreadsheet contains many sheets.

You can rename a sheet using one of the following methods:

- Enter the name in the **Name** text box when you create the sheet using the Insert Sheet dialog (Figure 107 on page 136).
- Right-click on a sheet tab and select **Rename Sheet** from the context menu to replace the existing name with a different one.
- Double-click on a sheet tab to open the **Rename Sheet** dialog.

 Note

> Sheet names must start with either a letter or a number; other characters, including spaces, are not allowed. Apart from the first character of the sheet name, permitted characters are letters, numbers, spaces, and the underscore character. Attempting to rename a sheet with an invalid name will produce an error message.

Viewing Calc

Changing document view

Use the zoom function to show more or fewer cells in the window when you are working on a spreadsheet. For more about zoom, see *Chapter 1 Introducing LibreOffice* in this guide.

Freezing rows and columns

Freezing locks a number of rows at the top of a spreadsheet or a number of columns on the left of a spreadsheet or both rows and columns. Then, when moving around within a sheet, the cells in frozen rows and columns always remain in view.

Figure 108 shows some frozen rows and columns. The heavier horizontal line between rows 3 and 23 and the heavier vertical line between columns F and Q indicate that rows 1 to 3 and columns A to F are frozen. The rows between 3 and 23 and the columns between F and Q have been scrolled off the page.

	A	B	C	D	E	F	Q	R
1		Surname	First Name	Address	City	Country		
2		Henderson	Sue	PO 876	Warman	Canada		
3		Alan	Darmack	76 Creek Road	Etton	USA		
23								
24								

Figure 108: Frozen rows and columns

Freezing rows or columns

1) Click into the cell that is immediately below the rows you want to freeze and immediately to the right of the columns you want frozen.

2) Click on the **Freeze Rows and Columns** icon 🔲 - in the main toolbar or go to **View** on the Menu bar and select **Freeze Cells > Freeze Rows and Columns**. A heavier line appears between the rows or columns indicating where the freeze has been placed.

Unfreezing

To unfreeze rows or columns, either go to **View** on the Menu bar and select **Freeze Cells > Freeze Rows and Columns** or click on the **Freeze Rows and Columns** icon in the main toolbar. The heavier lines indicating freezing will disappear.

Splitting the screen

Another way to change the view is by splitting the screen your spreadsheet is displayed in (also known as splitting the window). The screen can be split horizontally, vertically, or both, giving you up to four portions of the spreadsheet in view at any one time. An example of splitting the screen is shown in Figure 109 where a split is indicated by additional window borders within the sheet.

Why would you want to do this? For example, consider a large spreadsheet in which one cell contains a number that is used by three formulas in other cells. Using the split-screen technique, you can position the cell containing the number in one section and each of the cells with formulas in the other sections. You can then change the number in one cell and watch how it affects each of the formulas.

	A	B	C
1		Beta=	3.2
2		A0=	0.1
7	A1=	Beta*A0*(1*A0)	0.6421
8	A2=	Beta*A1*(1*A0)	0.6582
9	A3=	Beta*A0*(1*A0)	0.7219
10	A4=	Beta*A0*(1*A0)	0.6574
11	A5=	Beta*A0*(1*A0)	0.6597
12			

Figure 109: Split screen example

Splitting horizontally or vertically

1) Click on the row header below the rows where you want to split the screen horizontally or click on the column header to the right of the columns where you want to split the screen vertically.

2) Go to **View** on the Menu bar and select **Split Window.** Window borders appear between the rows or columns indicating where the split has been placed, as shown in Figure 110.

Alternatively:

- For a horizontal split, drag the new horizontal window border beneath the row where you want the horizontal split positioned.

- For a vertical split, drag the new vertical window border across to the right of the column where you want the vertical split positioned.

J	B	C	
	Beta=	3.2	
	A0=	0.1	
	Beta*A0*(1*A0)	0.6421	
	Beta*A1*(1*A0)	0.6582	
	Beta*A0*(1*A0)	0.7219	
	Beta*A0*(1*A0)	0.6574	
	Beta*A0*(1*A0)	0.6597	

Figure 110: Split screen window borders

Removing split views

To remove a split view, do one of the following:

- Drag the split window borders back to their places at the ends of the scroll bars.
- Go to **View** on the Menu bar and deselect **Split Window.**

Using the keyboard

Most data entry in Calc can be accomplished using the keyboard.

Numbers

Click in the cell and type in a number using the number keys on either the main keyboard or numeric keypad. By default, numbers are right aligned in a cell.

Minus numbers

To enter a negative number, either type a minus (–) sign in front of the number or enclose the number in parentheses (), for example (1234). The result for both methods of entry will be the same, for example -1234.

Leading zeroes

To retain a minimum number of integer characters in a cell when entering numbers in order to retain the number format, for example 1234 and 0012, leading zeros have to be added using one of the following methods.

Method 1

1) With the cell selected, right-click on the cell, select **Format Cells** from the context menu or go to **Format > Cells** on the Menu bar or use the keyboard shortcut *Ctrl+1* to open the **Format Cells** dialog (Figure 111).

2) Make sure the **Numbers** tab is selected then select *Number* in the *Category* list.

3) In **Options > Leading Zeros**, enter the minimum number of characters required. For example, for four characters, enter 4. Any number less than four characters will have leading zeros added, for example 12 becomes 0012.

4) Click **OK**. The number entered retains its number format and any formula used in the spreadsheet will treat the entry as a number in formula functions.

Figure 111: Format Cells dialog – Numbers page

Method 2

1) Select the cell.

2) Open the Sidebar (**View > Sidebar**) and click the **Open Panel (+)** icon on the **Number Format** panel to open it.

3) Select **Number** in the **Category** list box.

4) Set the **Leading zeroes** value box to **4**. Formatting is applied immediately.

Figure 112: Set Leading zeroes

If a number is entered with leading zeroes, for example 01481, without first setting the Leading zeros parameter, then by default Calc will automatically drop the leading 0. To preserve leading zeros in a number:

1) Type an apostrophe (') before the number, for example '01481.

2) Move the cell focus to another cell. The apostrophe is automatically removed, the leading zeros are retained and the number is converted to text left aligned.

Numbers as text

Numbers can also be entered as text using one of the following methods.

Method 1
1) With the cell selected, right-click on the cell and select **Format Cells** from the context menu or go to **Format > Cells** on the Menu bar or use the keyboard shortcut *Ctrl+1* to open the **Format Cells** dialog (Figure 111).
2) Make sure the **Numbers** page is selected, then select *Text* from the *Category* list.
3) Click **OK** and the number, when entered, is converted to text and, by default, left aligned.

Method 2
1) Select the cell.
2) Open the Sidebar (**View > Sidebar**) and click the **Open Panel (+)** icon on the **Number Format** panel.
3) Select **Text** in the **Category** list box. Formatting is applied to the cell immediately.
4) Click back on the cell. Enter the number and move focus from the cell to have the data formatted.

 Note

By default, any numbers that have been formatted as text in a spreadsheet will be treated as a zero by any formulas used in the spreadsheet. Formula functions will ignore text entries. You can change this feature in **Tools – Options – LibreOffice – Calc – Formula**, in **Detailed Calculation Settings**, select **Custom (conversion of text to numbers and more)** and then select the proper treatment in the **Convert from text to numbers** drop down list.

Text

Click in the cell and type the text. By default, text is left-aligned in a cell.

Date and time

Select the cell and type the date or time.

You can separate the date elements with a slash (/) or a hyphen (–) or use text, for example 10 Oct 2012. The date format automatically changes to the selected format used by Calc.

When entering a time, separate time elements with colons, for example 10:43:45. The time format automatically changes to the selected format used by Calc.

To change the date or time format used by Calc, use one of the following methods.

Method 1
1) With the cell selected, right-click on the cell and select **Format Cells** from the context menu, or go to **Format > Cells** on the Menu bar, or use the keyboard shortcut *Ctrl+1*, to open the **Format Cells** dialog (Figure 111).
2) Make sure the **Numbers** page is selected, then select *Date* or *Time* from the *Category* list.
3) Select the date or time format you want to use from the *Format* list. Click **OK**.

Method 2
1) With the cell selected, open the Sidebar (**View > Sidebar**) and (if necessary) click the **Open Panel (+)** icon on the **Number Format** panel.
2) Select **Date** in the **Category** list box.

3) Click the **More Options** button in the panel title bar to open the **Format Cells** dialog.

4) Select the date or time format you want to use from the *Format* list. Click **OK**.

AutoCorrection options

Calc automatically applies many changes during data input using autocorrection, unless you have deactivated any autocorrect changes. You can also undo any autocorrection changes by using the keyboard shortcut *Ctrl+Z* or manually by going back to the change and replacing the autocorrection with what you want to actually see.

To change the autocorrect options, go to **Tools > AutoCorrect Options** on the Menu bar to open the **AutoCorrect** dialog (Figure 113).

Replace

Edits the replacement table for automatically correcting or replacing words or abbreviations in the document.

Exceptions

Specify the abbreviations or letter combinations that you do not want LibreOffice to correct automatically.

Options

Select the options for automatically correcting errors as you type and then click **OK**.

Localized options

Specify the AutoCorrect options for quotation marks and for options that are specific to the language of the text.

Reset

Resets modified values back to the LibreOffice default values.

Figure 113: AutoCorrect dialog

Deactivating automatic changes

Some AutoCorrect settings are applied when you press the spacebar after you enter data. To turn off or on Calc AutoCorrect, go to **Tools** on the Menu bar and deselect or select **AutoInput**.

Speeding up data entry

Entering data into a spreadsheet can be very labor-intensive, but Calc provides several tools for removing some of the drudgery from input.

The most basic ability is to drag and drop the contents of one cell to another with a mouse. Many people also find AutoInput helpful. Calc also includes several other tools for automating input, especially of repetitive material. They include the fill tool, selection lists, and the ability to input information into multiple sheets of the same document.

Using the Fill tool

The Calc Fill tool is used to duplicate existing content or create a series in a range of cells in your spreadsheet (Figure 114).

1) Select the cell containing the contents you want to copy or start the series from.
2) Drag the mouse in any direction or hold down the *Shift* key and click in the last cell you want to fill.
3) Go to **Sheet > Fill Cells** on the Menu bar and select the direction in which you want to copy or create data (**Up**, **Down**, **Left** or **Right**) or **Series** and **Random Number...** from the submenu.

Alternatively, you can use a shortcut to fill cells.

1) Select the cell containing the contents you want to copy or start the series from.
2) Move the cursor over the small square in the bottom right corner of the selected cell. The cursor will change shape.
3) Click and drag in the direction you want the cells to be filled. If the original cell contained text, then the text will automatically be copied. If the original cell contained a number, a series will be created.

Figure 114: Using the Fill tool

Using a fill series

When you select a series fill from **Sheet > Fill Cells > Series...**, the **Fill Series** dialog (Figure 115) opens. Here you can select the type of series you want.

Figure 115: Fill Series dialog

- **Direction** – determines the direction of series creation.
  - *Down* – creates a downward series in the selected cell range for the column using the defined increment to the end value.
  - *Right* – creates a series running from left to right within the selected cell range using the defined increment to the end value.
  - *Up* – creates an upward series in the cell range of the column using the defined increment to the end value.
  - *Left* – creates a series running from right to left in the selected cell range using the defined increment to the end value.

- **Series Type** – defines the series type.
  - *Linear* – creates a linear number series using the defined increment and end value.
  - *Growth* – creates a growth series using the defined increment and end value.
  - *Date* – creates a date series using the defined increment and end date.
  - *AutoFill* – forms a series directly in the sheet. The AutoFill function takes account of customized lists. For example, by entering January in the first cell, the series is completed using the list defined in **Tools > Options > LibreOffice Calc > Sort Lists**. AutoFill tries to complete a value series by using a defined pattern. For example, a numerical series using 1,3,5 is automatically completed with 7,9,11,13; a date and time series using 01.01.99 and 15.01.99, an interval of fourteen days is used.

- **Unit of Time** – in this area you specify the desired unit of time. This area is only active if the Date option has been chosen in the Series type area.
  - *Day* – use the Date series type and this option to create a series using seven days.
  - *Weekday* – use the Date series type and this option to create a series of five day sets.
  - *Month* – use the Date series type and this option to form a series from the names or abbreviations of the months.
  - *Year* – use the Date series type and this option to create a series of years.

- **Start Value** – determines the start value for the series. Use numbers, dates or times.

- **End Value** – determines the end value for the series. Use numbers, dates or times.

- **Increment** – determines the value by which the series of the selected type increases by each step. Entries can only be made if the linear, growth or date series types have been selected.

Figure 116: Sort Lists dialog

Defining a fill series

To define your own fill series:

1) Go to **Tools > Options > LibreOffice Calc > Sort Lists** to open the Sort Lists dialog (Figure 116). This dialog shows the previously-defined series in the *Lists* box on the left and the contents of the highlighted list in the *Entries* box.

2) Click **New** and the *Entries* box is cleared.

3) Type the series for the new list in the *Entries* box (one entry per line).

4) Click **Add** and the new list will now appear in the *Lists* box.

5) Click **OK** to save the new list.

Defining a fill series from a range in a sheet

You can define a range of text values as a fill series.

1) Select the range containing the text values that you want to use as a fill series.

2) Go to **Tools > Options > LibreOffice Calc > Sort Lists** to open the Sort List dialog (Figure 116).

3) The selected range is in the box **Copy list from**. Click **Copy** to add the range to the sort list.

Using selection lists

Selection lists are available only for text and are limited to using only text that has already been entered in the same column.

1) Select a blank cell in a column that contains cells with text entries.

2) Right-click and select **Selection Lists** from the context menu. A drop-down list appears listing any cell in the same column that either has at least one text character or whose format is defined as text.

3) Click on the text entry you require and it is entered into the selected cell.

Sharing content between sheets

You might want to enter the same information in the same cell on multiple sheets, for example to set up standard listings for a group of individuals or organizations. Instead of entering the list on each sheet individually, you can enter the information in several sheets at the same time.

1) Go to **Edit > Select > Select Sheets...** on the Menu bar to open the **Select Sheets** dialog.

Figure 117: Select Sheets dialog

2) Select the individual sheets where you want the information to be repeated. Use the *Shift* and *Ctrl* (*Options* on Mac) keys to select multiple sheets.

3) Click **OK** to select the sheets and the sheet tabs will change color.

4) Enter the information in the cells on the first sheet where you want it to appear and it will be repeated in all the selected sheets.

 Note

> This technique automatically overwrites, without any warning, any information that is already in the cells on the selected sheets. Make sure you deselect the additional sheets when you are finished entering information that is going to be repeated before continuing to enter data into your spreadsheet.

Validating cell contents

When creating spreadsheets for other people to use, validating cell contents ensures that they enter data that is valid and appropriate for the cell. You can also use validation in your own work as a guide to entering data that is either complex or rarely used.

Fill series and selection lists can handle some types of data, but are limited to predefined information. To validate new data entered by a user, select a cell and go to **Data > Validity** on the Menu bar to define the type of contents that can be entered in that cell. For example, a cell may require a date or a whole number with no alphabetic characters or decimal points, or a cell may not be left empty.

Depending on how validation is set up, validation can also define the range of contents that can be entered, provide help messages explaining the content rules set up for the cell and what users should do when they enter invalid content. You can also set the cell to refuse invalid content, accept it with a warning, or start a macro when an error is entered. See the *Calc Guide Chapter 2 Entering, Editing, and Formatting Data* for more information on validating cell contents.

Editing data

Deleting data

Deleting data only

Data can be deleted from a cell without deleting any of the cell formatting. Click in the cell to select it and then press the *Delete* key.

Deleting data and formatting

Data and cell formatting can be deleted from a cell at the same time.

1) Click in the cell to select it.

2) Press the *Backspace* key, or right-click in the cell and select **Delete Contents** from the context menu, or go to **Edit > Delete Contents**) on the Menu bar to open the **Delete Contents** dialog (Figure 119). Here you can delete the different aspects of the data in the cell or to delete everything in the cell.

Figure 118: Delete Contents dialog

Replacing data

To completely replace data in a cell and insert new data, select the cell and type in the new data. The new data will replace the data already contained in the cell but will retain the original formatting used in the cell.

Alternatively, select the cell and click in the Input Line on the Formula Bar (Figure 94 on page 121), then double-click on the data to highlight it completely and type the new data.

Changing data

Sometimes it is necessary to edit the contents of cell without removing all of the data from the cell. For example, changing the phrase "Sales in Qtr. 2" to "Sales rose in Qtr" can be done as follows.

Using the keyboard

1) Click in the cell to select it.

2) Press the *F2* key and the cursor is placed at the end of the cell.

3) Use the keyboard arrow keys to reposition the cursor where you want to start entering the new data in the cell.

4) When you have finished, press the *Enter* key and your editing changes are saved.

Using the mouse

1) Double-click on the cell to select it and place the cursor in the cell for editing.

2) Either:

   • Reposition the cursor to where you want to start entering the new data in the cell.

- Single-click to select the cell.
- Move the cursor to the Input Line on the Formula Bar (Figure 94 on page 121) and click at the position where you want to start entering the new data in the cell.

3) When you have finished, click away from the cell to deselect it and your editing changes are saved.

Formatting data

Note

All the settings discussed in this section can also be set as a part of the cell style. See the *Calc Guide Chapter 4 Using Styles and Templates in Calc* for more information.

Multiple lines of text

Multiple lines of text can be entered into a single cell using automatic wrapping or manual line breaks. Each method is useful for different situations.

Automatic wrapping

To automatically wrap multiple lines of text in a cell, use one of the following methods.

Method 1
1) Right-click on the cell and select **Format Cells** from the context menu, or go to **Format > Cells** on the Menu bar, or press *Ctrl+1*, to open the Format Cells dialog.
2) Click on the *Alignment* tab (Figure 119).
3) Under **Properties**, select Wrap text automatically and click **OK**.

Figure 119: Format Cells dialog – Alignment page

Method 2
1) Select the cell.
2) Open the Sidebar (**View > Sidebar**) and click the **Open Panel (+)** icon on the **Alignment** panel.
3) Select the **Wrap text** option to apply the formatting immediately.

Figure 120: Wrap text formatting

Manual line breaks

To insert a manual line break while typing in a cell, press *Ctrl+Enter*. When editing text, double-click the cell, then reposition the cursor to where you want the line break. In the input line of the formula bar, press *Shift+Enter*.

When a manual line break is entered in a cell, the cell row height changes to display all the lines in the cell.

Shrinking text to fit the cell

The font size of the data in a cell can automatically adjust to fit inside cell borders. To do this, select the *Shrink to fit cell size* option under **Properties** in the Format Cells dialog (Figure 119) on the **Alignment** page. This dialog is also available by clicking the **More Options** button in the **Character** title bar of the **Properties** deck on the opened Sidebar, with text in the cell selected.

Formatting numbers

Several different number formats can be applied to cells by using icons on the Formatting toolbar (highlighted in Figure 121). Select the cell, then click the relevant icon to change the number format.

Figure 121: Number icons on Formatting toolbar

For more control or to select other number formats, use the *Numbers* page of the Format Cells dialog (Figure 112 on page 139):

- Apply any of the data types in the **Category** list to the data.
- Control the number of decimal places and leading zeros in **Options**.
- Enter a custom format code.
- The **Language** setting controls the local settings for the different formats such as the date format and currency symbol.

Some number formats are available from the Sidebar's **Number Format** panel in the Properties deck. Click the **More Options** button to open the Format Cells dialog described above.

Formatting fonts and text in cells

To quickly select a font and format text for use in a cell:

1) Select the cell.
2) Click the small triangle on the right of the Font Name box on the Formatting toolbar (highlighted in Figure 122) and select a font from the drop-down list.

3) Click on the small triangle on the right of the Font Size on the Formatting toolbar and select a font size from the drop down list.

Figure 122: Font Name and Size on Formatting toolbar

4) To change the character format, click on the **Bold**, *Italic*, or Underline icons.

5) To change the horizontal paragraph alignment, click on one of the four alignment icons (Left, Center, Right, Justified) ≣ ≣ ≣ ≣. For more options go to menu **Format – Cells – Alignment**, and select one of the options in the Horizontal drop down list.

6) To change the vertical alignment of the text in the cell, go to menu **Format – Cells – Alignment** and select one of the options in the Vertical drop down list.

7) To change the font color, click the arrow next to the Font Color icon ▲ to display the color palette, then select the desired color.

8) The **Format** menu also contains a quick access to direct text formatting in cells (Figure 123).

Figure 123: Direct formatting through Format menu

The **Properties** deck of the Sidebar has five panels, **Styles**, **Character**, **Number Format**, **Alignment** and **Cell Appearance**, which between them contain all the formatting controls from the Formatting toolbar and more.

To specify the language used in the cell, open the **Font** page on the Format Cells dialog. You can also select the **More Options** button on the Character panel of the Sidebar to open the Format Cells dialog. Changing language in a cell allows different languages to be used within the same document.

Use the *Font Effects* tab on the Format Cells dialog to set other font characteristics. See the *Calc Guide Chapter 4 Using Styles and Templates in Calc* for more information.

Formatting cell borders

To format the borders of a cell or a group of selected cells, click on the Borders icon ⊞ on the Formatting toolbar, and select one of the border options displayed in the palette.

To format the border line style, click on the line style icon ≡ and select the type from the palette. For the color of the borders lines of a cell, select the Border Color icon. A color palette is displayed.

The **Cell Appearance** panel of the **Properties** deck in the Sidebar contains **Cell border**, **Line style** and **Line color** controls.

For more control, including the spacing between cell borders and any data in the cell, use the *Borders* page of the Format Cells dialog (Figure 112 on page 139), where you can also define a shadow style. Clicking the **More Options** button on the **Cell Appearance** title bar, or clicking **More** in the panel's line style drop-down list, opens the Format Cells dialog at the *Borders* page.

See the *Calc Guide Chapter 4 Using Styles and Templates in Calc* for more information.

 Note

> Cell border properties apply only to the selected cells and can be changed only when you are editing those cells. For example, if cell C3 has a top border, that border can only be removed by selecting C3. It cannot be removed in C2 despite also appearing to be the bottom border for cell C2.

Formatting cell background

To format the background color for a cell or a group of cells, click the small arrow next to the Background Color icon 🖍 on the Formatting toolbar. A color palette, similar to the Font Color palette, is displayed. You can also use the *Background* tab of the Format Cells dialog (Figure 112 on page 139). The **Cell Appearance** panel of the **Properties** deck in the Sidebar contains a **Cell background** control with a color palette. See the *Calc Guide Chapter 4 Using Styles and Templates in Calc* for more information.

Formatting default cell styles

To add default styles for a cell or a group of cells, click Format > Styles. A menu displays the default styles. The default styles can be applied, deleted, or modified through the Styles and Formatting deck. You can create and use custom default cell styles for a cell by clicking **Format > Styles > New Styles...** Enter in a new name for the style or click an existing style name to update that style. Apply, delete, or modify the custom default style in the Styles and Formatting deck.

AutoFormatting of cells

Using AutoFormat

You can use Calc's AutoFormat feature to format a table (range of cells) quickly and easily. It also let you format different tables of the sheet with the same look and feel very easily. All formatting applied are direct formatting.

1) Select the cells in at least three columns and rows, including column and row headers, that you want to format.

2) Go to **Format > AutoFormat Styles** on the Menu bar to open the **AutoFormat** dialog (Figure 124).

3) Select the type of format and format color from the list.

4) Select the formatting properties to be included in the AutoFormat function. When selecting or deselecting a formatting property, the AutoFormat dialog displays the change instantly.

5) Click **OK**.

Figure 124: AutoFormat dialog

Defining a new AutoFormat

You can define a new AutoFormat so that it becomes available for use in all spreadsheets.

1) Format the data type, font, font size, cell borders, cell background, and so on for a range of cells.

2) Select the range.

3) Go to **Format > AutoFormat** to open the AutoFormat dialog. The **Add** button is now active.

4) Click **Add**.

5) In the *Name* box of the Add AutoFormat dialog that opens, type a meaningful name for the new format.

6) Click **OK** to save. The new AutoFormat is now available in the *Format* list in the AutoFormat dialog.

 Note

The new AutoFormat is stored in your computer user profile and is not available to other users. However, other users can import the new AutoFormat selecting the table range in the spreadsheet document and defining it as new AutoFormat.

Using themes

Calc comes with a predefined set of formatting themes (set of styles) that you can apply to your spreadsheet. While It is not possible to add new themes in Calc, you can modify the theme styles once the theme is applied to the spreadsheet. The modified styles become available for use in the whole spreadsheet.

To apply a theme to a spreadsheet:

1) Click the **Choose Themes** icon in the **Tools** toolbar. If this toolbar is not visible, go to **View > Toolbars** on the Menu bar and select **Tools**, and the **Theme Selection** dialog (Figure 125) opens. This dialog lists the available themes for the whole spreadsheet.

2) Select the theme that you want to apply. As soon as you select a theme, the theme styles are applied to the spreadsheet and are immediately visible.

3) Click **OK**.

4) If you wish, you can now open the Styles window to modify specific styles. These changes do not modify the theme; they only change the appearance of the style in the specific spreadsheet you are creating.

 Caution

Applying a new theme over an existing one will override all existing theme styles customization with the new theme styles.

Figure 125: Theme Selection dialog

The applied spreadsheet themes works with cell styles. Some themes even change the Default cell style. A new set of styles, including one named *Card* is added to your document. Figure 126 shows the styles added by the *Pastel* theme.

Theme Style	Effect
Background	1234.56
Card	1234.56
Card B	1234.56
Card BL	1234.56
Card BR	1234.56
Card L	1234.56
Card R	1234.56
Card T	1234.56
Card TL	1234.56
Card TR	1234.56
Column Header	1234.56
Heading1	1234.56
Input	$1,234.56
Result	$1,234.56
Result2	R$ 1.234,56

Figure 126: Cell styles of theme "Pastel"

Using conditional formatting

You can set up cell formats to change depending on conditions that you specify. For example, in a table of numbers, you can show all the values above the average in green and all those below the average in red. Multiple formatting options can be entered and arranged using assigned *priority rules* to order the importance of the conditions, allowing certain formatting options to take place before others, for example.

Conditional formatting depends upon the use of styles and the AutoCalculate feature must be enabled. Go to **Tools > Cell Contents > AutoCalculate** on the Menu bar to enable this feature. See the *Calc Guide Chapter 2 Entering, Editing, and Formatting Data* for more information.

Hiding and showing data

In Calc you can hide elements so that they are neither visible on a computer display nor printed when a spreadsheet is printed. However, hidden elements can still be selected for copying if you select the elements around them. For example, if column B is hidden, it is copied when you select columns A and C.

For more information on how to hide and show data, including how to use outline groups and filtering, see the *Calc Guide Chapter 2 Entering, Editing, and Formatting Data*.

 Note

When data in cells are hidden, the blank cells remain visible in the spreadsheet.

Hiding data

To hide *sheets*, select them, then go to **Sheet > Hide Sheets** on the Menu bar, or right-click and choose **Hide Sheets** on the context menu. You cannot hide all the sheets in a spreadsheet; at least one sheet must remain visible.

To hide *rows* or *columns*:

1) Select the row or column you want to hide.
2) Go to **Format** on the Menu bar and select **Rows** or **Columns**.
3) Select **Hide** from the submenu and the row or column can no longer viewed or printed.

Alternatively, right-click on the row header or column header and select **Hide Rows** or **Hide Columns** from the context menu.

Showing data

To show hidden sheets, rows, and columns:

1) Select the sheets, rows or columns each side of the hidden sheet, row or column.
2) Go to **Format** on the Menu bar and select **Sheet**, **Row** or **Column**.
3) Select **Show** from the menu and the sheet, row or column will be displayed and can be printed.

Alternatively, right-click on the sheet tabs, row headers or column headers and select **Show** from the context menu.

 Note

If the first column (A) or first row (1) is hidden, you must select the whole sheet to access the show command for this row or column.

Cell protection

All or some of the cells in a spreadsheet can be password protected to prevent changes being made by unauthorized users. This can be handy when multiple people have access to the spreadsheet itself, but for various reasons only a few can be allowed to modify the data it contains.

By default, *all* cells will be flagged as *Protected* (Figure 128).

Before protecting the sheet, you may wish to select certain cells that will be unprotected that can be changed by any users without the password.

To do this:

1) Using any of the methods previously discussed, select the cells that you wish to unprotect.

2) Open the Format Cells dialog by right-clicking and selecting *Format Cells* or by selecting **Format > Cells** from the Menu bar.

3) From the Cell Protection tab of the Format Cells dialog, the Protected status of individual or groups of cells can be toggled on or off.

In the *Cell Protection* tab of the Format Cells dialog is also the option to Hide all data contained in protected cells.

To toggle the hidden status of protected cells:

1) Go to **Tools > Protect Sheet**.

2) Enter the password to unprotect the sheet and click **OK**.

3) Go to **Format > Cells** on the Menu bar, or right-click and select **Format Cells** from the context menu, or use the keyboard shortcut *Ctrl+1* to open the **Format Cells** dialog.

4) Click the *Cell Protection* tab (Figure 127) and deselect the hide options for the cells.

5) Click **OK**.

Figure 127: Cell Protection page in Format Cells dialog

When all desired cells have been flagged with either a protected or unprotected status:

1) Go to **Tools > Protect Sheet**. The Protect Sheet dialog will open (Figure 128).

2) Select *Protect this sheet and the contents of protected cells*.

3) Type a password and then confirm the password.

4) Select or deselect the user selection options for cells.

5) Click **OK**.

Any cells that had been toggled as protected will no longer be editable by anyone that does not have the password.

Figure 128: Protect Sheet dialog

Alternatively, you can choose to protect the entire spreadsheet rather than individual cells on individual sheets by selecting **Tools > Protect Spreadsheet** from the Menu bar. The protected sheets has a lock icon in its tab, as shown in Figure 129.

*Figure 129: The lock icon
in a protected sheet*

Sorting records

Sorting within Calc arranges the cells in a sheet using the sort criteria that you specify. Several criteria can be used and a sort applies each criteria consecutively. Sorts are useful when you are searching for a particular item and become even more useful after you have filtered data.

Also, sorting is useful when you add new information to your spreadsheet. When a spreadsheet is long, it is usually easier to add new information at the bottom of the sheet, rather than adding rows in their correct place. After you have added information, you then carry out a sort to update the spreadsheet.

For more information on how to sort records and the sorting options available, see the *Calc Guide Chapter 2 Entering, Editing, and Formatting Data.*

Figure 130: Sort Criteria dialog

To sort cells in a spreadsheet:

1) Select the cells to be sorted.

2) Go to **Data > Sort** on the Menu bar to open the **Sort** dialog (Figure 130).

3) Select the sort criteria from the drop down lists. The selected lists are populated from the selected cells.

4) Select either ascending order (A-Z, 1-9) or descending order (Z-A, 9-1).

5) Click **OK** and the sort is carried out on your spreadsheet.

Cell comments

Comments are small notes and text that can serve as a reminder or an aside to the user. A comment is not considered a part of the spreadsheet for calculation or printing purposes, and will only appear when hovering the mouse over the particular cell that has been 'commented'.

The easiest way to insert a comment is by right-clicking on the desired cell and selecting *Insert Comment* from the *Context Menu* that appears. Alternatively, a comment can be inserted by selecting **Insert > Comment** from the Menu bar, by pressing the keyboard shortcut *(Ctrl+Alt+C)*, or by clicking the icon in the *Standard Toolbar*.

By default, comments will remain hidden and only appear when hovering the mouse. Cells that contain comments are marked with a red square in the upper right corner. To toggle the visibility of comments, select **View > Comments** from the Menu bar.

Using formulas and functions

You may need more than numbers and text on your spreadsheet. Often the contents of one cell depend on the contents of other cells. Formulas are equations that use numbers and variables to produce a result. Variables are placed in cells to hold data required by equations.

A function is a predefined calculation entered in a cell to help you analyze or manipulate data. All you have to do is enter the arguments and the calculation is made automatically. Functions help you create the formulas required to get the results that you are looking for.

The Function Wizard and Function Search

Functions and formulas can be entered directly into the formula bar or by accessing the function wizard. To launch the function wizard, click the Function Wizard icon to the right of the *Name box.*

Inside the function wizard, you can search, list, and narrow down the many Calc functions available. You can also choose to complete functions from within the wizard rather than having to type full formulas into the formula bar.

Each function, when selected, will display a brief explanation of its use and acceptable syntax. It will also display dialog boxes where you can enter the information required by that function and a *result window* showing the expected calculation from the data entered.

 Note

A fast alternative to the function wizard, the Calc Sidebar contains a *Functions tab* which allows you to quickly list and narrow down functions and provides brief explanations on their use and syntax, but does not provide the search or data entry functionalities of the full wizard.

For a more in-depth introduction to formulas and the function wizard, see the *Calc Guide Chapter 7 Formulas and Functions*.

Figure 131: Function Wizard with Search Bar

Analyzing data

Calc includes several tools to help you analyze the information in your spreadsheets, ranging from features for copying and reusing data, to creating subtotals automatically, to varying information to help you find the answers you need. These tools are divided between the Tools and Data menus.

Calc also includes many tools for statistical analysis of data, where you can obtain important numerical information on data obtained from physical measurements, polls, or even business transactions such as sales, stock quotations, and so on. These statistical data analyses are available in the menu **Data > Statistics**.

See the *Calc Guide Chapter 9 Data Analysis* for more information on the tools available in Calc to analyze your data.

Pivot tables and pivot charts

One of the most useful tools for analyzing data is the *Pivot Table*.

A pivot table is a way to organize, manipulate, and summarize large amounts of data to make it much easier to read and understand while also allowing you to answer different questions about your spreadsheet by rearranging --or pivoting-- the data you enter into it.

For example, let's say that you have a spreadsheet containing a list of donations to various charities by a group of recruiters in various months, but you are only interested in how much money each recruiter has collected in total. To determine your solution, you could manually calculate that amount by using the sorting and formatting options provided by Calc.

Alternatively, you could arrange a pivot table as shown below to make that data easier to organize and read.

Figure 132: Pivot Table dialog with raw data and results

To access the pivot table creation dialog, choose **Insert > Pivot Table** or **Data > Pivot Table > Create** from the Menu bar. The Pivot Table Layout dialog will intelligently guess the column headings from the provided raw data and insert them into the *Available Fields* selection box. From there, you can drag and drop your desired information into *column, row, or page fields* to organize accordingly and press **OK** to view the results.

To choose new information to display, or to alter the layout of the existing information, right-click anywhere in the existing pivot table to bring up the context menu and choose **Edit Layout.**

For a more in-depth explanation of pivot tables, see the *Calc Guide Chapter 8 Pivot Tables*.

Pivot charts

To get a quick visual representation of the data contained in a pivot table, a *Pivot Chart* can be generated.

Functionally, pivot charts are nearly identical to regular charts except in two key areas. First, as the data in the pivot table is altered, the pivot chart will adjust itself automatically to follow suit. The second difference is the inclusion of *Field Buttons*; graphical elements that allow you to filter the content of the pivot table from within the pivot chart itself, which is a useful time-saver if your pivot table and pivot chart are contained on different sheets.

For more information on Pivot Charts and Charts in general, see the *Calc Guide Chapter 3 Charts and Graphs* and the *Calc Guide Chapter 8 Pivot Tables*.

Printing

Printing from Calc is much the same as printing from other LibreOffice components (see *Chapter 10 Printing, Exporting, and Emailing* in this guide). However, some details for printing in Calc are different, especially regarding preparation for printing.

Print ranges

Print ranges have several uses, including printing only a specific part of the data or printing selected rows or columns on every page. For more information about using print ranges, see the *Calc Guide Chapter 6 Printing, Exporting, and E-mailing*.

Defining a print range

To define a new print range or modify an existing print range:

1) Select the range of cells to be included in the print range.
2) Go to **Format > Print Ranges > Define** on the Menu bar. Page break lines are displayed on screen.
3) To check the print range, go to **File > Print Preview** on the Menu bar or click on the **Print Preview** icon. LibreOffice will display the cells in the print range.

Adding to a print range

After defining a print range, you can add more cells to it by creating another print range. This allows multiple, separate areas of the same sheet to be printed while not printing the whole sheet.

1) After defining a print range, select an extra range of cells for adding to the print range.
2) Go to **Format > Print Ranges > Add** on the Menu bar to add the extra cells to the print range. The page break lines are no longer displayed on the screen.
3) To check the print ranges, go to **File > Print Preview** on the Menu bar or click on the **Print Preview** icon. LibreOffice will display the print ranges as separate pages.

 Note

The additional print range will print as a separate page, even if both ranges are on the same sheet.

Removing a print range

It may become necessary to remove a defined print range, for example, if the whole sheet needs to be printed later.

To remove all the defined print ranges, go to **Format > Print Ranges > Remove** on the Menu bar. After the print ranges have been removed, the default page break lines will appear on the screen.

Editing a print range

At any time, you can directly edit the print range, for example to remove or resize part of the print range. Go to **Format > Print Ranges > Edit** on the Menu bar to open the **Edit Print Ranges** dialog where you can define the print range.

Printing options

To select the printing options for page order, details, and scale to be used when printing a spreadsheet:

1) Go to **Format > Page** on the Menu bar to open the Page Style dialog (Figure 133).
2) Select the **Sheet** tab and make your selections from the available options.
3) Click **OK**.

For more information on printing options, see the *Calc Guide Chapter 6 Printing, Exporting, and E-mailing*.

Figure 133: Page Style dialog

Repeat printing of rows or columns

If a sheet is printed on multiple pages, you can set up certain rows or columns to repeat on each printed page. For example, if the top two rows of the sheet as well as column A need to be printed on all pages, do the following:

1) Go to **Format > Print Ranges > Edit** on the Menu bar to open the Edit Print Ranges dialog (Figure 134).

2) Type the row identifiers in the *Rows to repeat* box. For example, to repeat rows 1 and 2, type **$1:$2**. This automatically changes *Rows to repeat* from **- none -** to **- user defined -**.

3) Type the column identifiers in the *Columns to repeat* box. For example, to repeat column A, type **$A**. In the *Columns to repeat* list, **- none -** changes to **- user defined -**.

4) Click **OK**.

For more information on editing print ranges, see the *Calc Guide Chapter 6 Printing, Exporting, and E-mailing*.

Figure 134: Edit Print Ranges dialog

Page breaks

While defining a print range can be a powerful tool, it may sometimes be necessary to manually adjust the Calc printout manually using a *manual or page break*. A page break helps to ensure that your data prints properly according to your page size and page orientation. You can insert a horizontal page break above or a vertical page break to the left of the active cell.

For more information on manual breaks, see the *Calc Guide Chapter 6 Printing, Exporting, and E-mailing*.

Inserting a break

To insert a page break:

1) Navigate to the cell where the page break will begin.
2) Go to **Insert > Page Break** on the Menu bar.
3) Select **Row Break** to create a page break above the selected cell.
   Select **Column Break** to create a page break to the left of the selected cell.

Deleting a page break

To remove a page break:

1) Navigate to a cell that is next to the break you want to remove.
2) Go to **Edit > Delete Page Break** on the Menu bar.
3) Select **Row Break** or **Column Break** as needed.

 Note

> Multiple manual row and column breaks can exist on the same page. When you want to remove them, you have to remove each break individually.

Headers and footers

Headers and footers are predefined pieces of text that are printed at the top or bottom of a page when a spreadsheet is printed. Headers and footers are set and defined using the same method. For more information on setting and defining headers and footers, see the *Calc Guide Chapter 6 Printing, Exporting, and E-mailing*.

Headers and footers are also assigned to a page style. You can define more than one page style for a spreadsheet and assign different page styles to different sheets within a spreadsheet. For more information on page styles, see the *Calc Guide Chapter 4 Using Styles and Templates*.

Setting a header or footer

To set a header or footer:

1) Navigate to the sheet that you want to set the header or footer for.
2) Go to **Format > Page** on the Menu bar to open the **Page Style** dialog (Figure 135).
3) On the Page Style dialog, select **Header** or **Footer** tab.
4) Select the **Header on** or **Footer on** option.
5) Select **Same content left/right** option if you want the same header or footer to appear on all the printed pages.
6) Set the margins, spacing, and height for the header or footer. You can also select **AutoFit height** box to automatically adjust the height of the header or footer.
7) To change the appearance of the header or footer, click on **More** to open the borders and background dialog.
8) To set the contents, for example page number, date and so on, that appears in the header or footer, click on **Edit** to open the style dialog.

Figure 135: Header page of Page Style dialog

Getting Started Guide

Chapter 6
Getting Started with Impress

Presentations in LibreOffice

What is Impress?

Impress is the presentation (slide show) program included in LibreOffice. You can create slides that contain many different elements, including text, bulleted and numbered lists, tables, charts, and a wide range of graphic objects such as clipart, drawings, and photographs. Impress also includes a spelling checker, a thesaurus, text styles, and background styles.

This chapter includes instructions, screenshots, and hints to guide you through the Impress environment while designing your presentations. Although more difficult designs are mentioned in this chapter, explanations for creating them are in the *Impress Guide*. If you have a working knowledge of how to create slide shows, we recommend you use the *Impress Guide* for your source of information.

To use Impress for more than very simple slide shows requires some knowledge of the elements which the slides contain. Slides that contain text use styles to determine the appearance of that text. Creating drawings in Impress is similar to the Draw program included in LibreOffice. For this reason, we recommend that you also see *Chapter 3 Using Styles and Templates* and *Chapter 7 Getting Started with Draw* in this guide. You may also wish to consult the *Draw Guide* for more details on how to use the drawing tools.

Starting Impress

When you start Impress for the first time, the Impress window opens with the Presentation Template dialog displayed.

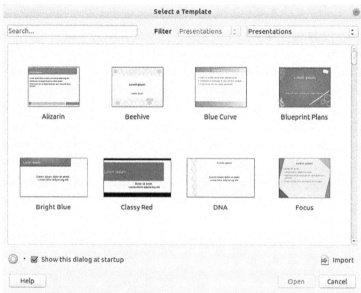

Figure 136: Template Selection Dialog

You can turn off the option to start Impress with a choice of available templates by unchecking the "*Show this dialog at startup*" box in the dialog, or through the **Tools > Options > LibreOffice Impress > General** option and deselecting **Start with Template Selection**.

For more detailed information about Templates, please read Chapter 3 of this guide.

Main Impress window

The main Impress window (Figure 137) has three parts: the *Slides pane*, *Workspace*, and *Sidebar*. Additionally, several toolbars can be displayed or hidden during the creation of a presentation.

 Tip

> You can close the *Slides pane* or the *Sidebar* by clicking the *X* in the upper right corner of each pane or go to **View > Slide Pane** or **View > Sidebar** on the Menu bar to deselect the pane. To reopen a pane, go to **View** on the Menu bar and select **Slide Pane** or **Sidebar** again.
>
> You can also maximize the *Workspace* area by clicking on the Hide/Show marker in the middle of the vertical separator line (highlighted in Figure 137). Using the Hide/Show marker hides, but does not close, the Slide pane or Sidebar. To restore a pane, click again on its Hide/Show marker.

Workspace

The *Workspace* (normally in the center of the main window) opens in the **Normal** view. It has five tabs: **Normal**, **Outline**, **Notes**, **Handout**, and **Slide Sorter**. These five tabs are called View buttons. Since LibreOffice 5.1, the View buttons are not shown by default; but they can be activated by choosing **View > Modes Tab Bar** from the menu bar.

The Workspace below the View buttons changes with the chosen view. The workspace views are described in "Workspace views" on page 168.

Figure 137: Main window of Impress; ovals indicate the Hide/Show markers. The View Tab Bar is visible in this image.

Slides pane

The *Slides pane* contains thumbnail pictures of the slides in your presentation in the order in which they will be shown, unless you change the slide show order. Clicking a slide in this pane selects it and places it in the *Workspace*. When a slide is in the Workspace, you can make changes to it.

Several additional operations can be performed on one or more slides simultaneously in the Slides pane:

- Add new slides to the presentation.
- Mark a slide as hidden so that it will not be shown as part of the presentation.
- Delete a slide from the presentation if it is no longer needed.
- Rename a slide.
- Duplicate a slide (copy and paste).
- Move a slide to another place in the slide stack by dragging and dropping it to the desired position. If the position is not visible in the slide pane, the slide stack will scroll up or down accordingly.

It is also possible to perform the following operations, although there are more efficient methods than using the Slides pane:

- Change the slide transition following the selected slide or after each slide in a group.
- Change the slide design.
- Change slide layout for a group of slides simultaneously.

Sidebar

The *Sidebar* has seven sections. To expand a section you want to use, click on its icon or click on the small triangle at the top of the icons and select a section from the drop down list. Only one section at a time can be open.

Properties

Shows the layouts included within Impress. You can choose the one you want and use it as it is, or modify it to meet your own requirements. However, it is not possible to save customized layouts.

Slide Transition

Provides a number of slide transition options. The default is set to *No Transition*, in which the following slide simply replaces the existing one. However, many additional transitions are available. You can also specify the transition speed (slow, medium, fast), choose between an automatic or manual transition, and choose how long the selected slide should be shown (automatic transition only).

Custom Animation

A variety of animations can be used to emphasize or enhance different elements of each slide. The Custom Animation section provides an easy way to add, change, or remove animations.

Master Pages

Here you define the page (slide) style for your presentation. Impress includes several designs for Master Pages (slide masters). One of them – Default – is blank, and the rest have background and styled text.

> ### 🔆 Tip
>
> Go to **Format > Styles > Styles and Formatting** on the Menu bar or press the *F11* key to open the Styles and Formatting dialog, where you can modify the styles used in any master page to suit your purpose. This can be done at any time.

Styles and Formatting

Here you can edit and apply graphics styles and create new ones, but you can only edit existing presentation styles. When you edit a style, the changes are automatically applied to all of the elements formatted with this style in your presentation. If you want to ensure that the styles on a specific slide are not updated, create a new master page for the slide.

Gallery

Opens the Impress gallery from which you can insert an object into your presentation either as a copy or as a link. A copy of an object is independent of the original object, so changes to the object have no effect on the copy. A link remains dependent on the original object and changes to the object are reflected in the link.

Navigator

Opens the Impress navigator, in which you can quickly move to another slide or select an object on a slide. It is recommended to give slides and objects in your presentation meaningful names so that you can easily identify them when using the navigator.

Toolbars

Many toolbars can be used during slide creation. They can be displayed or hidden by going to **View > Toolbars** on the Menu bar and selecting from the context menu.

You can also select the icons that you wish to appear on each toolbar. For more information, refer to Chapter 1, Introducing LibreOffice.

Many of the toolbars in Impress are similar to the toolbars in Draw. Refer to the *Draw Guide* for details on the functions available and how to use them.

Status bar

The *Status bar* (Figure 138), located at the bottom of the Impress window, contains information that you may find useful when working on a presentation. For details on the contents and use of these fields, see *Chapter 1 Introducing LibreOffice* in this guide and the *Impress Guide Chapter 1 Introducing Impress*.

Figure 138: Status bar

 Note

The sizes are given in the current measurement unit (not to be confused with the ruler units). This measurement unit is defined in **Tools > Options > LibreOffice Impress > General**.

From left to right, you will find:

- **Information area** – changes depending on the selection. For example:

Example selection	Examples of information shown
Text area	Text Edit: Paragraph x, Row y, Column z
Charts, spreadsheets	Embedded object (OLE) "ObjectName" selected
Graphics	Bitmap with transparency selected

- **Cursor position** – the position of the cursor or of the top left corner of the selection measured from the top left corner of the slide, followed by the width and height of the selection or text box where the cursor is located.

- **Unsaved changes** – a flag indicating that the file needs saving. Double-clicking on this flag opens the file save dialog.

- **Digital signature** – a flag indicating whether the document is digitally signed. After the file has been saved, double-clicking on this flag opens the digital signatures dialog.

- **Slide number** – the slide number currently displayed in the Workspace and the total number of slides in the presentation.

- **Page (slide) style** – the style associated with the slide, handout, or notes page currently in the Workspace. Double-clicking on the style name opens the slide design dialog.

- **Zoom slider** – adjusts the zoom percentage of the Workspace displayed.

- **Zoom percentage** – indicates the zoom percentage of the Workspace displayed. Double-clicking on zoom percentage opens the zoom and layout dialog.

You can hide the Status Bar and its information by going to **View** on the Menu bar and deselecting **Status Bar**.

Workspace views

Each of the Workspace views is designed to ease the completion of certain tasks. It is therefore useful to familiarize yourself with them in order to accomplish those tasks quickly.

 Note

Each Workspace view displays a different set of toolbars when selected. These toolbar sets can be customized by going to **View > Toolbars** on the Menu bar, then check or uncheck the toolbar you want to add or remove.

Normal view

View > *Normal view* is the main view for working with individual slides. Use this view to format and design and to add text, graphics, and animation effects.

To place a slide in the slide design area (Normal view) (Figure 137 on page 165), click the slide thumbnail in the Slides pane or double-click it in the Navigator (see *Chapter 1 Introducing LibreOffice* and the *Impress Guide* for more information on the Navigator).

Outline view

View > *Outline view* (Figure 139) contains all the slides of the presentation in their numbered sequence. It shows topic titles, bulleted lists, and numbered lists for each slide in outline format. Only the text contained in the default text boxes in each slide is shown, so if your slide includes other text boxes or drawing objects, the text in these objects is not displayed. Slide names are not included either.

Figure 139: Outline view

Figure 140: Outline level and movement arrows in Text Formatting toolbar

Use Outline view for the following purposes:

- Quickly inserting text for fast content creation or editing, when formatting and adding graphic objects is postponed until the final stages of creating the presentation.
- Making changes in the text of a slide:
  - Adding and deleting the text in a slide as in the Normal view.
  - Moving the paragraphs of text in the selected slide up or down by using the up and down arrow buttons (Move Up or Move Down) on the Text Formatting toolbar (highlighted in Figure 140).
  - Changing the outline level for any of the paragraphs in a slide using the left and right arrow buttons (Promote or Demote) on the Text Formatting toolbar.
  - Moving a paragraph and changing its outline level at the same time using a combination of these four arrow buttons.
- Comparing slides with your outline (if you have prepared one in advance). If you notice from your outline that another slide is needed, you can create it directly in the Outline view or you can return to the Normal view to create it.

Notes view

View > *Notes view* (Figure 141) to add notes to a slide. These notes are for your information and are not seen by the audience when the presentation is shown.

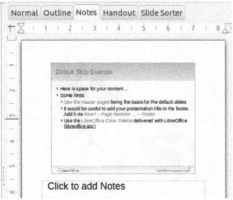

Figure 141: Notes view

1) Click the **Notes** tab in the Workspace.

2) Select the slide to which you want to add notes: click the slide in the Slides pane, or double-click the slide name in the Navigator.

3) In the text box below the slide, click on the words *Click to add notes* and begin typing.

You can resize the Notes text box using the colored resizing handles which appear when you click on the edge of the box. You can also move the box by placing the pointer on the border, then clicking and dragging. To make changes in the text style, click on the Styles and Formatting icon

T on the Sidebar.

Handout view

View > Master *Handout view* is for setting up the layout of your slide for a printed handout. Click the *Handout* tab in the workspace and the **Layouts** section opens on the Sidebar (Figure 142). Here you can choose to print 1, 2, 3, 4, 6, or 9 slides per page. If the Layouts section does not open, then click on the Properties icon at the side of the Sidebar.

Use this view also to customize the information printed on the handout. Refer to Chapter 10, Printing, E-mailing, Exporting, and Saving Slide Shows, in the *Impress Guide* for instructions on printing slides, handouts, and notes.

Go to **Insert > Page Number, Insert > Fields**, or **Insert > Header and Footer** on the Menu bar and the Header and Footer dialog opens. Click on the *Notes and Handouts* tab (Figure 143) and select the elements you want to appear on each handout page and their contents. More details on how to use this dialog are provided in the *Impress Guide*.

Figure 142: Handout layouts

Figure 143: Header and Footer dialog – Notes and Handouts page

Slide Sorter view

Slide Sorter view (Figure 144) contains all of the slide thumbnails. Use this view to work with a group of slides or with only one slide.

Figure 144: Slide Sorter view

Customizing Slide Sorter view

To change the number of slides per row:

1) Go to **View > Toolbars** and select **Slide Sorter** and **Slide View** to show or hide the Slide Sorter and Slide View toolbars (Figure 145).

2) Adjust the number of slides (up to a maximum of 15).

Figure 145: Slide Sorter and Slide View toolbars

Moving a slide using Slide Sorter

To move a slide in a presentation in the Slide Sorter:

1) Click the slide and the slide is highlighted (Figure 144).

2) Drag and drop the slide to the location you want.

Selecting and moving groups of slides

To select a group of slides, use one of these methods:

- Using the *Ctrl* key – click on the first slide and, while pressing the *Ctrl* key, select the other desired slides.

- Using the *Shift* key – click on the first slide, and while pressing the *Shift* key, select the final slide in the group. This selects all of the other slides between the first and the last slide selected.

- Using the mouse – click slightly to one side (left or right) of the first slide to be selected. Hold down the left mouse button and drag the cursor until all of the slides you want selected are highlighted.

To move a group of slides, select them and then drag and drop the group to their new location.

Working in Slide Sorter view

You can work with slides in the Slide Sorter view just as you can in the Slide pane. To make changes, right-click a slide and choose any of the following from the context menu:

- **New Slide** – adds a new slide after the selected slide (see "New slide" on page 172).

- **Duplicate Slide** – creates a duplicate of the selected slide and places the new slide immediately after the selected slide (see "Duplicate slide" on page 172).

- **Delete Slide** – deletes the selected slide.
- **Rename Slide** – allows you to rename the selected slide.
- **Slide Layout** – allows you to change the layout of the selected slide.
- **Slide Transition** – allows you to change the transition of one or a group of selected slides.
- **Hide Slide** – any slides that are hidden are not shown in the slide show.
- **Cut** – removes the selected slide and saves it to the clipboard.
- **Copy** – copies the selected slide to the clipboard without removing it.
- **Paste** – inserts a slide from the clipboard after the selected slide.

Formatting a presentation

A new presentation contains only one empty slide. In this section we will start adding new slides and preparing them for the intended contents.

Inserting slides

New slide

A new slide can be inserted into a presentation after the selected slide as follows:

- Go to **Slide** on the Menu bar and select **New Page/Slide**.Or, right-click on a slide in the Slides Pane or Slide Sorter view and select **New Slide** from the context menu.
- Or, right-click in an empty space in the Workspace and select **Slide > New Slide** from the context menu.
- Or click the **NewPage/Slide** icon in the Presentation toolbar. You can also select the desired layout of the new slide if you click on the small downward arrow of the icon. If the Presentation toolbar is not visible, go to **View > Toolbars** on the Menu bar and select **Presentation** from the list.
- Or use keyboard: *Ctrl+M* to insert a new slide.

Duplicate slide

Sometimes, rather than starting from a new slide you may want to duplicate a slide already included in your presentation. To duplicate a slide:

1) Select the slide you want to duplicate from the Slides Pane.
2) Go to **Slide** on the Menu bar and select **Duplicate Page/Slide**.
   - Or, right-click on the slide in the Slides Pane or Slide Sorter view and select **Duplicate Slide** from the context menu.
   - Or, right-click on a slide in the Workspace and select **Slide > Duplicate Slide** from the context menu.
   - Or, click on the triangle to the right of the **Slide** icon in the Presentation toolbar and select **Duplicate Page/Slide** from the context menu. If the Presentation toolbar is not visible, go to **View > Toolbars** on the Menu bar and select **Presentation** from the list.
3) A duplicate slide is inserted after the selected slide in the presentation.

Selecting slide layout

When creating a presentation, the first slide is normally a title slide. You can use either a blank layout or one of the title layouts as your title slide.

Click on the **Slide Layout** icon on the Presentation Toolbar to open **Layouts** section and display the available layouts

Figure 146: Available slide layouts

Or

Click on the Properties icon at the side of the Sidebar to open **Layouts** section and display the available layouts (Figure 147). The layouts included in LibreOffice range from a blank slide to a slide with six contents boxes and a title.

Figure 147: Available slide layouts

To create a title, if one of the title layouts has been selected, click on *Click to add title* and then type the title text. To add text content, depending on the slide layout selected, click on *Click to add text*. To adjust the formatting of the title, subtitle or content modify the presentation style; see the *Impress Guide Chapter 2 Using Slide Masters, Styles, and Templates*.

Note

Text and graphical elements can be readjusted at any time during the preparation of the presentation, but changing the layout of a slide that already contains some content can have an effect on the content format. Therefore, it is recommended that you pay particular attention to the layout you select to prevent any loss of content.

Tip

To view the names for the included layouts, use the Tooltip feature: position the cursor on an icon in the Layout section (or on any toolbar icon) and its name will be displayed in a small rectangle.

In **Tools > Options > LibreOffice > General > Help**, select the **Extended tips** option to get more detailed tooltip information.

To select or change the layout of a slide, select the slide in the Slides Pane so that it appears in the Workspace and select the desired layout from the Layouts section in the Sidebar. Several layouts contain one or more content boxes. Each of these content boxes can be configured to contain text, movies, images, charts or tables.

You can choose the type of content by clicking on the corresponding icon that is displayed in the middle of the content box as shown in Figure 148. If you intend to use the content box for text, click on *Click to add text*.

Figure 148: Selecting content type

Modifying slide elements

A slide contains elements that were included in the slide master, as well as those elements included in the selected slide layout. However, it is unlikely that the predefined layouts will suit all your needs for your presentation. You may want to remove elements that are not required or insert objects such as text and graphics.

Although Impress does not allow you to create new layouts, you can resize and move the layout elements. It is also possible to add elements without being limited to the size and position of the layout boxes.

To resize a contents box, click on the outer frame so that the resizing handles are displayed. To move it, place the mouse cursor on the frame so that the cursor changes shape. You can now click and drag the contents box to a new position on the slide.

To remove any unwanted element:

1) Click the element to highlight it. The resizing handles show that it is selected.
2) Press the *Delete* key to remove it.

Note

Changes to any of the layouts included in Impress can only be made using **View > Normal**, which is the default. Attempting any changes by modifying a slide master, although possible, may result in unpredictable results and requires extra care as well as a certain amount of trial and error.

Adding text

To add text to a slide that contains a text frame, click on *Click to add text* in the text frame and then type your text. The Outline styles are automatically applied to the text as you insert it. You can change the outline level of each paragraph as well as its position within the text by using the arrow buttons on the *Text Formatting* toolbar (see Figure 140 and "Outline view" on page 168) or using the Tab key while positioning the cursor at the beginning of the paragraph. For more information on text, see "Adding and formatting text" on page 176.

Adding objects

To add any objects to a slide, for example a picture, clipart, drawing, photograph, or spreadsheet, click on **Insert** then select from the drop down menu what type of object you want to insert. For more information, see "Adding pictures, tables, charts, and media" on page 181.

Modifying the appearance of all slides

To change the background and other characteristics of all slides in the presentation, you need to modify the master page or choose a different master page as explained in "Working with slide masters and styles" on page 183.

A *Slide Master* is a slide with a specified set of characteristics that acts as a template and is used as the starting point for creating other slides. These characteristics include slide background, objects in the background, formatting of any text used, and any background graphics.

 Note

LibreOffice uses three terms for a slide that is used to create other slides: *master slide*, *slide master*, and *master page*. This book uses the term *slide master*, except when describing the user interface.

Impress has a range of slide masters and these are found in the **Master Pages** section of the Sidebar. You can also create and save additional slide masters or add more from other sources. See the *Impress Guide Chapter 2 Using Slide Masters, Styles, and Templates* for more information on creating and modifying slide masters.

If all you need to do is to change the background, you can use a shortcut:

1) Select **Slide > Page/Slide Properties...** and go to the *Background* tab on the **Page Setup** dialog that opens.

2) Select the desired background between solid color, gradient, hatching, and bitmap.

3) Click **OK** to apply it.

4) A dialog opens asking if the background should be applied to all the slides. Click **Yes** if you want all the slides modified and Impress will automatically modify the master page for you.

 Note

Inserting and correctly formatting a background is beyond the scope of this chapter, but you can find all the information you need in the *Draw Guide Chapter 4 Changing Object Attributes* or in the *Impress Guide Chapter 6 Formatting Graphic Objects*.

Modifying the slide show

By default the slide show will display all the slides in the same order as they appear in the slide sorter, without any transition between slides. You need to use keyboard input or mouse interaction to move from one slide to the next.

You can use **Slide Show** on the Menu bar to change the order of the slides, choose which ones are shown, automate moving from one slide to the next, and other settings. To change the slide transition, animate slides, add a soundtrack to the presentation, and make other enhancements, you need to use functions in the Sidebar. See the *Impress Guide* for details on how to use all of these features.

Adding and formatting text

Many of your slides are likely to contain some text. This section gives some guidelines on how to add text and change its appearance. Text used in slides is contained in *text boxes*. For more information on adding and formatting text, see the *Impress Guide Chapter 3 Adding and Formatting Text*.

You can add two types of text boxes to a slide:

- Choose a predefined layout from the *Layouts* section of the Sidebar and do not select any special content type. These text boxes are called **AutoLayout** text boxes.

- Create a text box using the **Text** icon 🅣 on the Standard toolbar (Figure 149) or the Text toolbar (Figure 150), or use the keyboard shortcut *F2*.

Figure 149: Standard toolbar

Figure 150: Text toolbar

Using AutoLayout text boxes

1) Make sure Normal view is selected.
2) Click in the text box that reads **Click to add text**.
3) Type or paste your text in the text box.

Using text boxes

1) Make sure Normal view is selected.
2) Click on the **Text** icon on the Standard or Text toolbar or use the keyboard shortcut *F2*. If the Standard or Text toolbars are not visible, go to **View > Toolbars** on the Menu bar and select **Standard** or **Text**.
3) Click and drag to draw a box for the text on the slide. Do not worry about the vertical size and position as the text box will expand if needed as you type.
4) Release the mouse button when finished. The cursor appears in the text box, which is now in edit mode (a colored border shown in Figure 151).
5) Type or paste your text in the text box.
6) Click outside the text box to deselect it.

You can move, resize, and delete text boxes. For more information, see the *Impress Guide Chapter 3 Adding and Formatting Text*.

Vertical text

In addition to the normal text boxes where text is horizontally aligned, it is possible to insert text boxes where the text is aligned vertically. Vertical text is available only when Asian languages are enabled in **Tools > Options > Language Settings > Languages**. Click the **Vertical Text** icon in the Standard toolbar or Text toolbar to create a vertical text box.

Figure 151: Creating and editing text boxes

Quick font resizing

Impress has an **Increase Font** icon and a **Decrease Font** icon on the Text Formatting toolbar (highlighted in Figure 152) to increase or decrease the font size of selected text. The amount by which the font size changes depends on the standard sizes available for the font in use.

Figure 152: Quick font resizing on Text Formatting toolbar

> **Note**
>
> AutoLayout text boxes can automatically resize fonts to let the box contain all the text you insert. If you insert a long piece of text, the font size may shrink to fit into the box. Otherwise, the font keeps its default size.

Pasting text

Text may be inserted into the text box by copying it from another document and pasting it into Impress. However, pasted text will probably not match the formatting of the surrounding text on the slide or that of the other slides in the presentation. This may be what you want on some occasions; however, in most cases you want to make sure that the presentation style is consistent and does not become a patchwork of different paragraph styles, font types, bullet points and so on. There are several ways to ensure consistency in your presentation.

Pasting unformatted text

It is normally good practice to paste text without formatting and apply the formatting later. To paste text without formatting:

- Use the keyboard shortcut *Ctrl+Shift+V* and select **Unformatted text** from the Paste Special dialog that opens.

- Or click on the small triangle next to the **Paste** icon in the Standard toolbar and select **Unformatted text** from the context menu.

The unformatted text will be formatted with the outline or paragraph style at the cursor position in an AutoLayout text box or with the default graphic style in a normal text box.

Formatting pasted text

When formatting pasted text, you can use the tools available on the Text Formatting toolbar (Figure 152), or the tools available in the *Character* and *Paragraph* sections of the *Properties* deck in the Sidebar (Figure 153). If the *Character* and *Paragraph* sections do not automatically open after selecting some text, click on the Properties icon at the side of the Sidebar.

Figure 153: Sidebar Character section

If you are pasting the text into an **AutoLayout** text box, you need to apply the appropriate *outline style* to the text to give it the same look and feel as the rest of the presentation.

1) Paste the text in the desired position.

2) Select the text you have just pasted.

3) Select **Format > Default formatting** on the Menu bar.

4) Use the four arrow buttons on the Text Formatting toolbar (highlighted in Figure 140 on page 169) to move the text to the appropriate position and give it the appropriate outline level.

   – Left arrow promotes a list entry by one level (for example from Outline 3 to Outline 2). You can get the same result by placing the cursor at the beginning of the paragraph and pressing the *Shift + Tab* keys.

   – Right arrow button demotes a list entry by one level. Press the *Tab* key to get the same result after placing the cursor at the beginning of the paragraph.

   – Up arrow moves a list entry up in the list order.

   – Down arrow moves a list entry down in the list order.

5) Apply any necessary manual formatting to the text to change font attributes, tabs, and so on.

If you are pasting text in a **text box**, you can still use styles to format the text quickly. Only one graphic style can be applied to the pasted text, as follows:

1) Paste the text in the desired position.
2) Select the text you have just pasted.
3) Select the desired graphical style to format the text.
4) Apply any necessary manual formatting to the text to change font attributes, tabs, and so on.

Creating bulleted and numbered lists

The procedure to create a bulleted or numbered list is quite different depending on the type of text box used, although the tools to manage the list and customize the appearance are the same. In AutoLayout text boxes, the outline styles available are, by default, bulleted lists. For normal text boxes an additional step is required to create a bulleted list.

AutoLayout text boxes

AutoLayout text boxes included in the available layouts are already formatted as a bulleted list. Create a slide with a bulleted list as follows:

1) From the Layout pane, choose a slide design that contains a text box.
2) In the text box, click on **Click to add text.**
3) Type your text and press the *Enter* key to start a new bulleted point.

The default list type is a bulleted list. Methods for changing the appearance of a list are explained in "Changing list appearance" on page 180.

 Tip

> Press *Shift+Enter* to start a new line without creating a new bullet point. The new line will have the same indentation as the previous line. To switch off bullets altogether, click the **Bullets On/Off** icon ⠿ on the Text Formatting toolbar. If the Text Formatting toolbar is not displayed, go to **View > Toolbar > Text Formatting** on the Menu bar.

Text boxes

Create a bulleted list in a text box as follows:

1) Click the **Text** icon ⊤ on the Standard toolbar and draw a text box on your slide.
2) Click the **Bullets On/Off** icon ⠿ on the Text Formatting toolbar.
3) Type the text and press *Enter* to start a new bulleted line.

The default list type is a bulleted list. Methods for changing the appearance of a list are explained in "Changing list appearance" on page 180.

Creating a new outline level

In AutoLayout text boxes, create a new outline level as follows:

1) If necessary, press *Enter* to begin a new list entry.
2) To demote a list entry (move it to the right), press the *Tab* key or click the Demote (right arrow) icon on the Text Formatting toolbar or use the keyboard shortcut *Alt+Shift+Right*. The list entry moves to the right and is indented to the next outline level.
3) To promote a list entry (move it to the left), press *Shift+Tab* or click the Promote (left arrow) icon on the Text Formatting toolbar or use the keyboard shortcut *Alt+Shift+Left*. The list entry moves to the left and is indented at the next higher level.
4) To create a new list entry at the same level as the previous one, press *Enter* again.

In the AutoLayout text boxes, promoting or demoting an item in the list corresponds to applying a different outline style. The second outline level corresponds to Outline 2 style, the third outline level to Outline 3 style, and so on. A change in level and style produces other changes, for example, to font size, bullet type, and so on.

In text boxes, a new outline level can only be created by using the *Tab* key to demote the list entry and the *Shift+Tab* key combination to promote the list entry.

 Note

> Do not try to change the outline level by selecting the text and then clicking the desired outline style as you would in Writer. Due to the way that presentation styles work in Impress, it is not possible to change the level in this way.

Changing list appearance

You can fully customize list appearance by changing the bullet type or numbering for the entire list or for only a single entry. All of the changes can be made using the Bullets and Numbering dialog (Figure 154), which is accessed by going to **Format > Bullets and Numbering** on the Menu bar or by clicking on the **Bullets Icon** or the **Numbering** icon on the Text Formatting toolbar.

For the entire list:

1) Select the entire list or click on the border of the text box so that the resizing handles are displayed.

2) Select **Format > Bullets and Numbering** on the Menu bar or click on the **Bullets** or **Numbering** icon on the Text Formatting toolbar.

Figure 154: Bullets and Numbering dialog

3) The Bullets and Numbering dialog (Figure 154) contains five pages: Bullets, Numbering type, Image, Position, and Customize.

   – If a bullet list is needed, select the desired bullet style from the default styles available on the *Bullets* page.

   – If a graphics style is needed, select one from those available on the *Image* page.

   – If a numbered list is needed, select one of the default numbering styles on the *Numbering type* page.

- Use the *Position* page to set the indent and numbering spacing and alignment of your list.
- Use the *Customize* page to customize the numbering, color, relative size, and character used for your list.

4) For a single list entry, click anywhere in the text and then follow steps 2 and 3 above.

If the list was created in an AutoLayout text box, then an alternative way to change the entire list is to modify the Outline styles. Changes made to the outline style will apply to all the slides using them.

Adding pictures, tables, charts, and media

A contents box can contain pictures, tables, charts, or media as well as text. This section provides a quick overview of how to work with these objects. For more information on adding pictures, tables, charts, or media, please refer to the *Impress Guide*.

Adding pictures

To add a picture to a contents box:

1) Go to **Insert > Image** on the Menu bar and then select either **From file** or **Scan**.
2) Alternatively, after inserting a new slide, click the **Insert Image** icon (Figure 148 on page 174) on the new slide and select the file from the Insert Image dialog that opens. To see a preview of the picture, select **Preview** at the bottom of the Insert Image dialog.
3) Move the picture to the desired location.
4) The picture will automatically resize to fill the area of the content box. Follow the directions in the note below when manually resizing a graphic.

 Note

When resizing a graphic, right-click the picture. Select **Position and Size** from the context menu and make sure that **Keep ratio** is selected. Then adjust the height or width to the size you need. As you adjust one dimension, both dimensions will change to keep the width and height ratio the same, ensuring that the picture will not become distorted. Remember also that resizing a bitmap image will reduce its quality; it is better to create an image of the desired size outside of Impress.

Adding tables

To add basic tables to a slide:

1) Go to **Insert > Table** on the Menu bar, or click the **Table** icon ⊞ ˙ on the Standard toolbar.
2) If there is a table already on the slide and it is selected, click the **Table** icon ⊞ ˙ on the Table toolbar. The Table toolbar is only visible after selecting **View > Toolbars > Table** on the Menu bar and when a table is selected.
3) Alternatively, and after inserting a new slide into your presentation, click the **Insert Table** icon (Figure 148 on page 174).
4) Select the number of rows and columns required from the Insert Table dialog that opens.
5) Alternatively, click the small triangle to the right of the **Table** icon ⊞ ˙ and select the number of rows and columns by dragging the cursor.
6) Select a design style from the available options for your table in the Table Design deck in the Properties section of the Sidebar (Figure 155). If the *Table Design* section does not

automatically open after inserting or selecting a table, click on the Properties icon at the side of the Sidebar.

 Note

Selecting from any of the styles in the Table Design section in the Sidebar creates a table based on that style. If you create a table by another method, you can still apply a style of your choice later.

The Table toolbar in Impress offers the same functions as the Table toolbar in Writer, with the exception of the calculation functions Sort and Sum. To use Sum and Sort in your presentation, you have to insert a Calc spreadsheet.

After the table is created, you can modify it by adding and deleting rows and columns, adjusting width and spacing, adding borders, background colors and so on. For more information on working with tables see the *Impress Guide Chapter 3 Adding and Formatting Text* and the *Writer Guide Chapter 9 Working with Tables*.

Figure 155: Sidebar Table Design section

Entering data into table cells is similar to working with text box objects. Click in the cell you wish to add data to and begin typing. To move around cells quickly, use the following keyboard options:

- Press the *arrow* keys to move the cursor to another cell if the cell is empty, or to the next character if the cell already contains text.
- Press the *Tab* key to move to the next cell on the right and press *Shift+Tab* to move to the next cell on the left.

Adding charts

To insert a chart in a slide:

1) Go to **Insert > Chart** on the Menu bar or click on the **Chart** icon 🔵 in the Standard toolbar.

2) Alternatively and after inserting a new slide, click on the **Insert Chart** icon (Figure 148 on page 174).

3) Impress will insert a default chart and open the Chart dialog. To modify the chart type, insert your own data and change the formatting, refer to the *Impress Guide*.

Adding media files

To insert media files, such as music and movie clips, in a slide:

1) Go to **Insert > Audio or Video** on the Menu bar.

2) Alternatively and after inserting a new slide, click on the **Insert Audio or Video** icon (Figure 148 on page 174).

3) A media player will open at the bottom of the screen and you can preview the media.

4) When an audio file is inserted, the contents box will show a loudspeaker image.

Adding graphics, spreadsheets, and other objects

Graphics, such as shapes, callouts, and arrows, are often useful to complement the text on a slide. These objects are handled much the same way as graphics in Draw. For more information, see the *Draw Guide Chapter 7 Getting Started with Draw*, or the *Impress Guide Chapters 4, 5*, and 6.

Spreadsheets embedded in Impress include most of the functionality of Calc spreadsheets and are capable of performing extremely complex calculations and data analysis. If you need to analyze your data or apply formulas, these operations are best performed in a Calc spreadsheet and the results displayed in an embedded Calc spreadsheet or even better in an Impress table.

Alternatively, go to **Insert > Object > OLE Object** on the Menu bar. You can select from options that include a LibreOffice 5.0 Spreadsheet. This opens a spreadsheet in the middle of the slide and the menus and toolbars change to those used in Calc. You can start adding data, though you may have to resize the visible area on the slide. You can also insert an existing spreadsheet and use the viewport to select the data that you want to display on your slide.

Impress offers the capability of inserting into a slide various other types of objects such as Writer documents, Math formulas, Draw drawings, or another presentation. For details on using these objects, refer to the *Impress Guide Chapter 7 Including Spreadsheets, Charts, and Other Objects*.

Working with slide masters and styles

A slide master is a slide that is used as the starting point for other slides. It is similar to a page style in Writer and it controls the basic formatting of all slides based on it. A slide show can have more than one slide master.

 Note

> LibreOffice uses three terms for a slide that is used to create other slides: *master slide*, *slide master*, and *master page*. This book uses the term *slide master,* except when describing the user interface.

A slide master has a defined set of characteristics, including background colors, graphics, gradients; and other objects (such as logos, decorative lines and so on), headers and footers, placement and size of text frames, and text format.

Styles

All of the characteristics of slide masters are controlled by styles. New slides that you create using a slide master have styles that are inherited from the slide master which was used. Changing a style in a slide master results in changes to all slides based on that slide master, but you can modify individual slides without affecting the slide master.

 Note

Although it is highly recommended to use the slide masters whenever possible, there are occasions where manual changes are needed for a particular slide, for example to enlarge the chart area when the text and chart layout is used.

Slide masters have two types of styles associated with them: *presentation styles* and *image styles*. The prepackaged presentation styles can be modified, but new presentation styles cannot be created. For image styles, you can modify the prepackaged styles and also create new image styles.

Presentation styles affect three elements of a slide master: background, background objects (such as icons, decorative lines, and text frames), and text placed on the slide. Text styles are further divided into *Notes*, *Outline 1* through *Outline 9*, *Subtitle*, and *Title*. The outline styles are used for the different levels of the outline to which they belong. For example, Outline 2 is used for the sub-points of Outline 1, and Outline 3 is used for the sub-points of Outline 2, and so on.

Image styles are not restricted and can affect many of the elements of a slide. Note that text styles exist in both the presentation and image style selections.

Slide masters

Impress comes with a collection of slide masters. These slide masters are shown in the Master Pages section of the Sidebar (Figure 156), which has three subsections: *Used in This Presentation*, *Recently Used*, and *Available for Use*. Click the + sign next to the name of a subsection to expand it to show thumbnails of the slides, or click the – sign to collapse the subsection to hide the thumbnails.

Each of the slide masters shown in the *Available for Use* list is from a template of the same name. If you have created your own templates, or added templates from other sources, slide masters from those templates will also appear in this list.

Creating a slide master

Creating a new slide master is similar to modifying the default slide master.

1) Enable editing of slide masters by selecting **View > Master Slide** on the Menu bar and the **Master View** toolbar opens (Figure 157). If the Master View toolbar does not appear, go to **View > Toolbars** and select **Master View.**

2) On the Master View toolbar, click the **New Master** icon .

3) A new slide master appears in the Slides pane. Modify this slide master to suit your requirements.

4) It is also recommended that you rename this new slide master. Right-click on the slide in the Slides pane and select **Rename master** from the context menu.

5) When finished creating a slide master, click **Close Master View** on the Master View toolbar and return to normal slide editing mode.

Figure 156: Sidebar Master Pages section

Figure 157: Master View toolbar

Applying a slide master

To apply a slide master to all the slides in your presentation:

1) Click on the Master Pages icon ![icon] in the Sidebar to open the Master Pages section (Figure 156).

2) To apply one of the slide masters from the available selection to *all slides* in your presentation, right-click on it and select **Apply to All Slides** on the context menu.

To apply a different slide master to one or more selected slides:

1) In the Slide Pane, select the slide or slides where you want to use a new slide master.

2) In the Master Pages section on the Sidebar, right-click on the slide master you want to apply to the selected slides, and select **Apply to Selected Slides** on the context menu.

Loading additional slide masters

Sometimes, in the same set of slides, you may need to mix multiple slide masters that may belong to different templates. For example, you may need a completely different layout for the first slide of

---

the presentation, or you may want to add to your presentation a slide from a different presentation (based on a template available on the hard disk).

1) Go to **Slide > Slide Design** on the Menu bar or right-click on a slide in the Slides Pane and select **Slide Design** from the context menu to open the Slide Design dialog (Figure 158). This dialog shows the slide masters already available for use.

2) To add more slide masters, click the **Load** button to open the Load Slide Design dialog (Figure 159).

3) Select in the Load Slide Design dialog the template from which to load the slide master and click **OK**.

4) Click **OK** again to close the Slide Design dialog.

5) The slide masters in the template you selected to use are now shown in the *Available for use* subsection of Master Pages.

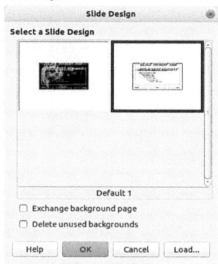

Figure 158: Slide Design dialog

Figure 159: Load Slide Design dialog

Note

The slide masters you have loaded will also be available the next time you load the presentation. If you want to delete the unused slide masters, click the corresponding checkbox in the Slide Design dialog. If the slide master was not used in the presentation, it is removed from the list of available slide masters.

 Tip

To limit the size of the presentation file, you may want to minimize the number of slide masters used.

Modifying a slide master

The following items can be changed on a slide master:

- Background (color, gradient, hatching, or bitmap)
- Background objects (for example, a logo or decorative graphics)
- Size, placement, and contents of header and footer elements to appear on every slide
- Size and placement of default frames for slide titles and content

For more information on modifying slide masters, see the *Impress Guide Chapter 2 Using Slide Masters, Styles, and Templates*.

1) Select **View > Slide Master** from the Menu bar. This unlocks the properties of a slide master so you can edit it.

2) Select a slide master in *Master Pages* in the Slides pane.

3) Select an object on the slide master in the Workspace and the Sidebar will display the property options that can be changed for the selected object. Figure 160 shows a graphic object selected with the *Graphic* properties section open on the Sidebar.

4) Make all necessary changes to the slide master, then click the **Close Master View** icon on the Master View toolbar or go to **View > Normal** on the Menu bar to exit from editing slide masters.

5) Save your presentation file before continuing.

 Caution

Any changes made to one slide when in Master View mode will appear on *all* slides using this slide master. Always make sure you Close Master View and return to Normal view before working on any of the presentation slides.

 Note

The changes made to one of the slides in Normal view (for example, changes to the bullet point style, the color of the title area, and so on) will not be overridden by subsequent changes to the slide master. There are cases, however, where it is desirable to revert a manually modified element of the slide to the style defined in the slide master. To revert back to default formatting, select the element and select **Format > Default Formatting** from the Menu bar.

Figure 160: Editing a master slide

Adding text, footers, and fields to all slides

A slide master can have text, footers, or fields added so that they appear on every slide in your presentation. Headers are not normally added to slides.

Text

1) Go to **View > Master Slide** on the Menu bar to open Master View (Figure 161).
2) On the Drawing toolbar, select the **Text** icon or press the *F2* key.
3) Click and drag in the master page to draw a text object and then type or paste your text into the text object.
4) Go to **View > Normal** on the Menu bar or click on **Close Master View** on the Master View toolbar when you have finished entering text objects that you want to appear on every slide in your presentation.

Footers

To add a footer to your slides:

1) Go to **View > Master Slide** on the Menu bar to open Master View (Figure 161).
2) Go to **Insert > Field** or **Insert > Page Number** on the Menu bar and time to open the Header and Footer dialog (Figure 162).
3) Select the type of date and time and type in the footer text and slide number from the available options in the dialog.
4) Click **Apply to All** to apply your changes to all the slide masters in your presentation, or click **Apply** to apply your changes to the selected slide master in your presentation.
5) Alternatively, you can add the date/time, footer text and slide number directly into their respective areas as shown in Figure 161.

 Note

Normally only footers are used on a slide. To create a header, you can use a text box as explained in "Text" on page 188.

Figure 161: Example master view

Figure 162: Footer dialog in Impress

Fields

To add a field into an object or as a separate object on a slide, select **Insert > Fields** on the Menu bar and select the required field from the submenu. If you want to edit this field in your slide, see the *Impress Guide Chapter 3 Adding and Formatting Text* for more information.

The fields you can use in Impress are as follows:

- Date (fixed)
- Date (variable): updates automatically when you reload a file
- Time (fixed)
- Time (variable): updates automatically when you reload a file
- Author: first and last names listed in the LibreOffice user data
- Page Number: the slide number in Impress
- Page Count: the number of slides in your presentation

- File Name

To change the author information, go to **Tools > Options > LibreOffice > User Data** on the Menu bar.

To change the number format (1,2,3 or a,b,c or i,ii,iii, and so on) for the number field, go to **Slide > Properties...** on the Menu bar and then select a format from the *Format* list in the **Layout Settings** area.

To change a paragraph style throughout your presentation, open the Styles and Formatting dialog and modify the appropriate presentation style.

Adding comments to a presentation

Impress supports comments similar to those in Writer and Calc.

In Normal View, go to **Insert > Comment** on the Menu bar to open a blank comment (Figure 163). A small box containing your initials appears in the upper left-hand corner of the slide, with a larger text box beside it. Impress automatically adds your name and the current date at the bottom of the text box.

Type or paste your comment into the text box. You can optionally apply some basic formatting to the comment by selecting it, right-clicking, and choosing from the context menu that opens. This menu allows you to apply formatting to selected text, delete the current comment, delete all comments from the same author, or delete all comments in the presentation.

Figure 163: Inserting comments

You can move the small comment markers to anywhere you wish on the slide. Typically you might place it on or near an object you refer to in the comment.

To show or hide the comment markers, choose **View > Comments**.

Select **Tools > Options > User Data** to configure the name you want to appear in the comment.

If more than one person edits the document, each author is automatically allocated a different background color for their comments.

Creating a photo album

Impress can create a photo album from a set of images, usually with one photo per slide. This photo album can source multimedia shows with graphics and images or even collect your latest vacation pictures into a presentation file.

To insert a photo album into your presentation

1) Open an existing or blank presentation.
2) Go to the slide that precedes the photo album.
3) Choose **Insert > Media > Photo Album**.
4) In the Create Photo Album dialog (Figure 164), click **Add**. A standard file browser opens.
5) Locate the files you want to insert.

Note

If several images are in the same folder, you can select a group of photos using the **Shift** or **Ctrl** keys while clicking on their filenames.

6) Click **Open** to add the files to the Photo Album.

Figure 164: The photo album dialog box with photo preview

Tip

Click on a file name to display it in the Preview area.

7) Select the number of images per slide in the **Slide layout** list box.
8) Select the **Add caption to each slide** option, if necessary, to insert a text box for the caption.
9) Create the required sequence by removing images or moving them up or down in the list of images. When the sequence of images is ready, click **Insert Slides**. (You can change the sequence and remove or insert images later, as you can with any slides.)

Impress will create a presentation with as many pages as determined by the Slide layout number of slides per page. If you selected **Add caption to each slide**, there will be a placeholder for the image caption (title) on each slide.

Tip

Use the slide sorter (see page 171) to reorder your photo album. Use slide transitions (page 192) to go smoothly to the following photo. Use audio resources (page 183) to insert a musical background.

Setting up a slide show

As mentioned in "Modifying the slide show" on page 176, Impress allocates reasonable default settings for slide shows, while at the same time allowing for customizing many aspects of the slide show experience. This section covers only some aspects; more advanced techniques are explained in the *Impress Guide Chapter 9 Slide Shows*.

Most of the tasks are best done in Slide Sorter view where you can see most of the slides simultaneously. Go to **View > Slide Sorter** on the Menu bar or click the Slide Sorter tab at the top of the Workspace.

One slide set – multiple presentations

In many situations, you may find that you have more slides than the time available to present them or you may want to provide a rapid overview without dwelling on the details. Rather than having to create a new presentation, you can use two tools that Impress offers: hiding slides and custom slide shows.

Hiding slides

1) Select the slide you want to hide in the Slide Pane or Slide Sorter view on the Workspace area.

2) Go to **Slide > Hide Slide** on the Menu bar or right-click on the slide thumbnail and select **Hide Slide** from the context menu. Hidden slides are marked by a diagonal bars across the slide.

Custom slide shows

If you want to create a custom slide show from the same presentation:

1) Select the slides you want to use in your custom slide show.

2) Go to **Slide Show > Custom Slide Show** on the Menu bar.

3) Click on the New button to create a new sequence of slides and save it with a different name. You can have as many slide shows as you want from a single presentation.

Slide transitions

Slide transition is the animation that is played when a slide is changed for the next slide in your presentation. You can configure the slide transition from the Slide Transition section in the Tasks Pane.

1) Go to **Slide > Slide Transition** on the Menu bar or click on the Slide Transition icon 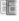 on the Sidebar to open the options available for slide transitions.

2) Select the desired transition, the speed of the animation, and whether the transition should happen when you click the mouse (preferred) or automatically after a certain number of seconds.

3) Click **Apply to All Slides** to apply the transition for all of your presentation or continue selecting transitions to place between each slide in your presentation.

 Tip

> The Slide Transition section has a very useful choice: Automatic preview. Select its checkbox and when you make any changes in a slide transition, the new slide is previewed in the Slide Design area, including its transition effect.

Slide advance

You can set the presentation to advance automatically to the next slide after a set amount of time from the Slide Transition section in the Sidebar.

1) Go to **Advance slide** and select the **Automatically after** option.
2) Enter the required amount of time in seconds that each slide will be displayed.
3) Click on the **Apply to All Slides** button to apply the same display time to all slides.

To apply a different display time to each slide in your presentation:

1) Go to **Slide Show > Rehearse Timings** on the Menu bar and the slide show starts.
2) When you are ready to advance to the next slide, mouse click on the display background or press the right arrow or space bar on your keyboard.
3) Impress will memorize the timings for each slide and will advance to the next slide automatically using these timings when you run the slide show.

To restart a slide show automatically after the last slide has been displayed:

1) Go to **Slide Show > Slide Show Settings** on the Menu bar.
2) Select **Auto** and the timing of the pause between slide shows.
3) Click **OK** when you have finished.

Running a slide show

To run a slide show, do one of the following:

- Click **Slide Show > Start from first Slide** on the Menu bar.
- Click the **Start from first Slide** icon on the Presentation toolbar.
- Press *F5* on the keyboard.

If the slide advance is set to *Automatically after X sec*, let the slide show run by itself.

If the slide advance is set to *On mouse click*, do one of the following to move from one slide to the next:

- Use the arrow keys on the keyboard to go to the next slide or to go back to the previous one.
- Click the mouse to move to the next slide.
- Press the spacebar on the keyboard to advance to the next slide.

Right-click anywhere on the screen to open a context menu where you can navigate through the slides and set other options.

To exit the slide show at any time including when the slide show has ended, press the *Esc* key.

Presenter Console

LibreOffice Impress has a Presenter Console function that can be used when an extra display for presentation has been connected to your computer. The Presenter Console (Figure 165) provides extra control over slide shows by using different views on your computer display and on the display that the audience sees. The view you see on your computer display includes the current slide, the upcoming slide, any slide notes, and a presentation timer.

For more information and details about using the Presenter Console, see the *Impress Guide Chapter 9 Slide Shows*.

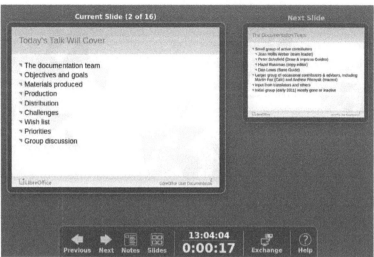

Figure 165: Impress Presenter Console

Using Impress Remote control

Impress Remote is a mobile application developed by the community for Android and iOS systems that allows you to control a live presentation with a mobile device such as a phone or tablet.

The connection between your mobile device and the computer running your presentation is made through a Bluetooth pairing or a local network connection between the two.

Getting Impress Remote

To get the software, access your mobile device application store, either Google Play Store for Android devices or Apple Store for IOs devices. Search for "Impress Remote" and select the one that is from The Document Foundation and install it in your device.

Connecting the mobile device to the computer

Activate Bluetooth on both devices, then pair the devices. (Refer to the manuals for your mobile device and computer operating system for instructions on enabling, setting up a Bluetooth identifier, and pairing.)

Once the pairing is established, your mobile device is ready to control your presentation.

Enabling remote control in Impress

An Impress slide show with remote control is not enabled by default. To enable it, go to **Tools > Options > LibreOffice Impress > General** and select **Enable Remote Control** checkbox in the Presentation area of the dialog (Figure 166).

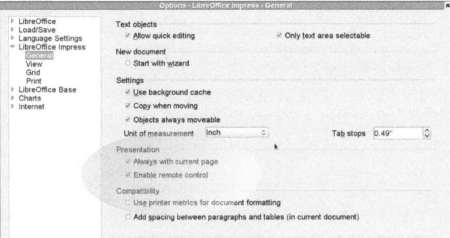
Figure 166: LibreOffice settings for Impress remote control

Running a slide show with Impress Remote

To run a slide show using Impress Remote, follow these steps:

1) On both devices, make sure Bluetooth is already enabled and configured.
2) On your computer, open the presentation you would like to present.
3) On your phone:
   a) Open Impress Remote from the main menu (Figure 167).
   b) To select your computer, tap its name. The presentation opened on the computer begins automatically (Figures 168 and 169).

Figure 167: Bluetooth visible device

Figure 168: Impress presentation as seen in mobile device

Figure 169: All slides

To advance the presentation

Tap the slide thumbnail or use the phone's physical volume up button.

To go backwards

Double-tap the slide thumbnail or use the phone's physical volume down button.

To skip slide animations and transitions

Swipe left to go to the next slide, or swipe right to go backwards.

To end the presentation, use the Back button of the phone, or open the menu and select **Stop slide show**.

Getting Started Guide

Chapter 7
Getting Started with Draw

Vector Drawing in LibreOffice

What is Draw?

LibreOffice Draw is a vector graphics drawing program, although it can also perform some operations on raster graphics (pixels). Using Draw, you can quickly create a wide variety of graphical images.

Vector graphics store and display an image as an assembly of simple geometric elements such as lines, circles, and polygons, rather than a collection of pixels (points on the screen). Vector graphics allow for easier storage and scaling of the image.

Draw is fully integrated into the LibreOffice suite, and this simplifies exchanging graphics with all components of the suite. For example, if you create an image in Draw, reusing it in a Writer document is as simple as copying and pasting the image. You can also work with drawings directly from within Writer or Impress, using a subset of the functions and tools from **Draw**.

The functionality of LibreOffice Draw is extensive and, even though it was not designed to rival high-end graphics applications, it possesses more functionality than the drawing tools that are generally integrated with most office productivity suites.

A few examples of the drawing functions are: layer management, magnetic grid-point system, dimensions and measurement display, connectors for making organization charts, 3D functions that enable small three-dimensional drawings to be created (with texture and lighting effects), drawing and page-style integration, and Bézier curves.

This chapter introduces some features of Draw and does not attempt to cover all of the Draw features. See the *Draw Guide* and the Help for more information.

Draw main window

The main components of the Draw main window are shown in Figure 170.

Workspace

The large area in the center of the window (Workspace) is where you create your drawings and this drawing area can be surrounded with toolbars and information areas. The number and position of the visible tools vary with the task in hand and user preferences, therefore your setup may look different from Figure 170.

In LibreOffice Draw, the maximum size of a drawing is 300 cm by 300 cm.

Pages pane

You can split drawings in Draw over several pages. Multi-page drawings are used mainly for presentations. The *Pages* pane gives an overview of the pages that you create in your drawing. If the Pages pane is not visible, go to **View** on the Menu bar and select **Page Pane**. To make changes to the page order, drag and drop one or more pages.

Layers bar

A layer is a workspace where you insert your drawings elements and objects. The layers bar is located on the bottom of the workplace and contains the guides for layer selection and layer command. For more information on layers see "Working with layers" on page 201.

Sidebar

The *Sidebar* has four main sections in Draw. To expand a section, click on its icon or click on the small triangle at the top of the icons and select a section from the drop down list. Only one section at a time can be open. If the Sidebar is not visible, go to **View** on the Menu bar and select **Sidebar** from the context menu.

Figure 170: LibreOffice Draw workspace

Properties

Opens sub-sections for object properties that you can change to suit your requirements. The sub-sections are *Insert Shapes*, *Character*, *Paragraph*, *Area*, *Line*, and *Position and Size*.

Styles and Formatting

Here you can edit and apply image styles to objects within your drawing. When you edit a style, the changes are automatically applied to all of the elements formatted with this image style in your drawing.

Gallery

Opens the Drawing gallery where you can insert an object into your drawing either as a copy or as a link. A copy of an object is independent of the original object. Changes to the original object have no effect on the copy. A link remains dependent on the original object. Changes to the original object are also reflected in the link.

Navigator

Opens the Drawing navigator, in which you can quickly move between pages in your drawing or select an object on the drawing. It is recommended to give pages and objects in your drawing meaningful names so that you can easily identify them when using the Navigator.

Rulers

You should see rulers (bars with numbers) on the upper and left-hand sides of the workspace. If they are not visible, you can enable them by selecting **View > Ruler** in the Menu bar. The rulers show the size of a selected object on the page using double lines (highlighted in Figure 171). When no object is selected, they show the location of the mouse pointer, which helps to position drawing objects more accurately.

You can also use the rulers to manage object handles and guide lines, making it easier to position objects.

The page margins in the drawing area are also represented on the rulers. You can change the margins directly on the rulers by dragging them with the mouse. The margin area is indicated by the grayed out area on the rulers as shown in Figure 171.

Figure 171: Rulers showing size of a selected object

To change the measurement units of the rulers, which can be defined independently, right-click on a ruler and select the measurement unit from the drop down list, as illustrated for the horizontal ruler in Figure 172.

Figure 172: Ruler units

Status bar

The Status bar is located at the bottom of the workspace in all LibreOffice components. It includes several Draw-specific fields. For details on the contents and use of these fields, see Chapter 1, Introducing LibreOffice, in this guide and Chapter 1, Introducing Draw, in the *Draw Guide*.

Figure 173: Draw status bar

Note

The sizes are given in the current measurement unit. They might not be the same as the ruler units. The measurement unit on the Status bar is defined in **Tools > Options > LibreOffice Draw > General**, where you can also change the scale of the page.

Toolbars

To display or hide the various Draw toolbars, go to **View > Toolbars** on the Menu bar. On the View menu, select which toolbars you want to display. For more about working with toolbars, see Chapter 1, Introducing LibreOffice, in this guide.

The tools available in the Draw toolbars are described below. The appearance of the toolbar icons may vary depending on your operating system and the selection of icon size and style in **Tools > Options > LibreOffice > View**.

Standard toolbar

The **Standard** toolbar is the same for all LibreOffice components and is not described in detail in this chapter. By default, it is located just under the Menu bar.

Drawing toolbar

The **Drawing** toolbar is the most important toolbar in **Draw**. It contains all the necessary functions for drawing various geometric and freehand shapes and for organizing them on the page. By default, it is docked vertically on the left side of the Draw window.

Line and Filling toolbar

Use the **Line and Filling** toolbar to modify the main properties of a drawing object. The icons and pull-down lists vary according to the type of object selected. For example, to change the style of a line, click on the up and down arrows for Line Style and select the required style.

The functions on this toolbar are also provided in the Properties pane of the sidebar when a drawing object is selected. By default, the Line and Filling toolbar is not shown, but you can display it from the **View > Toolbars** menu.

Text Formatting toolbar

If the selected object is text, the Sidebar shows relevant formatting choices in the Properties pane. By default, the Text Formatting toolbar is not shown, but you can display it from the **View > Toolbars** menu. If you have enabled both the Line and Filling toolbar and the Text Formatting toolbar, Draw switches between them depending on what object is selected.

Options toolbar

Use the **Options** toolbar to activate or deactivate various drawing aids. By default, the Options toolbar is not shown, but you can display it from the **View > Toolbars** menu.

Working with layers

Use layers to create a complex drawing by stacking simpler drawings in each layer. The area of a layer that does not contain an object is transparent. You can add any number of layers in a drawing document. A layer can be set to visible or hidden, it can be printable or not. Layers are common to all pages of the drawing.

A Draw document contains three default layers that you cannot delete or rename. Here are the common ways of using them:

- **Layout**: Here you place title, text, and object placeholders on your page.
- **Controls**: This layer is always on the top of any other. Here you put buttons and other controls of your drawing.
- **Dimension lines**: Here you place the dimension lines for your object, if relevant.

For more information on layers, see Chapter 11, Advanced Draw Techniques, in the *Draw Guide*.

Adding a layer

To add a layer to your drawing, select **Insert > Layer...** from the menu bar or right-click any layer tab in the Layers bar on the bottom of the workspace (Figure 170) and choose **Insert Layer...** The Insert Layer dialog opens (Figure 174).

Add a name, title, and description of the layer. Select if you want it printable or not, visible or hidden, or locked to prevent further changes or accidental edits.

A hidden layer still shows in the Layers bar, but its name is in blue. You cannot reorder layers in the Layers bar.

 Note

> Layers do not determine the stacking order of objects on the page, except for the Controls layer which is always in front of other layers. The stacking order of objects is determined by the sequence in which you add the objects. You can rearrange the stacking order by **Modify > Arrange**.

Figure 174: The Insert Layer dialog

Choosing and defining colors

To display the color palette currently in use (Figure 175), select **View > Toolbars > Color Bar**. By default, the Color Bar is displayed below the workspace. You can hide or show it by clicking on its Hide/Show button. Here you can rapidly choose the color of objects in your drawing (lines, areas, and 3D effects). The first box corresponds to none (no color).

Figure 175: Color bar

You can access several specialized color palettes in Draw, as well as change individual colors to your own taste. To do this, use the Area dialog by selecting **Format > Area** on the Menu bar or clicking the *Area* icon on the Sidebar, then selecting the **Colors** tab (Figure 176).

Figure 176: Area Dialog - Color

To choose another palette, click on the **Palette** drop down list and select one of the available LibreOffice palettes.

To add a custom color to the custom palette, first select your color by pressing the **Pick** button and adjusting your color using the color selection dialog that appears (Figure 177). In the color selection dialog, you can change any color by either dragging the round cursor to different locations on the visible color palette, or by modifying the numerical values in the fields provided to the right of the color palette in either CMYK or RGB color schemes.

Figure 177: Color Selection Dialog

For a more detailed description of color palettes and their options, as well as more on the difference between the CMYK and RGB color schemes, refer to Chapter 11:Advanced Draw Techniques, in the LibreOffice *Draw Guide*.

Drawing basic shapes

Draw provides a wide range of shapes, located in palettes accessed from the Drawing toolbar.

This section describes only a few of the basic shapes, including text, which are treated as objects in Draw. See the *Draw Guide* for a complete description of the shapes available.

Some of the icons on the Drawing toolbar will change according to the shape that has been selected from the choices available. Icons with tool palettes available are indicated by a small triangle to the right of the icon.

 Note

> When you draw a basic shape or select one for editing, the *Info* field at the left side in the status bar changes to reflect the present action: for example *Line created*, *Text frame xxyy selected*, and so on.

Drawing a straight line

Click on the **Line** icon and place the cursor at the point where you want to start the line (Figure 178). Drag the mouse while keeping the mouse button pressed. Release the mouse button at the point where you want to end the line. A selection handle appears at each end of the line, showing that this object is the currently selected object. The selection handle at the starting point of the line is slightly larger than the other selection handle.

Figure 178: Drawing a straight line

Keep the *Ctrl* key pressed while drawing a line to enable the end of the line to snap to the nearest grid point.

 Note

This is the default behavior of the *Ctrl* key. However, if the **Snap to Grid** option on the **View > Grid** menu has been selected, the *Ctrl* key deactivates the snap to grid activity.

Keep the *Shift* key pressed while you draw a line to restrict the drawing angle of the line to a multiple of 45 degrees (0, 45, 90, 135, and so on).

 Note

This is the default behavior of the *Shift* key. However, if the option *When creating or moving objects* in the *Snap position* section of **Tools > Options > LibreOffice Draw > Grid** has been selected, the action of the *Shift* key is the opposite. Lines will automatically be drawn at a multiple of 45 degrees *unless* the *Shift* key is pressed.

Hold down the *Alt* key while drawing a line to cause the line to extend outwards symmetrically in both directions from the start point. This lets you draw lines by starting from the middle of the line.

When a line is drawn, it uses default attributes. To change any of these attributes, select a line by clicking on it, then *right-click* and select **Line** from the context menu or go to **Format > Line** on the Menu bar to open the **Line** dialog (Figure 179). Alternatively, click on the Properties icon on the Sidebar and open the Line sub-section. Line style, line width, and line color can also be changed using the controls in the Line and Filling toolbar at the top of the workspace.

Figure 179: Line dialog

Drawing an arrow

Arrows are drawn like lines. Draw classifies *arrows* as a subgroup of lines: lines with arrowheads. The information field on the status bar shows them only as lines. Click on the **Line Ends with Arrow** icon on the Drawing toolbar or the *Insert Shapes* sub-section in Sidebar Properties to draw an arrow. The arrowhead is drawn at the end point of the arrow when you release the mouse button.

Choosing line endings

Several types of line endings (arrows, circles, squares, and others) are available in Draw. Click on the small triangle to the right of the **Lines and Arrows** icon on the Drawing toolbar or the *Insert Shapes* sub-section in Sidebar Properties to open a tool palette containing tools for drawing lines and arrows. Alternatively, go to **View > Toolbars > Arrows** to open the Arrows toolbar as a floating toolbar (Figure 180). The icon for the tool used most recently will be shown on the Drawing toolbar to make it easier to use the same tool again.

After drawing the line, you can change the arrow style by clicking on the **Arrowheads** icon in the Line and Filling toolbar and select the arrow start and end options.

Figure 180: Arrows toolbar and available tools

Drawing a dimension line

Dimension lines display a measurement of an object in the drawing (Figure 181). The dimension line does not belong to the object itself but it is usually placed close to it. An object can have as many dimension lines as necessary to indicate measures of its sides, edges, and distances.

Figure 181: Measuring an object with dimension lines

Dimension lines automatically calculate and display linear dimensions.

To draw a dimension line, open the **Arrows** toolbar (Figure 180) and click the **Dimension Line** icon. Move your pointer to where you want the line to start and drag to draw the dimension line. Release when finished.

You can control the display of the dimension line's components and appearance by selecting it, right-clicking, and choosing **Dimensions...** in the context menu to display the Dimension line dialog (Figure 182).

Figure 182: Dimension line settings dialog

 Note

> If the option *When creating or moving objects* has been selected in **Tools > Options > LibreOffice Draw > General**, the action of the *Shift* key is reversed: the Rectangle tool draws a square. To draw a rectangle, you have to press the *Shift* key when drawing. This *Shift* key reversal also applies when drawing ellipses and circles.

Drawing rectangles or squares

Drawing a rectangle is similar to drawing a straight line. Click on the **Rectangle** icon in the Drawing toolbar or the *Insert Shapes* sub-section in Sidebar Properties. As you draw the rectangle with the mouse cursor, the rectangle appears with its bottom right corner attached to the cursor.

Squares are rectangles with all sides of equal length. To draw a square, click on the **Rectangle** icon and hold down the *Shift* key while you draw a square.

To draw a rectangle or square from its center rather than the bottom right corner, position your cursor on the drawing, press the mouse button and then hold down the *Alt* key while dragging with the cursor. The rectangle or square uses the start point (where you first clicked the mouse button) as the center.

Drawing circles or ellipses

To draw an ellipse (also called an oval), click on the **Ellipse** icon on the Drawing toolbar or the *Insert Shapes* sub-section in Sidebar Properties. A circle is an ellipse with both axes the same length. To draw a circle, click on the **Ellipse** icon and hold down the *Shift* key whilst you draw a circle.

To draw an ellipse or circle from its center, position your cursor on the drawing, press the mouse button and then hold down the *Alt* key while dragging with the cursor. The ellipse or circle uses the start point (where you first clicked the mouse button) as the center.

 Note

> If you first press and hold down the *Ctrl* key and then click on one of the icons for Line, Rectangle, Ellipse, or Text, a standard sized object is drawn automatically in the work area; the size, shape, and color are all standard values. These attributes can be changed later, if desired. See the *Draw Guide* for more information.

Drawing curves or polygons

To draw a curve or polygon, click the **Curve** icon on the Drawing toolbar or the *Insert Shapes* sub-section in Sidebar Properties. Click on the triangle to the right of the icon to open the tool palette containing tools that are available for drawing curves and polygons (Figure 183). The icon for the tool used most recently is on the Drawing toolbar to make it easier to use the same tool again.

Move the mouse cursor over one of the icons to show a tooltip with a description of the function.

Figure 183: Curves (Lines) toolbar and available tools

 Note

> Hovering the mouse pointer over this icon gives a tooltip of *Curve*. If you open the floating toolbar, the title is *Lines*, as shown in Figure 183.
>
> Hold down the *Shift* key when drawing lines with the Curve or Polygon tools to restrict the angles between the lines to 45 or 90 degrees.

Curves

Click and hold the left mouse button to create the starting point of your curve, then, while holding down the left mouse button, drag from the starting point to draw a line. Release the left mouse button and continue to drag the cursor to bend the line into a curve. Click to set the end point of the curve and fix the line on the page. To continue with your line, drag the mouse cursor to draw a straight line. Each mouse click sets a corner point and allows you to continue drawing another straight line from the corner point. A double click ends the drawing of your line.

A filled curve automatically joins the last point to the first point to close off the figure and fills it with the current standard fill color. A curve without filling will not be closed at the end of the drawing.

Polygons

Click and draw the first line from the start point with the left mouse button held down. As soon as you release the mouse button, a line between the first and second points is drawn. Move the cursor to draw the next line. Each mouse click sets a corner point and allows you to draw another line. A double-click ends the drawing.

A filled polygon automatically joins the last point to the first point to close off the figure and fills it with the current standard fill color. A polygon without filling will not be closed at the end of the drawing.

Polygons 45°

Like ordinary polygons, these are formed from lines, but the angles between lines are restricted to 45 or 90 degrees.

Freeform lines

Using the freeform line tools is similar to drawing with a pencil on paper. Press and hold the left mouse button and drag the cursor to the line shape you require. It is not necessary to end the drawing with a double-click, just release the mouse button and the drawing is completed.

If Freeform Line Filled is selected, the end point is joined automatically to the start point and the object is filled with the appropriate color.

Adding text

To activate the text tool, click on the **Text** icon for horizontal text or the **Vertical Text** icon for vertical script. If the Vertical Text icon is not visible, check that *Asian* has been selected in **Tools > Options > Language Settings > Languages**. You can display the Text Formatting toolbar (**View > Toolbars**) or use the Character section in the Properties pane of the Sidebar to select font type, font size, and other text properties before you start typing.

After activating the Text command, click at the location where you want to position the text. A small text frame appears, containing only the cursor. This frame can be moved like any other object. A text frame is also dynamic and grows as you enter text.

The information field in the status bar shows that you are editing text and also provides details about the current cursor location using paragraph, row, and column numbers (Figure 184).

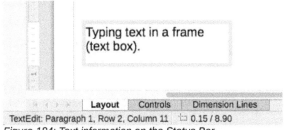

Figure 184: Text information on the Status Bar

You can insert a line break with the *Shift+Enter* key combination or start a new paragraph with the *Enter* key. The insertion of line breaks or new paragraphs does not terminate text editing or deselect the text frame. When you have finished typing text, click outside the text frame to cancel adding or editing text.

Text properties can also be changed during text input, with any changes taking effect from the cursor position onwards. To change the properties for all of the text in the text frame, you have to highlight all text in the text frame.

You can create Graphic styles that you can reuse for other text frames. Select **Format > Styles and Formatting** or press *F11* to open the Styles and Formatting dialog, or click on the Styles and Formatting icon on the Sidebar. Graphic styles affect all of the text within a text frame. To only format parts of the text, use direct formatting with the Text Formatting toolbar or the *Character* and *Paragraph* sub-sections in Sidebar Properties.

Text frames can also have fill colors, shadows, and other attributes, just like any other Draw object. You can rotate the frame and write the text at any angle. These options are available by right-clicking on the text frame itself.

If you double-click on a graphic object, or press *F2* or click on the **Text** icon when an object is selected, you can add text to the graphic object. This text then becomes part of the graphic object.

A graphic object is not dynamic and does not behave like a text frame. To keep text within the borders of the object, you have to use paragraphs, line breaks, or smaller text size, increase the object size, or combine all four methods.

For more information about text, see Chapter 2, Drawing Basic Shapes, and Chapter 9, Adding and Formatting Text, in the *Draw Guide*.

Glue points and connectors

Glue points

All Draw objects have glue points, which are not normally displayed. Glue points become visible when the **Connectors** icon is selected on the Drawing toolbar or the *Insert Shapes* sub-section in Sidebar Properties. Most objects have four glue points (Figure 185). You can add more glue points and customize glue points, using the **Glue Points** toolbar (Figure 186). Go to **View > Toolbars > Glue Points** on to open the toolbar.

Figure 185: Glue points

Glue points are not the same as the selection handles of an object. The handles are for moving or changing the shape of an object. Glue points are used to fix or glue a connector to an object so that when the object moves, the connector stays fixed to the object. For a more detailed description on the use of glue points, see Chapter 3, Working with Objects and Object Points, and Chapter 8, Connections, Flowcharts, and Organization Charts, in the *Draw Guide*.

Figure 186: Glue Points toolbar and available tools

Connectors

Connectors are lines or arrows whose ends automatically snap to a glue point of an object. Connectors are especially useful in drawing organization charts, flow diagrams, and mind-maps. When objects are moved or reordered, the connectors remain attached to a glue point. Figure 187 shows an example of two objects and a connector.

Draw offers a range of different connectors and connector functions. On the Drawing toolbar or the *Insert Shapes* sub-section in Sidebar Properties, click on the triangle next to the **Connector** icon to open the **Connectors** toolbar (Figure 188). For a more detailed description of the use of connectors, see Chapter 8, Connections, Flowcharts, and Organization Charts, in the *Draw Guide*.

Figure 187: A connector between two objects

Figure 188: Connectors toolbar

Drawing geometric shapes

The icons for drawing geometric shapes are located on the Drawing toolbar. The geometric shapes are explained in the following sections. Clicking on the triangle to the right of the icon on the Drawing toolbar opens a floating toolbar giving access to the tools for that shape.

 Tip

The use of these tools for geometric shapes is similar to the tool used for drawing rectangles or squares. For more information, see page 206 and Chapter 2, Drawing Basic Shapes, in the *Draw Guide*.

 Note

The icons for geometric shapes displayed on the Drawing toolbar will change shape according to the last tool selected and used to draw an object.

Basic shapes

Click on the triangle to the right of the **Basic Shapes** icon ◈ to open the **Basic Shapes** toolbar. This toolbar also includes a rectangle tool identical to the one on the Drawing toolbar.

Figure 189: Basic Shapes toolbar

Symbol shapes

Click on the triangle to the right of the **Symbol Shapes** icon ☺ to open the **Symbol Shapes** toolbar.

Figure 190: Symbol Shapes toolbar

Block arrows

Click on the triangle to the right of the **Block Arrows** icon ⬌ to open the **Block Arrows** toolbar.

Figure 191: Block Arrows toolbar

Flowcharts

Click on the triangle to the right of the **Flowcharts** icon to open the **Flowchart** toolbar for symbols used in drawing flowcharts. The creation of flowcharts, organization charts, and similar planning tools is further described in Chapter 8, Connections, Flowcharts, and Organization Charts in the *Draw Guide*.

Figure 192: Flowcharts toolbar

Callouts

Click on the triangle to the right of the **Callouts** icon to open the **Callouts** toolbar.

Figure 193: Callouts toolbar

Stars and banners

Click on the triangle to the right of the **Stars** icon to open the **Stars and Banners** toolbar.

Figure 194: Stars and Banners toolbar

> **Note**
>
> You can add text to all of these geometric shapes. For more information, see Chapter 2, Drawing Basic Shapes, and Chapter 11, Advanced Draw Techniques, in the *Draw Guide*.

Selecting objects

Direct selection

The easiest way to select an object is to click directly on it. For objects that are not filled, click on the object outline to select it. One click selects; a second click deselects. To select or deselect more than one object, hold the shift button down while clicking.

Selection by framing

You can also select several objects at once by dragging the mouse cursor around the objects. This cursor dragging draws a rectangle around the objects and only objects that lie entirely within the rectangle will be selected.

To select multiple objects by framing, the **Select** icon on the Drawing toolbar must be active.

Note

When dragging the mouse cursor to select multiple objects, the selection rectangle being drawn is also known as a marquee.

Selecting hidden objects

Even if objects are located behind others and not visible, they can still be selected. Hold down the *Alt* key and click on the object at the front of where the hidden object is located, then click again to select the hidden object. If there are several hidden objects, keep holding down the *Alt key* and clicking until you reach the object you want. To cycle through the objects in reverse order, hold down the *Alt+Shift keys* and click.

When you click on the selected object, its outline will appear briefly through the objects covering it.

 Note

Using the *Alt* key method works on computers using a Windows or Mac operating systems. On a computer using a Linux operating system the *Tab* key method, described below, has to be used.

To select an object that is covered by another object using the keyboard, use the *Tab* key to cycle through the objects, stopping at the object you want to select. To cycle through the objects in reverse order, press *Shift+Tab*. This is a very quick way to reach an object, but it may not be practical if there a large number of objects in a drawing.

Arranging objects

In a complex drawing, several objects may be stacked on top of one another. To rearrange the stacking order by moving an object forward or backward, select an object, click **Modify > Arrange** on the Menu bar and select **Bring Forward** or **Send Backward**. Alternatively, right-click the object, select **Arrange** from the context menu, then **Bring Forward** or **Send Backward**.

The arrange options are also available by clicking on the small triangle to the right of the **Arrange** icon ⬚ on the Line and Filling toolbar. This opens the **Position** toolbar giving access to the various arrangement options (Figure 195).

Figure 195: Position toolbar and available tools

Moving and adjusting object size

When moving an object or changing its size, check the left-hand area of the status bar at the bottom of the Draw window (Figure 196). The area on the left of the Status bar, from left to right, shows what object is selected, its position on the drawing in X/Y coordinates and dimensions of the object. The units of measurement are those selected in **Tools > Options > LibreOffice Draw > General**.

For more information on moving and adjusting object size, see Chapter 3, Working with Objects and Object Points, in the *Draw Guide*.

Figure 196: Left end of status bar when moving or adjusting an object

Moving objects

To move an object (or a group of objects), select it and then click within the object borders and hold down the left mouse button while dragging the mouse. During movement, a ghost image of the object appears to help with repositioning (Figure 197). To locate the object at its new location, release the mouse button.

Figure 197: Moving an object

Adjusting object size

To change the size of a selected object (or a group of selected objects), move the mouse cursor to one of the selection handles. The mouse cursor will change shape to indicate the direction of movement for that selection handle. As you change the size of the object, a ghosted outline of the object appears (Figure 198). When you have reached the desired size of the object, release the mouse button.

The results depend on which selection handle you use. To resize an object along one axis, use a side handle. To resize along both axes, use a corner handle.

Figure 198: Adjusting object size

 Note

If you press the *Shift* key while resizing an object, the change in size will be carried out symmetrically with respect to the two axes so that the aspect ratio of the object remains the same. This *Shift* key behavior works on all selection handles.

This is the default behavior of the *Shift* key. However, if *When creating or moving objects* has been selected in **Tools > Options > LibreOffice Draw > Grid**, the action of the *Shift* key is reversed and the aspect ratio will be preserved *unless* the *Shift* key is pressed.

Rotating and slanting an object

For more information on rotating and slanting an object, see Chapter 3, Working with Objects and Object Points, in the *Draw Guide*.

Rotating an object

To rotate an object (or a group of objects), select the object, then go to rotation mode using one of the following methods:

- Click on the Rotate icon on the Line and Filling toolbar.
- Go to **View > Toolbars > Mode** and select the Rotate icon .

The selection handles will change shape and color (Figure 199). Also a rotation point will appear in the center of the object. As you move the mouse cursor over the handles, the cursor changes shape. The corner handles are for rotating an object and the top, bottom and side handles are to slant an object.

Figure 199: Rotating an object

Move the mouse cursor to one of the corner handles and it normally changes to an arc with an arrow at each end. Click and hold the mouse button, then start to move the cursor to rotate the object. A ghost image of the object being rotated appears and the current angle of rotation is shown in the status bar.

 Note

> Rotation works differently for 3D objects because rotation occurs around global axes and not around a single axis. For more information, see Chapter 7, Working with 3D Objects, in the *Draw Guide*.

The rotation point is normally located at the center of an object. To change the position of the rotation point, click on the object with the mouse cursor and drag the object until the rotation point is at the desired position. This rotation point can even be outside of the object.

 Note

> If you press the *Shift* key while rotating an object, rotation will be restricted to 15° of movement.

> This is the default behavior of the *Shift* key. However, if *When creating or moving objects* has been selected in **Tools > Options > LibreOffice Draw > Grid**, the action of the *Shift* key is reversed and rotation will be restricted to 15° of movement *unless* the *Shift* key is pressed.

Slanting an object

To slant an object, use the handles located at the midpoints on the top, bottom and sides of a selected object. The mouse cursor changes when it hovers over one of these midpoint handles. The axis used for slanting an object is the object edge directly opposite the midpoint handle being used to slant the object. This axis stays fixed in location while the other sides of the object move in relation to it as you drag the mouse cursor.

Click and hold the mouse button, then move the cursor to shear the object. A ghost image of the object being slanted appears (Figure 200) and the current angle of slant is shown in the status bar.

 Note

If you press the *Shift* key while slanting an object, slanting will be restricted to 15° of movement. This is the default behavior of the *Shift* key. However, if *When creating or moving objects* has been selected in **Tools > Options > LibreOffice Draw > Grid**, the action of the *Shift* key is reversed and slanting will be restricted to 15° of movement *unless* the *Shift* key is pressed.

Figure 200: Slanting an object

Editing objects

To edit an object or change attributes such as color or border width, the Line and Filling toolbar, the Text Formatting toolbar, the Sidebar Properties section, or a context menu can be used. For more information on editing objects and changing attributes, see Chapter 4, Changing Object Attributes, in the *Draw Guide*.

Line and Filling toolbar

By default, the **Line and Filling** toolbar is not shown in Draw. To display it, go to **View > Toolbars > Line and Filling** on the Menu bar to open the toolbar (Figure 201) at the top of the workspace. The most common object attributes can be edited using this toolbar. You can also open the Line

dialog by clicking on the **Line** icon ⬛ and the Area dialog by clicking on the **Area** icon ⬛ for access to more formatting options.

Figure 201: Line and Filling toolbar and its available tools

Text Formatting toolbar

You can open the Text Formatting toolbar by selecting **View > Toolbars > Text Formatting** on the Menu bar. The tools on this toolbar will not become active until text has been selected.

Figure 202: Text Formatting toolbar and its available tools

Sidebar Properties

When you select an object in your drawing, the sub-sections in Sidebar Properties become active (Figure 203). You can change the properties or options of an object without having to open a dialog or use any of the available tools on the various toolbars provided by Draw. To expand a sub-section, click on the plus (+) sign or arrow next to the sub-section title.

Figure 203: Sub-sections in Sidebar Properties

Context menu

When an object is selected and you right-click on the object, a context menu (Figure 204) opens that applies to the selected object. You can change object attributes without having to open a dialog. Menu entries with a small arrow on the right-hand side contain a submenu.

Figure 204: Example of a context menu

Formatting lines and borders

In LibreOffice the term *line* indicates both a freestanding segment (line), outer edge of a shape (border), or an arrow. In most cases the properties of the line you can modify are its style (solid, dashed, invisible, and so on), its width, and its color.

Select the line you need to format and then use the controls on the Line and Filling toolbar to change the most common options (highlighted in Figure 205).

Figure 205: Common line properties (style, color, width)

If you need to fine tune the appearance of a line, choose **Format > Line** from the Menu bar, or right-click on the line and select **Line** from the context menu, or select the **Line** icon 🖉 from the Line and Filling toolbar. All of these methods open the **Line** dialog (Figure 180 on page 13), where you can set line properties. This dialog consists of three pages: *Line*, *Line Styles*, and *Arrow Styles*. Alternatively, use the *Line* sub-section in Sidebar Properties to change the appearance of a line.

Arrows, arrowheads, and line endings

Arrows, arrowheads, and other line endings are usually referred to as arrows and can be treated the same as lines when editing and changing attributes. Select a line and click on the **Arrow Style** icon 🔦 from the Line and Filling toolbar to open the **Arrowheads** menu (Figure 206).

Figure 206: Arrowheads menu

Several types of arrowheads are available. Each end of a line can have a different arrowhead or no arrowhead). Arrowheads are only applicable to lines and they have no effect on the border of an object.

Formatting area fill

The term **area fill** refers to the inside of an object, which can be a uniform color, gradient, hatching pattern, or bitmap (Figure 207). An area fill can be made partly or wholly transparent. In most cases, you will choose one of the standard fill options, which are all available from the Line and Filling toolbar, or the *Area* sub-section in Sidebar Properties. You can also define your own area fills. For more information on area fill, see Chapter 4, Changing Object Attributes, in the *Draw Guide.*

Figure 207: Different types of area fill

Using styles

Suppose that you want to apply the same area fill, line thickness, and border to a set of objects. This repetitive process can be greatly simplified by the use of styles. Styles allow you to define a format (a style) and then apply that format to multiple objects. For more information on styles, see Chapter 3, Using Styles and Templates, in this guide; Chapter 8, Introduction to Styles, in the *Writer Guide;* and Chapter 4, Changing Object Attributes, in the *Draw Guide.*

Positioning objects

Snap function

In Draw, objects can be accurately and consistently positioned using the snap function. Grid points, snap points and lines, object frames, individual points on objects, or page edges can all be used with the snap function.

Snap function is easier to work with at the highest zoom values that are practical for your display. Two different snap functions can be used at the same time; for example snapping to a guide line and to the page edge. It is recommended, however, to activate only the functions that you really need.

For more detailed information about the snap function, see Chapter 3, Working with Objects and Object Points, and Chapter 11, Advanced Draw Techniques, in the *Draw Guide*.

Snap to grid

Use Snap to grid to position an object to a grid point. Go to **View > Grid > Snap to Grid** on the Menu bar or click on the **Snap to Grid** icon on the **Options** toolbar to turn on or off the snap to grid function. If the Options toolbar is not visible, go to **View > Toolbars > Options** on the Menu bar.

Figure 208: Positioning with snap to grid

Displaying the grid

To display the grid in Draw or to switch off the grid, go to **View > Grid > Display Grid** on the Menu bar or click on the **Display Grid** icon on the Options toolbar.

Configuring the grid

The resolution, snap and snap position of the grid points can be configured. Go to **Tools > Options > LibreOffice Draw > Grid** on the Menu bar to open the options dialog for the grid.

- Vertical and horizontal spacing of the dots in the grid. You can also change the unit of measurement used in the general Draw options by going to **Tools > Options > LibreOffice Draw > General**.
- The resolution is the size of the squares or rectangles in the grid. If the resolution is 1 cm horizontal and 2 cm vertical, the grid consists of rectangles 2 cm high and 1 cm wide.
- Subdivisions are additional points that appear along the sides of each rectangle or square in the grid. Objects can snap to subdivisions as well as to the corners of the grid.
- The pixel size of the snap area defines how close you need to bring an object to a snap point or line before it will snap to it.
- The default color of the grid is light gray. To change the color of the grid points, go to **Tools > Options > LibreOffice > Appearance** on the Menu bar.

![Figure 209: Configuring the grid - Options dialog showing LibreOffice Draw Grid settings]

Figure 209: Configuring the grid

Help lines

Draw has help lines to easily allow you to position an object using the rulers at the top and left side of the workspace. To turn on or off the help lines, go to **Tools > Options > LibreOffice Draw > View** on the Menu bar and select **Snap Lines when moving** option or go to the Options toolbar and click on the **Helplines While Moving** icon .

Applying special effects

With Draw, you can apply many special effects to objects and groups of objects. This section is an introduction to some of these effects. For more information on special effects, see Chapter 4, Changing Object Attributes, *in the Draw Guide*.

To access the tools used for special effects, go to **View > Toolbars > Mode** (Figure 210). **Rotate** and **Flip** can also be accessed by going to **Modify** on the Menu bar or by right-clicking on the object and using the context menu.

Flipping objects

The quickest and easiest method to flip an object horizontally or vertically is as follows:

1) Click on a graphic object and the selection handles will show.

2) Right-click and select **Flip > Vertically** or **Horizontally**, or go to **Modify > Flip > Vertically** or **Horizontally** on the Menu bar and the selected object will be flipped to face the other direction.

However, the **Flip** tool on the Mode or Drawing toolbar provides greater control over the flipping process. You can use the Flip tool to change the position and angle that the object flips over, as described in Chapter 4, Changing Object Attributes, in the *Draw Guide*.

Figure 210: Mode toolbar and its tools

Mirror copies

At the moment no mirror command exists in Draw. However, mirroring an object can be emulated by using the **Flip** tool, as described in Chapter 4, Changing Object Attributes, in the *Draw Guide*.

Distorting an object

Three tools on the Mode toolbar let you drag the corners and edges of an object to distort the image.

 Distort tool distorts an object in perspective.

 Set to Circle (slant) creates a pseudo three-dimensional effect.

 Set in Circle (perspective) creates a pseudo three-dimensional effect.

In all three cases you are initially asked if you want to transform the object to a curve. This is a necessary first step, so click **Yes**. Then you can move the object handles to produce the desired effect. See Chapter 4, Changing Object Attributes, in the *Draw Guide* for more information on how to distort an object.

Dynamic transparency gradients

You can control transparency gradients in the same manner as color gradients. Both types of gradient can be used together. With a transparency gradient, the direction and degree of object fill color changes from opaque to transparent. In a regular gradient, the fill changes from one color to another, but the degree of transparency remains the same.

The **Transparency** and **Gradient** tools on the Mode toolbar dynamically control transparency and color gradients. See Chapter 4, Changing Object Attributes, in the *Draw Guide* for more information on how to create transparencies and gradients in an object.

Duplication

Duplication makes copies of an object while applying a set of changes such as color or rotation to the duplicates that are created.

1) Click on an object or group of objects and go to **Edit > Duplicate** on the Menu bar or use the keyboard shortcut *Shift+F3* to open the **Duplicate** dialog (Figure 211).

2) Select the required options chosen from the options available. For example, when the options in the dialog are applied to a rectangle, they produce the result shown in Figure 212.

Figure 211: Duplicate dialog

Figure 212: Duplication result

Cross-fading

Cross-fading transforms one object shape to another object shape and only works when two objects are selected.

1) Select two differently shaped objects.

2) Go to **Edit > Cross-fading** on the Menu bar to open the **Cross-fading** dialog (Figure 213).

3) Select **Increments** to determine the number of shapes between the two objects.

4) Select **Cross-fading attributes** to apply a gradual change of line and fill properties between the two objects.

5) Select **Same orientation** to apply a smooth transition between the two objects.

6) Click on **OK** and the result is a new group of objects with the first object selected as the start object and the second object selected as the end object. For example, when the options in the dialog are applied to a rectangle and a triangle, the cross fade produces the result shown in Figure 214.

Figure 213: Cross-fading dialog

Figure 214: Cross-fading result

Combining multiple objects

Using Draw, you can group or combine objects together allowing you to treat multiple objects as one unit, or to merge objects to form a new shape. For more information, see Chapter 5, Combining Multiple Objects, in the *Draw Guide*.

Grouping of objects is similar to putting objects into a container. You can move the objects as a group and apply global changes to the objects within the group. A group can always be undone and the objects that make up the group can always be manipulated separately. The objects within a group also retain their own individual properties.

Combining objects is a permanent merging of objects that creates a new object. The original objects are no longer available as individual entities and cannot be edited as individual objects. Any editing of a combined object affects all the objects that were used when combination was carried out.

Grouping

Temporary grouping

A temporary grouping is when several objects are selected using the Select icon on the Drawing toolbar or using the mouse to drag a rectangle around the objects (also known as a marquee). Any changes to object parameters you carry out are applied to all of the objects within the temporary group. For example, you can rotate a temporary group of objects in its entirety.

To cancel a temporary grouping of objects simply click outside of the selection handles displayed around the objects.

Permanent grouping

A permanent grouping of objects can be created after you have selected your objects. Go to **Modify > Group** on the Menu bar, or right-click on the selection and select **Group** from the context menu, or use the keyboard shortcut *Ctrl+Shift+G*. When you deselect your selection, the objects remain grouped together.

When objects are permanently grouped, any editing operations carried out on that group are applied to all members of the group. If you click on one member of the group, the whole group is selected.

You can edit an individual member of a group without ungrouping or breaking the group. Select the group and go to **Modify > Enter Group**, or right-click and select **Enter Group** from the context menu, or use the keyboard shortcut *F3*, or double-click on the group.

When you have finished editing an individual member of a group, go to **Modify > Exit Group**, or right-click and select **Exit Group** from the context menu, or use the keyboard shortcut *Shift+F3*.

Ungrouping

To ungroup or break apart a group of objects, select the group then go to **Modify > Ungroup** on the Menu bar, or right-click and select **Ungroup** from the context menu or use the keyboard shortcut *Ctrl+Alt+Shift+G*.

Combining objects

Combining objects is a permanent merging of objects that creates a new object. The original objects are no longer available as individual entities and cannot be edited as individual objects. Any editing of a combined object affects all the objects that were used when combination was carried out.

Select several objects, then go to **Modify > Combine** on the Menu bar, or right-click on the objects and select **Combine** from the context menu, or use the keyboard shortcut *Ctrl+Shift+K*.

After you have selected your objects, the **Merge**, **Subtract**, and **Intersect** functions also become available so that you can create a new object from your selected objects. See Chapter 5, Combining Multiple Objects, in the *Draw Guide* for more information on these functions.

Arranging, aligning, and distributing objects

In Draw you can arrange, align, and distribute selected objects in relation to each other:

- Arrange the position of an object by moving it either forward or backward in relation to the order of objects.
- Align objects with respect to each other using **Left**, **Centered**, or **Right** for horizontal alignment and **Top**, **Center**, or **Bottom** for vertical alignment.
- Distribute objects so that the space between each of the objects is the same.

See Chapter 5, Combining Multiple Objects, in the *Draw Guide* for more information on arranging and aligning objects in relation to each other.

Inserting and editing pictures

Draw contains a number of functions for editing pictures or raster graphics (bitmaps); for example, photos and scanned images. This includes the import and export of graphics, and conversion from one graphic format to another.

Draw includes a large range of graphic filters so that it can read and display several graphic file formats. It also includes several tools for working with raster graphics, but does not have the same functionality as specialized graphic programs like Gimp or Adobe Photoshop. See Chapter 6, Editing Pictures, in the *Draw Guide* for more information.

You can add pictures from several sources:

- Directly from a scanner (**Insert > Picture > Scan**)
- Images created by another program, including photographs from a digital camera (**Insert > Picture > From File**)

- The Draw Gallery; see Chapter 11, Graphics, the Gallery, and Fontwork, in this guide for more information.

Working with 3D objects

Although Draw does not match the functionality of the leading drawing or picture editing programs, it is capable of producing and editing very good 3D drawings.

Draw offers two types of 3D objects: *3D bodies* and *3D shapes*. Depending on which type you choose, there are different methods of editing of a 3D object (rotation, illumination, perspective, and so on) with 3D shapes being simpler to set up and edit than 3D bodies. However, 3D bodies currently allow for more customization.

See Chapter 7, Working with 3D Objects, in the *Draw Guide* for more information.

Exporting graphics

Draw saves graphics and images in the open source format *.odg. To save a graphic or the entire file in another format, use **File > Export** and select a format from the list displayed. The graphic formats that Draw can export and save to are listed in Appendix B, Open Source, Open Standards, OpenDocument in this guide.

You can also export Draw files to HTML, XHTML, PDF, or Flash. PDF export for modules of LibreOffice is described in Chapter 10, Printing, Exporting, and E-mailing, in this guide.

HTML export uses a conversion wizard that creates as many web pages as there are pages in your Draw document. You can optionally choose to display pages in frames with a navigator and set an index page. For more information, see Chapter 12, Creating Web Pages, in this guide.

Inserting comments in a drawing

You can insert comments into your drawing in a similar process to the one used in Writer and Calc.

1) Go to **Insert > Comment** on the menu bar. A small box containing your initials appears in the upper left-hand corner of your drawing with a larger text box beside it (Figure 215). Draw automatically adds your name and the date at the bottom of this text box.

2) Type or paste your comment into the text box. You can apply basic formatting to parts of the text by selecting it, right-clicking, and choosing from the context menu. From this menu, you can also delete the current comment, all the comments from the same author, or all the comments in the document.

3) You can move the small comment markers to anywhere you wish on the drawing. Typically you might place it on or near an object you refer to in the comment.

4) To show or hide the comment markers, go to **View > Comments** on the Menu bar.

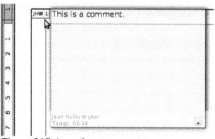

Figure 215: Inserting comments

You can go to **Tools > Options > User Data** to enter the name you want to appear in the Author field of the comment.

If more than one person edits the document, each author is automatically allocated a different background color.

Getting Started Guide

Chapter 8
Getting Started with Base

Relational Databases in LibreOffice

Introduction

A data source, or database, is a collection of pieces of information that can be accessed or managed by LibreOffice. For example, a list of names and addresses is a data source that could be used for producing a mail merge letter. A shop stock list could be a data source managed through LibreOffice.

This chapter covers creating a database, showing what is contained in a database and how the different parts are used by LibreOffice.

Note

> LibreOffice uses the terms "Data Source" and "Database" to refer to the same thing, which could be a database such as MySQL or dBase or a spreadsheet or text document holding data.

A *database* consists of a number of *fields* that contain the individual pieces of data. Each *table* of the database is a group of fields. When creating a table, you also determine the characteristics of each field within it. *Forms* are for data entry into the fields of one or more tables which have been associated with the form. They can also be used for viewing fields from one or more tables associated with the form. A *query* creates a new table from the existing tables based upon how you create the query. A *report* organizes the information from the fields of a query into a document according to your requirements.

Caution

> To use Base, you need to use a Java Runtime Environment (JRE). Please go to **Tools > Options > LibreOffice > Advanced** to select a JRE from those installed on your computer.
>
> If a JRE is not already installed, you will need to download and install one. For Windows, you need to get Java from www.java.com. For Linux, you can download it from the same website or you can use openjdk-7-jre, available from the repository of your Linux version. macOS users can install a JRE from Apple Inc.

Base creates *relational databases*. This makes it fairly easy to create a database in which the fields of the database have relationships with each other.

For example: Consider a database for a library. It will contain a field for the names of the authors and another field for the names of the books. There is an obvious relationship between the authors and the books they have written. The library may contain more than one book by the same author. This is what is known as a one-to-many relationship: one author and more than one book. Most if not all the relationships in such a database are one-to-many relationships.

Consider an employment database for the same library. One of the fields contains the names of the employees while others contain the social security numbers, and other personal data. The relationship between the names and social security numbers is one-to-one: only one social security number for each name.

If you are acquainted with mathematical sets, a relational database can easily be explained in terms of sets: elements, subsets, unions, and intersections. The fields of a database are the elements. The tables are subsets. Relationships are defined in terms of unions and intersections of the subsets (tables).

To explain how a database works and how to to use it, we will create one for automobile expenses.

Planning a database

The first step in creating a database is to ask yourself many questions. Write them down, and leave some space between the questions to write the answers later. At least some of the answers should seem obvious after you take some time to think.

You may have to go through this process a few times before everything becomes clear in your mind and on paper. Using a text document for these questions and answers makes it easier to move the questions around, add additional questions, or change the answers.

Here are some of the questions and answers I developed before I created a database for automobile expenses. I had an idea of what I wanted before I started, but as I began asking questions and listing the answers, I discovered that I needed additional tables and fields.

What are the fields going to be? My expenses divided into three broad areas: fuel purchases, maintenance, and vacations. The annual cost for the car's license plate and driver's license every four years did not fit into any of these. It will be a table of its own: license fees.

What fields fit the fuel purchases area? Date purchased, odometer reading, fuel cost, fuel quantity, and payment method for it. (Fuel economy need not be included, as it can be calculated using a query.)

What fields fit the maintenance area? Date of service, odometer reading, type of service, cost of service, and next scheduled service of this type (for example, for oil changes, list when the next oil change should be). But it would be nice if there was a way to write notes. So a field for notes was added to the list.

What fields fit the vacations area? Date, odometer reading, fuel (including all the fields of the fuel table), food (including meals and snacks), motel, total tolls, and miscellaneous. Since these purchases are made by one of two bank cards or with cash, I want a field to state which payment type was used for each item.

What fields fit into the food category? Breakfast, lunch, supper, and snacks seem to fit. Do I list all the snacks individually or list the total cost for snacks for the day? I chose to divide snacks into two fields: number of snacks and total cost of snacks. I also need a payment type for each of these: breakfast, lunch, supper, and total cost of snacks.

What are the fields that are common to more than one area? Date appears in all of the areas as does odometer reading and payment type.

How will I use this information about these three fields? While on vacation, I want the expenses for each day to be listed together. The date fields suggest a relationship between the vacation table and the dates in each of these tables: fuel and food, This means that the date fields in these tables will be linked as we create the database.

The type of payment includes two bank cards and cash. So we will create a table with a field for the type of payment and use it in list boxes in the forms.

 Tip

While we have listed fields we will create in the tables of the database, there is one more field that may be needed in a table: the field for the primary key, an identifier unique to each record. In some tables, a suitable field for the primary key has already been listed. In other tables such as the payment type, an additional field for the primary key must be created.

Creating a new database

To create a new database, select **File > New > Database** from the menu bar, or click the arrow next to the **New** icon on the Standard toolbar and select **Database** from the drop-down menu. Both methods open the Database Wizard.

On the first page of the Database Wizard, select **Create a new database** and then click **Next**.

The second page has two questions. Make sure the choice for the first question is **Yes, register the database for me** and the choice for the second question is **Open the database for editing**. Click **Finish**.

 Note

> In Writer, the *Ctrl+Shift+F4* key opens and closes the Data Source window containing the list of registered databases. In Calc, press *Ctrl+Shift+F4* to open the Data Source window. If a database is not registered, this window will not contain it, so you cannot access the database in Writer or Calc.

Save the new database with the name *Automobile*. This opens the Automobile – LibreOffice Base window. Figure 216 shows part of this window.

Figure 216: Creating database tables using HSQLDB

 Tip

> Every time the *Automobile* database is opened, the *Automobile – LibreOffice Base* window opens. Changes can then be made to the database. The title for this window is always <database name> – LibreOffice Base.

Caution

As you create a database, you should save your work regularly. This means more than saving what you have just created. You must save the whole database as well.

For example, when you create your first table, you must save it before you can close it. This makes it part of the database in memory. But it is only when you save the database file that the table is written to disk.

 Note

Database files in Open Document Format are stored with the ***.odb** extension. This file format is actually a container of all elements of the database, including forms, reports, tables, and the data itself. The same format can also store a connection to an external database server instead of the local data, for example, to access a MySQL or PostgresSQL database server in your network.

Creating database tables

In a database, a table stores information in a group of things we call fields. For example, a table might hold an address book, a stock list, a phone book or a price list. A database must have at least one table and may have several.

Each field of a table contains information of a single type. For example, the Phone field of an address book would only contain phone numbers. Similarly, a price list table could contain two fields: Name and Price. The Name field would contain the names of the items; the Price field would contain the amount of each item.

To work with tables, click the *Tables* icon in the *Database* list, or press *Alt+a*. The three tasks that you can perform on a table are in the *Tasks* list (see Figure 216).

Using the Wizard to create a table

Wizards are designed to do the basic work. Sometimes this is not sufficient for what we want; in those cases we can use a wizard as a starting point and then build upon what it produces.

The Table Wizard in Base contains two categories of suggested tables: business and personal. Each category contains sample tables from which to choose. Each table has a list of available fields. We can delete some of these fields and add other fields.

A field in a table is one bit of information. For example, a price list table might have one field for item name, one for the description, and a third for the price.

Since none of the fields we need for our Automobile database are contained in any of the sample wizard tables, we will create a simple table using the wizard that has nothing to do with our database. This section is merely an exercise in explaining how the Wizard works.

The Wizard permits the fields of the table to come from more than one suggested table. We will create a table with fields from three different suggested tables in the Wizard.

 Caution

Every table requires a *Primary key field*. (What this field does will be explained later.) We will use this field to number our entries and want that number to automatically increase as we add each entry.

Click *Use Wizard to Create Table*. This opens the Table Wizard (Figure 217).

Step 1: Select fields

We will use the *CD-Collection* Sample table in the Personal category and Employees in the Business category to select the fields we need.

1) *Category*: Select *Personal*. The *Sample Tables* drop down list changes to a list of personal sample tables.

2) *Sample tables*: Select *CD-Collection*. The *Available fields* box changes to a list of available fields for this table.

3) *Selected fields*: Using the **>** button, move the following fields from the *Available fields* window to the *Selected fields* window in this order: *CollectionID, AlbumTitle, Artist, DatePurchased, Format, Notes,* and *NumberofTracks*.

4) *Selected Fields from another sample* table. Click Business as the Category. Select *Employees* from the drop down list of sample tables. Use the **>** button to move the *Photo* field from the *Available fields* window to the *Selected fields* window. It will be at the bottom of the list directly below the *NumberofTracks* field.

5) If you make a mistake in selecting fields, click on the field name in the *Selected fields* list and use the **<** button to move it from the *Selected fields* list back to the *Available fields* list.

6) If you make a mistake in the order of the selected fields, **click** on the field name that is in the wrong order and use the **Up** or **Down arrow** on the right side of the Selected fields list to move the field name to the correct position.

7) Click **Next**.

Figure 217: Selecting fields for the table

Step 2: Set field types and formats

Figure 218: Changing field types

In this step you give the fields their properties. When you click a field, the information on the right changes. (See Figure 218.) You can then make changes to meet your needs. Click each field, one at a time, and make the changes listed below.

 Note

If any of these fields requires a mandatory entry, set *Entry required* to **Yes**. A blank field will then not be allowed. In general, only set *Entry required* to **Yes** if something must always be put in that field. By default, *Entry required* is set to **No**.

*   *CollectionID*: Change *AutoValue* from **No** to **Yes**. (example of a mandatory entry)
*   *AlbumTitle*:
    *   *Entry required*: Leave *Entry required* as *No*, unless all of your music is in albums.
    *   *Length*: Unless you have an album title that exceeds 100 characters counting the spaces, do not change the length.
*   *Artist*: Use the Default setting. Since music always has artists, set *Entry Required* to *Yes*.
*   *Date Purchased*: *Field type*: default date setting. *Entry required* should be No. (You may not know the date.)

 Note

In Base the maximum length of each field must be specified on creation. It is not easy to change this later, so if in doubt specify a greater length. Base uses VARCHAR as the field format for text fields. This format uses only the actual number of characters in a field up to the limit set, so a field containing 20 characters will occupy only 20 characters even if the limit is set at 100. Two album titles containing 25 and 32 characters respectively will use space for 25 and 32 characters and not 100 characters.

*   *Format*: Only change the *Entry Required* setting: from *No* to *Yes*.
*   *Notes*: No changes are required.
*   *NumberofTracks*: Change the *Field Type* to *Tiny Integer [TINYINT]*. Your allowable number of tracks will be 127. Small Integer [SMALLINT] would allow 32768 tracks if you needed more than 127 tracks.
*   *Photo*: Use the default settings.

When you have finished, click **Next**.

 Note

Each field has a *Field Type*, which must be specified. Types include text, integer, date, and decimal. If the field is going to have general information in it (for example, a name or a description), use text. If the field will always contain a number (for example, a price), the type should be decimal or another numerical field. The wizard picks the right field type, so to get an idea of how this works, see what the wizard has chosen for different fields.

Step 3: Set primary key

1) *Create a primary key* should be checked.
2) Select option *Use an existing field as a primary key*.
3) In the *Fieldname drop down* list, select *CollectionID*.
4) Check *Auto value* if it is not already checked. Click **Next**.

Note

A primary key uniquely identifies an item (or record) in the table. For example, you might know two people called "Randy Herring" or three people living at the same address and the database needs to distinguish between them.

The simplest method is to assign a unique number to each one: number the first person 1, the second 2, and so on. Each entry has one number and every number is different, so it is easy to say "record ID 172". This is the option chosen here: CollectionID is just a number assigned automatically by Base to each record of this table.

Step 4: Create the table

1) If desired, rename the table at this point. If you rename it, make the name meaningful to you. For this example, make no changes.

2) Leave the option *Insert data immediately* checked.

3) Click **Finish** to complete the table wizard. Close the window created by the table wizard. You are now back to the main window of the database with the listing of the tables, queries, forms, and reports. Notice that a table named "CD-Collection" is now listed in the Tables portion of the window.

4) Click the **Save** button at the top of the main window.

Creating a table by copying an existing table

If you have a large collection of music, you might want to create a table for each type of music you have. Rather than creating each table from the wizard, you can make copies of the original table, naming each according to the type of music contained in it.

1) Click on the **Tables** icon in the Database pane to see the existing tables.

2) Right-click on the *CD-Collection* table icon. Choose **Copy** from the context menu.

3) Move the mouse pointer below this table, right-click, and select **Paste**. The Copy table dialog opens.

4) Change the table name to *CD-Jazz* and click **Next**.

5) Click the **>>** button to move all the fields from the left box to the right box and click **Next**.

6) Since all the fields already have the proper Field type, no changes should be needed. However, this is the time and place to make any changes if they are needed. (See Caution below for the reason why.) Click **Create**. The new table is created.

7) Click the **Save** button at the top of the main database window.

 Caution

Once tables have been created using the wizard, and data has been entered, editing a table should be very limited. You can add or delete fields, but adding a field requires you to enter the data for that one field for every existing record with an entry for that field.

Deleting a field deletes **all the data** once contained in that field. Changing the field type of a field can lead to data being lost either partially or completely. When creating a new table, it pays to create the fields with the correct names, length, and format before you add any data.

Deleting a table removes all of the data contained in every field of the table. **Unless you are sure, do not delete a table**.

Creating tables in Design View

Design View is a more advanced method for creating a new table, in which you directly enter information about each field in the table. We will use this method for the tables of our database.

 Note

While the *Field type* and *formatting* are different in Design View, the concepts are the same as in the Wizard.

The first table to be created is *Fuel*. Its fields are *FuelID, Date, FuelCost, FuelQuantity, Odometer*, and *PaymentType*.

1) Click Create Table in Design View (which opens the Table Design dialog).

2) *FuelID* field: Type *FuelID* as the first Field Name. Press the *Tab* key to move to the Field Type column. Select *Integer [INTEGER]* as the Field Type from the drop down list. (The default setting is Text [VARCHAR].)

 Tip

A shortcut for selecting from the Field Type drop down list: press the key for the first letter of the choice. You can cycle through the choices for a given letter by repeatedly pressing that key.

   a) Change the Field Properties in the bottom section.
      Change *AutoValue* from *No* to *Yes*.

   b) Set *FuelID* as the *Primary key*.
      Click in the Field Name cell directly below FuelID. The dialog automatically sets FuelID as the primary key and places a key icon in front of FuelID (Figure 219).

Figure 219: Defining the primary key field

 Tip

Certain of the Integer filed types (Integer and BigInt for example) have an AutoValue Field Property. When using one of these field types, your selection of *Yes* for the AutoValue value automatically makes the field the primary key.

Primary keys for any other field type must be selected by right-clicking the rectangle before the field and selecting *Primary key* in the context menu.

Note

The primary key serves only one purpose: to identify each record uniquely. Any name can be used for this field. We have used *FuelID* for convenience, so we know to which table it belongs.

3) All other fields (*Date, FuelCost, FuelQuantity, Odometer*, and *PaymentType*):

   a) Type the next field name in the Field Name column.

   b) Select the Field Type for each field.

   – For *Date* use Date[DATE]. (Press the *D* key to select it.)

   – All other fields use Number [NUMERIC]. (Press the *N* key once to select it.)

   – *PaymentType* uses Text [VARCHAR], the default setting.

   c) *FuelCost, FuelQuantity*, and *Odometer* need changes in the Field Properties section (Figure 220).

   – *FuelCost*: Change the Length to 5 and Decimal places to 2. Click the *Format example* ellipse button (...) (Figure 220). This opens the Field Format window (Figure 221). Use *Currency* as the Category and your currency as the Format. My currency has two decimal places. Use what is appropriate for yours.

   – *FuelQuantity*: Change *Length* to 6 and *Decimal places* to 3. (Many fuel pumps measure fuel to thousandths of a gallon in the USA.) *Odometer*: Change the *Length* to 10 and the *Decimal places* to 1.

   d) Repeat steps a) through c) until you have entered all of the fields.

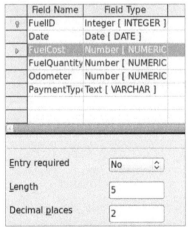

Figure 220: Changing field properties

   e) To access additional formatting options, click the ellipse button (...) to the right of the Format example field.

   Description can be any of the categories listed in the figure below, or can be left blank.

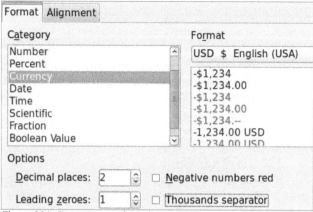

Figure 221: Format example options

4) To save and close the table, select **File > Save**. Name the table *Fuel*. Close the Fuel table.

5) In the main database window, click the **Save** button.

	Field Name	Field Type	Description
🔑	Date	Date [DATE]	
	Odometer	Number [NUMERIC	odometer reading
	Motel	Number [NUMERIC	
	MPayment	Text [VARCHAR]	payment type for motels
	Tolls	Number [NUMERIC	total tolls
	Breakfast	Number [NUMERIC	
	BPayment	Text [VARCHAR]	payment type for breakfast
	Lunch	Number [NUMERIC	
	LPayment	Text [VARCHAR]	payment type for lunch
	Supper	Number [NUMERIC	
	SPayment	Text [VARCHAR]	payment type for supper
	SnackNo	Text [VARCHAR]	
	SnCost	Number [NUMERIC	
	SnPayment	Text [VARCHAR]	payment type for snacks
	Miscellaneous	Number [NUMERIC	
▷	MiscPayment	Text [VARCHAR]	payment type for misc.|
	Notes	Memo [LONGVARCl	

Figure 222: Fields in Vacations table

Follow the same steps to create the *Vacations* table. The fields, field types, and Descriptions are listed in Figure 222.

Making Date the primary key has to be done in a different way because this field's field type is *Date*, not *Integer*.

1) Right-click to the left of the field name *Date*.

2) Select Primary Key in the context menu.

Defining relationships

Now that the tables have been created, what are the relationships between our tables? This is the time to define them based upon the questions we asked and answered in the beginning.

When on vacation, we want to enter all of our expenses at once each day. Most of these expenses are in the Vacations table, but the fuel we buy is not. So we will link these two tables using the Date fields. Since the Fuel table may have more than one entry per date, this relationship between the Vacations and Fuel tables is one to many (it is designated 1:n.)

The Fuel and Maintenance tables do not really have a relationship even though they share similar fields: Date and Odometer readings.

 Tip

> As you create your own databases, you will also need to determine if tables are related and how.

1) To begin defining relationships, select **Tools > Relationships**. The Automobile – LibreOffice Base: Relation Design window opens and the Add Tables dialog pops up. (You can also open it by clicking the Add Tables icon on the Relation Design window if you ever need to do so.)

2) In the Add Tables dialog, use either of these ways to add a table to the Relation Design window:
   - Double-click the name of the table. In our case, do this for both *Vacations* and *Fuel*.
   - Or, for each table, click the name of the table and then click **Add**.

3) Click **Close** to close the Add Tables dialog when you have added the tables you want.

4) Define the relationship between the Vacations and Fuel tables: click the **New Relation** icon. This opens the Relations window (Figure 224). Our two tables are listed in the *Tables involved* section.
   a) In the *Fields involved* section, click the drop-down list under the Fuel label.
   b) Select *Date* from the Fuel table list.
   c) Click in the cell to the right of this drop-down list. This opens a drop down list for the Vacations table.
   d) Select *Date* from the Vacations table list. It should now look like Figure 224.
   e) Modify the Update options and Delete options section of the Relation window (Figure 225).
      i) Select **Update cascade**.
      ii) Select **Delete cascade**.

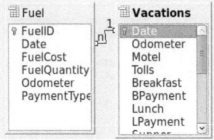

Figure 223: Designation for a 1:n relationship

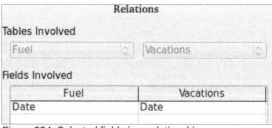

Figure 224: Selected fields in a relationship

The primary key can contain more than one field. (Its foreign key[1] will contain the same number of fields.) If this were the case in Figure 224, the other fields of the primary field for the Fuel table would be listed under Date. The corresponding fields of the foreign key would be listed under Vacations. Detailed information about this is in the *Base Guide*.

Figure 225: Update options and Delete options section

f) Click **OK**.

g) Save the Relation Design dialog if the **Save** button is active.

h) Close the Relation Design dialog.

i) Click the **Save** button at the top of the main database window.

While these options are not strictly necessary, they do help. Having them selected permits you to update a table that has a relationship defined with another table which has been modified. It also permits you to delete a field from the table without causing inconsistencies.

Creating a database form

Databases are used to store data. But, how is the data put into the database? Forms are used to do this. In the language of databases, a form is a front end for data entry and editing.

A simple form consists of the fields from a table (Figure 226). More complex forms can contain much more, including additional text, graphics, selection boxes, and many other elements. Figure 227 is made from the same table with a text label (Fuel Purchases), a list box placed in PaymentType, and a graphic background.

---

1   A field in a table that stores values of the primary key of records in another table.

Tip

A list box is useful when a field contains a fixed choice of options. It saves you from having to type data by hand, and ensures that invalid options are not entered.

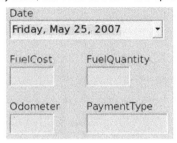

Figure 226: Fields of a simple form

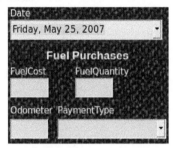

Figure 227:Simple form with additions

In our database, payments for food or fuel might be made from one of two credit cards (Dan or Kevin) or in cash, so these would be the available options for all boxes that contain payments.

To create a list box, we first need to create a small, separate table containing the options. This is then linked to the corresponding field in the form. The topic is dealt with in detail in the Base User Guide and will not be pursued further here.

Using the Wizard to create a form

We will use the Form Wizard to create a Vacations form, which will contain a form and a subform.

In the main database window (Figure 216), click the **Forms** icon in the left column. In the Tasks list, double-click **Use Wizard to Create Form** to open the Form Wizard (Figure 228). Simple forms require only some of these steps, while more complex forms may use all of them.

Step 1: Select fields

1) Under Tables or queries, select Table: Vacations. *Available fields* lists the fields for the Vacations table.

2) Click the right double arrow to move all of these fields to the *Fields in the form* list. Click **Next**.

Figure 228: Form Wizard steps

Step 2: Set up a subform

Since we have already created a relationship between the Fuel and Vacations tables, we will use that relationship. If no relationship had been defined, this would need to be done in step 4.

1) Click the box labeled *Add Subform.*
2) Click Subform based upon existing relation.
3) Fuel is listed as a relation we want to add. So click Fuel to highlight it, as in Figure 229. Click **Next**.

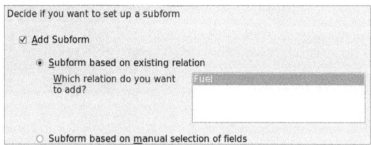

Figure 229: Adding a subform

Step 3: Add subform fields

This step is similar to step 1. The only difference is that not all of the fields will be used in the subform.

1) Fuel is preselected under *Tables or queries.*
2) Use the **>>** button to move all the fields to the right.
3) Click the *FuelID* field to highlight it.
4) Use the **<** button to move the *FuelID* to the left (Figure 230).
5) Click **Next**.

Figure 230: Selecting fields of a sub form

Step 4: Get joined fields

This step is for tables or queries for which no relationship has been defined. Because we have already defined the relationship, the wizard skips this step.

Note

It is possible to create a relationship between two tables that is based upon more than one pair of fields. How to do that and why is discussed in the *Base Guide*.

Caution

When selecting a pair of fields from two tables to use as a relationship, they have to have the same field type. That is why we used the Date field from both tables: both their field types are Date[DATE].

Whether a single pair of fields from two tables are chosen as the relationship, or two or more pairs are chosen, certain requirements must be met for the form to work.

– One of the fields from the main form must be the Primary key for its table. (Date would have to be used.)

– No field from the subform can be the Primary key for its table. (*FuelID* cannot be used.)

– Each pair of joined fields must have the same file type.

Step 5: Arrange controls

A control in a form consists of two parts: label and field. This step in creating the form determines where a control's label and field are placed relative to each other. The four choices from left to right are *Columnar left, Columnar—Labels on top*, As *Data Sheet, and In Blocks – Labels Above*.

1) Arrangement of the main form: Click the second icon (*Columnar—Labels on top*). The labels will be placed above their field.

2) Arrangement of the sub form: Click the third icon (*As Data Sheet*). (The labels are column headings and the field entries are in spreadsheet format.) Click **Next**.

Figure 231: Arrange controls

Step 6: Set data entry

Unless you have a need for any of these entries to be checked, accept the default settings. Click **Next**.

Step 7: Apply styles

1) Select the color you want in the *Apply Styles* list. (I chose the beige.)
2) Select the Field border you want. (I prefer the 3D look. You might want to experiment with the different possible settings.)
3) Click **Next**.

Step 8: Set name

1) Enter the name for the form. In this case, it is *Fuel*.
2) Click *Modify the form*.
3) Click **Finish**. The form opens in Edit mode.

Modifying a form

We will be moving the controls to different places in the form and changing the background to a picture. We will also modify the label for the PaymentType field as well as change the field to a list box.

First, we must decide what we want to change. The discussion will follow this ten step outline of our planned changes.

- Provide a drop-down capability for the Date field in the main form, and lengthen the field to show the day of the week, month, day, and year.
- Shorten the length of the payment fields (all fields containing the word Payment).
- Move the controls into groups: food, fuel subform, and miscellaneous.
- Change the wording of some of the labels. Some single words should be two words. Some abbreviations should be used if possible (Misc. for miscellaneous).
- Change the lengths of several fields and labels. Only Lunch, Supper, Motel, and Tolls have acceptable lengths. But for a better appearance, changes will be made to these as well.
- Lengthen the Note field vertically, add a scroll bar, and move it.
- Make changes in the Date and PaymentType columns of the subform to match the changes in the main form.
- Add headings for each group in the main form.
- Change the background to a picture, then modify some of the labels so that they can be read clearly against this background. Change the font color of the headings.

Here are some methods that we will be using in these steps. The controls in the main form consist of a label and its field. Sometimes we want to work with the entire control, sometimes with only the label or the field, and there are times when we want to work with a group of controls.

- Clicking a label or field selects the entire control. A border appears around the control with eight green handles. You can then drag and drop it where you want.

Figure 232: A selected control

- *Ctrl+click* a label or field selects only the label or the field. You can press the *Tab* key to change the selection from the field to the label or the label to the field.

Figure 233: Selecting a field of a control

- Moving a group of controls is almost as easy as moving one of them.
  a) Click the field of the top left control to be moved, to select it.
  b) Move the cursor to just above and to the left of the selected control.
  c) Drag the cursor to the bottom right of the group of controls and release the mouse button.

As you drag the cursor, a dashed box appears, showing what is contained in your selection. Make sure it is big enough to include the entire length of all the controls.

When you release the mouse button, a border with its green handles appears around the controls you selected.

Figure 234: Selecting multiple controls

Move the cursor over one of the fields. It changes to a drag icon. Drag the group of controls to where you want them.

- Click the Tolls control to select it. Then drag it to the right close to the Lunch control.

 Tip

When either changing size or moving a control, two properties of the Form Design toolbar should be selected: *Snap to Grid*, and *Guides when Moving*. Your controls will line up better, and an outline of what you are moving moves as the cursor moves. You should also have both rulers active (**View > Ruler**).

Step 1: Change the Date field

1) *Open the Form Design toolbar. (Figure 245) If it is not visible, select* **View > Toolbars > Form Controls***.*
2) *Ctrl+click* the Date field to select it.
3) Move the cursor over the middle green handle on the right side. It should change to a double-headed arrow.
4) Hold the left mouse button down as you drag the cursor to the right until the length is 6 cm. The vertical dashed line is lined up with the 6. Release the mouse button.
5) Click the Control icon (circled in red). The *Properties: Date Field* window opens. Each line contains a property of the field.

Figure 235: Form Design toolbar

   – Scroll down to the *Date format* property. This is a drop down list with Standard (short) as the default setting. Click it to open the list. Select the *Standard (long)* entry.

– Scroll down to the *Drop down* property. Its default setting is No. It is also a drop down list. Click to open the list. Select *Yes*.

Step 2: Shorten the width of some fields

All of the fields with a label containing the word payment are too wide. They need to be shortened before the controls are moved.

Figure 236: Selecting a field

1) *Ctrl+click* the BPayment field.
2) Move the cursor over the middle green handle on the right end. The cursor becomes a double-headed arrow.
3) Drag the cursor to the left until the field is 2.5 cm (1 inch) wide.
4) Repeat these steps to shorten these fields: Lpayment, SPayment, SnPayment, Mpayment, and MiscPayment.

Step 3: Move the controls to group them by category

We want to move the controls so that they look like Figures 237 and 238.

1) Click the first control you want to move. A border appears around the control with eight green handles.
2) Move the cursor over the label or field of the control. It changes shape to a drag icon.
3) Drag and drop the control to where you want it.
4) Use the same steps to move the rest of the controls to where they belong.

Figure 237a: Positioning of controls (left side of form)

Figure 238: Positioning of controls (right side of form)

Step 4: Change the label wording

Field names are required to be single words. However, the labels for the fields in a form can be more than one word. So we will change them by editing the text in the label.

1) *Ctrl+click* the SnackNo label. Do one of the following:
   - Right-click the SnackNo label and select **Control** from the context menu.
   - Or click the Control icon in the Form Control toolbar (Figure 235).

2) The dialog that opens is labeled Properties: Label Field. It contains all the properties of the selected label.
   - In the Label selection, make SnackNo into two words: Snack No.
   - Close the Properties dialog.

3) Use the same procedure to change these labels as well: BPayment to Payment, LPayment to Payment, SPayment to Payment, Miscellaneous to Misc., SnackCost to Snack Cost, MPayment to Payment, MiscPayment to Misc. Payment, and MiscNotes to Misc. Notes.

 Tip

> You can modify all of the listings in the Properties window. For example, if you change the Alignment from Left to Center, the word or words in the label are centered within the label. When you have some time, you might want to experiment with different settings just to see the results you get.

Step 5: Change the widths of the labels and fields

We want the fields of the following controls to be 2 cm wide (0.8 inches): Breakfast, Lunch, Supper, Odometer, Snack No., Tolls, Snack Cost, Motel, and Misc. All of the payment fields were changed in step 2, but Misc. Payment needs to be changed to 3 cm (1.2 inches).

1) Right-click Breakfast and select the **Position and Size icon**. (Icon to the left of the Anchor.) On the Position and Size dialog, change Width to 2 cm.

2) Click OK to close the Position and Size dialog.

3) Repeat for the other listed controls, using 3 cm for MiscPayment.

Caution

When changing the position or size of an entire control, use the Position and Size dialog or the drag and drop method.

When working with either the label or the field (but not both at the same time), you can use the Properties dialog to make these changes when you want to be exact. However, you need to be careful not to accidentally select the entire control for use with the Properties dialog or you will apply exactly the same values to both the label and field. For example, if you enter the values for a new position, both the field and the label moves to the same position and the field is positioned on top of the label. Then you will have to move each of them to where you really want them.

 Tip

To open the Properties dialog, right-click a control and select **Control** from the context menu. Or, you can click the Control icon in the *Form Design* toolbar. Just be careful, and use *Ctrl+Z* to undo any mistakes you may make. Detailed instructions on how to use the Properties window are given in the *Base Guide*.

Step 6: Change the Misc. Notes field

We want the Misc. Notes control, which has a field type of Memo, to have a vertical scroll bar for additional text space if desired.

Figure 239: Scroll bar selections in the Properties window

1) *Ctrl+click* the *Misc. Notes* field. The green handles should surround the field but not its label.

2) Click the **Control** icon to open the Properties window (Figure 239).

3) Scroll down to the *Text type* property with *single-line* as the default value.

   – Change it to Multi-line.

4) Scroll down to the *Scrollbars* setting. Change the selection from *None* to *Vertical* in this list.

5) Close the Properties window. (*Esc* key)

6) Lengthen the Misc. Notes field by moving the cursor over the middle green handle at the bottom of the field and dragging down until the length is 6 cm (2.4 inches).

Step 7: Change labels and fields in the subform

The subform is located at the bottom of the form. We want to widen the Date column, and change the label for the PaymentType column to two words.

- To widen the Date column, move the mouse pointer over the dividing line between the Date and FuelCost columns. When the pointer changes shape, click and drag to move the divider to the right.
- To change the PaymentType column:
  - Right-click the label PaymentType to open the context menu.
  - Select **Column** to open the Properties dialog. In the *Label* property, change PaymentType to Payment Type.
  - Close the Properties dialog.

Figure 240: Properties

Step 8: Add headings to groups

This step is easier to do if you have end-of-paragraph markers visible. Choose **View > Non printing Characters** to turn them on.

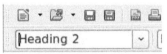

Figure 241: Apply Styles list

1) Make sure the cursor is in the upper left corner. If it is not, click in that corner to move it there.
2) Press the *Enter* key to move the cursor down to the space between the Date field and the Breakfast field.
3) Change the *Apply Styles drop down list from Default* to *Heading 2*.
4) Use the space bar to move the cursor to where you want the heading to start.
5) Type the heading *Meals*.
6) Use the space bar to move the cursor to the center of snack area.
7) Type the heading *Snacks*.
8) Use the *Enter* key to move the cursor between the Supper control and the subform.
9) Use the space bar to move the cursor to the center of the subform.
10) Change the *Apply Styles* drop down list from *Default to Heading 2*.
11) Type the heading *Fuel Data*.

 Tip

If you know how to use styles, you can open the Styles and Formatting window using *F11*. Right-clicking the Heading 2 paragraph style allows you to modify the appearance of all three headings. See Chapter 6 of the *Writer Guide* for details.

Step 9: Change the background of a form

The background for a form can be a color, or a graphic (picture). You can use any of the colors in the Color Table at **Tools > Options > LibreOffice > Colors**. If you know how to create custom colors, you can use them. You can also use a picture (graphic file) as the background.

To add a color to the form background:

1) Right-click the form to open a context menu.
2) Select **Page**.
3) Make sure the *Area* tab has been selected. (It should have a white background while the other tabs have a gray one.)

Figure 242: Page style dialog

4) Select Color from the drop-down list below *Fill*. (List contains None, Color, Gradient, Hatching, and Bitmap.)
5) Scroll down through the colors and then Click *Cyan 2*.
6) Click **Apply** to see the effects of adding the color. OR, click **OK** to close the dialog.

To create other form backgrounds:

1) Perform steps 1-3 for adding color to the background.
2) Select the type of background from the drop-down list below *Fill*.
3) Scroll down to background you want from the list of backgrounds based upon your choice in 2) above.
   - *None*: No background.
   - *Gradient*: You can select increments between the colors to be automatic or you can select the amount of it. Remove the check to specify the amount.
   - *Hatching*: Select the hatching design. Then if you want a background color, check Background color and select the color.
   - *Bitmap*: Select the bitmap design that you want.
4) Click **Apply** to see what your selection will look like in your form.

5) Change if necessary.

6) Click **OK** to select your final decision.

If you selected *Bitmap* and *Sky* from the Bitmap list, the form should look like Figure 243.

Figure 243: Finished form

Tip

On the left side of the form window are four icons (Figure 244). You can use the Gallery as a source for backgrounds. Click it and click Backgrounds (Figure 245). Right-click the background you want to use. Select **Insert as Background > Page**.

Properties

Styles and
Formatting

Gallery

Navigator

Figure 244: Often used items

Figure 245: Open Gallery

Note

You can create custom Gradients, Hatchings, and Bitmaps using the Draw component of LibreOffice. See the *Draw Guide* for information how to do this.

Modifying a form | 251

Step 10: Change the tab order

The *Tab* key moves the cursor from field to field. This is much easier to do than to click each field to enter data into it. It also permits us to group our expenses into areas before we begin entering data. For example, all of our meal receipts can be grouped together as can our snacks and also our fuel purchases.

Figure 246: Form Design toolbar with Activation Order icon circled

1) *Ctrl+click* the Date field.
2) Select **View > Toolbar > Form Design** to open this toolbar.
3) Click the **Activation Order** icon (circled).
4) Rearrange the order of the fields in the Tab Order window.
   a) Find the txtMPayment listing near the bottom of the list and click it.
   b) Click the **Move Up** button until txtPayment is just below fmtMotel.
   c) Use the same two steps to put the fields in the same order as in Figure 247. Click **OK**.
5) Save and close the form.
6) Save the database.

Creating forms and sub forms in Design View

This method requires using the *Form Controls* and *Form Design* toolbars extensively. These techniques are beyond the scope of this document. Instructions for creating forms using Design view will be described in the *Database Guide*.

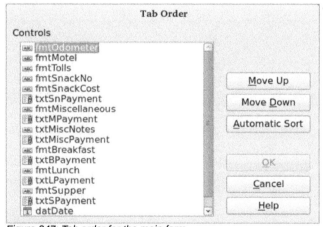

Figure 247: Tab order for the main form

Entering data in a form

Records are used to organize the data we enter into a form. They also organize the data we enter into a subform.

Different types of fields allow different methods of data entry. In many cases, more than one method can be used.

The first step to entering data in a form is to open it from the main database window (Figure 216).

1) Click the Forms icon in the *Database* list.
2) Find the form's name in the *Forms* list (Vacations).
3) Double-click the form's name.

The quickest way to enter a date in the Date field is to click the arrow that opens the drop down calendar (Figure 248). Then click the day the you want. Then press the *Tab* key to go to the Odometer field.

Figure 248: Calendar drop down

The Odometer, Tolls, and Motel fields are numeric fields. Enter values directly into them, or use the *up* and *down arrows*. When the value has been entered, use the *Tab* key to go to the next field.

- Typing the *up arrow* increases the value, and the *down arrow* decreases the value by one unit.
- These two arrows only change the numerals to the left of the decimal place.
- Numerals to the right of the decimal place must be changed by deleting them and typing the desired ones.

The Motel's Payment field is a drop-down list. If, as in my case, all of the elements of the list start with different letters, typing the first letter selects the desired entry.

- If two or more elements of the list have the same first letter, repeated typing of the first letter will cycle through these elements.
- When the selection is correct, use the *Tab* key to go to the Misc. field.

The rest of the fields of the main form are either numeric fields or drop-down lists until we reach the Misc. Notes field. It is a text field. Type anything you desire in this field just as you would any simple text editor.

 Note

Since the *Tab* key is used to move between fields, it cannot be used in a text field. All spacing must be done by the space bar. Furthermore in text fields, the *Enter* key acts only as a line break to move the cursor to the next line. While the *Enter* key will move between non-text fields, it will not do so from a text field. Use the *Tab* key instead.

If we did not have a subform for fuel data, pressing the *Tab* key in the last field would save all of the fields, clear them, and make the form ready to accept data on the second record.

Since we have a subform, using the *Tab* key places the cursor in the first Date field of the subform with the date automatically entered to match the Date field of the main form.

The FuelCost, FuelQuantity, and Odometer fields are numeric fields. The Payment field is a drop-down list. Enter the data just as you did in the main form, and use the *Tab* key to go to the next field.

When you use the *Tab* key to leave the Payment field, it goes to the Date field of the next line and automatically enters the date. Now you can enter your second set of fuel data for this day.

To move to another record when the form has a subform, click any of the fields of the main form. In this case, click the Date field of the main form. Then use the directional arrows at the bottom; from left to right: *First Record, Previous Record, Next Record*, and *Last Record*. To the right of these arrows is the *New Record* icon.

To create a new record while in the last record of the main form, click either the *Next Record* icon or the *New Record* icon.

 Tip

> The number in the Record box is the number of the record whose data is shown in the form.
>
> If you know the number of the record you want, you can enter it into the record box and then press *Enter* to take you to that record.

Figure 249 is a record with data inserted in its fields.

Figure 249: Sample record of the Vacation form and sub form

Quickly populate a table with data from a spreadsheet

If you have data in a spreadsheet document that represents the layout of a database table, and you want to copy it into a table of your database, then it is possible to load the sheet contents quickly by dragging and dropping the sheet into a database table:

1) Open the database file in the LibreOffice Base window (Figure 216) and select the Table view.

2) Open the spreadsheet in LibreOffice Calc. Select the sheet you want to insert in the database.

3) Place the two windows side by side on your desktop.

4) Drag the sheet tab in the bottom of the Calc window into the table list of the database file. The mouse pointer shows a square with a + sign. (Sheet tab: This has the name of the sheet on it.)

5) Drop the sheet by releasing the mouse button.

6) The Copy table wizard appears to help you migrate the content to the database table.

7) On the first page of the wizard, select the options of the copy operation and name the database table. Each option is explained in the Help (F1).

8) On the second page of the wizard, select the sheet columns you want to copy into the table.

9) On the third page of the wizard, define the data type of each column of your table.

10) Click **Create** to populate the new table with the spreadsheet data.

 Note

The Copy table operation copies only values and strings from the Calc spreadsheet. It does not copy formulas.

Creating queries

Queries are used to get specific information from a database. Their results are special tables within the database.

To demonstrate the use of queries, we will use two different methods:

- Using our CD-Collection table, we will create a list of albums by a particular artist. We will do this using the Wizard.

- The information we might want from the Fuel table includes what our fuel economy is. We will do this using Design View. (Queries that require calculations are best created with Design view.)

Using the Wizard to create a query

Queries created by the wizard provide a list or lists of information based upon what one wants to know. It is possible to obtain a single answer or multiple answers, depending upon the circumstances.

In the main database window (Figure 216), click the Queries icon in the Database section, then in the Tasks section, click *Use Wizard to Create Query*. The Query Wizard window opens (Figure 250). The information we want is what albums are by a certain musical group or individual (the album's author). We can include when each album was bought.

 Note

When working with a query, more than one table can be used. Since different tables may contain the same field names, the format for naming fields in a query is *Table name.field name*, with a period (.) between the table name and the field name. For example, the Lunch field of the Vacation table used in a query has the name *Vacation.Lunch*.

Figure 250: First page of the Query Wizard

Step 1: Select the fields

1) Select the CD-Collection table from the drop down list of tables.
2) Select fields from the CD-Collection table in the *Available fields* list.

   a) Click *Artist*, and use the **>** button to move it to the *Fields in the Query* list.

   b) Move the *AlbumTitle* and *DatePurchased* fields in the same manner.

   c) Click **Next**.

 Tip

> To change the order of the fields, select the field you want to move and click the up or down arrow to the right of the *Fields in the Query* list.

Step 2: Select the sorting order

Up to four fields can be used to sort the information of our query. A little simple logic helps at this point. Which field is most important?

In our query, the artist is most important. The album title is less important, and the date purchased is of least importance. Of course, if we were interested in what music we bought on a given day, the date purchased would be the most important.

Figure 251: Sorting order page

1) Click the first *Sort by* drop down list.

   a) Click *CD-Collection.Artist* to select it.

   b) To list the artists in alphabetical order (a-z), select *Ascending* on the right.

2) Click the second *Sort by* drop down list.

   – Click *CD-Collection.ArtistTitle*. and select *Ascending*.

3) Repeat this process for *CD-Collection.DatePurchased*. Click **Next**.

Step 3: Select the search conditions

The search conditions allow us to compare the name we entered with the names of the artist in our database and decide whether to include a particular artist in our query results or not.

- *is equal to*: the same as
- *is not equal to*: not the same as
- *is smaller than*: comes before
- *is greater than*: comes after
- *Is equal or less than*: the same as or comes before
- *is equal or greater than*: the same as or comes after
- *like*: similar to in some way

 Note

These conditions apply to numbers, letters (using alphabetical order), and dates.

1) Since we are only searching for one thing, we will use the default setting of *Match all of the following*.
2) We are looking for a particular artist, so select *CD-Collection. Artist* in the Fields list and *is equal to* as the Condition.
3) Type the name of the artist in the *Value* box. Click **Next**.

Step 4: Select type of query

We want simple information, so the default setting: *Detailed query* is what we want.

- Click **Next** at the bottom of the window.

 Note

Since we have a simple query, the *Grouping* and *Grouping conditions* are not needed. Steps 5 and 6 of the wizard are skipped in our query.

Step 7: Assign aliases if desired

The fields, AlbumTitle and DatePurchased, have names made up of two words. Instead, aliases can be made containing two words each (Album Title and Date Purchased, respectively).

1) Change AlbumTitle to Album Title.
2) Change DatePurchased to Date Purchased.
3) Click **Next**.

Step 8: Overview

1) Make sure that the query conditions listed in the Overview list are the ones you wanted. (There are only two that you need to check.)
2) If something is wrong, use the **Back** button to move to the step that contains the error.
3) Then use the Next button to move to step 8.
4) Name the query (suggestion: *Query_Artists*).
5) To the right of this are two choices. Select *Display Query*.
6) Click **Finish**.

Using the Design View to create a query

Creating a query using Design View is not as difficult as it may first seem. It may take multiple steps, but each step is fairly simple.

What fuel economy is our vehicle getting (miles per gallon in the USA)? This question requires creating two queries, with the first query used as part of the second query.

Step 1: Open the first query in Design View

- Click **Create Query in Design View**.

Step 2: Add tables

1) Click *Fuel* to highlight it.
2) Click **Add**.
3) Click **Close**.

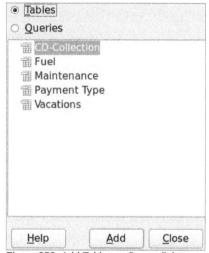

Figure 252: Add Tables or Query dialog

 Tip

Move the cursor over the bottom edge of the fuel table (Figure 253) and drag the edge to make it longer and easier to see all of the fields in the table.

Figure 253: Fuel table in query

Step 3: Add fields to the table at the bottom

1) Double-click the *FuelID* field in the Fuel table.
2) Double-click the Odometer field.
3) Double-click the FuelQuantity field.

The table at the bottom of the query window should now have three columns.

Field	FuelID	Odometer	FuelQuantity
Alias			
Table	Fuel	Fuel	Fuel
Sort			
Visible	☑	☑	☑

Figure 254: Query table

Step 4: Set the criterion for the query

We want the query's FuelID to begin with the numeral 1.

1) Type *>0* in the Criterion cell under FuelID in the query table.
2) Click the *Run Query* icon in the Query Design toolbar. (Circled in Red.)

Figure 255: Query Design toolbar

Figure 256 contains the Fuel table with my entries. The query results based upon the Fuel table are in Figure 257.

FuelID	Date	FuelCost	FuelQuantity	Odometer
0	05/25/07	$16.00	14.690	704.2
1	05/25/07	$7.00	6.430	778.7
2	05/26/07	$20.00	19.570	1032.3
3	05/26/07	$16.00	15.150	1239.4
4	05/26/07	$16.00	15.144	1639.4
<AutoField				

Figure 256: Fuel table

FuelID	Odometer	FuelQuantity	FuelCost
1	778.7	6.430	$7.00
2	1032.3	19.570	$20.00
3	1239.4	15.150	$16.00
4	1639.4	15.144	$16.00
<AutoField			

Figure 257: Query of Fuel table

Step 5: Save and close the query

Since this query contains the final odometer reading for our calculations, name it *End-Reading* when saving it. Then close the query. Now click the Save icon in the main database window.

Step 6: Create the query to calculate the fuel economy

1) Click **Create Query in Design View** to open a new query.
2) Add the Fuel table to the query just as you did in step 2: Add tables but **do not** close the Add Tables window.

3) Add the End-Reading query to this query.
   a) Click *Queries* to get the list of queries in the database (Figure 258).
   b) Click End-Reading.
   c) Click **Add**, and then click **Close**.

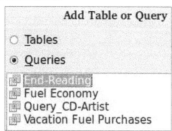

Figure 258: Selecting queries to add to another query

Step 7: Add fields to the table at the bottom of the query

We are going to calculate the fuel economy. To do this we need the FuelQuantity and distance traveled. Since the FuelQuantity we want to use is the final odometer reading, we will use the End-Reading query to get it. We will also use the Odometer field from both the Fuel table and End-Reading queries.

Figure 259: Tables in this query

1) Double-click *FuelQuantity* in the End-Reading query.
2) Double-click *Odometer* in the End-Reading query.
3) Double-click *Odometer* in the Fuel table.

Field	FuelQuantity	Odometer	Odometer
Alias			
Table	End-Reading	End-Reading	Fuel
Sort			
Visible	☑	☑	☑

Figure 260: Added fields to the query

Step 8: Enter the FuelID difference field

We want the difference between the FuelID value of the Fuel table and FuelID value of the End-Reading query to equal one (1).

1) Type "End-Reading"."FuelID" - "Fuel"."FuelID" in the field to the right of the Odometer field of the Fuel Table. (Figure 261)
2) Type ='1' in the Criterion cell of this column.
3) Leave the *Visible* cell of this column unchecked.

4) Calculate the distance traveled:
   - Type in the Field cell (Figure 262):
     `"End-Reading"."Odometer" - "Fuel"."Odometer"`
   - In the Alias row, type *Distance*.
   - Type `>'0'` in the Criterion cell.
5) Calculate fuel economy: Type
   `("End-Reading"."Odometer" - "Fuel"."Odometer")/"End-Reading"."FuelQuantity"`
   in the next column to the right of the word Field (Figure 263).
6) Type Fuel Economy as the alias.

Figure 261: Typing in calculation of fields

Figure 262: Field for distance traveled calculations

("End-Reading"."Odometer" - "Fuel"."Odometer") / "End-Reading"."FuelQuantity"

Fuel Economy

☑

Figure 263: Fuel economy calculation field

Note

When entering fields for these calculations, you must follow this format: table or query name followed by a period followed by the field name. For hyphenated or multiple-word names (table or query), use double quotes around the table or query name. The query will then add the rest of the double quotes as in Figure 263.

Use the arithmetical symbol between the two. More than one calculation can be done by using parentheses to group the arithmetical operations.

Step 9: Run the query and make some modification

After we run the query to make sure it works correctly, we will hide all of the fields that we do not need.

FuelQuantity	Odometer	Odometer	Distance	Fuel Economy
6.430	704.2	778.7	74.5	11.59
19.570	778.7	1032.3	253.6	12.96
15.150	1032.3	1239.4	207.1	13.67
15.144	1239.4	1493.4	254	16.77

Figure 264: Result of running the fuel economy query

1) Click the Run Query icon in the Design Query toolbar (Figure 255). The results are in Figure 264.

   Two of the column headers are identical. By giving these two headers different aliases, we can distinguish them.

2) Add Aliases:

   Type the aliases as they are listed in Figure 265.

Field	FuelQuantity	Odometer	Odometer	"End-Reading"."Od ("End-Reading".
Alias		Begin|	End	Distance	Fuel Economy
Table	End-Reading	Fuel	End-Reading	

Figure 265: Query table with aliases added

3) Run the query again. The results are in Figure 266.

FuelQuantity	Begin	End	Distance	Fuel Economy	FuelCost	cents per mi
6.430	704.2	778.7	74.5	11.59	7.00	9
19.570	778.7	1032.3	253.6	12.96	20.00	8
15.150	1032.3	1239.4	207.1	13.67	16.00	8
15.144	1239.4	1493.4	254	16.77	16.00	6

Figure 266: Query run with aliases

Step 10: Close, save, and name the query

My suggestion for a name is *Fuel Economy*.

1) Click the Save icon.
2) Name the query.
3) Close the query.
4) Save the database file.

There are obviously other calculations that can be made in this query such as cost per distance traveled and how much of the cost belongs to each of the payment types.

Creating reports

Reports provide information found in the database arranged in a useful way. In this respect, they are similar to queries. They are different in that they are designed to be distributed to people. Queries are only designed to answer a question about the database. Reports are generated from the database's tables, views, or queries.

All reports are based upon a single table, view, or query, so you need first to decide what fields you want to use in the report. If you want to use fields from different tables, you must first combine these fields in a single query or view. Then you can create a report from this.

For example, a report on vacation expenses includes both fuel costs and meal costs. These values are contained in fields of two different tables: Vacations and Fuel. So this report requires you to create a query or view.

 Caution

Dynamic reports update only the *data* that is changed or added to a table or query. They do **not** show any modifications made to the table or query itself. For example, **after** creating the report below, open the fuel economy query created in the previous section. For the "End-Reading"."Odometer" – "Fuel."Odometer" column, change the number 1 to the number 3. (See Figure 261The report will be identical before and after you make the change. But if you add more data to the query and run the report again, it will contain the new data. However, all data will be based upon "End-Reading"."Odometer" – "Fuel."Odometer" having the value 1. **No data** will be present in the report for which "End-Reading"."Odometer" – "Fuel."Odometer" has the value 3.

Creating a report: Example

We will create a report on vacation expenses. Certain questions need to be asked before creating the report.

- What information do we want in the report?
- How do we want the information arranged?
- What fields are required to provide this information?
- Will a query or view have to be created because these fields are in different tables?
- Are any calculations required in the data before being added to the report?

The expenses for our vacation are motel, tolls, miscellaneous, breakfast, lunch, supper, snacks, and fuel. One possible report could list the totals of each of these expense groups. Another could list the expense totals for each day of the vacation. A third could list the totals for each expense group for each type of payment. (This would let us know where the money came from to pay the expenses.) Once you create a query to do any one of these, you can create a report based upon the query.

We will create two reports, one listing the expenses each day (other than fuel) and the second listing fuel statistics. The fields we need for the first report from the Vacations table are: Date, Motel, Toll, Breakfast, Lunch, Supper, SnackCost, and Miscellaneous. This report only requires the Vacation table. Had the report listed the total expenses for each of these fields, we would have to create a query to provide us with these totals, which is beyond the scope of this chapter.

The second report involves the Fuel table. Since this table includes fuel purchases at times other than during the vacation, we need to create a query that contains only the fuel purchased during vacation periods.

Report wizard vs Report Design View

1) When you open the Report Wizard, the Report Builder also opens. As you make your selections in the wizard, these appear in layout in the Report Builder. When you have finished making your selections, you save the report, name it and then close it.

2) When using Design View to create a report, you open the Report Builder to design the layout of it. (There is only one layout available when the wizard is used.)

Vacations table report

To create a new report.

1) Click the *Reports* icon in the Database list in the Automobile – LibreOffice Base window (Figure 216).

2) In the Tasks list, click **Use Wizard to Create Report**. The Report Wizard and then the Report Builder opens.

Step 1: Field selection

1) Select *Table: Vacations* in the Tables or Queries drop down list.

2) Use the **>** to move these fields from the *Available fields* list to the *Fields in report* list: Date, Motel, Tolls, Miscellaneous, Breakfast, Lunch, Supper, and SnackCost. Click **Next**.

Figure 267: Adding fields to a report

Step 2: Labeling fields

Change any field labels you wish. We will shorten Miscellaneous to Misc. and make SnackCost into two words.

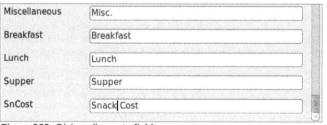

Figure 268: Giving aliases to fields

1) Shorten Miscellaneous to Misc.
2) Add a space to separate SnackCost into Snack Cost.
3) Click **Next**.

Step 3: Grouping

Since we are grouping by the date, use the **>** button to move the *Date* field to the Groupings list. Click **Next**.

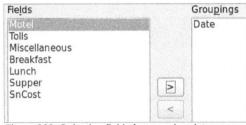
Figure 269: Selecting fields for grouping data

Step 4: Sort options

We do not want to do any additional sorting.

- Click **Next**.

Step 5: Choose layout

Use *Columnar, three columns* for the layout.

1) Select *Columnar, three columns* for the Layout of data.
2) *Layout of headers and footers* has no possible selections.
3) Select Landscape as the Orientation for the page layout.
4) Click **Next**.

Figure 270: Report Builder template determined by the Report Wizard

Step 6: Create report

1) Label the report: Vacation Expenses.
2) Select *Dynamic report*.
3) Select *Create report now*.
4) Click **Finish**.

The report (Figure 271) has been created, but it needs some editing. The date could be formatted better, and all the numbers need to be formatted as currency. It could use a heading that includes its name, its author, and the date it was prepared. If the report had more than one page, the page numbers could be put in a footer of each page, perhaps including the total number of pages. But to do these things, you must use Report Builder.

Date	05/25/07					
Motel	50	Breakfast	11	Snack Cost	5
Tolls		Lunch	15		
Misc.	2	Supper	13		
Date	05/26/07					
Motel	48	Breakfast	13	Snack Cost	7
Tolls	4	Lunch	10		
Misc.		Supper	15		
Date	05/27/07					
Motel		Breakfast		Snack Cost	
Tolls		Lunch			
Misc.		Supper			
Date	09/10/08					
Motel		Breakfast		Snack Cost	
Tolls		Lunch			
Misc.		Supper			

Figure 271: Report without modifications

Report Builder: another way to create reports

With Report Builder, you can create complex and stylish database reports. You can define group and page headers, group and page footers, and calculation fields. Report Builder is installed with LibreOffice.

When we used the Report Wizard, we created a template in Report Builder for our report. If we edit our report, we open Report Builder with this template. By modifying the template, we also modify the report. For example, we can change the Date field's format, and it will change the format of all the dates contained in that field in the above report. Similarly, we can change the field formatting of any of the other fields and change the format everywhere that field appears in the report.

Report Builder can also create reports by itself. To do this, click **Create Report in Design View**. For instructions on how to use the Report Builder, see Chapter 6, Reports, in the *Base Handbook*.

Accessing other data sources

LibreOffice allows data sources to be accessed and then linked into LibreOffice documents. For example, a mail merge links an external document containing a list of names and addresses into a letter, with one copy of the letter being generated for each entry.

To access a data source that is not a *.odb file:

1) **File > New > Database** opens the *Database Wizard* window.

2) Select **Connect to an existing database**. Click the arrow next to the *Database type* field and select the database type from the drop down list. Click **Next**.

3) Click *Browse* and select the database. Click **Next**.

4) Accept the default settings: *Register the database for me,* and *Open the database for editing*. Click **Finish**. Name and save the database in the location of your choice.

 Caution

One of the choices available when you select *Connect to an existing database* is *LDAP Address Book*. Beginning with LibreOffice 4.0.0, this option no longer works.

Accessing a spreadsheet as a data source

Accessing a spreadsheet is similar to accessing other databases:

1) Choose **File > New > Database**.

2) Select *Connect to an existing database*. Select *Spreadsheet* as the *Database type*.

3) Click **Browse** to locate the spreadsheet you want to access. If the spreadsheet is password protected, check the *Password required* box. Click **Next**.

4) If the spreadsheet requires a user's name, enter it. If a password is also required, check its box. Click **Next**.

 Note

> Using this method of accessing a spreadsheet, you cannot change anything in the spreadsheet. You can only view the contents of the spreadsheet, run queries, and create reports based upon the data already entered into the spreadsheet.
>
> All changes in a spreadsheet must be made in the spreadsheet itself, using Calc. After modifying the spreadsheet and saving it, you will see the changes in the database. If you create and save an additional sheet in your spreadsheet, the database will have a new table the next time you access it.

Registering *.odb databases

Databases created by LibreOffice are in the *.odb (OpenDocument Base) format. Other programs can also produce databases in this format. Registering a *.odb database is simple:

1) Choose **Tools > Options > LibreOffice Base > Databases**.

2) Under *Registered databases*, click **New**.

3) Browse to where the database is located.

4) Make sure the registered name is correct.

5) Click **OK**.

 Note

> Sometimes after updating LibreOffice to a newer version, your list of registered database files disappears. When that happens, you can use these steps to re-register your database files with your latest version of LibreOffice.

Using data sources in LibreOffice

Having registered the data source, whether a spreadsheet, text document, external database or other accepted data source, you can use it in other LibreOffice components including Writer and Calc.

Viewing data sources

Open a document in Writer or Calc. To view the data sources available, press *Ctrl+Shift+F4* or select **View > Data Sources** from the pull-down menu. This brings up a list of registered databases, which will include Bibliography and any other registered database, such as the Automobile database created earlier in this chapter.

To view each database, click on the arrow to the left of the database's name (see Figure 272). This brings up Queries and Tables. Click on the ▷ next to Tables to view the individual tables created. Now click on a table to see all the records held in it.

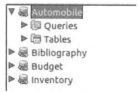
Figure 272: Databases

Editing data sources

Some data sources (but not spreadsheets) can be edited in the Data View window. A record can be edited, added, or deleted.

View a table's data

If you click on a table, its rows and columns of data appear on the right side of the Data Source window. Editing this data requires only a click in the cell whose data should be changed, change the data, and click in the row above or below it to save the new data.

Beneath the records are five tiny buttons. The first four move the cursor to the beginning, to the left, to the right, and to the end respectively. The fifth button, with a small star, inserts a new record.

Figure 273: View Data Sources navigation buttons

To delete a record, right-click on the gray box to the left of a row to highlight the entire row, and select **Delete Rows** to remove the selected row.

FuelID	Date	FuelCost	FuelQuantity	Odometer	PaymentType
Table Format...	y, May 25, 2007	$16.00	14.690	704.2	Kevin
Row Height...	y, May 25, 2007	$7.00	6.430	778.7	Dan
	rday, May 26, 2007	$20.00	19.570	1032.3	Kevin
Copy	rday, May 26, 2007	$16.00	15.150	1239.4	Dan
	rday, May 26, 2007	$16.00	15.144	1639.4	Dan
Delete Rows					

Figure 274: Deleting a row in the Data View window

Launching Base to work on data sources

You can launch LibreOffice Base at any time from the Data Source window. Just right-click on a database or its Tables or Queries icons and select **Edit Database File**. Once in Base, you can edit, add, and delete tables, queries, forms, and reports.

Using data sources in Writer and Calc

Data can be placed into Writer and Calc documents from the tables in the data source window. In Writer, values from individual fields can be inserted. Or a complete table can be created in the Writer document. One common way to use a data source is to perform a mail merge.

Figure 275: Toolbar for the Data Sources window

Writer documents

To insert a field from a table opened in the data source window into a Writer document, click on the field name (the gray square at the top of the field list) and, with the left mouse button held down, drag the field onto the document. In a Writer document, it will appear as <FIELD> (where FIELD is the name of the field you dragged).

For example, to enter the cost of meals and who paid for them on a certain date of a vacation:

1) Open the list of data sources (Ctrl+Shift+F4) and select the Vacations table in the Automobile database.

2) Use this sentence: "On (date), our breakfast cost (amount) paid by (name), our lunch cost (amount) paid by (name), and our supper cost (amount) paid by (name)." But only type "On, our breakfast cost paid by, our lunch cost paid by , and our supper cost paid by ."

3) To replace (date), click the field name Date in the data source window and drag it to the right of the word *On*. The result: On <Date>. If you have Field shadings turned on (**View > Field shading**), <Date> has a gray background. Otherwise it does not.

4) To replace first (amount), click the Breakfast field name and drag it to the right of *our breakfast cost*. Make sure you have the proper spacing between the field names and the words before and after them. Result: breakfast cost <Breakfast>.

5) To replace the first (name), click the Bpayment field name and drag it to the right of *paid by*. Result: paid by <Bpayment>.

6) In the same way, fill in the rest of the fields in the sentence.
   - Use <Lunch> and <LPayment> for the second set of (amount) and (name) in the sentence.
   - Use <Supper> and <SPayment> for the third set of (amount) and (name) in the sentence.

7) Final result: On <Date>, our breakfast cost <Breakfast> paid by <BPayment>, our lunch cost <Lunch> paid by <LPayment>, and our supper cost <Supper> paid by <SPayment>.

8) Add data to the fields of the sentence:
   - Click the gray box to the left of the row of data you want to add. That row should be highlighted like the second row of Figure 276.
   - Click the *Data to Fields* icon (circled). This should fill the fields with the data from the row you chose.
   - Click another row and then click this icon again. The data in the sentence changes to this selected row of data.
   - Save the document if you want to use it as an example later.

Date	Odometer	Motel	Tolls	Breakfast	BPayment
Friday, June 26,	530	$50.00		$11.00	Dan
Saturday, June 2	778	$48.00	$4.00	$13.00	Dan

Figure 276: Selected row in data source window

Adding data in table format is a little easier and takes perhaps fewer steps. Some of the steps will be quite similar.

1) Navigate to the place you want to place the table and click the location.

2) *Ctrl+Click* the gray box to the left of each row of the data source that you want to be a row in your table if the rows are not consecutive. To select consecutive rows, click the gray box to the left of the top desired row and *Shift+click* the bottom desired row.

3) Click the *Data to text* icon to open the Insert Database Columns dialog (Figure 277). (The *Data to text* icon is to the left of the Data to Fields icon in Figure 276.)

Figure 277: Insert Database Columns dialog

4) Move the fields you want in your table from the *Database Columns* list to the *Table column(s)* list.

   – To place the fields in the order you select, click the field and use the *single arrow* to move the fields in the order you desire. You can also limit the fields you use to less than all of the fields available.

   – If you want to use all of the fields, use the *double arrow* pointing to the right to move all of them at one time. The order of the fields in the table you create will be the same as in the data source table.

   – To remove a single field from the *Table Column(s)* list, click the field and use the *single arrow* pointing to the left.

5) To start over, click the *double arrow pointing to the left.*

6) Select the settings for your table. Use the default settings as in Figure 277.

7) Click **OK**. Save the document.

Calc spreadsheets

There are two ways to transfer data into a Calc spreadsheet. One enters the data into the spreadsheet cells. The other creates complete new records in the spreadsheet. While you can directly access the data inserted into the spreadsheet cells, new records created in the spreadsheet are read-only.

Entering data directly to the spreadsheet cells uses the *Data to Text* icon as when making a table in a Writer document. But there are certain differences.

The steps are straightforward.

1) Click the cell of the spreadsheet which you want to be the top left cell of your data, including the column names.
2) Use *Ctrl+Shift+F4* to open the database source window and select the table whose data you want to use.
3) Select the rows of data you want to add to the spreadsheet:
   - Click the gray box to the left of the row (the row header) you want to select if only selecting one row. That row is highlighted.
   - To select multiple rows, hold down the *Ctrl* key while clicking the gray box of the rows you need. Those rows are highlighted.
   - To select all the rows, click the gray box in the upper left corner. All rows are highlighted.
4) Click the *Data to text* icon to insert the data into the spreadsheet cells.
5) Save the spreadsheet.

Adding records to a spreadsheet is fairly easy. You need to have the Data Source window open, your spreadsheet open, and the table you want to use selected.

1) Click the gray box containing the field name for the table's ID field (the column header).
2) Drop and drag the gray box for the table's ID field to where you want the record to appear in the spreadsheet.
3) Repeat until you have moved all of the fields you need to where you want them.
4) Name and save the spreadsheet.
5) Click a row of the table in the Data Source window.
6) Drag the data in the ID field in the selected row onto the ID field in the spreadsheet. The Save icon should activate.
7) Click the *Edit File* button to make the spreadsheet read-only. Click **Save** when asked if you want to save the file.

   The Data Sources window goes blank, the fields in the spreadsheet are populated with data from the row you selected, and the Form Navigation toolbar appears at the bottom of the spreadsheet.
8) Click the arrows on the Form Navigation toolbar to view the different records of the table. (The arrows are circled in red.) The number in the box changes when you change the record number by clicking an arrow. The data in the fields changes correspondingly to the data for that particular record number.

Figure 278: Navigation arrows of a form

Getting Started Guide

Chapter 9
Getting Started with Math

LibreOffice's Formula (Equation) Editor

Introduction

LibreOffice Math is a formula editor you can use to create or edit formulas (equations) in a symbolic form within LibreOffice documents or as standalone objects. Example formulas are shown below. However, if you want to evaluate numeric values using formulas, then refer to the Calc Guide for more information; Math does not carry out any actual calculation.

$$\frac{df(x)}{dx} = \ln(x) + \tan^{-1}(x^2) \quad or \quad NH_3 + H_2O \rightleftharpoons NH_4^+ + OH^-$$

The Formula Editor in Math uses a markup language to represent formulas. This markup language is designed to be easily read wherever possible, for example, a over b produces the fraction $\frac{a}{b}$ when used in a formula.

Getting started

Using the Formula Editor, you can create a formula as a separate document or file for a formula library, or insert formulas directly into a document using LibreOffice Writer, Calc, Impress, or Draw.

Formulas as separate documents or files

Figure 279: An empty formula document in Math

To create a formula as a separate document or file, use one of the following methods to open an empty formula document in LibreOffice Math (Figure 279):

- On the menu bar, go to **File > New > Formula**.
- From the Start Center, click **Math Formula**.
- On the Standard toolbar, click the triangle to the right of the **New** icon and select **Formula** from the context menu.
- In Math, use the keyboard shortcut *Ctrl+N*.
- Use command **Import MathML** from the clipboard.

As you enter the markup language in the Formula Editor, the formula will appear in the Preview window during and after input of the markup. The Elements window to the left of the Preview window may also appear, if it has been selected in **View** on the menu bar. For more information on creating formulas, see "Creating formulas" on page 275.

File formats for formulas

LibreOffice's native file format for formulas is ODF Formula, with extension *.odf. You can also embed formula objects in other documents like presentations, spreadsheets, or text documents. LibreOffice can also read and save formulas in MathML 1.01 format, with extension .mml.

LibreOffice Math can import MathML Presentations directly from the clipboard. To import a MathML Presentation formula, copy the formula from the external equation editor and issue **Tools > Import MathML from Clipboard**. For example, the MathML code on the left of Table 4 displays the equation on the right.

Table 4: MathML 1.01 language imported from the clipboard

``` <math xmlns="http://www.w3.org/1998/Math/MathML" display="block"> <semantics> <mrow> <mi>E</mi> <mo stretchy="false">=</mo> <msup> <mi mathvariant="italic">mc</mi> <mn>2</mn> </msup> </mrow> </semantics> </math> ```	$E = mc^2$

Formulas in LibreOffice documents

To insert a formula into a LibreOffice document, open the document in Writer, Calc, Draw, or Impress. The LibreOffice module in use affects how you position the cursor to insert the formula.

- In Writer, click in the paragraph where you want to insert the formula.
- In Calc, click in the spreadsheet cell where you want to insert the formula.
- In Draw and Impress, the formula is inserted into the center of the drawing or slide.

Then, go to **Insert > Object > Formula** on the menu bar to open the Formula Editor. Alternatively, go to **Insert > Object > OLE Object** on the menu bar to open the Insert OLE Object dialog, select **Create new** option and *Formula* from the sub-menu, then click OK to open the Formula Editor. The Elements window to the left of the Preview window may also appear, if it has been selected in **View** on the menu bar. For more information on creating formulas, see "Creating formulas" on page 275.

Figure 280 shows an example Writer document with the formula box selected ready for a formula to be entered.

When you have completed entering the markup for the formula, close the Formula Editor by pressing the *Esc* key or by clicking an area outside the formula in the document. Double-clicking on the formula object in the document will open the Formula Editor again so that you can edit the formula.

Formulas are inserted as OLE objects into documents. As with any OLE object, you can change how the object is placed within the document. For more information on OLE objects, see the user guides for *Math, Writer, Calc, Draw,* and *Impress*.

Figure 280: Empty formula in a Writer document

If you frequently insert formulas into documents, you might like to add the Formula button to the Standard toolbar or create a keyboard shortcut. See Chapter 14, Customizing LibreOffice, for more information.

Creating formulas

You can insert elements into a formula using one of the following methods:

- Select a category from the drop-down list, then a symbol using the Elements window.
- Right-click in the Formula Editor and select a category, then a symbol from the context menu.
- Enter markup language directly in the Formula Editor.

 Note

> Using the Elements window or the context menus to insert a formula provides a convenient way to learn the markup language used by LibreOffice Math.

Elements window

The Elements window can easily be used when entering formula data. In addition to the list of categories at the top of the window, it also provides an Example category with example formulas to use as a starting point for a formula or equation.

1) Go to **View** on the menu bar and select **Elements** to open the Elements window.
2) Select the category you want to use in the formula from the drop-down list at the top of the Elements window.
3) Select the symbol you want to use in the formula from the Elements window. The symbols that are available change according to the selected category.

Note

The Elements window is positioned by default to the left of the Preview and Formula Editor windows, as shown in Figure 279 and Figure 280. It can be floated in the same way as other docked windows.

Context menu

The Formula Editor also provides a context menu to access categories and symbols when creating a formula. Right-click in the Formula Editor to open the context menu. Select a category and then select the markup example that you want to use from the sub-context menu. An example is shown in Figure 281.

Figure 281: Context menu in Formula Editor

 Note

The Elements window and the context menu contain only the most common commands that are used in formulas. For some seldom-used commands, you must always enter the command using the markup language. For a complete list of commands, see the *Math Guide*.

Markup language

Markup language is entered directly into the Formula Editor. For example, typing the markup 5 times 4 into the Formula Editor creates the simple formula 5×4. If you are experienced in using markup language, it can be the quickest way to enter a formula. Table 5 shows some examples of using markup language to enter commands. For a full list of commands that can be used in the Formula Editor, see the *Math Guide*.

Table 5: Example commands using markup language

Display	Command	Display	Command
$a=b$	a = b	$\sqrt{a}$	sqrt {a}
a^2	a^2	a_n	a_n
$\int f(x)\,dx$	int f(x) dx	$\sum a_n$	sum a_n
$a \leq b$	a <= b	∞	infinity
$a \times b$	a times b	$x \cdot y$	x cdot y

Greek characters

Using markup language

Greek characters are commonly used in formulas, but Greek characters cannot be entered into a formula using the Elements window or the context menu. Use the English names of Greek characters in markup language when entering Greek characters into a formula. See Appendix A, Commands Reference, in the *Math Guide* for a list of Greek characters that can be entered using markup language.

- For a lowercase Greek character, type a percentage % sign, then type the character name in lowercase using the English name. For example, typing %lambda creates the Greek character λ.

- For an UPPERCASE Greek character, type a percentage % sign, then type the character name in UPPERCASE using the English name. For example, typing %LAMBDA creates the Greek character Λ.

- For an *italic* Greek character, type a percentage % sign followed by the i character, then the English name of the Greek character in lower or UPPER case. For example, typing %iTHETA creates the *italic* Greek character Θ.

Symbols dialog

Greek characters can also be entered into a formula using the Symbols dialog.

1) Make sure the cursor is in the correct position in the Formula Editor.

2) Go to **Tools > Symbols** on the menu bar or click on the **Symbols** icon on the Tools toolbar to open the Symbols dialog (Figure 282).

3) Select *Greek* from the **Symbol set** drop-down list. For *italic* characters, select *iGreek* from the drop-down list.

4) Select the Greek character from the symbol list, then click **Insert**. When selected, the name of a Greek character is shown below the symbol list.

5) Click **Close** when you have finished entering Greek characters into the formula.

Figure 282: Symbols dialog

Formula examples

Example 1

The simple formula 5×4 can be created using LibreOffice Math as follows:

1) Make sure the cursor is flashing in the Formula Editor, then select the category **Unary/Binary Operators** and symbol **Multiplication** using one of the following methods:

   – In the Elements window, select **Unary/Binary Operators** from the drop-down list and then select the **Multiplication** icon □×□.

- Right-click in the Formula Editor and select **Unary/Binary Operators > a times b** from the context menu.

2) Select the first placeholder <?> before the word `times` in the Formula Editor and replace it with the character 5. The formula in the document updates automatically.

3) Select the second placeholder <?> after the word `times` in the Formula Editor and replace it with the character 4. The formula in the document updates automatically.

This method initially places the formula text <?> `times` <?> in the Formula Editor and the symbol appears in the document. These placeholders must then be replaced with real numbers. Using markup language in the Formula Editor places the formula 5×4 directly into the document. To use markup language, enter 5 `times` 4 in the Formula Editor. 5×4 appears in the document.

> ### 💡 Tip
>
> To move forward from one placeholder to the next placeholder in a formula, press the *F4* key. To move backward from one placeholder to the previous placeholder in a formula, use the key combination *Shift+F4*.

> ### 📝 Note
>
> If necessary, you can prevent a formula in a document from updating automatically. Go to **View** on the menu bar and deselect **AutoUpdate display**. To then manually update a formula, press *F9* key or select **View > Update** on the menu bar.

Example 2

You want to enter the formula $\pi \simeq 3.14159$ where the value of pi is rounded to 5 decimal places. You know the name of the Greek character (pi), but do not know the markup associated with the Is Similar Or Equal symbol $\simeq$.

1) Make sure the cursor is flashing in the Formula Editor.

2) Enter %pi in the Formula Editor to enter the Greek character for pi (π).

3) Select the category **Relations** and symbol **Is Similar Or Equal** using one of the following methods:
   - In the Elements window, select **Relations** from the drop-down list and then select the **Is Similar Or Equal** icon .
   - Right-click in the Formula Editor and select **Relations > a simeq b** from the context menu.

4) Delete the first placeholder <?> before the word `simeq` in the Formula Editor.

5) Select the second placeholder <?> after the word `simeq` in the Formula Editor and replace it with the characters 3.14159. The formula $\pi \simeq 3.14159$ now appears in the document.

Editing formulas

How you edit a formula and switch into formula editing mode depends on whether the formula is in Math or another LibreOffice component.

1) In Math, double-click on a formula element in the formula that appears in the Preview window to select the formula element in the Formula Editor, or directly select a formula element in the Formula Editor. Alternatively, right click on a selected formula in the *formula*

editor to bring up the context menu and choose from the standard editing options that appear (Figure 283).

Figure 283: Context Menu Edit Commands

2) In Writer, Calc, Impress, or Draw, double-click on the formula, or right-click on the formula and select **Edit** from the context menu, to open the Formula Editor in editing mode. The cursor is positioned at the start of the formula in the Formula Editor.

 Note

If you cannot select a formula element using the cursor, click on the **Formula Cursor** icon ⌶ in the Tools toolbar to activate the formula cursor.

3) Select the formula element you want to change, using one of the following methods:
   – Click on the formula element in the preview window, position the cursor at the beginning of the formula element in the Formula Editor, then select the formula element in the Formula Editor.
   – Double-click on the formula element in the preview window to select the formula element in the Formula Editor.
   – Position the cursor in the Formula Editor at the formula element you want to edit, then select that formula element.
   – Double-click directly on the formula element in the Formula Editor to select it.

4) Make your changes to the selected formula element.

5) Go to **View > Update** on the menu bar, or press the *F9* key, or click on the **Update** icon in the Tools toolbar to update the formula in the preview window or the document.

6) In Math, save your changes to the formula after editing.
   In Writer, Calc, Impress, or Draw, click anywhere in your document away from the formula to leave editing mode, then save the document to save your changes to the formula.

Formula layout

This section provides some advice on how to layout complex formulas in Math or in a LibreOffice document.

Using braces

LibreOffice Math knows nothing about order of operation within a formula. You must use braces (also known as curly brackets) to state the order of operations that occur within a formula. The following examples show how brackets can be used in a formula.

Example 1

`2 over x + 1` gives the result $\frac{2}{x}+1$

Math has recognized that the 2 before and the x after the over as belonging to the fraction, and has represented them accordingly. If you want x+1 rather than x to be the denominator, you must bracket them together using braces so that both will be placed there.

Inserting braces into `2 over {x + 1}` gives the result $\frac{2}{x+1}$ where x+1 is now the denominator.

Example 2

`- 1 over 2` gives the result $\frac{-1}{2}$

Math has recognized the minus sign as a prefix for the 1 and has therefore placed it in the numerator of the fraction. If you wish to show that the whole fraction is negative, with the minus sign in front of the fraction, you must put the fraction in braces to signify to Math that the characters belong together.

Adding braces to into the markup language `- {1 over 2}` gives the result $-\frac{1}{2}$ and the whole fraction is now negative.

Example 3

When braces are used in markup language, they are used to define the layout of the formula and are not displayed or printed. If you want to use braces within your formula, you use the commands `lbrace` and `rbrace` within the markup language.

`x over {-x + 1}` gives the result $\frac{x}{-x+1}$

Replace the braces using the commands lbrace and rbrace in the markup language. Writing

`x over lbrace -x + 1 rbrace` and the result is $\frac{x}{\{-x+1\}}$

Brackets and matrices

If you want to use a matrix in a formula, you have to use a matrix command. For example, `matrix { a # b ## c # d }` gives the resulting matrix $\begin{matrix} a & b \\ c & d \end{matrix}$ in the formula, where rows are separated by two hashes (#) and entries within each row are separated by one hash (#).

Normally, when you use brackets within a matrix, the brackets do not scale as the matrix increases in size. For example, `( matrix { a # b ## c # d } )` gives the result $(\begin{smallmatrix} a & b \\ c & d \end{smallmatrix})$.

To overcome this problem, LibreOffice Math provides scalable brackets that grow in size to match the size of a matrix. The commands `left(` and `right)` have to be used to create scalable brackets within a matrix. For example, `left( matrix { a # b ## c # d } right)` gives the result $\begin{pmatrix} a & b \\ c & d \end{pmatrix}$ where the matrix is now bracketed by scalable brackets.

Scalable brackets can be used with any element of a formula, such as a fraction or square root.

Unpaired brackets

When using brackets in a formula, Math expects that for every opening bracket there will be a closing one. If you forget to add a closing bracket, Math places an inverted question mark next to where the closing bracket should have been placed. This inverted question mark disappears when all the brackets are paired. However, an unpaired bracket is sometimes necessary and you have the following options.

Non-scalable brackets

A backslash \ is placed before a non-scalable bracket to indicate that the following character should not be regarded as a bracket, but as a literal character.

For example, the unpaired brackets in the formula [a; b [are deliberate, but gives the result $a;b$. To remove the inverted question marks and create unpaired brackets, backslashes are added. The formula now becomes \ [a; b \ [and the result $[a;b[$ shows unpaired brackets without the inverted question marks.

Scalable brackets

To create unpaired scalable brackets or braces in a formula, the markup commands `left`, `right`, and `none` are used.

Example

You want to create the formula $|x| = \begin{cases} x \text{ for } x \geq 0 \\ -x \text{ for } x < 0 \end{cases}$ and in the Formula Editor you enter

`abs x = lbrace stack {x "for" x >= 0 # -x "for" x < 0.`

However, this gives the incorrect result $\begin{matrix} x \text{ for } x \geq 0 \\ -x \text{ for } x < 0 \end{matrix}$.

To remove the inverted question marks and create the correct formula, you have to use the markup commands `left`, `right`, and `none`.

To create the correct formula, change the entry in the Formula Editor to

`abs x = left lbrace stack {x "for" x >= 0 # -x "for" x < 0} right none.`

Recognizing functions

In the basic installation of Math, Math outputs functions in normal characters and variables in italic characters. However, if Math fails to recognize a function, you can tell Math that you have just entered a function. Enter the markup command `func` before a function forces Math to recognize the following text as a function and uses normal characters.

For a full list of functions within Math, see the *Math Guide*.

Some Math functions have to be followed by a number or a variable. If these are missing, Math places an inverted question mark where the missing number or variable should be. To remove the inverted question mark and correct the formula, you have to enter a number, a variable, or a pair of empty brackets as a placeholder.

Formulas over multiple lines

Suppose you want to create a formula that requires more than one line, for example $\begin{aligned}x=3\\y=1\end{aligned}$.

Your first reaction would normally be to press the *Enter* key. However, if you press the *Enter* key, the markup language in the Formula Editor goes to a new line, but the resulting formula is written on one line. You must type the macro command `newline` each time you want to create and display a new line in a formula.

Example
```
x = 3
y = 1
```
gives the incorrect result $x=3\,y=1$

`x = 3 newline y = 1` gives the correct result $\begin{aligned}x=3\\y=1\end{aligned}$

It is not possible in Math to create multiple-line formulas when a line ends with an equals sign and you want to continue the calculation on a new line without completing the term on the right side of the equals sign. If you require a multiple line formula to have an equals sign at the end of a line without a term after the equals sign, then use either empty quotes "" or empty braces {} or the space characters grave ` or tilde ~.

By default, a multiple line formula is centrally aligned. For more information on alignment using the equals sign, see the *Math Guide*.

Spacing between the elements in a formula is not set by using space characters in the markup language. If you want to add spaces into the formula, use one of the following options:

- Grave ` to add a small space.
- Tilde ~ for a large space.
- Add space characters between quotes " ". These spaces will be considered as text.

Any spaces at the end of a line in the markup language are ignored by default. For more information, see the *Math Guide*.

Adding limits to sum/integral commands

The sum and integral commands can take the parameters `from` and `to` if you want to set the lower and upper limits respectively. The parameters `from` and `to` can be used singly or together as shown by the following examples. For more information on the sum and integral commands, see the *Math Guide*.

Examples

sum from k = 1 to n a_k gives the result $\sum_{k=1}^{n} a_k$

int from 0 to x f(t) dt gives the result $\int_0^x f(t)\,dt$

int_0^x f(t) dt gives the result $\int_0^x f(t)\,dt$

int from Re f gives the result $\int_{\Omega} f$

sum to infinity 2^{-n} gives the result $\sum^{\infty} 2^{-n}$

Writing derivatives

When writing derivatives, you have to tell Math that it is a fraction by using the over command. The over command is combined with the character d for a total derivative or the partial command for a partial derivative to achieve the effect of a derivative. Braces {} are used each side of the element to surround the element and make the derivative as shown by the following examples.

Examples

{df} over {dx} gives the result $\dfrac{df}{dx}$

{partial f} over {partial y} gives the result $\dfrac{\partial f}{\partial y}$

{partial^2 f} over {partial t^2} gives the result $\dfrac{\partial^2 f}{\partial t^2}$

Note

To write function names with primes, as is normal in school notation, you must first add the symbols to the catalog. See the *Math Guide* for more information.

Markup language characters as normal characters

Characters that are used as controls in markup language cannot be entered directly as normal characters. These characters are: %, {, }, &, |, _, ^ and ". For example, you cannot write 2% = 0.02 in markup language and expect the same characters to appear in the formula. To overcome this limitation, use one of the following methods:

- Use double quotes either side of the character to mark that character as text, for example 2"%"= 0.02 will appear in the formula as 2%=0.02 . However, this method cannot be used for the double-quote character itself, see "Text in formulas" below.
- Add the character to the Math Catalog, for example the double quote character.
- Use commands, for example lbrace and rbrace give literal braces {} .

Note

The Special Characters dialog used by other LibreOffice modules is not available in Math. If you regularly require special characters in Math, the characters should be added to the catalog of Math symbols. See the *Math Guide* for more information.

Text in formulas

To include text in a formula, you have to enclose it in double-quotes, for example x " for " x >= 0 in markup language will create the formula x for $x \geq 0$. All characters, except double quotes, can be used in text. However, if you require double quotes in the formula text, then you have to create the text with double quotes in LibreOffice Writer, then copy and paste the text into the Formula Editor as shown in Figure 284.

The font used for text in a formula will be the default font that has been set in the Fonts dialog. For more information on how to change fonts used for in formulas, see "Changing formula appearance" on page 285.

By default, text alignment is left-justified in formulas. To change text alignment, see "Adjusting formula alignment" on page 288.

Formatting commands are not interpreted within text used in formulas. If you want to use formatting commands within formula text, then you must break up the text using double quotes in the Formula Editor.

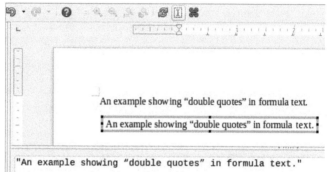

Figure 284: Example of double quotes in formula text

Example

Enter the following in the Formula Editor:

```
"In " color blue bold "isosceles" "triangles, the base angles are
equal"
```

creates the following text in a formula   In *isosceles* triangles, the base angles are equal

Aligning formulas using equals sign

LibreOffice Math does not have a command for aligning formulas on a particular character. However, you can use a matrix to align formulas on a character and this character is normally the equals sign (=).

Example

Creating the matrix:

```
matrix{ alignr x+y # {}={} # alignl 2 ## alignr x   # {}={} # alignl 2-y }
```

gives the following result, where formulas are aligned on the equals sign $\begin{matrix} x+y & = & 2 \\ x & = & 2-y \end{matrix}$

Note

The empty braces each side of the equals sign are necessary because the equals sign is a binary operator and requires an expression on each side. You can use spaces, or `` ` `` or ~ characters each side of the equals sign, but braces are recommended as they are easier to see within the markup language.

You can reduce the spacing on each side of the equals sign if you change the inter-column spacing of the matrix. See "Adjusting formula spacing" on page 287 for information on how to adjust adjust formula spacing.

Changing formula appearance

Formula font size

Current formula font size

To change the font size used for a formula already inserted in Math or another LibreOffice module:

1) Click in the markup language in the Formula Editor.

2) Go to **Format > Font size** on the menu bar to open the Font Sizes dialog (Figure 285).

3) Select a different font size using the *Base size* spinner or type a new font size in the *Base Size* box.

4) Click **OK** to save your changes and close the dialog. An example result when you change font size is shown below.

Example

Default font size 12pt: $\pi \simeq 3.14159$

After font size change to 18pt: $\pi \simeq 3.14159$

Figure 285: Font Sizes dialog

Default formula font size

To change the default font size used for all formulas in Math or another LibreOffice module:

1) Before inserting any formulas into a document, go to **Format > Font size** on the menu bar to open the Font Sizes dialog (Figure 285).

2) Select a different font size using the Base size spinner or type a new font size in the Base Size box.

3) Click **Default** and confirm your changes to the base size font. Any formulas created from this point on will use the new base size font for formulas.

4) Click **OK** to save your changes and close the Font Sizes dialog.

 Note

If you have already inserted formulas into a document and you change the default font size, only formulas inserted after the change in default font size will use the new default settings. You have to individually change the font size of formulas already inserted if you want these formulas to use the same font size as the default settings. For more information on changing the font size, see the *Math Guide*.

Formula fonts

Current formula fonts

To change the fonts used for the current formula in Math or another LibreOffice module:

1) Click in the markup language in the Formula Editor.
2) Go to **Format > Fonts** on the menu bar to open the Fonts dialog (Figure 286).
3) Select a new font for each the various options from the drop-down lists.
4) If the font you want to use does not appear in the drop-down list, click **Modify** and select the option from the context menu to open a fonts dialog. Select the font you want to use and click **OK** to add it to the drop-down list for that option.
5) Click **OK** to save your changes and close the Fonts dialog.

Figure 286: Fonts dialog

Default formula fonts

To change the default fonts used for all formulas in Math or another LibreOffice module:

1) Before inserting any formulas into a document, go to **Format > Fonts** on the menu bar to open the Fonts dialog (Figure 286).
2) Select a new font where required for each of the various options from the drop-down lists.
3) If the font you want to use does not appear in the drop-down list, click **Modify** and select the option from the context menu to open a fonts dialog. Select the font you want to use and click **OK** to add it to the drop-down list for that option.
4) Click **Default** and confirm your changes to the fonts. Any formulas created from this point on will use the new fonts for formulas.
5) Click **OK** to save your changes and close the Fonts dialog.

Note

If you have already inserted formulas into a document and you change the default fonts, only formulas inserted after the change in default fonts will use the new default settings. You have to individually change the font of formulas already inserted if you want these formulas to use the same font as the default settings. For more information on changing the font, see the *Math Guide*.

Adjusting formula spacing

Use the Spacing dialog (Figure 287) to determine the spacing between formula elements. The spacing is specified as a percentage in relation to the defined base size for fonts.

Current formula spacing

To change the spacing used for the current formula in Math or another LibreOffice module:

1) Click in the markup language in the Formula Editor.
2) Go to **Format > Spacing** on the menu bar to open the Spacing dialog (Figure 287).
3) Click **Category** and select one of the options from the drop-down list. The options in the Spacing dialog change according to the category selected.
4) Enter new values for the spacing category and click **OK**.
5) Check the result in your formula. If it is not to your satisfaction, repeat the above steps.

Figure 287: Spacing dialog

Default formula spacing

To change the default spacing used for all formulas in Math or another LibreOffice module:

1) Before inserting any formulas into a document, go to **Format > Spacing** on the menu bar to open the Spacing dialog (Figure 287).
2) Click **Category** and select one of the options from the drop-down list. The options in the Spacing dialog change according to the category selected.
3) Click **Default** and confirm your changes to the formula spacing. Any formulas created from this point on will use the new spacing for formulas.
4) Click **OK** to save your changes and close the Spacing dialog.

 Note

If you have already inserted formulas into a document and you change the spacing, only formulas inserted after the change in spacing will use the new default settings. You have to individually change the spacing of formulas already inserted if you want these formulas to use the same spacing as the default settings. For more information on changing the formula spacing, see the *Math Guide*.

Adjusting formula alignment

The alignment settings determine how formula elements located above one another are aligned horizontally relative to each other.

 Note

> It is not possible to align formulas on a particular character and formula alignment (using the method described below) does not apply to text elements, which are always aligned left.
>
> Independent of using formula alignment given below, it is possible to align formulas using the commands `alignl`, `alignc` and `alignr`. These commands also work for text elements.

Current formula alignment

To change the alignment used for the current formula in Math or another LibreOffice module:

1) Click in the markup language in the Formula Editor.
2) Go to **Format > Alignment** on the menu bar to open the Alignment dialog (Figure 288).
3) Select either *Left*, *Centered*, or *Right* for horizontal alignment.
4) Click **OK** and check the result in your formula. If it is not to your satisfaction, repeat the above steps.

Figure 288: Alignment dialog

Default formula alignment

To change the default alignment used for all formulas in Math or another LibreOffice module:

1) Before inserting any formulas into a document, go to **Format > Alignment** on the menu bar to open the Alignment dialog (Figure 288).
2) Select either *Left*, *Centered*, or *Right* for horizontal alignment.
3) Click **Default** and confirm your changes to the formula alignment. Any formulas created from this point on will use the new alignment for formulas.
4) Click **OK** and check the result in your formula. If it is not to your satisfaction, repeat the above steps.

 Note

> If you have already inserted formulas into your document and you change the formula alignment, only formulas inserted after the change in alignment will use the new default settings. You have to individually change the alignment of formulas already inserted if you want these formulas to use the same alignment as the default settings.

Changing formula color

Character color

To change the color of the characters used in a formula, use the command color in the markup language. This command only works on the formula element immediately after the color name. For example, entering the markup language `color red ABC 5 times 4` gives the result $ABC\,5{\times}4$.

To change the color of the whole formula, you have to enclose the whole formula within brackets. For example, entering the markup language `color red {ABC 5 times 4}` gives the result $ABC\,5{\times}4$.

For information on the colors available in Math, see the Math Guide.

 Tip

> For ease of use, the Elements window includes the category *Attributes*, which lists standard colors. Click on the required color to insert the command into your formula.

Background color

It is not possible to select a background color for formulas in LibreOffice Math. The background color for a formula is by default the same color as the document or frame that the formula has been inserted into. However, in LibreOffice documents, you can use object properties to change the background color for a formula. For more information on using a background color (area fill for objects) with a formula, please refer to the user guides for *Writer*, *Calc*, *Draw*, and *Impress*.

Formula library

If you regularly insert the same formulas into your documents, you can create a formula library using formulas that you have created using the Formula Editor. Individual formulas can be saved as separate files using the ODF format for formulas with the file suffix of .odf, or in MathML format with the file suffix of .mml.

You can use LibreOffice Math, Writer, Calc, Draw, or Impress to create formulas and build up your formula library.

Using Math

1) Create a folder on your computer to contain your formulas. Give the folder a memorable name, for example Formula Library.

2) In LibreOffice, go to **File > New > Formula** on the menu bar, or click on **Math Formula** in the opening splash screen to open LibreOffice Math and create your formula using the Formula Editor. See "Formulas as separate documents or files" on page 273 for more information.

3) Go to **File > Save As** on the menu bar or use the keyboard shortcut *Ctrl+Shift+S* to open a Save As dialog.

4) Navigate to the folder you have created for your formula library.

5) Type a memorable name for your formula in the **File name** text box.

6) Select from the drop-down list for **File type** either *ODF Formula (.odf)* or *MathML 1.01 (.mml)* as the file type for your formula.

7) Click **Save** to save the formula and close the Save As dialog.

Using Writer, Calc, Draw, or Impress

1) Create a folder on your computer to contain your formulas. Give the folder a memorable name, for example Formula Library.

2) Open a document using Writer, Calc, Draw, or Impress.

3) Go to **Insert > Object > Formula** on the menu bar to open the Formula Editor and create your formula. See "Formulas in LibreOffice documents" on page 274 for more information.

4) Right-click on the formula object and select **Save Copy as** from the context menu to open a Save As dialog.

5) Navigate to the folder you have created for your formula library.

6) Type a memorable name for your formula in the **File name** text box.

7) Select from the drop-down list for **File type** either *ODF Formula (.odf)* or *MathML 1.01 (.mml)* as the file type for your formula.

8) Click **Save** to save the formula and close the Save As dialog.

Using your formula library

You cannot insert a formula from your library into a document by dragging and dropping using the mouse, nor by using **Insert > File** on the menu bar. You must insert a formula from your library into your document as an OLE object.

1) Open the document in Writer, Calc, Draw, or Impress.

2) Go to **Insert > Object > OLE Object** on the menu bar to open the Insert OLE Object dialog.

3) Select the option **Create from file**.

4) Click **Search** to open a file browser dialog.

5) Navigate to the folder you have created for your formula library.

6) Select the formula you want to insert and click **Open**, or double-click on the formula you want to insert.

7) Click **OK** to insert the formula as an OLE object in the document and close the OLE Object dialog.

Formulas in Writer

When a formula is inserted into a document, LibreOffice Writer inserts the formula into a frame and treats the formula as an OLE object. Double-clicking on an inserted formula will open the Formula Editor in LibreOffice Math, where you can edit the formula.

This section explains what options you can change for each individual formula within a Writer document. Please refer to the chapters on styles in the *Writer Guide* for information on how to change the default settings for frame styles for OLE objects.

Automatic formula numbering

Automatic numbering of formulas for cross-reference purposes can only be carried out in LibreOffice Writer.

Numbering

1) Start a new line in your document.

2) Type *fn* (mnemonic for *formula numbered*) and then press the *F3* key. A two-column table with no borders is inserted into the document with the left column containing a sample formula and the right column containing a reference number, as shown below.

$$ABC\,5\times4 \hspace{8cm} (1)$$

3) Delete the sample formula and insert your formula as an object in the left column. See "Creating formulas" on page 275 for more information on inserting formulas.

Alternatively, you can first insert your formula into the document, then carry out Steps 1 and 2 above, replacing the sample formula with your formula.

 Note

> If you want to use square parentheses instead of round ones around the formula number, or if you want the formula number to be separated from the formula by tabs instead of using a table, then you need to modify the AutoText entry for fn. Refer to the section on AutoText in Chapter 4, Getting Started with Writer.

Cross-referencing

1) Click in the document where you want the cross-reference to appear.

2) Go to **Insert > Cross-reference** on the menu bar to open the Fields dialog (Figure 289).

3) Click on the **Cross-references** tab, then select *Text* in the **Type** section.

4) In the **Selection** section, select the formula number you want to refer to.

5) In the **Insert reference to** section, select *Reference* and click **Insert**.

6) When you have finished creating cross-references, click **Close** to close the Fields dialog.

 Tip

> To insert the cross-reference number without parentheses, select *Numbering* instead of *Reference* in the **Insert** reference to section.

Figure 289: Fields dialog – Cross-references page

Anchoring formulas

A formula is treated as an object within Writer and its default anchoring is **As character** within a paragraph when it is inserted into a document. To change the anchoring of a formula object:

1) Right-click on the selected formula object and select **Anchor** from the context menu.

2) Select a new anchoring option from the context sub-menu. The anchoring positions available are **To page**, **To paragraph**, **To character**, or **As character**.

Alternatively,

1) Right-click on the selected formula object and select **Object** from the context menu, or go to **Format > Frame/Object** on the menu bar to open the Object dialog (Figure 290).

2) Make sure the **Type** page is selected and select a new anchoring position from the *Anchor* section.

3) Click **OK** to save your changes and close the Object dialog.

 Note

> The anchoring options are not available in the Object dialog when you are making changes to the various options available for frame styles. For more information on how to modify frame styles, please refer to the chapters on styles in the *Writer Guide*.

Figure 290: Object dialog – Type page with Anchor options

Vertical alignment

The normal default setting for vertical alignment for formula objects is to use the text base line as a reference. This default setting can be changed by modifying the formula frame style. See the chapters on styles in the *Writer Guide* for more information.

To change the vertical alignment position of an individual formula object:

1) Right-click on the selected formula object and select **Object** from the context menu, or go to **Format > Frame/Object** to open the Object dialog (Figure 290).

2) Make sure the **Type** page is selected and select a new alignment position from the drop-down list in the *Position* section. The vertical alignment options available are **Top**, **Bottom**, **Center** or **From bottom**.

---

3) If necessary, type in the text box a plus or minus value for vertical alignment. This option is only available if **From bottom** vertical alignment has been selected.

4) Select the type of text alignment from the drop-down list in the *Position* section. The text alignment options available are **Base line**, **Character** and **Row**.

5) Click **OK** to save your changes and close the Object dialog.

 Note

> If the *Position* section in the Object dialog is grayed out and not available, then go to **Tools > Options > LibreOffice Writer > Formatting Aids** and uncheck the option *Math baseline alignment*. This setting is stored with the document and applies to all formulas within it. Any new documents created will also use this setting for *Math baseline alignment*.

Figure 291: Object dialog – Wrap page

Object spacing

A formula object, when inserted into a Writer document, has spacing on each side. The default value used for spacing is set within the frame style for formula objects and can be changed by modifying the formula frame style, see the chapters on styles in the *Writer Guide* for more information.

You can individually adjust the spacing for each formula object within a document as follows:

1) Create the formula in your Writer document.

2) Right-click on the selected formula object and select **Object** from the context menu, or go to **Format > Frame/Object** on the menu bar to open the Object dialog.

3) Click on the **Wrap** tab to open the Wrap page in the Object dialog (Figure 291).

4) In the **Spacing** section, enter the spacing value for *Left*, *Right*, *Top* and *Bottom* spacing.

5) Click **OK** to save your changes and close the Object dialog.

Text mode

In large formulas placed within a line of text, the formula elements can often be higher than the text height. Therefore, to make large formulas easier to read, it is recommended to always insert them into a separate paragraph of their own.

However, if it is necessary to place a large formula within a line of text, double-click on the formula to open the Formula Editor and then go to **Format > Text Mode** on the menu bar. The Formula Editor will try to shrink the formula to fit the text height. The numerators and denominators of fractions are shrunk, and the limits of integrals and sums are placed beside the integral/sum sign, as shown in the following example.

Example

A formula in a separate paragraph:

$$\sum_{i=2}^{5} i^2$$

and the same formula embedded into a line of text using text mode format: $\sum_{i=2}^{5} i^2$

Background and borders

The default setting for background (area fill) and borders for formula objects is set by the formula frame style. To change this default setting for formula frame style, refer to the chapters on styles in the *Writer Guide*. However, for individual formulas in a document, you can change the background and borders.

 Note

> The size of the frame that a formula is placed in when inserted into a document cannot be changed. The frame size for a formula object depends on the setting of the formula font size; see the *Math Guide* for more information.

Backgrounds

1) In the document, select the formula where you wish to change the background.

2) Right-click on the formula and select **Object** from the context menu, or go to **Format > Frame/Object** on the menu bar to open the object dialog.

3) Click on the **Area** tab and select the type of fill you want to use for the formula from the *Fill* drop-down list (Figure 292).

4) Select the options you want to use for the formula background. The options change depending on the type of fill selected.

5) Click **OK** to save your changes and close the Object dialog.

Figure 292: Object dialog – Area page

Borders

1) In the document, select the formula where you want to change the borders.

2) Right-click on the formula and select **Object** from the context menu, or go to **Format > Frame/Object** on the menu bar to open the object dialog.

3) Click on the **Borders** tab and select the options you want to use for the formula borders (Figure 293).

4) Click **OK** to save your changes and close the Object dialog.

Figure 293: Object dialog – Borders page

Quick insertion of formulas

To quickly insert a formula into a Writer document without opening the Formula Editor, where you know the markup language for the formula:

1) Enter the formula markup language into the document at the position where you want the formula.

2) Select the markup language.

3) Go to **Insert > Object** on the menu bar and select **Formula**, or click on the **Formula** icon on the Standard toolbar to create a formula from the selected markup language.

> **Note**
>
> If the **Formula** icon is not displayed on the Standard toolbar, then right-click in an empty area on the toolbar, select **Visible Buttons** from the context menu, then select **Formula** from the available options.

Formulas in Calc, Draw, and Impress

In Calc, Draw, and Impress, formulas are inserted as OLE objects without any background (area fill) or borders. See the *Math Guide* for more information.

Each formula object is inserted into a spreadsheet, drawing, or slide as follows:

• In Calc, formulas are inserted into a selected cell in a spreadsheet with no style assigned to the formula object.

- In Draw and Impress, formulas are inserted into a central position on a drawing or slide and, by default, are assigned the drawing object style *Object with no fill and no line*. For more information on how to modify or assign drawing object styles, see the *Draw Guide* or the *Impress Guide*.

Anchoring formulas

Calc

A formula object can be anchored into a spreadsheet as **To Page** (default setting), or as **To Cell**. To change the anchoring type of formulas in a Calc spreadsheet:

1) Select the formula object in the spreadsheet.
2) Right-click on the formula and select **Anchor > To Page** or **To Cell** from the context menu
3) Alternatively, go to **Format > Anchor** on the menu bar and select **To Page** or **To Cell**.

Draw and Impress

When a formula is inserted into a drawing or slide, it is inserted as a floating OLE object and is not anchored to any particular position in a drawing or slide.

Formula object properties

Formula objects in Calc, Draw, and Impress can be modified just like any other object that has been placed in a spreadsheet, drawing, or presentation, with the exception of formula object size and changing the format of any text within a formula. For more information on how to change object properties, see the *Calc Guide*, *Draw Guide*, and *Impress Guide*. For more information on formula object size and formatting formula text, see the *Math Guide*.

The following points will help you select which dialog to use if you want to change the properties of formula objects.

- For formula backgrounds, use the various options in the pages of the Area dialog.
- For formula borders, use the various options in the Line dialog. Note that formula borders are separate from cell borders in a Calc spreadsheet.
- To accurately re-position a formula object, use the various options in pages of the Position and Size dialog.
- In Draw and Impress, you can arrange, align, group, flip, convert, break, combine, and edit points of formula objects.
- You cannot change the text attributes of a formula object. The text used in a formula is set when you create the formula in the Formula Editor.
- Formula object size is set by the formula font size when the formula is created in the Formula Editor. The formula object size is protected in the Position and Size dialog, but this can be deselected if you so wish. However, this is not recommended, as resizing a formula object using the Position and Size dialog could lead to distortion of a formula making it difficult to read.

Formulas in charts

A chart in a Calc spreadsheet is itself an OLE object; therefore you cannot use the Formula Editor to create and insert a formula into a chart.

To insert a formula into a chart, create the formula first using the Formula Editor and copy the formula to the clipboard. You then create the chart in Calc and paste the formula into the chart. The formula is automatically converted into the correct format for insertion into a chart.

If you want to change the formula at a later date, then you must repeat the whole process of creating, copying, and pasting.

Getting Started Guide

Chapter 10
Printing, Exporting, E-mailing
and Signing Documents

Quick printing

Click the **Print File Directly** icon ( ) to send the entire document to the default printer defined for your computer.

Note

You can change the action of the **Print File Directly** icon to send the document to the printer defined for the document instead of the default printer for the computer. Go to **Tools > Options > Load/Save > General** and select the **Load printer settings with the document** option.

Controlling printing

For more control over printing, use the Print dialog (**File > Print** or *Ctrl+P*).

Figure 294: The Print dialog

Note

The options selected on the Print dialog apply to this printing of this document only.

To specify default printing settings for LibreOffice, go to **Tools > Options > LibreOffice > Print** and **Tools > Options > LibreOffice [Component] > Print**. See Chapter 2, Setting Up LibreOffice, for more details.

The Print dialog has four pages, from which you can choose a range of options, as described in the following sections.

The different components of LibreOffice have different print settings available, as summarized in Table 6.

Table 6: Print options in LibreOffice components

Feature	Writer	Calc	Impress	Draw
Select pages/sheets/slides to print	Yes	Yes	Yes	Yes
Print multiple pages/sheets/slides on one page	Yes	Yes	Yes	Yes
Print a brochure	Yes	No	Yes	Yes
Print envelopes	Yes	No	No	No
Print labels or business cards	Yes	No	No	No
Preview pages/sheets before printing	Yes	Yes	No	No

Selecting general printing options

On the *General* tab of the Print dialog, you can choose:

- The **printer** (from the list of available printers)
- Which **pages** to print, the number of copies to print, and whether to collate multiple copies (*Range and copies* section).
- Whether to print any **comments** that are in the document, and where to print the comments.

Some selections may not be available all the time. For example, if the document contains no comments, the Print – Comments drop-down list is disabled..

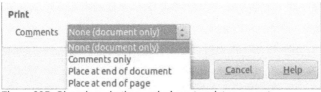
Figure 295: Choosing whether and where to print comments

Select the **Properties** button to display the selected printer's properties dialog where you can choose portrait or landscape orientation, which paper tray to use, and the paper size to print on.

On the Options tab of the Print dialog (Figure 296), the last item, *Use only paper tray from printer preference*, is not available in Calc.

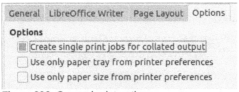
Figure 296: General print options

Printing multiple pages on a single sheet of paper

You can print multiple pages of a document on one sheet of paper. To do this:

1) In the Print dialog, select the Page Layout tab (Figure 297).

Figure 297: Printing multiple page per sheet of paper

2) In the *Layout* section, select from the drop-down list the number of pages to print per sheet. The preview panel on the left of the Print dialog shows how the printed document will look.

When printing more than 2 pages per sheet, you can choose the order in which they are printed across and down the paper.

Figure 298: Print order options

3) In the *Page sides* section, select whether to print all pages or only some pages. Click the **OK** button.

 Tip

In Writer, to print two pages per sheet in "facing pages" (book layout) style, print from Print Preview instead. See page 305.

Selecting pages/sheets/slides to print

In addition to printing a full document, you can choose to print individual pages/sheets/slides, ranges of pages/sheets/slides, or a selection of a document. The details vary slightly between Writer, Calc, Draw, and Impress, as described in this section.

Writer

Printing an individual page:

1) Choose **File > Print** from the Menu bar, or press *Ctrl+P*.

2) On the Print dialog, select the page to print.

a) In the *Range and copies* section of the General page, select the **Pages** option. The text input box displays the current page number.

b) Enter the page number of the page you want to print. The preview box changes to show the selected page.

3) Click **OK**.

Printing a range of pages:

1) Choose **File > Print** from the Menu bar, or press *Ctrl+P*.

2) On the Print dialog, select the range of pages to print.

a) In the *Range and copies* section of the General page, select the **Pages** option.

b) Enter the sequence numbers of the pages to print (for example, 1–4 or 1,3,7,11).

3) Click **OK**.

Printing a selection of text:

1) In the document, select the material (text and graphics) to print.

2) Choose **File > Print** from the Menu bar, or press *Ctrl+P*.

3) The *Range and copies* section of the Print dialog now includes a **Selection** option and the preview box shows the selected material. See Figure 299.

4) Click **OK**.

Figure 299: Printing a selection of text

Calc

You can choose single sheets, multiple sheets, and selections of cells for printing (Figure 300).

Figure 300: Choosing what to print in Calc

Printing an individual sheet:

1) In the spreadsheet, click on the sheet tab to select the sheet you want to print.
2) Choose **File > Print** from the Menu bar, or press *Ctrl+P*.
3) In the *Range and copies* section of the Print dialog, choose the **Selected sheets** option.
4) Click **OK**.

Printing a range of sheets:

1) In the spreadsheet, select the sheets to print.
    a) Select the first sheet.
    b) Hold down the *Control* key.
    c) Click on the additional sheet tabs.
    d) Release the *Control* key when all required sheets are selected.
2) Choose **File > Print** from the Menu bar, or press *Ctrl+P*.
3) In the *Range and copies* section of the Print dialog, choose the **Selected sheets** option.
4) Click **OK**.

Printing a selection of cells:

1) In the document, select the section of cells to print.
2) Choose **File > Print** from the Menu bar, or press *Ctrl+P*.
3) In the *Ranges and copies* section of the Print dialog, select the *Selected cells* option.
4) In the sub-section *From which print* select the *Pages* option and type 1 in the edit box.
5) Click **OK**.

 Caution

> After printing, be sure to deselect the extra sheets. If you keep them selected, the next time you enter data on one sheet, you enter data on all the selected sheets. This might not be what you want.

Impress and Draw

You can choose individual slides, ranges of slides, or selections of slides for printing.

Figure 301: Choosing what to print in Impress and Draw

Printing an individual slide:

1) Choose **File > Print** from the Menu bar, or press *Ctrl+P*.
2) Select the slide to print (Figure 301).

     a) In the *Range and copies* section of the Print dialog, select the **Slides** option.

     b) Enter the number of the slide to print.

  3) Click **OK**.

Printing a range of slides:

  1) Choose **File > Print** from the Menu bar, or press *Ctrl+P*.

  2) Select the slides to print.

     a) In the *Range and copies* section of the Print dialog, select the **Slides** option.

     b) Enter the slide numbers to print (for example 1-4 or 1,3,7,11).

  3) Click **OK**.

Printing a selection from a slide, or a selection from multiple slides:

  1) In the document, select the section of the slide to print.

  2) Choose **File > Print** from the Menu bar, or press *Ctrl+P*.

  3) Select the **Selection** option in the *Range and copies* section of the Print dialog.

  4) Click **OK**.

Printing handouts, notes, or outlines in Impress

Handouts prints the slides in reduced size on the page, from one to nine slides per page. The slides can be printed horizontally (landscape orientation) or vertically (portrait orientation) on the page.

Notes prints a single slide per page with any notes entered for that slide in Notes View.

Outline prints the title and headings of each slide in outline format.

To print handouts, notes, or outlines:

  1) Choose **File > Print** from the Menu bar, or press *Ctrl+P*.

  2) In the Print section of the Print dialog, select the required option.

  3) For Handouts, you can then choose how many slides to print per page, and the order in which they are printed (Figure 302).

  4) Click **OK**.

Figure 302: Handouts

Printing a brochure

In Writer, Impress, and Draw, you can print a document with two pages on each side of a sheet of paper, arranged so that when the printed pages are folded in half, the pages are in the correct order to form a booklet or brochure.

Plan your document so it will look good when printed half size; choose appropriate margins, font sizes, and so on. You may need to experiment.

To print a brochure on a single-sided printer:

1) Choose **File > Print**, or press *Ctrl+P*.
2) In the Print dialog, click **Properties**.
3) Check that the printer is set to the same orientation (portrait or landscape) as specified in the page setup for your document. Usually the orientation does not matter, but it does for brochures. Click **OK** to return to the Print dialog.
4) Select the *Page layout* tab in the Print dialog (Figure 303).
5) Select the **Brochure** option.
6) In the *Page sides* section, select the **Back sides / left pages** option from the **Include** drop-down list. Click **OK**.

Figure 303: Selecting which pages to print

7) Take the printed pages out of the printer, turn the pages over, and put them back into the printer in the correct orientation to print on the blank side. You may need to experiment a bit to find out what the correct arrangement is for your printer.
8) On the Print dialog, in the Page sides section, select the **Front sides / right pages** option from the Include drop-down box. Click **OK**.

If your printer can print double-sided automatically, choose **All pages**.

Printing envelopes, labels, business cards

Printing envelopes, labels, or business cards using Writer involves two steps: setup and printing.

For details of how to set these up, see Chapter 11, Using Mail Merge, in the *Writer Guide*. To print:

1) Choose **File > Print** from the Menu bar, or press *Ctrl+P*.
2) On the Print dialog, under *Range and copies*, choose **Pages** and type 1 in the box. Click **OK**.

Printing in black and white (on a color printer)

You may wish to print documents in black and white on a color printer. Several choices are available.

Change the printer settings to print in black and white or grayscale:

1) Choose **File > Print**, or press *Ctrl+P*, to open the Print dialog.

2) Click **Properties** to open the Properties dialog for the printer. The available choices vary from one printer to another, but you should find options for the Color settings. See your printer's help or user manual for more information.

3) The choices for color might include *black and white* or *grayscale*. Choose the required setting.

4) Click **OK** to confirm your choice and return to the Print dialog,

5) Click **OK** to print the document.

 Tip

Grayscale is better if you have any graphics in the document.

Change the LibreOffice settings to print all color text and graphics as grayscale:

1) Choose **Tools > Options > LibreOffice > Print**.

2) Select the **Convert colors to grayscale** option. Click **OK** to save the change.

3) Open the Print dialog (**File > Print**), or press *Ctrl+P*.

4) Click **OK** to print the document.

Change the LibreOffice Writer (or Calc, Impress, Draw) settings to print all color text as black, and all graphics as grayscale:

1) Choose **Tools > Options > LibreOffice Writer > Print**.

2) Under *Contents*, select the **Print text in black** option. Click **OK** to save the change.

3) Open the Print dialog (**File > Print**), or press *Ctrl+P*.

4) Click **OK** to print the document.

Previewing pages/sheets before printing

You can use the previewing options in Writer and Calc to view the document as it will be printed. Different viewing options are available.

Writer

The normal page view in Writer shows you what each page will look like when printed and you can edit the pages in that view. If you are designing a document to be printed double-sided, you may want to see what facing pages look like. Writer provides two ways to do this:

- View Layout (editable view): use the Facing Pages (Book view) button on the status bar.

- Print Preview (read-only view).

To use Print Preview:

1) Choose **File > Print Preview**, click the **Print Preview** button ( ) on the Standard toolbar or press *Ctrl+Shift+O*.

Writer now displays the **Print Preview** toolbar instead of the Formatting toolbar.

Figure 304: Print Preview toolbar (Writer)

2) Select the required preview icon: **Two Pages** (⊟⊟), **Multiple Pages** (⊞⊞ ▾) or **Book Preview** (⊟⊟).

3) To print the document from this view, click the **Print** icon (🖨) to open the Print dialog. Choose the print options and click the **OK** button.

Calc

To preview the sheets in Calc before printing:

1) Choose **File > Print Preview**.

The Calc window now displays the **Print Preview** toolbar instead of the Formatting toolbar.

Figure 305: Print Preview toolbar (Calc)

2) To print the document from this view, click the **Print** icon (🖨) to open the Print dialog.

3) Choose the print options and click the **Print button**.

Exporting to PDF

LibreOffice can export documents to PDF (Portable Document Format). This industry-standard file format is ideal for sending the file to someone else to view using Adobe Reader or other PDF viewers.

 Warning

> A document in PDF format is not protected against contents tampering or editing by default. The PDF document contents can be edited by specialized software tools, including LibreOffice Draw.

The process and dialogs are the same for Writer, Calc, Impress, and Draw, with a few minor differences mentioned in this section.

 Tip

> Unlike **Save As**, the **Export** command writes a copy of the current document in a new file with the chosen format, but keeps the current document and format open in your session.

Quick export to PDF

Click the **Export Directly as PDF** icon (📄) to export the entire document using the PDF settings you most recently selected on the PDF Options dialog (see below). You are asked to enter the file name and location for the PDF file, but you do not get a chance to choose a page range, the image compression, or other options.

Controlling PDF content and quality

For more control over the content and quality of the resulting PDF, use **File > Export as PDF**. The PDF Options dialog opens. This dialog has six pages (General, Initial View, User Interface, Links, Security, and Digital Signatures). Select the appropriate settings, and then click **Export.** Then you are asked to enter the location and file name of the PDF to be created, and click **Save** to export the file.

 Note

> Another choice is to use **File > Export**. This opens the Export dialog. Select the PDF file format, file name and location and click **Export**. This then opens the PDF Options dialog. Click **Export** when all the selections have been made.

General page of PDF Options dialog

On the *General* page (Figure 308), you can choose which pages to include in the PDF, the type of compression to use for images (which affects the quality of images in the PDF), and other options.

Figure 306: General page of PDF Options dialog

Range section
- **All**: Exports the entire document to PDF.
- **Pages**: To export a range of pages, use the format **3-6** (pages 3 to 6). To export single pages, use the format **7;9;11** (pages 7, 9 and 11). You can also export a combination of page ranges and single pages, by using a format like **3-6;8;10;12**.
- **Selection**: Exports all the selected material.

Images section
- **Lossless compression**: Images are stored without any loss of quality. Tends to make large files when used with photographs. Recommended for other kinds of images or graphics.
- **JPEG compression**: Allows for varying degrees of quality. A setting of 90% works well with photographs (small file size, little perceptible loss of quality).
- **Reduce image resolution**: Lower DPI (dots per inch) images have lower quality. For viewing on a computer screen, generally a resolution of 72dpi (for Windows) or 96dpi

(GNU/Linux) is sufficient, while for printing it is generally preferable to use at least 300 or 600dpi, depending on the capability of the printer. Higher DPI settings greatly increase the size of the exported file.

 Note

EPS (Encapsulated PostScript) images with embedded previews are exported only as previews. EPS images without embedded previews are exported as empty placeholders.

Watermark section
- **Sign with Watermark:** When this option is selected, a transparent overlay of the text you enter into the **Watermark Text** box will appear on each page of the PDF.

General section
- **Hybrid PDF (embed ODF file)**: Use this setting to export the document as a PDF file containing two file formats: PDF and ODF. In PDF viewers it behaves like a normal PDF file, and it remains fully editable in LibreOffice.

- **Archive PDF/A-1a (ISO 19005-1)**: PDF/A is an ISO standard for long-term preservation of documents, by embedding all the information necessary for faithful reproduction (such as fonts) while forbidding other elements (including forms, security, and encryption). PDF tags are written. If you select PDF/A-1a, the forbidden elements are grayed-out (not available).

- **Tagged PDF**: Tagged PDF contains information about the structure of the document's contents. This can help to display the document on devices with different screens, and when using screen reader software. Some tags that are exported are table of contents, hyperlinks, and controls. This option can increase file sizes significantly.

- **Create PDF form – Submit format:** Choose the format of submitting forms from within the PDF file. This setting overrides the control's URL property that you set in the document. There is only one common setting valid for the whole PDF document: PDF (sends the whole document), FDF (sends the control contents), HTML, and XML. Most often you will choose the PDF format.

  Allow duplicate field names: If enabled, the same field name can be used for multiple fields in the generated PDF file. With this option enabled, you can enter data in the first occurrence of the named field in the PDF document and all fields with the same name will carry your entry. If disabled, field names will be exported using generated unique names.

- **Export bookmarks**: Exports headings in Writer documents, and page or slide names in Impress and Draw documents, as "bookmarks" (a table of contents list displayed by most PDF viewers, including Adobe Reader).

- **Export comments**: Exports comments as PDF notes. You may not want this!

- **Export automatically inserted blank pages**: If selected, automatically inserted blank pages are exported to the PDF. This is best if you are printing the PDF double-sided. For example, books usually have chapters set to always start on an odd-numbered (right-hand) page. When the previous chapter ends on an odd page, LibreOffice inserts a blank page between the two odd pages. This option controls whether to export that blank page.

- **View PDF after export:** Your default PDF viewer will open and display the newly exported PDF.

Initial View page of PDF Options dialog

On the *Initial View* page (Figure 307), you can choose how the PDF opens by default in a PDF viewer. The selections should be self-explanatory.

If you have Complex Text Layout enabled (in **Tools > Options > Language settings > Languages**), an additional selection is available under *Continuous facing*: **First page is left** (normally, the first page is on the right when using the *Continuous facing* option).

Figure 307: Initial View page of PDF Options dialog

User Interface page of PDF Options dialog

On the *User Interface* page (Figure 308), you can choose more settings to control how a PDF viewer displays the file. Some of these choices are particularly useful when you are creating a PDF to be used as a presentation or a kiosk-type display.

Figure 308: User Interface page of the PDF Options dialog

Window options section
- **Resize window to initial page.** Causes the PDF viewer window to resize to fit the first page of the PDF.
- **Center window on screen.** Causes the PDF viewer window to be centered on the computer screen.
- **Open in full screen mode.** Causes the PDF viewer to open full-screen instead of in a smaller window.
- **Display document title.** Causes the PDF viewer to display the document's title in the title bar.

User interface options section
- **Hide menubar.** Causes the PDF viewer to hide the menu bar.
- **Hide toolbar.** Causes the PDF viewer to hide the toolbar.
- **Hide window controls.** Causes the PDF viewer to hide other window controls.

Transitions

In Impress, displays slide transition effects as their respective PDF effects.

Bookmarks

Select how many heading levels are displayed as bookmarks, if *Export bookmarks* is selected on the General page.

Links page of PDF Options dialog

On the Links page (Figure 309), you can choose how links are exported to PDF.

Figure 309: Links page of PDF Options dialog

Export bookmarks as named destinations

If you have defined Writer bookmarks, Impress or Draw slide names, or Calc sheet names, this option exports them as "named destinations" to which Web pages and PDF documents can link.

Convert document references to PDF targets

If you have defined links to other documents with OpenDocument extensions (such as .odt, .ods, and .odp), this option converts the files' extensions to .pdf in the exported PDF document.

Export URLs relative to file system

If you have defined relative links in a document, this option exports those links to the PDF.

Cross-document links

Defines the behavior of links clicked in PDF files. Select one among the following alternatives:

- **Default mode**: The PDF links will be handled as specified in your operating system.

- **Open with PDF reader application**: Use the same application used to display the PDF document to open linked PDF documents.

- **Open with Internet browser**: Use the default Internet browser to display linked PDF documents.

Security page of PDF Options dialog

PDF export includes options to encrypt the PDF (so that it cannot be opened without a password) and apply some digital rights management (DRM) features.

- With an *open password* set, the PDF can only be opened with the password. Once opened, there are no restrictions on what the user can do with the document (for example, print, copy, or change it).

- With a *permissions password set*, the PDF can be opened by anyone, but its permissions can be restricted. See Figure 310. After you set a password for permissions, the other choices on the Security page become available.

- With *both* the open password and permission password set, the PDF can only be opened with the correct password, and its permissions can be restricted.

 Note

Permissions settings are effective only if the user's PDF viewer respects the settings.

Figure 310: Security page of PDF Options dialog

Figure 311 shows the pop-up dialog displayed when you click the **Set passwords** button on the Security page of the PDF Options dialog.

When you have set all the options you require, click on **Export** to open the Export dialog, where you can set the file name and the save location.

Figure 311: Setting a password to encrypt a PDF

Digital Signatures page of PDF Options dialog

This page contains the options related to exporting a digitally signed PDF.

Digital signatures are used to ensure that the PDF was really created by the original author (that is, you), and that the document has not been modified since it was signed.

The signed PDF export uses the keys and X.509 certificates already stored in your default key store location or on a smartcard. The key store to be used can be selected under **Tools > Options > LibreOffice > Security > Certificate Path**. When using a smartcard, it must already be configured for use by your key store. This is usually done during installation of the smartcard software. Details about using these features is outside the scope of this chapter.

Figure 312: Digital signature page for PDF

- **Use this certificate to digitally sign PDF documents:** Click **Select** to open the Select Certificate dialog, where all certificates found in your selected key store are displayed. If the key store is protected by a password, you are prompted for it. When using a smartcard that is protected by a PIN, you are also prompted for that.

  Select the certificate to use for digitally signing the exported PDF, then click **OK**.

  All other fields on the Digital Signatures tab are accessible only after a certificate has been selected.

- **Certificate password:** Enter the password used for protecting the private key associated with the selected certificate. Usually this is the key store password. If the key store password has already been entered in the Select Certificate dialog, the key store may already be unlocked and not require the password again.

When using a smartcard, enter the PIN here. Some smartcard software will prompt you for the PIN again before signing.

- **Location, Contact information, Reason:** Optionally enter additional information about the digital signature that will be applied to the PDF. This information will be embedded in the appropriate PDF fields and will be visible to anyone viewing the PDF. Each or all of the three fields may be left blank.

- **Time Stamp Authority:** Optionally select a Time Stamping Authority (TSA) URL. During the PDF signing process, the TSA will be used to obtain a digitally signed timestamp that is then embedded in the signature. Anyone viewing the PDF can use this timestamp to verify when the document was signed.

  The list of TSA URLs that can be selected is maintained under **Tools > Options > LibreOffice > Security > TSAs**. If no TSA URL is selected (the default), the signature will not be timestamped, but will use the current time from your local computer.

Exporting to EPUB format

EPUB format is becoming popular since mobile devices such as smartphones, tablets and e-readers appeared on the market. The EPUB format is implemented as an archive file consisting of HTML files carrying the content, along with images and other supporting files.

Quick export to EPUB

Choose menu **File > Export > Export Directly as EPUB** to export the entire document using the EPUB settings you most recently selected on the EPUB Options dialog (see below). You are asked to enter the file name and location for the PDF file, but you do not get a chance to select other options.

Export to EPUB

For more control over the content and quality of the resulting EPUB file, use **File > Export as EPUB**. The EPUB Export dialog opens (Figure 313).

Figure 313: EPUB Export

The EPUB Export dialog is rather simple:

- **Version**: choose the EPUB version for the exported file. Values are *EPUB 2.0* and *EPUB 3.0*.

- **Split method**: Select the method to split the document for pagination. The heading method splits the pages by Heading 1 or Chapters style and the page method tries to honor the pagination of the original document.

Exporting to other formats

LibreOffice uses the term "export" for some file operations involving a change of file type. If you cannot find what you want under **File > Save As**, look under **File > Export** as well.

LibreOffice can export files to XHTML. In addition, Draw and Impress can export to Adobe Flash (SWF) and a range of image formats.

To export to one of these formats, choose **File > Export**. On the Export dialog, specify a file name for the exported document, then select the required format in the *File format* list and click the **Export** button.

E-mailing documents

LibreOffice provides several ways to send documents quickly and easily as e-mail attachments in one of three formats: OpenDocument (LibreOffice's default format), Microsoft Office formats, or PDF.

 Note

> With Linux operating system, documents can only be sent from the LibreOffice menu if a mail program has been set up in **Tools > Options > Internet > E-mail.** With Windows operating system, LibreOffice uses the e-mail program defined in the Windows Standard Applications.

To send the current document in OpenDocument format:

1) Choose **File > Send > Document as E-mail**. LibreOffice opens your default e-mail program. The document is attached.

2) In your e-mail program, enter the recipient, subject, and any text you want to add, then send the e-mail.

File > Send > E-mail as OpenDocument [Text, **Spreadsheet**, or **Presentation]** has the same effect.

If you choose **E-mail as Microsoft [Word**, **Excel**, or **PowerPoint]**, LibreOffice first creates a file in one of those formats and then opens your e-mail program with the file attached.

Similarly, if you choose **E-mail as PDF**, LibreOffice first creates a PDF using your default PDF settings (as when using the **Export Directly as PDF** toolbar button) and then opens your email program with the PDF file attached.

E-mailing a document to several recipients

To e-mail a document to several recipients, you can use the features in your e-mail program or you can use LibreOffice's mail merge facilities to extract email addresses from an address book.

You can use LibreOffice's mail merge to send e-mail in two ways:

• Use the Mail Merge Wizard to create the document and send it. See Chapter 11, Using Mail Merge, in the *Writer Guide* for details.

• Create the document in Writer without using the Wizard, then use the Wizard to send it. This method is described here.

To use the Mail Merge Wizard to send a previously-created Writer document:

1) Click **Tools > Mail Merge Wizard**. On the first page of the wizard, select **Use the current document** and click **Next**.

Figure 314: Select starting document

2) On the second page, select **E-mail message** and click **Next**.

Figure 315: Select document type

3) On the third page, click the **Select Address List** button. Select the required address list (even if only one is shown) and then click **OK**. (If the address list you need is not shown here, you can click **Add** to find it and add it to the list.)

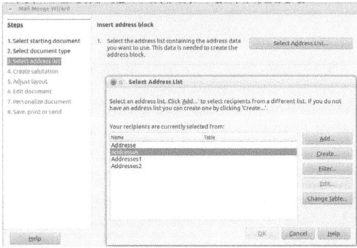

Figure 316: Selecting an address list

4) Back on the Select address list page, click **Next**. On the Create salutation page, deselect **This document should contain a salutation**.

Figure 317: Deselecting a salutation

5) In the left-hand list, click **8. Save, print or send**. LibreOffice displays a "Creating documents" message and then displays the *Save, print or send* page of the Wizard.

6) Select **Send merged document as E-Mail**. The lower part of the page changes to show e-mail settings choices. See Figure 318.

7) Type a subject for your email and click **Send documents**. LibreOffice sends the e-mails.

Figure 318: Sending a document as an email message

Digital signing of documents

To sign a document digitally, you need a personal key, also known as a *certificate*. A personal key is stored on your computer as a combination of a private key, which must be kept secret, and a public key, which you add to your documents when you sign them. You can get a certificate from a certification authority, which may be a private company or a governmental institution.

When you apply a digital signature to a document, a kind of checksum is computed from the document's content plus your personal key. The checksum and your public key are stored together with the document.

When someone later opens the document on any computer with a recent version of LibreOffice, the program will compute the checksum again and compare it with the stored checksum. If both are the same, the program will signal that you see the original, unchanged document. In addition, the program can show you the public key information from the certificate. You can compare the public key with the public key that is published on the web site of the certificate authority. Whenever someone changes something in the document, this change breaks the digital signature.

On Windows operating systems, the Windows features of validating a signature are used. On Solaris and Linux systems, files that are supplied by Thunderbird, Mozilla or Firefox are used. For a more detailed description of how to get and manage a certificate, and signature validation, see "About Digital Signatures" in the LibreOffice Help.

To sign a document:

1) Choose **File > Digital Signatures**. If you have set LibreOffice to warn you when the document contains comments (see "Removing personal data" below), you may see a message box asking whether you want to want to continue signing the document.

2) If you have not saved the document since the last change, a message box appears. Click **Yes** to save the file.

3) The Digital Signatures dialog opens. Click **Sign Document** to add a public key to the document.

4) In the Select Certificate dialog, select your certificate and click **OK** to return to the Digital Signatures dialog.

5) The certificate used is displayed in the dialog with an icon next to its name.

   This icon indicates the status of the digital signature.

   – An icon with a red seal (🔖) indicates that the document was signed and the certificate was validated.

   – An icon with a yellow caution triangle overlaying the red seal (🔖) indicates that the document is signed but that the certificate could not be validated.

   – An icon of a yellow caution triangle by itself (⚠) indicates an invalid digital signature.

6) Click **Close** to apply the digital signature.

A signed document shows an icon in the status bar. You can double-click the icon to view the certificate. More than one signature can be added to a document.

Signing multiple times with same signature

In the past, LibreOffice prohibited creating multiple signatures by the same author on a document, because there was no semantic meaning of signing the same document multiple times. LibreOffice now provides a signature description, so multiple signatures from the same author are now allowed, because each signature can have a different meaning.

When you select **File > Digital Signatures**, the dialog (Figure 319) lists existing signatures together with their description (if they have any):

Figure 319: Signatures of the document

When you click on the **Sign Document** button, the dialog (Figure 320) for certificate selection now also asks for an optional description.

Changing the value of an existing description invalidates the signature.

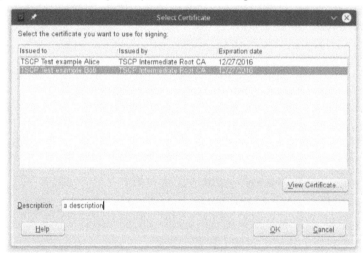

Figure 320: Signatures can now have a description

Removing personal data

You may wish to ensure that personal data, versions, notes, hidden information, or recorded changes are removed from files before you send them to other people or create PDFs from them.

In **Tools > Options > LibreOffice > Security > Options**, you can set LibreOffice to remind (warn) you when files contain certain information and remove personal information automatically on saving.

To remove personal and some other data from a file, go to **File > Properties**. On the *General* tab, uncheck **Apply user data** and then click the **Reset Properties** button. This removes any names in the created and modified fields, deletes the modification and printing dates, and resets the editing time to zero, the creation date to the current date and time, and the version number to 1.

To remove version information, either go to **File > Versions**, select the versions from the list and click **Delete;** or use **File > Save As** and save the file with a different name.

Getting Started Guide

Chapter 11
Graphics, Gallery, Fontwork

Introduction

You can add graphic and image files, including photos, drawings, and scanned images, to LibreOffice documents. LibreOffice can import various vector (line drawing) and raster (bitmap) file formats. The most commonly used graphic formats are GIF, JPG, PNG, and BMP. See Appendix B for a full list of the graphic formats LibreOffice can import.

Graphics in LibreOffice are of three basic types:

- Image files, such as photos, drawings, PDF Documents, and scanned images
- Diagrams created using LibreOffice's drawing tools
- Charts created using LibreOffice's Chart component

This chapter covers images and diagrams.

More detailed descriptions on working with drawing tools can be found in the *Draw Guide* and *Impress Guide*. Instructions on how to create charts are given in the *Calc Guide*.

Adding images to a document

Images can be added to a document in several ways: by inserting an image file, directly from a graphics program or a scanner, by dragging them from the clip art internal gallery, or by copying and pasting from a source being viewed on your computer.

Inserting an image file

When the image is in a file stored on the computer, you can insert it into a LibreOffice document using either of the following methods.

Drag and drop

1) Open a file browser window and locate the image you want to insert.
2) Drag the image into the LibreOffice document and drop it where you want it to appear. A faint vertical line marks where the image will be dropped.

This method embeds (saves a copy of) the image file in the document. To link the file instead of embedding it, hold down the *Ctrl+Shift* keys while dragging the image.

Insert Image dialog

1) Click in the LibreOffice document where you want the image to appear.
2) Choose **Insert > Image** from the menu bar.
3) On the Insert Image dialog, navigate to the file to be inserted, and select it.
4) At the bottom of the dialog (Figure 321) a **Link option**. See page 322 for the use of **Link**.
5) Click **Open**.

 Note

> If you choose the **Link** option, a message box appears when you click **Open**. It asks if you want to embed the graphic instead. Choose **Keep Link** if you want the link, or **Embed Graphic** if you do not. To prevent this message from appearing again, deselect the option **Ask when linking a graphic** at the bottom of the message.

Figure 321: Insert Image dialog

Linking an image file

If the **Link** option in the Insert picture dialog is selected, LibreOffice creates a link to the file containing the image instead of saving a copy of the image in the document. The result is that the image is displayed in the document, but when the document is saved, it contains only a reference to the image file, not the image itself. The document and the image remain as two separate files, and they are merged together only when you open the document again.

Linking an image has two advantages and one disadvantage:

- Advantage – Linking can reduce the size of the document when it is saved, because the image file itself is not included. File size is usually not a problem on a modern computer with a reasonable amount of memory, unless the document includes many large graphics files; LibreOffice can handle quite large files.

- Advantage – You can modify the image file separately without changing the document because the link to the file remains valid, and the modified image will appear when you next open the document. This can be a big advantage if you (or someone else, perhaps a graphic artist) is updating images.

- Disadvantage – If you send the document to someone else, or move it to a different computer, you must also send the image files, or the receiver will not be able to see the linked images. You need to keep track of the location of the images and make sure the recipient knows where to put them on another machine, so that the document can find them. For example, you might keep images in a subfolder named Images (under the folder containing the document); the recipient of the file needs to put the images in a subfolder with the same name and in the same place relative to the document.

 Note

When inserting the same image several times in the document, it would appear beneficial to link rather than embed; however, this is not necessary as LibreOffice embeds only one copy of the image file in the document.

Embedding linked images

If you originally linked the images, you can easily embed one or more of them later if you wish. To do so:

1) Open the document in LibreOffice and choose **Edit > Links to External Files**.
2) The Edit Links dialog (Figure 322) shows all the linked files. In the *Source file* list, select the files you want to change from linked to embedded.
3) Click the **Break Link** button.
4) Click the **Close** button.
5) Save the document.

Figure 322: The Edit Links dialog

 Note

> Going the other way, from embedded to linked, is not so easy—you must replace the images, one at a time, selecting the **Link** option when you do so.

Inserting an image from the clipboard

Using the clipboard, you can copy images into a LibreOffice document from another LibreOffice document and from other programs. To do this:

1) Open both the source document and the target document.
2) In the source document, select the image to be copied.
3) Click once on the selected image and press *Ctrl+C* to copy the image to the clipboard.
4) Switch to the target document.
5) Click to place the cursor where the graphic is to be inserted.
6) Press *Ctrl+V* to insert the image.

 Caution

> If the application from which the graphic was copied is closed before the graphic is pasted into the target, the image stored on the clipboard could be lost.

Inserting an image using a scanner

If a scanner is connected to your computer, LibreOffice can call the scanning application and insert the scanned item into the LibreOffice document as an image. To start this procedure, and choose **Insert > Media > Scan > Select Source**. Then place the cursor where you want the graphic to be inserted, and choose **Insert > Media > Scan > Request**.

Although this practice is quick and easy, it is unlikely to result in a high-quality image of the correct size. You may get better results by passing scanned material into a graphics program and cleaning it up there before inserting the resulting image into LibreOffice.

Inserting an image from the Gallery

The Gallery (Figure 323) provides a convenient way to group reusable objects such as graphics and sounds that you can insert into your documents. The Gallery is available in all components of LibreOffice. See "Managing the LibreOffice Gallery" on page 326. You can copy or link an object from the Gallery into a document.

To insert an object:

1) Click the **Gallery** icon in the Sidebar.
2) Select a theme.
3) Select an object with a single click.
4) Drag and drop the image into the document.

   You can also right-click on the object and choose **Insert**.

Figure 323: The Gallery in the Sidebar

To insert an object as a link:

1) Choose **Insert > Media > Gallery** and select a theme.
2) Select an object with a single click, then while pressing the *Shift* and *Ctrl* keys, drag and drop the object into the document.

Inserting an image as a background

To insert an image as the background to a page or paragraph:

1) Choose **Insert > Media > Gallery** and select a theme.

2) Select an object with a single click, right-click on the object, and choose **Insert as Background > Page** or **> Paragraph**.

Modifying, handling, and positioning graphics

LibreOffice provides many tools for cropping, resizing, modifying, filtering, and positioning graphics; wrapping text around graphics; and using graphics as backgrounds and watermarks. These tools are described in relevant chapters of the other guides. Some sophisticated adjustments of the graphics are best done in an image manipulation program and the results brought into LibreOffice, rather than using LibreOffice's built-in tools.

Exporting images

If you need to make complex adjustments to the image, or want to save the image for use in another document, you can export the image directly from your document. Right-click on the image to select it and open the context menu. Then choose **Save** to open the Image Export dialog. Depending on the original format of the image, LibreOffice will let you save the picture in many different formats. Give a name to the image, select the desired image format in the *File Type* filter list, and click **Save**. Before the image is finally saved another dialog (not shown) opens, where you can choose various image size and format options.

Compressing images

If you insert a large image in your document and resize it to fit into the layout of the page, the complete full size original image is stored in the document file to preserve its content, resulting in a large document file to store or send by mail.

If you can accept some loss of quality of the image rendering or want to resize it, you can compress or resize the image object to reduce its data volume while preserving its display in the page layout.

Figure 324: Compressing an image

Right-click to select the image and open the context menu. Then choose **Compress** to open the Compress Image dialog (Figure 324). Note that the **Calculate** button updates the image information on the dialog on each parameter set you change. Click **OK** to apply the compression settings. If the resulting image is not acceptable, press *Ctrl+Z* to undo and choose another compression setting. For more information, see the Help.

Managing the LibreOffice Gallery

Graphics in the Gallery are grouped by themes, such as Arrows, Diagrams, and People. You can create other groups or themes and add your own pictures or find extensions containing more graphics. Click on a theme to see its contents displayed in the Gallery window.

You can display the Gallery in *Icon View* (Figure 323) or *Detailed View* (Figure 325), and you can hide or show the Gallery by clicking on the Sidebar's *Hide* button.

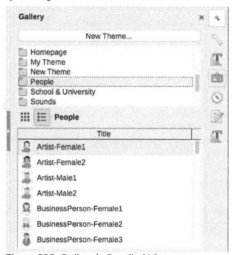

Figure 325: Gallery in Detailed View

 Note

In some installations, only the *My themes* theme is customizable, although new themes can be added as explained in "Adding a new theme to the Gallery" on page 327. The locked themes are easily recognizable by right-clicking on them; the only available option in the context menu is **Properties**.

Adding objects to the Gallery

You may wish to add to the My Theme folder in the Gallery any images that you use frequently, for example, a company logo. You can then easily insert these graphics into a document later.

1) Right-click on the My Theme folder and select **Properties** from the context menu.

2) In the theme's Properties dialog, click the *Files* tab (Figure 326).

Figure 326: Gallery Properties dialog

To add several files at once:

1) Click the **Find Files** button.

2) The *Select path* dialog (not shown) opens. You can enter the path for the file's directory in the *Path* text box, or you can navigate to locate the file's directory.

3) Click the **Select** button to start the search. A list of graphic files is then displayed in the Properties dialog. You can use the *File type* drop-down list to limit the files displayed.

4) To add all of the files shown in the list, click **Add All.** Otherwise, select the files to add and then click **Add** (hold down either the Shift key or the *Ctrl* key while clicking on the files).

To add a single file:

1) Click **Add** to open the Gallery dialog.

2) Use the navigation controls to locate the image to add to the theme. Select it and then click **Open** to add it to the theme.

3) Click **OK** on the Properties dialog to close it.

Deleting images from the Gallery

To delete an image from a theme:

1) Right-click on the name of the image file or its thumbnail in the Gallery.

2) Click **Delete** in the context menu. A message appears, asking if you want to delete this object. Click **Yes.**

 Note

Deleting the name of a file from the list in the Gallery does not delete the file from the hard disk or other location.

Adding a new theme to the Gallery

To add a new theme to the Gallery:

1) Click the **New Theme** button above the list of themes (Figure 325).

2) In the Properties of New Theme dialog, click the **General** tab and type a name for the new theme.

3) Click the **Files** tab and add images to the theme, as described earlier.

Deleting a theme from the Gallery

To delete a theme from the Gallery:

1) Go to **Insert > Media > Gallery.**

2) Select from the list of themes the theme you wish to delete.

3) Right-click on the theme, then click **Delete** on the context menu.

Location of the Gallery and the objects in it

Graphics and other objects shown in the Gallery can be located anywhere on your computer's hard disk, on a network drive, or other removable media. When you add graphics to the Gallery, the files are not moved or copied; the location of each new object is simply added as a reference.

In a workgroup, you may have access to a shared Gallery (where you cannot change the contents unless authorized to do so) and a user Gallery, where you can add, change, or delete objects.

The location of the user Gallery is specified in **Tools > Options > LibreOffice > Paths**. You can change this location, and you can copy your gallery files (SDV) to other computers.

Gallery contents provided with LibreOffice are stored in a different location. You cannot change this location.

 Note

> Gallery themes can be packed for distribution through the LibreOffice extensions framework. In that case, the location of the graphic files is determined by the extension settings. To get more gallery themes, visit the LibreOffice extensions website at http://extensions.libreoffice.org.

Creating an image map

An image map defines areas of an image (called *hotspots*) with hyperlinks to web addresses, other files on the computer, or parts of the same document. Hotspots are the graphic equivalent of text hyperlinks (described in Chapter 12). Clicking on a hotspot causes LibreOffice to open the linked page in the appropriate program (for example, the default browser for an HTML page; LibreOffice Calc for an ODS file; a PDF viewer for a PDF file). You can create hotspots of various shapes and include several hotspots in the same image.

To use the image map editor:

1) In your LibreOffice document, click on the picture in which you want to create the hotspots.
2) Choose **Edit > ImageMap** from the menu bar. The ImageMap Editor (Figure 327) opens.
3) Select the hotspot drawing shape from the toolbar and draw on the image.
4) Use the fields in the dialog (described below) to define the hotspots and links necessary.
5) Click the **Apply** icon ✅ to apply the settings.
6) When done, click the **Save** icon 🖫 to save the image map to a file, then click the **X** in the upper right corner to close the dialog.

The main part of the dialog shows the image on which the hotspots are defined. A hotspot is identified by a line indicating its shape.

The toolbar at the top of the dialog contains the following tools:

- **Apply** button: click this button to apply the changes.
- **Load, Save,** and **Select** icons.
- Tools for drawing a hotspot shape: these tools work in exactly the same way as the corresponding tools in the Drawing toolbar.
- **Edit**, **Move**, **Insert**, **Delete Points**: advanced editing tools to manipulate the shape of a polygon hotspot. Choose the Edit Points tool to activate the other tools.
- **Active** icon: toggles the status of a selected hotspot between active and inactive.
- **Macro**: associates a macro with the hotspot instead of just associating a hyperlink.
- **Properties**: sets the hyperlink properties and adds the Name attribute to the hyperlink.

Figure 327: The dialog to create or edit an image map

Below the toolbar, specify for the selected hotspot:

- **Address:** the address pointed to by the hyperlink. You can also point to an anchor in a document; to do this, write the address in this format: file:///<path>/document_name#anchor_name

- **Text:** type the text that you want to be displayed when the mouse pointer is moved over the hotspot.

- **Frame:** where the target of the hyperlink will open: pick among _blank (opens in a new browser window), _self (opens in the active browser window), _top or _parent.

 Tip

The value _self for the target frame will usually work just fine. It is therefore not recommended to use the other choices unless absolutely necessary.

Using LibreOffice's drawing tools

You can use LibreOffice's drawing tools to create graphics such as simple diagrams using rectangles, circles, lines, text, and other predefined shapes. You can also group several drawing objects to make sure they maintain their relative position and proportion.

You can place the drawing objects directly on a page in your document, or you can insert them into a frame.

You can also use the drawing tools to annotate photographs, screen captures, or other illustrations produced by other programs, but this is not recommended because:

- You cannot include images in a group with drawing objects, so they may not remain aligned in your document.

- If you convert a document to another format, such as HTML, the drawing objects and the graphics will not remain associated; they are saved separately.

In general, if you need to create complex drawings, it is recommended to use LibreOffice Draw, which includes many more features such as layers, styles, and so on.

Creating drawing objects

To begin using the drawing tools, display the Drawing toolbar (Figure 328) by clicking **View > Toolbars > Drawing** or by clicking on the **Show Draw Functions** icon on the standard toolbar.

> ### 💡 Tip
>
> If you are planning to use the drawing tools repeatedly, you can tear off (undock) this toolbar and move it to a convenient place it as a floating toolbar in the window.

1	Select	**7**	Rectangle	**13**	Right Triangle	**19**	Flowchart
2	Insert Line	**8**	Rectangle, Rounded	**14**	Insert Basic Shapes	**20**	Callouts
3	Lines and Arrows	**9**	Square	**15**	Symbol	**21**	Insert Text Box
4	Curve, Freehand	**10**	Ellipse	**16**	Arrow	**22**	Fontwork
5	Curve, Bézier	**11**	Circle	**17**	Star	**23**	Points
6	Polygon	**12**	Isosceles Triangle	**18**	Callout	**24**	Toggle extrusion

Figure 328: The Drawing Toolbar

To use a drawing tool:

1) Click in the document where you want the drawing to be anchored. You can change the anchor later, if necessary.

2) Choose the tool from the Drawing toolbar (Figure 328). The mouse pointer changes to a drawing-functions pointer and the normal Formatting Toolbar changes to Drawing Object Properties toolbar (Figure 329).

3) Move the cross-hair pointer to the place in the document where you want the graphic to appear and then click and drag to create the drawing object. Release the mouse button. The selected drawing function remains active, so that you can draw another object of the same type.

4) To cancel the selected drawing function, press the *Esc* key or click on the **Select** icon (the arrow) on the Drawing toolbar.

5) You can now change the properties (fill color, line type and weight, anchoring, and others) of the drawing object using either the Drawing Object Properties toolbar (Figure 329) or the choices and dialogs reached by right-clicking on the drawing object.

Setting or changing properties for drawing objects

To set the properties for a drawing object before you draw it:

1) On the Drawing toolbar (Figure 328), click the **Select** tool.

2) On the Drawing Object Properties toolbar (Figure 329), click on the icon for each property and select the value you want for that property.

3) For more control, or to define new attributes, you can click on the **Area** or **Line** icons on the toolbar to display detailed dialogs.

1	Line Color	8	Wrap Off	15	Align	22	Group
2	Arrow Style	9	Page Wrap	16	Bring to Front	23	Enter Group
3	Line Style	10	Optimal Page Wrap	17	Forward One	24	Exit Group
4	Line Width	11	Wrap Left	18	Back One	25	Ungroup
5	Area Style / Filling	12	Wrap Right	19	Send to Back	26	Insert Caption
6	Fill Color	13	Wrap Through	20	To Foreground		
7	Anchor	14	Rotate	21	To Background		

Figure 329: Drawing Object Properties toolbar

The default you set applies to the current document and session. It is not retained when you close the document or close Writer, and it does not apply to any other document you open. The defaults apply to all the drawing objects except text objects.

To change the properties for an existing drawing object:

1) Select the object.

2) Continue as described above.

You can also specify the position and size, rotation, and slant and corner radius properties of the drawing object:

1) Right-click on the drawing object and then choose **Position and Size** from the context menu. The Position and Size dialog is displayed.

2) Choose any properties, as required.

Resizing a drawing object

An object is resized in a similar way to an image. Select the object, click on one of the eight handles around it and drag it to its new size. The object will be scaled up or down.

When you grab the corner handle of an object and drag it, LibreOffice will resize proportionately. If you also press the *Shift* key, the resizing will not keep object proportions. Conversely, if you grab one of the edges, LibreOffice will scale disproportionately in the direction perpendicular to the edge; if you also press the *Shift* key, LibreOffice will scale proportionately.

For more sophisticated control of the size of the object, choose **Format > Frame and Object > Properties** from the Menu bar. Use the **Type** tab to set the position and size independently. If the **Keep ratio** option is selected, then the two dimensions change so that the proportion is maintained, resulting in a scaled resizing.

Grouping drawing objects

Grouping drawing objects makes it easier to handle several objects as a single entity, while preserving their relative sizes and positions.

To group drawing objects:

1) Select one object, then hold down the *Shift* key and select the others you want to include in the group. The bounding box expands to include all the selected objects.

2) With the objects selected, hover the mouse pointer over one of the objects and choose **Format > Group > Group** from the Menu bar, or click the Group icon on the Drawing Object Properties toolbar, or right-click and choose **Group > Group** from the pop-up menu.

 Note

You cannot include an embedded or linked graphic in a group with drawing objects.

Using Fontwork

With Fontwork you can create graphical text art objects to make your work more attractive. There are many different settings for text art objects (line, area, position, size, and more), so you have a large choice.

Fontwork is available with each component of LibreOffice, but you will notice small differences in the way that each component displays it.

Creating a Fontwork object

1) On the Fontwork toolbar (**View > Toolbars > Fontwork**) or the Drawing toolbar (**View > Toolbars > Drawing**), click the Fontwork Gallery icon , or choose **Insert > Media > FontWork Gallery**.

2) In the Fontwork Gallery (Figure 330), select a Fontwork style, then click **OK**. The Fontwork object will appear in your document. Notice the colored squares around the edge (indicating that the object is selected) and the yellow dot; these are discussed in "Moving and resizing Fontwork objects" on page 336.

Figure 330: The Fontwork Gallery

3) Double-click the object to edit the Fontwork text (see Figure 331). Select the text and type your own text in place of the black *Fontwork* text that appears over the object.

Figure 331: Editing Fontwork text

4) Click anywhere in a free space or press *Esc* to apply your changes.

Editing a Fontwork object

Now that the Fontwork object is created, you can edit some of its attributes. To do this, you can use the Fontwork toolbar, the Formatting toolbar, or menu options as described in this section. If the selected Fontwork object is a 3-D object, you can also use the 3D-Settings toolbar.

Using the Fontwork toolbar

Make sure that the Fontwork toolbar, shown in Figure 332, is visible. If you do not see it, go to **View > Toolbars > Fontwork**. Click on the different icons to edit Fontwork objects.

Figure 332: The floating Fontwork toolbar

Fontwork Shape: Edits the shape of the selected object. You can choose from a palette of shapes.

Figure 333: Fontwork toolbar showing palette of shapes

Fontwork Same Letter Heights: Changes the height of characters in the object. Toggles between normal height (some characters taller than others, for example capital letters, d, h, l and others) and all letters the same height.

Figure 334: Left: normal letters; right: same letter heights

Fontwork Alignment: Changes the alignment of characters. Choices are left align, center, right align, word justify, and stretch justify. The effects of the text alignment can only be seen if the text spans over two or more lines. In the stretch justify mode, all the lines are filled completely.

Fontwork Character Spacing: Changes the character spacing and kerning in the object. Select from the choices in the drop-down list.

Using the Formatting toolbar

Now let us go further and customize the Fontwork object with several more attributes.

Click on the Fontwork object. The Formatting toolbar changes to The Drawing Object Properties toolbar (Figure 329) when you use Fontwork in Writer.)

The Formatting toolbar provides a large choice of options for customizing your object. These choices are the same as the ones for other drawing objects. For more information, see the *Draw Guide*.

Line options

Line icon: Opens a dialog with three tabs: **Line**, **Line Styles**, **Arrow Styles**. Use the **Line** tab to edit the most common properties of the line around the selected Fontwork object, by choosing from previously-defined attributes including line style, line color, and arrow styles. Use the **Lines Styles** and **Arrow Styles** tabs to edit the properties of line and arrow styles, and define new styles.

Arrow Style icon: Choose from the different arrow styles.

Line Style box: Choose from the available line styles.

Line Width box: Set the width of the line.

Line Color box: Select the color of the line.

Area options

Area icon: Opens a dialog with seven tabs: **Area, Shadow, Transparency, Colors, Gradients, Hatching, Bitmaps**.

- **Area** tab: Choose from the predefined list a color, bitmap, gradient or hatching pattern to fill the selected object.
- **Shadow** tab: Set the shadow properties of the selected object.
- **Transparency** tab: Set the transparency properties of the selected object.
- **Colors** tab: Modify the available colors or add new ones to appear on the Area tab.
- **Gradients** tab: Modify the available gradients or add new ones to appear on the Area tab.
- **Hatching** tab: Modify the available hatching patterns or add new ones to appear on the Area tab.

- **Bitmaps** tab: Create simple bitmap patterns and import bitmaps, to make them available on the Area tab.

Area Style / Filling boxes: Select the type of the fill of the selected object. For more detailed settings, use the Area icon.

Positioning options

Rotate icon: Rotate the selected object manually using the mouse to drag the object.

To Foreground icon: Move the selected object in front of the text.

To Background icon: Move the selected object behind the text.

Alignment icon: Modify the alignment of the selected objects.

Bring to front icon: Move the selected object in front of the others.

Send to back icon: Move the selected object behind the others.

Change Anchor icon: Choose between anchoring options:

- To Page—The object keeps the same position in relation to the page margins. It does not move as you add or delete text.
- To Paragraph—The object is associated with a paragraph and moves with the paragraph. It may be placed in the margin or another location.
- To Character—The object is associated with a character but is not in the text sequence. It moves with the paragraph but may be placed in the margin or another location. This method resembles anchoring to a paragraph.
- As Character—The object is placed in the document like any character and moves with the paragraph as you add or delete text before the object.

Ungroup icon: Ungroup a selection of grouped objects, so that they can be managed individually.

Group icon: Group the selected objects, so you can manage them as a single object.

Using menu options

You can use some the choices on the **Format** menu to anchor, align, arrange, and group selected Fontwork objects, wrap text around them, and flip them horizontally and vertically.

You can also right-click on a Fontwork object and choose many of the same options from the pop-up menu. The pop-up menu also provides quick access to the Line, Area, Text, and Position and Size dialogs. The Text dialog offers only a few options for Fontwork objects and is not discussed here. On the Position and Size dialog, you can enter precise values for size and position. For more information on all of these menu options, see the *Draw Guide*.

Using the 3D-Settings toolbar

If the selected Fontwork object is a 3-D object, you can also use the options on the 3D-Settings toolbar. You can also change a 2-D Fontwork object into a 3-D object (or change a 3-D object into a 2-D object) by clicking the Extrusion On/Off icon on the 3D-Settings toolbar. For more information, see the *Draw Guide*.

Figure 335: 3D-Settings toolbars

Moving and resizing Fontwork objects

When you select a Fontwork object, eight colored squares (known as *handles*) appear around the edge of the object, as shown below. You can drag these handles to resize the object.

A yellow dot also appears on the object. This dot may be along an edge of the object, or it may be somewhere else; in the example on the right. If you hover the pointer over this yellow dot, the pointer turns into a hand symbol. You can drag the dot in different directions to distort the object.

Hovering the pointer over other parts of the object turns the pointer into the usual symbol for dragging the object to another part of the page.

For precise control of the location and size of the object, use the Position and Size areas of the Type tab in the Properties dialog.

Getting Started Guide

Chapter 12
Creating HTML Files

Saving Documents as HTML Files

Introduction

HTML capabilities in LibreOffice make it possible to save and export documents in HTML format.

This chapter describes how to do the following in Writer, Calc, Impress, and Draw:

- Create hyperlinks within a document, also to other documents such as web pages, PDFs, and other files.
- Create, edit, and save HTML documents using Writer/Web.

When creating a document that you plan to deliver as an HTML file, you need to consider the following:

- In an HTML document, hyperlinks are active (clickable), but other cross-references inserted by LibreOffice are not active links.
- An object such as an image is saved as a separate file. However, if that object has been placed in a frame (for example, with an associated caption), it is not saved and does not appear in the HTML document; instead, the name of the frame appears.

Relative and absolute hyperlinks

Hyperlinks stored within a file can be either relative or absolute.

A relative hyperlink says, *Here is how to get there starting from where you are now* (meaning from the folder in which your current document is saved) while an absolute hyperlink says, *Here is how to get there no matter where you start from*.

An absolute link will stop working if the target is moved. A relative link will stop working if the start and target locations change relative to each other. For instance, if you have two spreadsheets in the same folder linked to each other and you move the entire folder to a new location, an absolute hyperlink will break but a relative one will not.

To change the way that LibreOffice stores the hyperlinks in your file, select **Tools > Options > Load/Save > General** and choose if you want URLs saved relatively when referencing the *File System*, or the *Internet*, or both.

Calc will always display an absolute hyperlink. Do not be alarmed when it does this even when you have saved a relative hyperlink. This 'absolute' target address will be updated if you move the file.

 Note

HTML Files containing links as relative to the file system that will be uploaded to a web server requires the files be in a file structure matching that of the web server. Otherwise, the links will point to the wrong folder.

 Tip

When you rest the mouse pointer on a hyperlink, a help tip displays the absolute reference, because LibreOffice uses absolute path names internally. The complete path and address can only be seen when you view the result of the HTML export (saving a spreadsheet as an HTML file), by loading the HTML file as text, or by opening it with a text editor.

Creating hyperlinks

When you type text (such as a website addresses or URL) that can be used as a hyperlink, and then press the space bar or the *Enter* key, LibreOffice automatically creates the hyperlink and applies formatting to the text (usually a color and underlining). If this does not happen, you can enable this feature by going to **Tools > AutoCorrect Options > Options** on the menu bar and selecting the **URL Recognition** option.

If you do not want LibreOffice to convert a specific URL to a hyperlink, go to **Edit > Undo Insert** on the menu bar, or press *Ctrl+Z* immediately after the formatting has been applied, or place the cursor in the hyperlink, right-click, and select **Remove Hyperlink** from the context menu.

 Tip

> To change the color of hyperlinks, go to **Tools > Options > LibreOffice > Application colors**, scroll to *Unvisited links* and/or *Visited links*, pick the new colors and click **OK**. Caution: this will change the color for all hyperlinks in all components of LibreOffice; this may not be what you want.
>
> In Writer and Calc (but not Draw or Impress), you can also change the *Internet link* character style or define and apply new styles to selected links.

Using the Navigator

You can insert hyperlinks using the Navigator and this is an easy way to insert a hyperlink to another part of the same document.

1) Open the documents containing the items you want to cross-reference.

2) Click on the Navigator icon in the Sidebar or press **F5**.

3) Click the triangle to the right of the **Drag Mode** icon and select **Insert as Hyperlink** (Figure 336). The Drag Mode icon changes shape depending on the type of insert that was previously selected. The default icon for Drag Mode is to show the Hyperlink icon.

Figure 336: Inserting hyperlink using the Navigator

4) Select the document from the drop-down list at the bottom of the Navigator that contains the item that you want to link to.

5) In the Navigator list, select the item that you want to insert as a hyperlink.

6) Drag the item to where you want to insert the hyperlink in the document. The name of the item is inserted in the document as an active hyperlink.

When using the Navigator to insert a hyperlink to an object such as a graphic, it is recommended to have the hyperlink show a useful name, for example *2009 Sales Graph*. You need to give such objects useful names instead of leaving them as the default names, for example Graphics6, or you will have to edit the name of the resulting link using the Hyperlink dialog, as described below.

You can also use the Navigator to insert a hyperlink from one document (the source) to a specific place in another document (the target). Open the Navigator in the target document and drag the item to the position in the source document where you want the hyperlink to appear.

Using the Hyperlink dialog

You can use the Hyperlink dialog to insert a hyperlink and modify all hyperlinks.

1) Highlight the existing text you want to use as a link.

2) Click the **Hyperlink** icon on the Standard toolbar or go to **Insert > Hyperlink** on the menu bar to open the Hyperlink dialog (Figure 337).

3) On the left side, select one of the four categories of hyperlink:
   – **Internet**: the hyperlink points to a web address, normally starting with http://.
   – **Mail**: the hyperlink opens an email message that is pre-addressed to a particular recipient.
   – **Document**: the hyperlink points to another document or to another place in the current document.
   – **New document**: the hyperlink creates a new document.

4) The Hyperlink dialog changes depending on the type of hyperlink selected. Enter all necessary details to create the hyperlink.

5) Click **Apply** or **OK** button to create the hyperlink. If the **Apply** button is clicked the Hyperlink dialog remains open allowing you to create another hyperlink.

6) Click **Close** to close the Hyperlink dialog.

Figure 337: Hyperlink dialog showing details for Internet links

The dialog changes according to the choice made for the hyperlink category in the left panel. A full description of all the choices and their interactions is beyond the scope of this chapter. Here is a summary of the most common choices.

- For an *Internet* hyperlink, choose the type of hyperlink (Web or FTP), and enter the required web address (URL).

- For a *Mail* hyperlink, specify the address of the receiver and the subject.

- For a *Document* hyperlink, specify the document path (clicking **Open File** opens a file browser) or leave this blank if you want to link to a target in the same document. Optionally specify the target in the document (for example a specific slide). Click the **Target in Document** icon to open the Target in Document dialog where you can select the type of target; or, if you know the name of the target, you can type it into the box.

- For a *New Document* hyperlink, specify whether to edit the newly created document immediately (**Edit now**) or just create it (**Edit later**). Enter the file name and select the type of document to create (text, spreadsheet, and so on). Click the **Select Path** icon to open a file browser and choose where to store the file.

The *Further settings* section in the bottom right part of the dialog is common to all the hyperlink categories, although some choices are more relevant to some types of links.

- **Frame** value determines how the hyperlink will open. This applies to documents that open in a Web browser.

- **Form** specifies if the link is to be presented as text or as a button. See the *Writer Guide Chapter 15 Using Forms in Writer* for more information.

- **Text** specifies the text that will be visible to the user. If you do not enter anything here, LibreOffice uses the full URL or path as the link text. Note that if the link is relative and you move the file, this text will not change, though the target will.

- **Name** is applicable to HTML documents. It specifies text that will be added as a NAME attribute in the HTML code behind the hyperlink.

- **Events**: click this icon to open the Assign Macro dialog and select a macro to run when the link is clicked. See *Chapter 13 Getting Started with Macros* for more information.

Editing hyperlinks

To edit an existing link:

1) Click anywhere in the hyperlink text.

2) Click the **Hyperlink** icon on the Standard toolbar, or go to **Edit > Hyperlink** on the menu bar, or right-click and select **Edit Hyperlink** from the context menu. The Hyperlink dialog opens.

3) Make your changes and click **Apply** to save your changes. The Hyperlink dialog remains open, allowing you to continue editing hyperlinks. Click **Apply** after editing each hyperlink.

4) When you are finished editing hyperlinks, click **Close**.

The standard (default) behavior for activating hyperlinks within LibreOffice is to use *Ctrl+click*. This behavior can be changed in **Tools > Options > LibreOffice > Security > Options** by deselecting the option **Ctrl-click required to follow hyperlinks**. If clicking in your links activates them, check that page to see if the option has been deselected.

Removing hyperlinks

You can remove the link from hyperlink text and leave just the text by right-clicking on the link and selecting **Remove Hyperlink** from the context menu. You may then need to re-apply some formatting to match the text with the rest of your document.

To erase the link text or button from the document completely, select it and press the *Backspace* or *Delete* key.

Saving and exporting documents as HTML files

The easiest way to create HTML documents in LibreOffice is to start with an existing document. You can get a good idea of how it will appear as a web page by using **View > Web**. However, web layout view does not show you which features will or will not be saved correctly in HTML format. Refer to "Relative and absolute hyperlinks" on page 338 on what to consider before creating a web page from a document.

Writer documents

Saving a Writer document as an HTML file

To save a Writer document as a single HTML file, go to **File > Save As** on the menu bar and specify **HTML Document (Writer)** as the file type.

Saving a document as HTML document produces a set of files on your disk. LibreOffice will generate the image files and the HTML files necessary to create an HTML page in the browser.

 Tip

Use an empty folder to save your document as HTML file and images, The number of files generated by the format conversion depends on the number of images and objects in the original text document.

The file names are created following a simple rule summarized in Table 7.

Table 7: Summary of the file types created when saving as HTML format

File	Contents
Myfile.html	The text contents, page layout, text attributes, meta tags, and styles.
Myfile_html_[random number].gif	Gif image of visible contents of OLE objects.
Myfile_html_[random number].png, jpg, or bmp	Images inserted in the text document as PNG, BMP, or JPEG keep their original format.

 Note

The HTML transformation of the text document is limited by the HTML 4.0 Transitional specification. Text documents in office suites have a richer set of resources that will not appear in HTML, for example page formatting. Do not expect the same layout fidelity when saving a file with HTML format.

Saving as HTML may require more work directly on the HTML code to adjust the layout of the web page. See "Creating, editing, and saving HTML files using Writer/Web" on page 348.

Exporting a single web page

Another way to create a HTML file is to use **File > Export** and specify **XHTML** as the file type. LibreOffice will generate one XHTML file per text document. The image files are embedded in the XHTML file. XHTML files created by exporting a text document in LibreOffice have significant better layout rendering but fail to render objects other than images.

Notes

Writer does not replace multiple spaces in the original document with the HTML code for non-breaking spaces. If you want to have extra spaces in your HTML file or web page, you need to insert non-breaking spaces in LibreOffice. To do this, press *Ctrl+Spacebar* instead of just *Spacebar*.

The tab character is not rendered on exporting to XHTML. Instead, use borderless tables to position contents instead of the tab character in a line. This also affects bullet and number lists that insert by default a tab character between the bullet or number and the text. Use a list style where the tab character is replaced by a space.

Objects different than usual image formats are not rendered in LibreOffice XHTML output. These include drawings, spreadsheets, charts, and OLE object in general. To render an OLE object in XHTML, first transform its visible contents into an image and then replace the object in your document with the image.

The use of styles in the text document is strongly recommended for getting the best results when exporting to HTML or XHTML.

Saving as a series of web pages

Writer can save a large document as a series of web pages (HTML files) with a table of contents page.

1) Decide which headings in the document should start on a new page and make sure all those headings have the same paragraph style (for example, Heading 1).

2) Go to **File > Send > Create HTML Document** on the menu bar to open the Name and Path of the HTML Document dialog (Figure 338).

Figure 338: Creating a series of web pages from one document

3) Type the file name to save the pages under.

4) Specify which style indicates a new page by using the **separated by** drop-down list at the bottom of the dialog (for example, Heading 1).

5) Click **Save** to create the multi-page HTML document. The resulting HTML files conform to the HTML 4 Transitional standard.

Calc spreadsheets

Calc can save files as HTML documents by going to **File > Save As** on the menu bar and select **HTML Document (Calc)** format as the file type.

If the file contains more than one sheet, the additional sheets will follow one another in the HTML file. Links to each sheet will be placed at the top of the document.

Calc also allows the insertion of links directly into the spreadsheet using the Hyperlink dialog. See "Creating hyperlinks" on page 339 for more information on hyperlinks.

Impress presentations

 Note

Saving in HTML format does not retain animation and slide transitions.

Impress presentations cannot be saved in HTML format, but have to be exported as HTML documents. Note that you can click **Create** at any step in the following procedure. The HTML files created will then use the default settings that you have not changed in any way.

1) Go to **File > Export** on the menu bar and specify the file name and location of where to save the web page version of your presentation.

2) Select **HTML document (Impress)** as the file type and click **Save** to open the HTML Export dialog (Figure 339).

Figure 339: HTML Export dialog - Assign design page

3) On the *Assign design* page, you can choose to create a new design and select or delete an existing design. Specify a *New design* or an *Existing design* and click **Next >>**. If you have not previously saved a web page design, the *Existing Design* choice is not available.

– *New design* – creates a new design in the next pages of the Wizard.

– *Existing design* – loads an existing design from the design list to use as a starting point for the steps that follow. The list box displays all existing designs.

– *Delete Selected Design* deletes the selected design from the design list. If you delete a design, you will only delete the design information. An export file will not be deleted by this action.

4) Specify the *Publication type* for the web pages (Figure 348), then click **Next>>**. The publication type defines the basic settings for the intended export. The choices are:

 – *Standard HTML format* – creates standard HTML pages from export pages.

 – *Standard HTML with frames* – creates standard HTML pages with frames. The exported page will be placed in the main frame and the frame to the left will display a table of contents in the form of hyperlinks.

 – *Automatic* – creates a default HTML presentation as a kiosk export in which the slides are automatically advanced after a specified amount of time.

 – *WebCast* – in a WebCast export, automatic scripts will be generated with Perl or ASP support. This enables the speaker (for example, a speaker in a telephone conference using a slide show on the Internet) to change the slides in the web browsers used by the audience.

For more information on the options available for this page of the HTML Export dialog, click **Help** to open the help pages.

Figure 340: HTML Export dialog – Publication type page

5) Specify the options for *Save graphics as, Monitor resolution*, and *Effects* used for the web pages (Figure 341), then click **Next>>**. The options for this page of the HTML Export dialog are as follows:

 – *Save graphics as* – determines the image format. You can also define the compression value for the export.

 – *Monitor resolution* – defines the resolution for the target screen. Depending on the selected resolution, the image will be displayed in a reduced size. You can specify a reduction of up to 80% from the original size. When selecting a resolution, consider what the majority of your viewers might be using. If you specify a high resolution, then a viewer with a medium-resolution monitor will have to scroll sideways to see the entire slide, which is probably not desirable.

 – *Effects* – specifies whether sound files defined as an effect for slide transitions are exported and whether any hidden slides are exported.

For more information on the options available for this page of the HTML Export dialog, click **Help** to open the help pages.

Figure 341: HTML Export dialog – graphics and monitor resolution

6) Specify the *Information for the title page* to be used with the web version of your presentation (Figure 342). The title page normally contains the author's name, an e-mail address and home page, along with any additional information you may want to include. This page is not available if you have selected not to create a title page and either Automatic or WebCast publication type.

Figure 342: HTML Export dialog – title page information

7) Select *Link to a copy of the original presentation* if you want to create a hyperlink to download a copy of the presentation file and then click **Next>>**.

8) *Select button style* to be used for the web pages from the designs available (Figure 343) and then click **Next>>**.

   If you do not select a button style, LibreOffice will create a text navigator.

   This page is not available if you have selected either Automatic or WebCast publication type.

Figure 343: HTML Export dialog – button style page

9) *Select color scheme* to be used for the web pages (Figure 344) such as the color scheme and colors for text and background. This page is not available if you have selected either Automatic or WebCast publication type.

Figure 344: HTML Export dialog – color scheme page

10) Click **Create**.

11) If you have created a new design for your web pages, type in a name for your design and click **Save**.

 Note

Depending on the size of your presentation and the number of graphics it contains, the HTML export function creates several HTML, JPG, and GIF files. It is recommended to create a folder to hold all the files created for the web version of your presentation. If you simply save to your desktop and not in a specific folder, these separate HTML and graphics files will be placed all over your desktop.

Draw documents

Draw documents cannot be saved in HTML format, but have to be exported as HTML documents. Exporting drawings from Draw is similar to exporting a presentation from Impress. Go to **File > Export** and select **HTML Document (Draw)** as the file type, then follow the procedure above for exporting Impress presentations.

Creating, editing, and saving HTML files using Writer/Web

LibreOffice Writer can create, edit, and save files in HTML format using a configuration called Writer/Web.

To create a new HTML file use the menu option **File > New > HTML Document**.

Figure 345: Web display mode for Writer/Web

Writer/Web display modes

In addition to the Normal and Web display modes for editing (Figure 345), Writer/Web has a third editing mode called HTML Source mode (Figure 346). With the HTML Source mode, you can directly edit HTML tags such as <p>, <ul>, <table>, and so on to compose web page elements. In that mode you must know the HTML markup language.

You normally add content to an HTML document using the Web display mode, because it will render the contents as if displayed in a browser. Use the HTML Source editing mode to tweak the formatting.

 Note

> Because HTML markup language has fewer formatting possibilities than a text document in OpenDocument Format, Writer/Web cannot provide all formatting features for HTML documents and some formatting dialogs have fewer options available. For example, an HTML paragraph has no tab settings.

```
Writer HTML Test.html - LibreOfficeDev Writer/Web

File   Edit   View   Insert   Format   Table   Tools   Window   Help

<!DOCTYPE HTML PUBLIC "-//W3C//DTD HTML 4.0 Transitional//EN">
<html>
<head>
    <meta http-equiv="content-type" content="text/html; charset=windows-1252"/>
    <title></title>
    <meta name="generator" content="LibreOfficeDev 6.0.0.0.alpha0 (Windows)"/>
    <meta name="created" content="2017-09-17T15:53:10.209000000"/>
    <meta name="changed" content="2017-09-17T15:55:30.669000000"/>
</head>
<body lang="en-AU" dir="ltr">
<h1>Writer in HTML Mode.</h1>
<p>Just a simple test file.</p>
</body>
</html>
```

Figure 346: HTML Source view mode

Creating and editing an HTML document

To create an HTML document, choose **File > New > HTML Document**. Writer/Web opens a blank document in web display mode. You can now add content to the document by typing or pasting text, images, tables, and other objects. Use all the Writer/Web formatting resources including styles to format the content. When you have finished, save the document with the HTML file type.

If you need to add HTML content directly into the document, enter HTML Source editing mode by clicking the **HTML Source** icon on the toolbar or choosing **View > HTML Source** from the menu bar. In that mode, Writer/Web turns into a notepad-like text editor (Figure 346).

 Note

> The HTML markup content generated by Writer/Web is limited to the production of a displayable document in a web browser. It does not consider other components of a website such as external cascading style sheets (CSS), external JavaScript, or other script languages. Use the HTML Source mode to manually insert links to these external components into the page.

Checking a web page in a browser

It is important to check your web pages (HTML documents) in a web browser such as Mozilla Firefox, Google Chrome, Microsoft Edge, or Safari. Not all browsers render HTML files the same way, so if possible, check the contents in several browsers.

To make LibreOffice open your default web browser and display the contents of a document, go to **File > Preview in Web Browser**. You can also open any web browser and then open the HTML file in it.

Getting Started Guide

Chapter 13
Getting Started with Macros

Using the Macro Recorder … and Beyond

Introduction

A macro is a saved sequence of commands that are stored for later use. An example of a simple macro is one that "types" your address. The LibreOffice macro language is very flexible, allowing automation of both simple and complex tasks. Macros are very useful when you have to repeat the same task in the same way over and over again.

LibreOffice macros are usually written in a language called LibreOffice Basic, sometimes abbreviated to Basic. Although you can learn Basic and write macros, there is a steep learning curve to writing macros from scratch. The usual methods for a beginner are to use macros that someone else has written or use the built-in macro recorder, which records keystrokes and saves them for use.

Most tasks in LibreOffice are accomplished by "dispatching a command" (sending a command), which is intercepted and used. The macro recorder works by recording the commands that are dispatched (see "Dispatch framework" *on page* 361).

Your first macros

Adding a macro

The first step in learning macro programming is to find and use existing macros. This section assumes that you have a macro that you want to use, which may be in an email, on a web page, or even in a book. For this example, the macro in Listing 1 is used. You should create a library and module to contain your macro; see "Macro organization" on page 362 for more information.

Listing 1: Simple macro that says hello

```
Sub HelloMacro
  Print "Hello"
End Sub
```

Use the following steps to create a library which will contain your macro:

1) Go to **Tools > Macros > Organize Macros > LibreOffice Basic** to open the LibreOffice Basic Macros dialog (Figure 347).

2) Click **Organizer** to open the Basic Macro Organizer dialog (Figure 348) and select the *Libraries* tab.

3) Set the *Location* to *My Macros & Dialogs*, which is the default location.

4) Click **New** to open the New Library dialog.

5) Enter a library name, for example TestLibrary, and click **OK**.

6) Select the *Modules* tab.

7) In the *Module* list, expand *My Macros* and select your librery (in the example TestLibrary). A module named Module1 already exists and can contain your macro. If you wish, you can click **New** to create another module in the library.

8) Select Module1, or the new module that you created, and click **Edit** to open the Integrated Development Environment (IDE) (Figure 349). The IDE is a text editor included with LibreOffice that allows you to create and edit macros.

9) When a new module is created, it contains a comment and an empty macro named Main, which does nothing.

10) Add the new macro either before Sub Main or after End Sub. Listing 2 shows the new macro has been added before Sub Main.

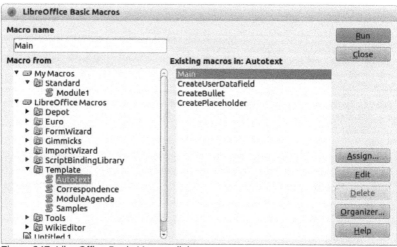
Figure 347: LibreOffice Basic Macros dialog

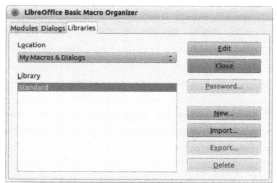
Figure 348: LibreOffice Basic Macro Organizer dialog

11) Click the **Compile** icon on the Macro toolbar to compile the macro.

12) Place the cursor in the HelloMacro subroutine and click the **Run BASIC** icon on the Macro toolbar, or press the *F5* key, to run the HelloMacro in the module. A small dialog will open with the word "Hello" displayed. If the cursor is not in a subroutine or function, a dialog will open; select the macro to run.

13) Click **OK** to close this small dialog.

14) To select and run any macro in the module, click the **Select Macro** icon on the Standard toolbar or go to **Tools > Organize Macros > LibreOffice Basic**.

15) Select a macro and then click **Run**.

Figure 349: Integrated Development Environment window

Listing 2: Module1 after adding the new macro.

```
REM  *****  BASIC  *****

Sub HelloMacro
  Print "Hello"
End Sub

Sub Main

End Sub
```

Recording a macro

If you have to repeatedly enter the same information, you can copy this information after it has been entered into your document for the first time, then paste the information into your document each time you want to use it. However, if something else is copied to the clipboard, the contents on the clipboard are changed. This means that you have to re-copy your repeated information. To overcome this problem, you can create a macro that enters your repeated information.

Note

> For some cases when you want to repeatedly use information into a document, it may be more convenient to create an AutoText. See the *Writer Guide Chapter 2 Working with Text:Basics* for more information.

Make sure macro recording is enabled by going to **Tools > Options > LibreOffice > Advanced** on the main menu bar and selecting the option **Enable macro recording**. By default, this feature is turned off in LibreOffice.

1) Go to **Tools > Macros > Record Macro** on the main menu bar to start recording a macro. A small dialog is displayed indicating that LibreOffice is recording a macro.

2) Type the desired information or perform an appropriate series of operations. As an example, type your name.

3) Click **Stop Recording** on the small Recording dialog to stop recording and the LibreOffice Basic Macros dialog opens (Figure 347 on page 352).

4) Open the library container *My Macros*.

5) Find the library named *Standard* in My Macros. Note that every library container has a library named Standard.

6) Select the Standard library and click **New Module** to create a new module to contain the macro. This opens the New Module dialog.

7) Type a descriptive name for the new module, for example *RecordsInsertText*, and click **OK** to create the module. The LibreOffice Basic Macros dialog now displays the name of the new module in the Standard library.

8) In the **Macro name** text box, type a name for the macro you have just recorded, for example *EnterMyName*.

9) Click **Save** to save the macro and close the LibreOffice Basic Macros dialog.

If you followed all of the above steps, the Standard library now contains a module named Records*InsertText* and this module contains the EnterMyName macro.

 Note

When LibreOffice creates a new module, it automatically adds the macro named Main.

Running a macro

1) Go to **Tools > Macros > Run Macro** on the main menu bar to open the Macro Selector dialog (Figure 350).

2) For example, select your newly created macro EnterMyName and click **Run.**

3) Alternatively, go to **Tools > Macros > Organize Macros > LibreOffice Basic** on the main menu bar to open the LibreOffice Basic Macros dialog, select your macro and click **Run.**

Figure 350: Macro Selector dialog

Viewing and editing macros

To view and/or edit the macro that you created:

1) Go to **Tools > Macros > Organize Macros > LibreOffice Basic** to open the LibreOffice Basic Macros dialog.

2) Select your new macro EnterMyName and click **Edit.**The Basic IDE will be opened andthe macro EnterMyName will be shown as in Listing 3.

This first macro is not complicated. A little explanation will significantly help you in understanding macros. The discussion starts with first line of the macro and describes features through whole listing.

Listing 3: Generated "EnterMyname" macro

```
REM  *****  BASIC  *****
Sub Main

End Sub

sub EnterMyName
rem ----------------------------------------------------------------
rem define variables
dim document    as object
dim dispatcher as object
rem ----------------------------------------------------------------
rem get access to the document
document    = ThisComponent.CurrentController.Frame
dispatcher = createUnoService("com.sun.star.frame.DispatchHelper")

rem ----------------------------------------------------------------
dim args1(0) as new com.sun.star.beans.PropertyValue
args1(0).Name = "Text"
args1(0).Value = "Your name"

dispatcher.executeDispatch(document, ".uno:InsertText", "", 0, args1())
end sub
```

Commenting with REM

All comments in macro coding begin with REM, which stands for remark. All text after REM on the same line is ignored.

 Note

As a short cut, you can use the single quote character (') to start a comment.

LibreOffice Basic is not case-sensitive for keywords, so REM, Rem, and rem can all start a comment. If you use symbolic constants defined by the Application Programming Interface (API), it is safer to assume that the names are case-sensitive. Symbolic constants are an advanced topic not covered by this user guide and are not required when using the macro recorder in LibreOffice.

Defining subroutines with SUB

Individual macros are stored in subroutines and these subroutines begin with the keyword SUB. The end of a subroutine is indicated by the words END SUB. The code starts by defining the subroutine named Main, which is empty and does nothing. The next subroutine, EnterMyName, contains the generated code for your macro.

 Note

LibreOffice always creates an empty subroutine named Main when it creates a module.

There are advanced topics that are beyond the scope of this user guide, but knowing about them might be of interest:

- You can write a macro so that values can be passed to the subroutine. The values are called arguments. However, recorded macros in LibreOffice do not accept arguments.

- Another kind of subroutine is called a function, which is a subroutine that can return a value as a result of the work. Functions are defined by the keyword FUNCTION at the beginning. Recorded macros in LibreOffice creates subroutines only.

Defining variables using Dim

You can write information on a piece of paper so that you can look at it later. A variable, like a piece of paper, contains information that can be changed and read. The Dim keyword originally stood for Dimension and was used to define the dimensions of an array. The dim statement used in the EnterMyName macro is similar to setting aside a piece of paper to be used to store a message or note.

In the EnterMyName macro, the variables document and dispatcher are defined as the type *object*. Other common variable types include *string*, *integer*, and *date*. A third variable, named *args1*, is an array of property values. A variable of type *array* allows a single variable to contain multiple values, similar to storing multiple pages in a single book. Values in an array are usually numbered starting from zero. The number in the parentheses indicates the highest usable number to access a storage location. In this example, there is only one value, and it is numbered zero.

Explaining macro code

The following is an explanation of the code used in the EnterMyName macro. You may not understand all the details, but the explanation of each line of code may give you some idea of how a macro works.

```
sub EnterMyName
```

Defines the start of the EnterMyName macro.

```
dim document    as object
```

Defines document as an object variable. Objects are a specific variable type with multiple *fields* (sometimes they are called *properties*) and *actions* (also they are called *methods*). The fields can be perceived like variables (including an object) and actions like subroutines which allow us to operate with the object.

 Note:

Sometimes the word *service* is used. A service is supplied by a type of object which are distinguished in order to point out how they are used.

```
dim dispatcher as object
```

Defines dispatcher as an object variable.

```
document = ThisComponent.CurrentController.Frame
```

ThisComponent refers to the current document.

CurrentController is a property referring to a service that controls the document. For example, when you type, it is the current controller that takes note of what you type. CurrentController then dispatches the changes to the document frame.

Frame is a controller property that returns the main frame for a document. Therefore, the variable named document refers to a document's frame, which receives dispatched commands.

```
dispatcher = createUnoService("com.sun.star.frame.DispatchHelper")
```

Most tasks in LibreOffice are accomplished by dispatching a command. LibreOffice includes a DispatchHelper service, which provides an easy way to dispatch an URL using one call instead of multiple ones and does most of the work when using dispatches in macros. The method CreateUnoService accepts the name of a service and it tries to create an instance of that service. On completion, the dispatcher variable contains a reference to a DispatchHelper.

```
dim args1(0) as new com.sun.star.beans.PropertyValue
```

Declares the *args1* array of properties. Each property has a name and a value. In other words, it is a name/value pair. The created array has one property at index zero.

The com.sun.star.beans.PropertyValue expression is an Universal Network Objects (UNO) *srtucture*. Structures are special variable type that contane other variables united by logical basis. They can be convenient to operate with sets of heterogeneous information that should be treated as a single whole. An explanation of UNO and user *structures* goes far beyond the scope of this book. For more information on creating and using structures , see the LibreOffice Help system and other Basic guids.

```
args1(0).Name = "Text"
args1(0).Value = "Your name"
```

Gives the property the name "Text" and the value "Your name", which is the text that is inserted when the macro is run.

```
dispatcher.executeDispatch(document, ".uno:InsertText", "", 0, args1())
```

This is where the magic happens. The dispatch helper sends a dispatch to the document frame (stored in the variable document) with the command .uno:InsertText. The next two arguments, frame name and search flags, are beyond the scope of this book . The last argument is the array of property values to be used while executing the command InsertText.

```
end sub
```

The last line of the code ends the subroutine.

Creating a macro

When creating a macro, it is important to ask two questions before recording:

1) Can the task be written as a simple set of commands?
2) Can the steps be arranged so that the last command leaves the cursor ready for the next command or entering text or data into the document?

A more complicated example of a macro

A common task is to copy rows and columns of data from a web site and format them as a table in a text document as follows:

1) Copy the data from the web site to the clipboard.
2) To avoid strange formatting and fonts, paste the text into a Writer document as unformatted text.
3) Reformat the text with tabs between columns so that it can be converted into a table using **Table > Convert > Text to Table** on the main menu bar.

With the two questions given above in mind, inspect the text to see if a macro can be recorded to format the text. An example of copied data showing the FontWeight constants group from the API web site (Figure 351). The first column in this example indicates a constant name and each name is followed by a space and a tab, and each line has two trailing spaces.

The first column in the table should contain a numeric value, the second column the name, and the third column the description. This conversion is easily accomplished for every row except for DONTKNOW and NORMAL, which do not contain a numeric value, but the values are between 0 and 100 and can be entered manually.

DONTKNOW	The font weight is not specified/known.
THIN	specifies a 50% font weight.
ULTRALIGHT	specifies a 60% font weight.
LIGHT	specifies a 75% font weight.
SEMILIGHT	specifies a 90% font weight.
NORMAL	specifies a normal font weight.
SEMIBOLD	specifies a 110% font weight.
BOLD	specifies a 150% font weight.
ULTRABOLD	specifies a 175% font weight.
BLACK	specifies a 200% font weight.

Figure 351: Example of copied data

The data can be cleaned up in several ways, all of them easy to accomplish. The example given below uses keystrokes that assume the cursor is at the start of the line with the text THIN.

1) Make sure macro recording is enabled by going to **Tools > Options > LibreOffice > Advanced** on the main menu bar and selecting the option **Enable macro recording**. By default, this feature is turned off when LibreOffice was installed on your computer.
2) Go to **Tools > Macros > Record Macro** on the main menu bar to start recording.
3) Press *Ctrl+Right Arrow* to move the cursor to the start of "specifies".
4) Press *Backspace* twice to remove the tab and the space.
5) Press *Tab* to add the tab without the space after the constant name.
6) Press *Delete* to delete the lower case s and then press *Shift+S* to add an upper case S.
7) Press *Ctrl+Right Arrow* twice to move the cursor to the start of the number.
8) Press *Ctrl+Shift+Right Arrow* to select and move the cursor before the % sign.
9) Press *Ctrl+C* to copy the selected text to the clipboard.
10) Press *End* to move the cursor to the end of the line.
11) Press *Backspace* twice to remove the two trailing spaces.
12) Press *Home* to move the cursor to the start of the line.
13) Press *Ctrl+V* to paste the selected number to the start of the line.
14) Pasting the value also pasted an extra space, so press *Backspace* to remove the extra space.
15) Press *Tab* to insert a tab between the number and the name.
16) Press *Home* to move to the start of the line.
17) Press *down arrow* to move to the next line.
18) Stop recording the macro and save the macro, see "Recording a macro" on page 353.

It takes much longer to read and write the steps than to record the macro. Work slowly and think about the steps as you do them. With practice this becomes second nature.

The generated macro code in Listing 4 has been modified to contain the step number in the comments to match the code to the step above.

Listing 4: Copying numeric value to start of the column

```
sub CopyNumToCol1
rem ----------------------------------------------------------------
rem define variables
dim document    as object
```

```
dim dispatcher as object
rem ---------------------------------------------------------------
rem get access to the document
document    = ThisComponent.CurrentController.Frame
dispatcher = createUnoService("com.sun.star.frame.DispatchHelper")

rem (3) Press Ctrl+Right Arrow to move the cursor to the start of "specifies".
dispatcher.executeDispatch(document, ".uno:GoToNextWord", "", 0, Array())

rem (4) Press Backspace twice to remove the tab and the space.
dispatcher.executeDispatch(document, ".uno:SwBackspace", "", 0, Array())

rem ---------------------------------------------------------------
dispatcher.executeDispatch(document, ".uno:SwBackspace", "", 0, Array())

rem (5) Press Tab to add the tab without the space after the constant name.
dim args4(0) as new com.sun.star.beans.PropertyValue
args4(0).Name = "Text"
args4(0).Value = CHR$(9)

dispatcher.executeDispatch(document, ".uno:InsertText", "", 0, args4())

rem (6) Press Delete to delete the lower case s ....
dispatcher.executeDispatch(document, ".uno:Delete", "", 0, Array())

rem (6) ... and then press Shift+S to add an upper case S.
dim args6(0) as new com.sun.star.beans.PropertyValue
args6(0).Name = "Text"
args6(0).Value = "S"

dispatcher.executeDispatch(document, ".uno:InsertText", "", 0, args6())

rem (7) Press Ctrl+Right Arrow twice to move the cursor to the number.
dispatcher.executeDispatch(document, ".uno:GoToNextWord", "", 0, Array())

rem ---------------------------------------------------------------
dispatcher.executeDispatch(document, ".uno:GoToNextWord", "", 0, Array())

rem (8) Press Ctrl+Shift+Right Arrow to select the number.
dispatcher.executeDispatch(document, ".uno:WordRightSel", "", 0, Array())

rem (9) Press Ctrl+C to copy the selected text to the clipboard.
dispatcher.executeDispatch(document, ".uno:Copy", "", 0, Array())

rem (10) Press End to move the cursor to the end of the line.
dispatcher.executeDispatch(document, ".uno:GoToEndOfLine", "", 0, Array())

rem (11) Press Backspace twice to remove the two trailing spaces.
dispatcher.executeDispatch(document, ".uno:SwBackspace", "", 0, Array())

rem ---------------------------------------------------------------
dispatcher.executeDispatch(document, ".uno:SwBackspace", "", 0, Array())

rem (12) Press Home to move the cursor to the start of the line.
dispatcher.executeDispatch(document, ".uno:GoToStartOfLine", "", 0, Array())

rem (13) Press Ctrl+V to paste the selected number to the start of the line.
```

```
dispatcher.executeDispatch(document, ".uno:Paste", "", 0, Array())

rem (14) Press Backspace to remove the extra space.
dispatcher.executeDispatch(document, ".uno:SwBackspace", "", 0, Array())

rem (15) Press Tab to insert a tab between the number and the name.
dim args17(0) as new com.sun.star.beans.PropertyValue
args17(0).Name = "Text"
args17(0).Value = CHR$(9)

dispatcher.executeDispatch(document, ".uno:InsertText", "", 0, args17())
rem (16) Press Home to move to the start of the line.
dispatcher.executeDispatch(document, ".uno:GoToStartOfLine", "", 0, Array())

rem (17) Press Down Arrow to move to the next line.
dim args19(1) as new com.sun.star.beans.PropertyValue
args19(0).Name = "Count"
args19(0).Value = 1
args19(1).Name = "Select"
args19(1).Value = false

dispatcher.executeDispatch(document, ".uno:GoDown", "", 0, args19())
end sub
```

Cursor movements are used for all operations (as opposed to searching). If run on the DONTKNOW line, the word *weight* is moved to the front of the line, and the first "The" is changed to "She". This is not perfect, but you should not run the macro on the lines that did not have the proper format. You need to do these manually.

Running a macro quickly

It is tedious to repeatedly run the macro using **Tools > Macros > Run Macro** on the main menu bar when the macro can be run from the IDE (Figure 349 on page 353).

Here are a few tips to do the life easier. If you create a temporary macro using same name, you can add its macro into the Main subroutine and to delete your macro after using.

1) Go to **Tools > Macros > Organize Macros > LibreOffice Basic** on the main menu bar to open the LibreOffice Basic Macro dialog (Figure 347 on page 352).

2) Select your macro and click **Edit** to open the macro in the IDE.

3) Unless you change the first macro, it is the empty macro named Main. Modify Main so that it reads as shown in Listing 5.

4) Now, you can run CopyNumToCol1 when run the Mine macro by clicking the **Run Basic** icon in the Macro toolbar of the IDE, or press *F5* key to run you macro.

5) Go to **Tools > Customize** on the main menu bar and select the Keyboard tab in the Customize dialog.

6) Select a shortcut key what you want in the Shortcut keys list. Then select LibreOffice Macros, and further, a library container, a library, and a module in the Category list where your modified Main macro is. Select the Main macro in the Function list and click the Modify button.

Now you can run your macro by the shortcut. This is very fast and easy, especially for temporary macros that will be used a few times and then discarded. See "How to run a macro" on page 365 for more information.

Listing 5: Modify Main to call CopyNumToCol1.

```
Sub Main
   CopyNumToCol1
End Sub
```

Macro recorder failures

Sometimes the macro recorder has a failure and knowledge of LibreOffice internal workings helps to understand how and why the macro recorder sometimes fails. The primary offender is related to the dispatch framework and its relationship to the macro recorder.

Dispatch framework

The purpose of the dispatch framework is to provide uniform access to components (documents) for commands that usually correspond to menu items. Using **File > Save** from the main menu bar, the shortcut keys *Ctrl+S*, or clicking the **Save** icon are all of commands that are translated into the same "dispatch command".

The dispatch framework can also be used to send "commands" back to the User Interface (UI). For example, after saving a new document, the list of recent files is updated.

A dispatch command is text, for example .uno:InsertObject or .uno:GoToStartOfLine. The command is sent to the document frame and this passes on the command until an object is found that can handle the command.

How the macro recorder uses the dispatch framework

The macro recorder records the generated dispatches. The recorder is relatively simple tool to use and the same commands that are issued are recorded for later use. The problem is that not all dispatched commands are complete. For example, inserting an object generates the following code:

```
dispatcher.executeDispatch(document, ".uno:InsertObject", "", 0, Array())
```

It is not possible to specify what kind of object to create or insert. If an object is inserted from a file, you cannot specify which file to insert.

If while recording a macro you use **Tools > Options** on the main menu bar to open and modify configuration items, the generated macro does not record any configuration changes. In fact, the generated code is commented so it will not even be run.

```
rem dispatcher.executeDispatch(document, ".uno:OptionsTreeDialog", "", 0, Array())
```

If a dialog is opened, a command to open the dialog is likely to be generated. Any work done inside the dialog is not usually recorded. Examples of this include macro organization dialogs, inserting special characters, and similar types of dialogs. Other possible problems using the macro recorder include things such as inserting a formula, setting user data, setting filters in Calc, actions in database forms, and exporting a document to an encrypted PDF file. You never know for certain what will work unless you try it. For example, the actions from the search dialog *are* properly captured.

Other options

When the macro recorder is not able to solve a specific problem, the usual solution is to write code using the LibreOffice objects. Unfortunately, there is a steep learning curve for these LibreOffice objects. It is usually best to start with simple examples and then increase the scope of macros as you learn more. Learning to read generated macros is a good place to start.

Macro organization

In LibreOffice, macros are grouped in modules, modules are grouped in libraries, and libraries are grouped in library containers. A library is usually used as a major grouping for either an entire category of macros, or for an entire application. Modules usually split functionality, such as user interaction and calculations. Individual macros are subroutines and functions. Figure 352 shows an example of the hierarchical structure of macro libraries in LibreOffice.

Go to **Tools > Macros > Organize Macros > LibreOffice Basic** on the main menu bar to open the LibreOffice Basic Macros dialog (Figure 347 on page 352). All available library containers are shown in the *Macro from* list. Every document is a library container, capable of containing multiple libraries. The application itself acts as two library containers, one container for macros distributed with LibreOffice called LibreOffice Macros, and one container for personal macros called My Macros.

The LibreOffice Macros are stored with the application runtime code, which may not be editable to you unless you are an administrator. This helps protect these macros because they should not be changed and you should not store your own macros in the LibreOffice container.

Unless your macros are applicable to a single document, and only to a single document, your macros will probably be stored in the My Macros container. The My Macros container is stored in your user area or home directory.

Figure 352: Macro Library hierarchy

If a macro is contained in a document, then a recorded macro will attempt to work on that document; because it primarily uses "ThisComponent" for its actions.

Every library container contains a library named *Standard*. It is better to create your own libraries with meaningful names than to use the Standard library. Not only are meaningful names easier to manage, but they can also be imported into other library containers whereas the Standard library cannot.

 Caution

LibreOffice allows you to import libraries into a library container, but it will not allow you to overwrite the library named Standard. Therefore, if you store your macros in the Standard library, you cannot import them into another library container.

Just as it makes good sense to give your libraries meaningful names, it is prudent to use meaningful names for your modules. By default, LibreOffice uses names such as Module1, Module2 and so on.

As you create your macros, you must decide where to store them. Storing a macro in a document is useful if the document will be shared and you want the macro to be included with the document. Macros stored in the application library container named My Macros, however, are globally available to all documents.

Macros are not available until the library that contains them is loaded. However, in contrast to other libraries the Standard and Template libraries are automatically loaded. A loaded library is displayed differently from a library that is not loaded. To load the library and the modules it contains, double-click on the library.

Where are macros stored?

LibreOffice stores user-specific data in a subdirectory of the home directory for the user. The location is operating system specific. Go to **Tools > Options > LibreOffice > Paths** on the main menu bar to view where other configuration data are stored. For example, on computer running Windows Vista or later, this is `C:\Users\<user name>\AppData\Roaming` (a part of the path may be localized on non-English versions). User macros are stored in `LibreOffice\4\user\basic`. Each library is stored in its own directory off the basic directory.

For casual use, it is not necessary to understand where macros are stored. If you know where they are stored, however, you can create a backup, share your macros, or inspect them if there is an error.

Go to **Tools > Macros > Organize Dialogs** on the main menu bar to open the LibreOffice Macro Organizer dialog (Figure 348 on page 352). Alternatively, go to **Tools > Macros > Organize Macros > LibreOffice Basic** on the main menu bar to open the LibreOffice Basic Macros dialog (Figure 347 on page 352) and then click the **Organizer** button.

Importing macros

The LibreOffice Macro Organizer dialog allows you to import macro libraries into your document as well as creating, deleting, and renaming libraries, modules, and dialogs.

1) Select the library container to use and then click **Import** to import macro libraries (Figure 353 on page 364).

2) Navigate to the directory containing the library to import (Figure 353). There are usually two files from which to choose, dialog.xlb and script.xlb. It does not matter which of these two files you select; both will be imported. Macros can be stored in libraries inside LibreOffice documents. Select a document rather than a directory on disk to import libraries contained in a document.

 Note

You cannot import the library named Standard.

Figure 353: Navigating to a macro library

 Tip

On a computer operating Linux, the LibreOffice specific files are stored in the home directory of a user, in a subdirectory whose name begins with a dot prefix (usually .config/). Directories and files with names beginning with a dot prefix may be hidden and not shown in a normal selection dialog. If using LibreOffice dialogs, rather than the operating system specific dialogs, type the name of the desired directory in the Name field.

3) Select a file and click **Open** to continue and open the Import Libraries dialog (Figure 354).

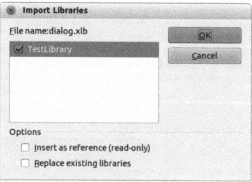

Figure 354: Choose library import options

4) Select the following options for importing libraries:

a) If no options are selected, the library is copied to your user macro directory. However, if the library you are importing has the same name and you are importing into the same location, it will not be copied.

b) Select **Replace existing libraries** if the library you want to import has the same name and you want to replace the existing library.

c) Select **Insert as reference (read only)** if you want to use the library as reference, but not import the library into your document. When a library is used as a reference, it remains in its current location and is fully functional, but cannot be modified in the Basic IDE.

5) Click **OK** to import the macro library you selected.

Downloading macros to import

Macros are available for download. Some macros are contained in documents, some as regular files that you must select and import, and some as macro text that should be copied and pasted into the Basic IDE. See "Adding a macro" on page 351 on how to add macros to your macro library and "Viewing and editing macros" on page 354 on how to edit macros using the Basic IDE.

Some macros are available as free downloads on the Internet (see Table 347).

Table 8. Macro examples

Location	Description
http://www.pitonyak.org/oo.php	Reference materials regarding macros.
http://www.pitonyak.org/database/	Reference materials regarding database macros.
https://wiki.documentfoundation.org/Macros	Lots of links to macros.
http://forum.openoffice.org/en/forum/	Forums, with many examples and help.

How to run a macro

Although you can use **Tools > Macros > Run Macro** to run all macros, this is not efficient for frequently run macros. See "Running a macro" on page 354 for more information.

A more common technique for frequently used macros is to link the macro to a toolbar icon, menu item, keyboard shortcut, or a button embedded in a document. While choosing a method, it is also good to ask questions such as:

- Should the macro be available for only one document, or globally for all documents?
- Is the macro for a specific document type, such as a Calc document?
- How frequently will the macro be used?

The answers will determine where to store the macro and how to make it available. For example, you will probably not add a rarely used macro to a toolbar. To help determine your choices, see Table 9.

Table 9. Where to store a macro

Type of macro	LibreOffice (for all components)	A specific document type	One document
Toolbar	No	Yes	Yes
Menu	No	Yes	Yes
Shortcut	Yes	Yes	No
Event	Yes	No	Yes

Toolbars, menu items, and keyboard shortcuts

To add a menu item, keyboard shortcut, or toolbar icon that calls a macro, use the Customize dialog (Figure 355).

Figure 355: Menus tab in Customize dialog

The Customize dialog contains pages to configure menus, keyboard shortcuts, toolbars, and events. To open this dialog, go to **Tools > Customize** on the main menu bar or right-click on a toolbar and select **Customize Toolbar** from the context menu.

Complete coverage of the Customize dialog is beyond the scope of this chapter. Click the **Help** button to access the help pages included with LibreOffice or see *Chapter 14 Customizing LibreOffice*.

Events

Whenever something happens in LibreOffice, it is called an event. For example, opening a document, changing status of modified, or moving the mouse cursor are all events. LibreOffice allows events to trigger the execution of a macro; the macro is then called an event handler. Full coverage of event handlers is well beyond the scope of this document, but a little knowledge can accomplish much.

 Caution

> Be careful when you configure an event handler. For example, assume that you write an event handler that is called every time that a document is modified, but you make a mistake so the event is not properly handled. One possible result is that your event handler will consume all changing status, forcing you to kill LibreOffice.

1) Go to **Tools > Customize** on the main menu bar to open the Customize dialog and select the Events tab (Figure 356). The events in the Customize dialog are related to the entire application and specific documents.

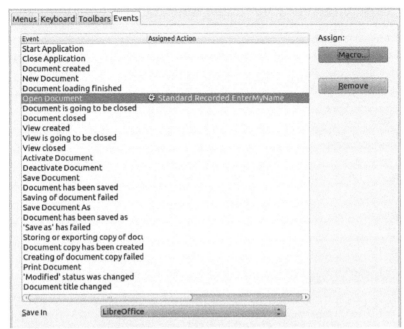

Figure 356: Events tab in Customize dialog

2) In **Save In**, select LibreOffice, or a specific document from the drop down menu to save your event.

3) A common use is to assign the Open Document event to call a specific macro. The macro then performs certain setup tasks for the document. Select the desired event and click **Macro** to open the Macro Selector dialog (Figure 350 on page 354).

4) Select the desired macro and click **OK** to assign the macro to the event. The Events tab shows that the event has been assigned to a macro.

Many objects in a document can be set to call macros when events occur. The most common use is to add a control, such as a button, into a document. Even double-clicking on a graphic opens a dialog with a Macros tab that allows you to assign a macro to an event.

Extensions

An extension is a package that can be installed into LibreOffice to add new functionality. Extensions can be written in almost any programming language and may be simple or sophisticated. Extensions can be grouped into types:

• Calc Add-Ins, which provide new functionality for Calc, including new functions that act like normal built-in functions.

• New components and functionality, which normally include some level of User Interface (UI) integration such as new menus or toolbars.

• Pivot Tables that are used directly in Calc.

• Chart Add-Ins with new chart types.

• Linguistic components such as spelling checkers.

• Document templates and images.

Although individual extensions can be found in several places, there is currently an extension repository at: http://extensions.libreoffice.org/ and some documentation at http://libreplanet.org/wiki/Group:OpenOfficeExtensions/List.

For more about obtaining and installing extensions, see Chapter 14, Customizing LibreOffice.

Writing macros without the recorder

The examples covered in this chapter are created using the macro recorder and the dispatcher. You can also write macros that directly access the objects that comprise LibreOffice if you are confident in writing computer code. In other words, you can create a macro that directly manipulates a document.

Directly manipulating LibreOffice internal objects is an advanced topic that is beyond the scope of this chapter. A simple example, however, demonstrates how this works.

Listing 6: Append the text "Hello" to the current document.

```
Sub AppendHello
   Dim oDoc
   Dim sTextService$
   Dim oCurs

   REM ThisComponent refers to the currently active document.
   oDoc = ThisComponent

   REM Verify that this is a text document
   sTextService = "com.sun.star.text.TextDocument"
   If NOT oDoc.supportsService(sTextService) Then
     MsgBox "This macro only works with a text document"
     Exit Sub
   End If
   REM Get the view cursor from the current controller.
   oCurs = oDoc.currentController.getViewCursor()

   REM Move the cursor to the end of the document
   oCurs.gotoEnd(False)

   REM Insert text "Hello" at the end of the document
   oCurs.Text.insertString(oCurs, "Hello", False)
End Sub
```

Finding more information

Numerous resources are available that provide help with writing macros. Use **Help > LibreOffice Help** to open the LibreOffice help pages. The upper left corner of the LibreOffice help system contains a drop-down list that determines which help set is displayed. To view the help for Basic, choose *LibreOffice Basic* from this list.

Included material

Many excellent macros are included with LibreOffice. Use **Tools > Macros > Organize Macros > LibreOffice Basic** to open the LibreOffice Basic Macros dialog. Expand the Tools library in the LibreOffice library container. Inspect the Debug module — some good examples include WritedbgInfo(document) and printdbgInfo(sheet).

Online resources

The following links and references contain information regarding macro programming:

https://wiki.documentfoundation.org/Macros

http://ask.libreoffice.org/ (a Q & A site where volunteers answer questions related to LibreOffice)

http://forum.openoffice.org/en/forum/ (Apache OpenOffice community forum; volunteers answer questions about LibreOffice as well)

https://wiki.documentfoundation.org/Documentation/Other_Documentation_and_Resources (look in Programmers section for *BASIC Programmers' Guide* and *Developers' Guide*; the latter contains a detailed explanation)

Printed and eBook materials

There are currently no books specific to LibreOffice macros that are available for download.

Information in the following books is mostly applicable to LibreOffice; the books are available for purchase in both printed and eBook form from their publishers:

Dr. Mark Alexander Bain's *Learn OpenOffice.org Spreadsheet Macro Programming*. See http://www.packtpub.com/openoffice-ooobasic-calc-automation/book.

Roberto Benitez's *Database Programming with OpenOffice.org Base & Basic*. See http://www.lulu.com/product/paperback/database-programming-with-openofficeorg-base-basic/3568728

Getting Started Guide

Chapter 14
Customizing LibreOffice

Introduction

This chapter describes some common customization that you may wish to carry out.

You can customize menus, toolbars, and keyboard shortcuts in LibreOffice, add new menus and toolbars, and assign macros to events. However, you cannot customize context (right-click) menus.

Other customization are made easy by extensions that you can install from the LibreOffice website or from other providers.

Note

Since LibreOffice 5.1, the menu bars in Writer, Calc, and Impress have been reorganized to improve the usability of the application. The most used application commands were put together in the Styles, Sheets, and Slide menus, respectively.

Note

Customization to menus and toolbars can be saved in a template or file. To do so, first save them in a document and then save the document as a template as described in Chapter 3, Using Styles and Templates.

Customizing menu content

In addition to changing the menu font (described in Chapter 2, Setting up LibreOffice), you can add and rearrange categories on the menu bar, add commands to menus, and make other changes.

To customize menus:

1) Choose **Tools > Customize** to display the Customize dialog. Choose the **Menus** page (Figure 357).

Figure 357: The Menus page of the Customize dialog

2) In the upper left drop-down list, choose whether to save this changed menu for the application (for example, LibreOffice Writer) or for a selected document (for example, SampleDocument.odt).

3) In the section **LibreOffice [name of the program** (example: Writer)] **Menus**, select from the *Menu* drop-down list the menu that you want to customize. The list includes all the main menus as well as submenus (menus that are contained under another menu). For example, in addition to *File, Edit, View,* and so on, there is *File | Send* and *Edit | Changes.* The commands available for the selected menu are shown in the left part of the dialog.

4) To customize the selected menu, browse the left part of the dialog, where each line is a command. You can narrow the search by either typing the command in the upper left **Search** box or selecting the **Category** in the drop-down list.

5) Once the command found click on the right arrow at the center of the dialog box to add the command to the selected menu on the right. Use the up and down arrows on the far right to move the selected menu item to a different position.

6) When you have finished making all your changes, click **OK** to save them.

Creating a new menu

In the *Menus* page of the Customize dialog, click on the plus sign (**+**) to display the New Menu dialog (Figure 358).

1) Type a name for your new menu in the **Menu name** box.

2) Use the up and down arrow buttons to move the new menu into the required position on the menu bar.

3) Click **OK** to save.

The new menu now appears on the list of menus in the Customize dialog. (It will appear on the menu bar itself after you save your customizations.)

After creating a new menu, you need to add some commands to it, as described in "Adding a command to a menu" on page 373.

Figure 358: Adding a new menu

Modifying existing menus

To modify an existing menu, either user-made or inbuilt, select it in the *Menu* list and click the **Modify** button to drop down the **Rename** command. Proceed to enter a new name for the command to be displayed in the menu. To move a menu (such as *File*), use the up and down arrows on the right.

To move submenus (such as *File | Send*), select the main menu (**File**) in the Menu list and then, in the *Menu Content* section of the dialog, select the submenu (**Send**) in the *Entries* list and use the arrow keys to move it up or down in the sequence. Submenus are easily identified in the *Entries* list by a small black triangle on the right hand side of the name.

In addition to renaming, you can allocate a letter in a custom menu's name, which will become underlined, to be used as a keyboard shortcut, allowing you to select that menu by pressing *Alt+* that letter. Existing submenus can be edited to change the letter which is used to select their default shortcut.

1) Select a custom menu or a submenu in the *Menu* drop-down list.

2) Click the **Menu** button and select **Rename**.

3) Add a tilde (~) in front of the letter that you want to use as an accelerator. For example, to select the **Send** submenu command by pressing *S* (after opening the File menu using *Alt+F*), enter **~Send**. This changes it from the default *d*.

 Note

> It is possible to use a letter already in use in the menu list (for example, in the Insert menu, the letter *v* is used in *Envelope* and in *Movie and sound* as an accelerator). However, you should use an unused letter if possible, to make it simpler to navigate.

Adding a command to a menu

You can add commands to both the supplied menus and menus you have created. On the Customize dialog, select the menu in the *Menu* list.

Start choosing the command in the left pane of the Customize dialog (Figure 357) and click on the Right arrow to add it to the menu. Use the up and down arrows on the right to position the command in the menu list. To remove an unwanted entry of the current menu, select it in the right pane and click on the left arrow. Click **OK** to save your menu customization.

Modifying menu entries

In addition to changing the sequence of entries on a menu or submenu, you can add submenus, rename or delete the entries, and add group separators.

To begin, select the menu or submenu to be modified from the *Menu* list on the right. Click the **Modify** button to rename the entry. Click on the Let arrow to remove from the menu.

You can add menu separators, a horizontal line that takes the place of a command and is useful to group many related commands in a pseudo-section in the menu. To add a separator, highlight the command just below the position of the separator and then click on the Insert drop-down and choose **Insert separator.** The horizontal line will appear in the right pane of the menu.

Use the **Insert submenu** of the Insert button to add a submenu to your menu.

Customizing context menu contents

Context menus are a dynamic set of menus that displays different commands and options depending on the selected object in you document. For instance, the context menu of a table object is different from the context menu of a frame object.

To customize context menus:

1) Choose **Tools > Customize** to display the Customize dialog. Choose the **Context Menus** page (Figure 357, and the context menu tab is identical).

2) All procedures and options of the LibreOffice menus applies to the contexts menu.

Customizing toolbars

You can customize toolbars in several ways, including choosing which icons are visible and locking the position of a docked toolbar (as described in Chapter 1, Introducing LibreOffice), and adding or deleting icons (commands) in the list of those available on a toolbar. You can also create new toolbars. This section describes how to create new toolbars and add or delete icons on existing ones.

To get to the toolbar customization dialog (Figure 359), do any of the following:

- On the toolbar, right-click in the toolbar and choose **Customize Toolbar**.
- Choose **View > Toolbars > Customize** from the menu bar.
- Choose **Tools > Customize** from the menu bar and go to the *Toolbars* page.

Figure 359: The Toolbars page of the Customize dialog

Modifying existing toolbars

You will recognize the same dialog layout as for the menus. Indeed, the procedures for creating, modifying and deleting a toolbar are very similar (Figure 359).

To modify an existing toolbar:

1) In the upper right drop-down list, choose whether to save this changed toolbar for the application (for example, Writer) or for a selected document.

2) Just below, select from the *Toolbar* drop-down list the toolbar that you want to customize. The current toolbar content is displayed in the right pane below.

3) Select the commands on the right. You can narrow your search by performing a search on the top left search box or choosing a category in the drop-down list just below.

4) Click on the right arrow to add the command to the toolbar. Use the up and down arrows in the far right to position the command in the bar.

5) When you have finished making all your changes, click **OK** to save them.

Creating a new toolbar

To create a new toolbar:

1) Choose **Tools > Customize > Toolbars** from the menu bar.

2) Click on the plus sign (+) on the top right part of the dialog.

3) On the *Name* dialog (Figure 360), type the new toolbar's name and choose from the **Save In** drop-down list where to save this changed menu: for the application (for example, Writer) or for a selected document.

4) Click **OK**.

The new toolbar now appears on the list of toolbars in the Customize dialog. After creating a new toolbar, you need to add some commands to it, as described above.

Figure 360: Naming a new toolbar

Choosing icons for toolbar commands

Toolbar buttons usually have icons, not words, on them, but not all of the commands have associated icons.

To choose an icon for a command, select the command and click **Modify > Change icon**. On the Change Icon dialog, you can scroll through the available icons, select one, and click **OK** to assign it to the command (Figure 361).

Figure 361: Change Icon dialog

To use a custom icon, create it in a graphics program and import it into LibreOffice by clicking the **Import** button on the Change Icon dialog. Custom icons should be 16 x 16 pixels in size to achieve the best quality and should not contain more than 256 colors.

Assigning shortcut keys

In addition to using the built-in keyboard shortcuts (listed in Appendix A), you can define your own. You can assign shortcuts to standard LibreOffice functions or your own macros and save them for use with the entire LibreOffice suite.

 Caution

> Be careful when reassigning your operating system's or LibreOffice's predefined shortcut keys. Many key assignments are universally understood shortcuts, such as *F1* for Help, and are always expected to provide certain results. Although you can easily reset the shortcut key assignments to the LibreOffice defaults, changing some common shortcut keys can cause confusion, especially if other users share your computer.

To adapt shortcut keys to your needs, use the Customize dialog, as described below.

1) Select **Tools > Customize > Keyboard**. The Customize dialog (Figure 362) opens.

2) To have the shortcut key assignment available in all components of LibreOffice, select **LibreOffice** in the upper right.

3) Next select the required function from the *Category* and *Function* lists.

4) Now select the desired shortcut keys in the *Shortcut keys* list and click the **Modify** button.

5) Click **OK** to accept the change. Now the chosen shortcut keys will execute the function chosen in step 3 above whenever they are pressed.

 Note

> All existing shortcut keys for the currently selected *Function* are listed in the *Keys* selection box. If the *Keys* list is empty, it indicates that the chosen key combination is free for use. If it were not, and you wanted to reassign a shortcut key combination that is already in use, you must first delete the existing key.
>
> Shortcut keys that are grayed-out in the listing on the Customize dialog, such as *F1* and *F10*, are not available for reassignment.

Example: Assigning styles to shortcut keys

You can configure shortcut keys to quickly assign styles in your document. Some shortcuts are predefined, such as *Ctrl+0* for the *Text body* paragraph style, *Ctrl+1* for the *Heading 1* style, and *Ctrl+2* for *Heading 2*. You can modify these shortcuts and create your own.

1) Click **Tools > Customize > Keyboard**. The Keyboard page of the Customize dialog opens.

2) To have the shortcut key assignment available only with one component (for example, Writer), select that component's name in the upper right corner of the page; otherwise select **LibreOffice** to make it available to every component.

3) Choose the shortcut keys you want to assign a style to. In this example, we have chosen *Ctrl+9*. This enables the **Modify** button.

4) In the *Functions* section at the bottom of the dialog, scroll down in the *Category* list to *Styles*. Click the expansion symbol (usually a + sign or triangle) to expand the list of styles.

5) Choose the category of style. (This example uses a paragraph style, but you can also choose character styles and others.) The *Function* list will display the names of the available styles for the selected category. The example shows some of LibreOffice's predefined styles.

6) To assign *Ctrl+9* to be the shortcut key combination for the List 1 style, select *List 1* in the *Function* list, and then click **Modify**. *Ctrl+9* now appears in the *Keys* list on the right, and *List 1* appears next to *Ctrl+9* in the Shortcut keys box at the top.

7) Make any other required changes, and then click **OK** to save these settings and close the dialog.

Figure 362: Defining keyboard shortcuts for applying styles

 Warning

If you assign a custom style to a shortcut key, the shortcut will be effective only in documents that contains a custom style with the same name and family (paragraph, character, frame...). As consequence, a new default document may not have the custom style defined and the shortcut will apply a non-existing style.

Saving changes to a file

Changes to the shortcut key assignments can be saved in a keyboard configuration file for use a later time, thus permitting you to create and apply different configurations as the need arises, or in another way, create a standard keyboard configuration file to be distributed among many users in a company. To save keyboard shortcuts to a file:

1) After making your keyboard shortcut assignments, click the **Save** button at the right of the Customize dialog (Figure 362).

2) In the Save Keyboard Configuration dialog, select *All files* from the **Save as Type** list.

3) Next enter a name for the keyboard configuration file in the **File name** box, or select an existing file from the list. If you need to, browse to find a file from another location.

4) Click **Save**. A confirmation dialog appears if you are about to overwrite an existing file, otherwise there will be no feedback and the file will be saved.

Loading a saved keyboard configuration

To load a saved keyboard configuration file and replace your existing configuration, click the **Load** button at the right of the Customize dialog, and then select the configuration file from the Load Keyboard Configuration dialog.

Resetting the shortcut keys

To reset all of the keyboard shortcuts to their default values, click the **Reset** button near the bottom right of the Customize dialog. Use this feature with care as no confirmation dialog will be displayed; the defaults will be set without any further notice or user input.

Assigning macros to events

In LibreOffice, when something happens, we say that an event occurred. For example, a document was opened, a key was pressed, or the mouse moved. You can associate a macro with an event, so the macro is run when the event occurs. A common use is to assign the "open document" event to run a macro that performs certain setup tasks for the document.

To associate a macro with an event, use the Events page of the Customize dialog. For more information, see Chapter 13, Getting Started with Macros.

Adding functionality with extensions

An extension is a program that can be installed into LibreOffice to add new functionality and improve your productivity with LibreOffice. Template sets, spelling dictionaries, clipart galleries, macros, and dialog libraries can be packaged as LibreOffice extensions.

Several extensions are shipped bundled with LibreOffice and are installed with the program. These can only be removed by changing the installation options. Others can be downloaded from various websites. The official extension repository is located at https://extensions.libreoffice.org/. These extensions are free of charge.

Some extensions from other sources are free of charge; others are available for a fee. Check the descriptions to see what licenses and fees apply to the ones that interest you.

Download the extension to your computer in any folder that you want (Usually folder Download).

Installing extensions

Extensions can be installed in any of these ways:

- Directly from the *.oxt file in your system's file browser: double-click the file.
- From your web browser, if it can be configured to open this file type from a web page hyperlink: select the hyperlink, and then select to Open the file.

  In both cases, after the Extension Manager opens, a warning dialog opens for you to verify the installation and then continue. The file is installed as a "user only" file in a multi-user system.

- Directly from **Tools > Extension Manager**, as follows:

1) In LibreOffice, select **Tools > Extension Manager** from the menu bar. The option to view the extensions bundled with LibreOffice can be deselected to view more easily those installations that have been added by a user.
2) In the Extension Manager dialog (Figure 10), click **Add**.
3) A file browser window opens. Find and select the extension you want to install and click **Open**.

4) Users with administrator or root privileges will see a dialog where they can choose to install extensions "for all users" (**shared**) or "only for me" (**user**). Normal users without those privileges can install, remove, or modify extensions only for their own use (**user**).

In all cases, during the process you may be asked to accept a license agreement. When the installation is complete, the extension is listed in the Extension Manager dialog.

 Tip

To get extensions that are listed in the repository, you can open the Extension Manager and click the **Get more extensions online** link. You do not need to download them separately.

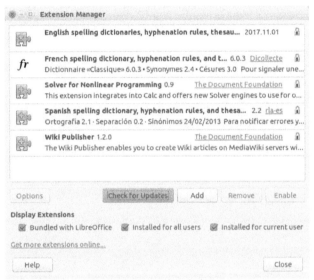

Figure 363: Extension Manager Main Window

Update extensions

Using the Check For Updates on the bottom of the main window of the Extension Manager, you can look for updates for the installed extensions, if there is any new version (Figure 364).

Figure 364: Extension Update Window

Removing and disabling extensions

You can remove whatever extension that you had installed. For this, select the extension in the main windows of Extension Manager and click the **Remove** button.

Finally you can disable an extension without uninstalling it, by selecting the extension in the main window of Extension Manager and clicking the button **Disable**. After that, the button Disable changes to Enable.

Getting Started Guide

Appendix A
Keyboard Shortcuts

Introduction

You can use LibreOffice without requiring a pointing device, such as a mouse or touchpad, by using its built-in keyboard shortcuts.

This appendix lists some of the most common built-in keyboard shortcuts that apply to all components of LibreOffice. For shortcuts specific to Writer, Calc, Impress, Draw, or Base, read the relevant component guide or search the application Help.

 Warning

> Some of the shortcuts listed here may not work if your operating system uses the same shortcuts for other tasks.

> To resolve any conflicts, assign different keys to these shortcuts by reconfiguring either LibreOffice (see Chapter 14) or your operating system (see system documentation).

Assistive tools in LibreOffice

In addition to keyboard shortcuts, LibreOffice supports some assistive technology tools like screen magnification software, screen readers, and on-screen keyboards. Please note that except for the Windows platform, accessibility support relies on Java technology for communications with assistive technology tools. This means that the first program startup may take a few seconds longer, because the Java runtime environment has to be started as well.

A current list of supported assistive tools can be found on the Wiki at http://wiki.documentfoundation.org/Accessibility.

Tip for Macintosh users

Some keystrokes are different on a Mac from those used in Windows and Linux. The following table gives some common substitutions for the instructions in this chapter. For a more detailed list, see the application Help.

Windows or Linux	Mac equivalent	Effect
Right-click	Control+click and/or right-click depending on computer setup	Open a context menu
Ctrl (Control)	⌘ (Command)	Used with other keys
F5	Shift+⌘+F5	Open the Navigator
F11	⌘+T	Open the Styles and Formatting window

Getting help

Shortcut Keys	Result
F1	Opens the LibreOffice Help contents in the user default browser. If the local Help package is not installed, LibreOffice opens the online Help located in http://help.libreoffice.org
Shift+F1	Turns the cursor into the *What's This?* question mark. Shows the tip for an item underneath the cursor. The shortcut does not work with the online help.
Shift+F2	Shows tip for a selected item. The shortcut does not work with the online help.
Esc	In LibreOffice Help: goes up one level. For Help online, the key is handled by the browser.

General keyboard shortcuts

Opening menus and menu items

Shortcut Keys	Result
Alt+<?>	Opens a menu where <?> is the underlined character of the menu you want to open. For example, *Alt+F* opens the menu **File.** With the menu open, you will again find underlined characters. You can access these menu items directly by pressing the underlined character key. Where two menu items have the same underlined character, press the character key again to move to the next item. Example: to access the **Printer Settings** item of the **File** menu after opening it, press *R* twice to move from the initial **Digital Signatures** selection to **Printer Settings.** There may be instances where an item in a menu has no underlined character. This will have to be clicked directly.
Esc	Closes an open menu.
F6	Repeatedly pressing *F6* switches the focus and circles through the following objects: • Menu bar • Every toolbar from top to bottom and from left to right • Every free window from left to right • Document
Shift+F6	Switches through objects in the opposite direction.
Ctrl+F6	Switches the focus to the document.
F10 or Alt	Switches to the Menu bar and back.
Esc	Closes an open menu.

Accessing a menu command

Press *Alt* or *F6* or *F10* to select the first item on the menu bar (the **File** menu). With the *right-arrow*, the next menu to the right is selected; with the *left-arrow*, the previous menu. The *Home* and *End* keys select the first and the last item on the Menu bar.

The *down-arrow* opens a selected menu. An additional *down-arrow* or *up-arrow* moves the selection through the menu commands. The *right-arrow* opens any existing submenus.

Press *Enter* to run the selected menu command.

Running a toolbar command

Press *F6* repeatedly until the first icon on the toolbar is selected. Use the right and left arrows to select any icon on a horizontal toolbar. Similarly, use the up and down arrows to select any icon on a vertical toolbar. The *Home* key selects the first icon on a toolbar, and the *End* key the last.

 Note

If the first object in the toolbar has an editable text field, like the **Load URL** or the **Paragraph Style**, the *Home*, *End*, *Left* and *Right* keys work on the text instead.

Press *Enter* to run the selected icon. If the selected icon normally demands a consecutive mouse action, such as inserting a rectangle, then pressing the *Enter* key is not sufficient: in these cases press *Ctrl+Enter*.

Press *Ctrl+Enter* on an icon for creating a draw object. A draw object will be placed into the middle of the view, with a predefined size.

Press *Ctrl+Enter* on the Selection tool to select the first draw object in the document. If you want to edit, size, or move the selected draw object, first use *Ctrl+F6* to move the focus into the document.

Navigating and selecting with the keyboard

You can navigate through a document and make selections with the keyboard.

* To move the cursor, press the key or key combination given in the following table.
* To select the characters under the moving cursor, additionally hold down the *Shift* key when you move the cursor.

Key	Function	Plus Ctrl key
Right, left arrow keys	Moves the cursor one character to the left or to the right.	Moves the cursor one word to the left or to the right.
Up, down arrow keys	Moves the cursor up or down one line.	(Ctrl+Alt) Moves the cursor up or down one paragraph.
Home	Moves the cursor to the beginning of the current line.	Moves the cursor to the beginning of the document.
End	Moves the cursor to the end of the current line.	Moves the cursor to the end of the document.
PgUp	Scrolls up one page.	Moves the cursor to the header.
PgDn	Scroll down one page.	Moves the cursor to the footer.

Controlling dialogs

When you open any dialog, one element (such as a button, an option field, an entry in a list box, or a checkbox) is highlighted or indicated by a dotted box around the field or button name. This element is said to have the focus on it.

Shortcut Keys	Result
Enter	Activates selected button. In most cases where no button is selected, *Enter* is equivalent to clicking **OK**.
Esc	Closes dialog without saving any changes made while it was open. In most cases, *Esc* is equivalent to clicking Cancel. When an open drop-down list is selected, *Esc* closes the list.
Spacebar	Checks an empty checkbox. Clears a checked checkbox.
Up, down arrow keys	Moves focus up and down a list. Increases or decreases value of a variable. Moves focus vertically within a section of dialog.
Left, right arrow keys	Moves focus horizontally within a section of a dialog.
Tab	Advances focus to the next section or element of a dialog.
Shift+Tab	Returns focus to the previous section or element in a dialog.
Alt+Down Arrow	Shows items in a drop-down list.

Controlling macros

Shortcut Keys	Result
Ctrl+* (multiplication sign: on number pad only)	Runs a macro field. (See Chapter 9 for more about macros.)
Shift+Ctrl+Q	Stops a running macro.

Managing documents

Shortcut Keys	Result
Ctrl+F4 or Alt+F4	Closes the current document. Closes LibreOffice when the last open document is closed.
Ctrl+O	Launches the Open dialog to open a document.
Ctrl+S	Saves the current document. If you are working on a previously unsaved file, the shortcut launches the Save As dialog.
Ctrl+N	Creates a new document.
Shift+Ctrl+N	Opens the Templates and Documents dialog.
Ctrl+P	Opens the Print dialog to print the document.
Ctrl+Q	Closes the application.
Del	In the Save and Open dialogs, deletes the selected files or folders. Items can be retrieved from the Recycle Bin (Trash), if your desktop has one.
Shift+Del	In the Save and Open dialogs, deletes the selected files or folders. Items are permanently deleted: they can not be retrieved from the Recycle Bin.
Backspace	In the Save and Open dialogs, shows contents of the current directory's parent folder.

Editing

Shortcut Keys	Result
Ctrl+X, Shift+Del	Cuts selected items.
Ctrl+C, Ctrl+Ins	Copies selected items to the clipboard.
Ctrl+V, Shift+Ins	Pastes copied or cut items from the clipboard.
Ctrl+Shift+V	Opens the Paste Special dialog.
Ctrl+A	Selects all.
Ctrl+Z	Undoes last action.
Ctrl+Y	Redoes last action.
Ctrl+Shift+Y	Repeats last command.
Ctrl+F	Opens the Find dialog
Ctrl+H	Opens the Find & Replace dialog.
Ctrl+Shift+F	Searches for the last entered search term.
Ctrl+Shift+R	Refreshes (redraws) the document view.
Ctrl+Shift+I	Shows or hides the cursor in read-only text.

Selecting rows and columns in a database table opened by Ctrl+Shift+F4

Shortcut keys	Result
Spacebar	Toggles row selection, except when the row is in edit mode.
Ctrl+Spacebar	Toggles row selection.
Shift+Spacebar	Selects the current column.
Ctrl+Page Up	Moves pointer to the first row.
Ctrl+Page Down	Moves pointer to the last row.

Shortcut keys for drawing objects

Shortcut keys	Result
Select the toolbar with F6. Use the Down Arrow and Right Arrow to select the desired toolbar icon and press Ctrl+Enter.	Inserts a Drawing Object.
Select the document with Ctrl+F6 and press Tab.	Selects a Drawing Object.
Tab	Selects the next Drawing Object.
Shift+Tab	Selects the previous Drawing Object.
Ctrl+Home	Selects the first Drawing Object.
Ctrl+End	Selects the last Drawing Object.
Esc	Ends Drawing Object selection.
Esc (in Handle Selection Mode)	Exit Handle Selection Mode and return to Object Selection Mode.
Up/Down/Left/Right Arrow	Move the selected point (the snap-to-grid functions are temporarily disabled, but end points still snap to each other).
Alt+Up/Down/Left/Right Arrow	Moves the selected Drawing Object one pixel (in Selection Mode).
	Re-sizes a Drawing Object (in Handle Selection Mode).
	Rotates a Drawing Object (in Rotation Mode).
	Opens the properties dialog for a Drawing Object.
	Activates the Point Selection mode for the selected drawing object.
Spacebar	Select a point of a drawing object (in Point Selection mode) / Cancel selection.
	The selected point blinks once per second.
Shift+Spacebar	Select an additional point in Point Selection mode.
Ctrl+Tab	Select the next point of the drawing object (Point Selection mode).
	In Rotation mode, the center of rotation can also be selected.
Ctrl+Shift+Tab	Select the previous point of the drawing object (Point Selection mode).
Ctrl+Enter	A new drawing object with default size is placed in the center of the current view.
Ctrl+Enter at the Selection icon	Activates the first drawing object in the document.

Esc	Leave the Point Selection mode. The drawing object is selected afterwards.
	Edit a point of a drawing object (Point Edit mode).
Any text or numerical key	If a drawing object is selected, switches to edit mode and places the cursor at the end of the text in the drawing object. A printable character is inserted.
Alt key while creating or scaling a graphic object	The position of the object's center is fixed.
Shift key while creating or scaling a graphic object	The ratio of the object's width to height is fixed.

Defining keyboard shortcuts

In addition to using the built-in keyboard shortcuts listed in this Appendix, you can define your own. See Chapter 14, Customizing LibreOffice, for instructions.

Further reading

For help with LibreOffice's keyboard shortcuts, or using LibreOffice with a keyboard only, search the application Help using the "shortcut keys" or "accessibility" keywords.

Getting Started Guide

Appendix B
Open Source,
Open Standards,
OpenDocument

Introduction

LibreOffice is a productivity suite that is compatible with other major office suites and available on a variety of platforms. It is open source software and therefore free to download, use, and distribute. If you are new to LibreOffice, this appendix will provide some information regarding its history, its community, and some of its technical specifications.

A short history of LibreOffice

The OpenOffice.org project began when Sun Microsystems released the source code ("blueprints") for its StarOffice® software to the open source community on October 13, 2000. OpenOffice.org 1.0, the product, was released on April 30, 2002. Major updates to OpenOffice.org included version 2.0 in October 2005 and version 3.0 in October 2008. On January 26, 2010, Oracle Corporation acquired Sun Microsystems.

On September 28, 2010, the community of volunteers who develop and promote OpenOffice.org announce a major change in project structure. After ten years' successful growth with Sun Microsystems as founding and principle sponsor, the project launched an independent foundation called The Document Foundation, to fulfill the promise of independence written in the original charter. This foundation is the cornerstone of a new ecosystem where individuals and organizations can contribute to and benefit from the availability of a truly free office suite.

Unable to acquire the trademarked OpenOffice.org name from Oracle Corporation, The Document Foundation named its product LibreOffice. Continuing the version numbers from OpenOffice.org, LibreOffice 3.3 was released in January 2011 and version 6.0 was release in February 2018.

In February 2012, The Document Foundation was incorporated in Berlin as a German Stiftung. You can read more about The Document Foundation at: http://www.documentfoundation.org/

The LibreOffice community

The Document Foundation's mission is:

"...to facilitate the evolution of the OpenOffice.org Community into a new open, independent, and meritocratic organizational structure within the next few months. An independent Foundation is a better match to the values of our contributors, users, and supporters, and will enable a more effective, efficient, transparent, and inclusive Community. We will protect past investments by building on the solid achievements of our first decade, encourage wide participation in the Community, and co-ordinate activity across the Community."

Some of our corporate supporters include Canonical, The GNOME Foundation, Google, Novell and Red Hat. Additionally, over 450,000 people from nearly every part of the globe have joined this project with the idea of creating the best possible office suite that all can use. This is the essence of an "open source" community!

With its open source software license, LibreOffice is key in the drive to provide an office suite that is available to anyone, anywhere, for commercial or personal use. The software has been translated into many languages and runs on all major operating systems. New functionality can be added in the form of extensions.

The LibreOffice community invites contributors in all areas, including translators, software developers, graphic artists, technical writers, editors, donors, and end-user support. Whatever you do best, you can make a difference in LibreOffice. The community operates internationally in all time zones and in many languages, linked through the internet at www.libreoffice.org and www.documentfoundation.org.

How is LibreOffice licensed?

LibreOffice is distributed under both the Mozilla Public License (MPL) 2.0 (https://www.libreoffice.org/about-us/licenses/) and the GNU Lesser General Public License (LGPL) 3.0+ (https://www.gnu.org/licenses/lgpl-3.0.en.html).

What is "open source"?

The four essential rights of open-source software are embodied within the Free Software Foundation's family of the *GNU General Public License* (GPL):

- The right to use the software for any purpose.
- Freedom to redistribute the software for free or for a fee.
- Access to the complete source code of the program (that is, the "blueprints").
- The right to modify any part of the source, or use portions of it in other programs.

The basic idea behind open source is very simple: When programmers can read, redistribute, and modify the source code for a piece of software, the software evolves. People improve it, people adapt it, people fix bugs.

For more information on Free and Open Source software, visit these websites:

Open Source Initiative (OSI): http://www.opensource.org

Free Software Foundation (FSF): https:///www.fsf.org

What are "open standards"?

An open standard provides a means of doing something that is independent of manufacturer or vendor, thus enabling competing software programs to freely use the same file formats. HTML, XML, and ODF are examples of open standards for documents.

An open standard meets the following requirements:

- It is well documented with the complete specification publicly available, either free or at a nominal charge.
- It can be freely copied, distributed and used. The intellectual property of the standard is made irrevocably available on a royalty-free basis.
- It is standardized and maintained in an independent, open forum (also called "standards organization") using an open process.

What is OpenDocument?

OpenDocument (ODF) is an XML-based file format for office documents (text documents, spreadsheets, drawings, presentations and more), developed at OASIS (http://www.oasis-open.org/who/), an independent, international standards group. OpenDocument version 1.2 was adopted by the International Standards Organization and named ISO IEC 26300:2015 standard[2].

Unlike other file formats, ODF (ISO-IEC 26300:2015) is an open standard. It is publicly available, royalty-free, and without legal or other restrictions; therefore ODF files are not tied to a specific office suite and anybody can build a program that interprets these files. For this reason ODF is quickly becoming the preferred file format for government agencies, schools and other companies who prefer not to be too dependent on any one software supplier.

---

2   http://www.iso.org/iso/catalogue_detail.htm?csnumber=66363

LibreOffice saves documents in OpenDocument Format by default. LibreOffice 3 adopted version 1.2 of the OpenDocument standard and LibreOffice 6 continues to use this standard. LibreOffice can also open and save many other file formats, as summarized below.

For a full list of file formats that LibreOffice can read and write, see https://en.wikipedia.org/wiki/LibreOffice#Supported_file_formats

OpenDocument filename extensions

The most common filename extensions used for OpenDocument documents are:

- *.odt for word processing (text) documents
- *.ods for spreadsheets
- *.odp for presentations
- *.odb for databases
- *.odg for graphics (vector drawings)
- *.odc for charts
- *.odf for formulas (scientific formulas and equations)

File formats LibreOffice can open

LibreOffice can open a wide variety of file formats in addition to the OpenDocument formats, including Portable Document Format (PDF).

Opening text documents

In addition to OpenDocument formats (.odt, .ott, .oth, .odm, and .fodt), Writer can open the formats used by OpenOffice.org 1.x (.sxw, .stw, and .sxg), the following text document formats, and a variety of legacy formats not listed below:

Microsoft Word 6.0/95/97/2000/XP/Mac) (.doc and .dot)	
Microsoft Word 2003 XML (.xml)	
Microsoft Word 2007/2010 XML (.docx, .docm, .dotx, .dotm)	
Microsoft WinWord 5 (.doc)	WordPerfect Document (.wpd)
Microsoft Works (.wps)	Lotus WordPro (.lwp)
Abiword Document (.abw, .zabw)	ClarisWorks/Appleworks Document (.cwk)
MacWrite Document (.mw, .mcw)	Rich Text Format (.rtf)
Text CSV (.csv and .txt)	StarWriter formats (.sdw, .sgl, .vor)
DocBook (.xml)	Unified Office Format text (.uot, .uof)
Ichitaro 8/9/10/11 (.jtd and .jtt)	Hangul WP 97 (.hwp)
T602 Document (.602, .txt)	eBook (.pdb)
Apple Pages 4 (.pages)	HTML Document (.htm, .html)
... and many others	

Most of these file types are automatically detected by LibreOffice, so they can be opened without explicitly selecting the document type in the file picker.

When opening .htm or .html files (used for web pages), LibreOffice customizes Writer for working with these files.

Opening spreadsheets

In addition to OpenDocument formats (.ods, .ots, and .fods), Calc can open the formats used by OpenOffice.org 1.x (.sxc and .stc) and the following spreadsheet formats:

> Microsoft Excel 97/2000/XP (.xls, .xlw, and .xlt)
> Microsoft Excel 4.x–5.0/95 (.xls, .xlw, and .xlt)
> Microsoft Excel 2003 XML (.xml)
> Microsoft Excel 2007/2013 XML (.xlsx, .xlsm, .xlts, .xltm)
> Microsoft Excel 2007/2010 binary (.xlsb)
> Lotus 1-2-3 (.wk1, .wks, and .123)
> Data Interchange Format (.dif)
> Rich Text Format (.rtf)
> Text CSV (.csv and .txt)
> StarCalc formats (.sdc and .vor)
> dBASE (.dbf)
> SYLK (.slk)
> Unified Office Format spreadsheet (.uos, .uof)
> HTML Document (.htm and .html files, including Web page queries)
> Quattro Pro 6.0 (.wb2)
> Apple Numbers 2 (.numbers)
> ... and many others

Opening presentations

In addition to OpenDocument formats (.odp, .odg, .otp, and .fopd), Impress can open the formats used by OpenOffice.org 1.x (.sxi and .sti) and the following presentation formats:

> Microsoft PowerPoint 97/2000/XP (.ppt and .pot)
> Microsoft PowerPoint 2007/2010 (.pptx, .pptm, .potx, .potm)
> StarDraw and StarImpress (.sda, .sdd, .sdp, and .vor)
> Unified Office Format presentation (.uop, .uof)
> CGM – Computer Graphics Metafile (.cgm)
> Portable Document Format (.pdf)
> Apple Keynote 5 (.key)
> ... and many others

Opening graphic files

In addition to OpenDocument formats (.odg and .otg), Draw can open the formats used by OpenOffice.org 1.x (.sxd and .std) and the following graphic formats:

> Adobe Photoshop (*.psd)
> AutoCAD Interchange Format (*.dxf)
> Corel Draw (*.cdr)
> Corel Presentation Exchange (*.cmx)
> Microsoft Publisher 98-2010 (*.pub)
> Microsoft Visio 2000-2013 (*.vdx; *.vsd; *.vsdm; *.vsdx)
> WordPerfect Graphics (*.wpg)

BMP	JPEG, JPG	PCX	PSD	SGV	WMF
DXF	MET	PGM	RAS	SVM	XBM
EMF	PBM	PLT	SDA	TGA	XPM
EPS	PCD	PNG	SDD	TIF, TIFF	
GIF	PCT	PPM	SGF	VOR	

Opening formula files

In addition to OpenDocument Formula (.odf) files, Math can open the format used by OpenOffice.org 1.x (.sxm), StarMath, (.smf), and MathML (.mml) files.

When opening a Word document that contains an embedded equation editor object, if the option for it (MathType to LibreOffice Math or reverse) is checked in **Tools > Options > Load/Save > Microsoft Office**, the object will be automatically converted to a LibreOffice Math object.

File formats LibreOffice can save to

Saving in an OpenDocument format guarantees the correct rendering of the file when it is transferred to another person or when the file is reopened with a later version of LibreOffice or with another program. It is strongly recommended that you use OpenDocument as the default file formats. However, you can save files in other formats, if you wish.

 Tip

> When sharing a document that you do not expect the recipient to modify, the preferred option is to convert the document to PDF. LibreOffice provides a very straightforward way to convert documents to PDF. See Chapter 10 Printing, Exporting, and E-Mailing in this guide.

Saving text documents

In addition to OpenDocument formats (.odt, .ott, and .fodt), Writer can save in these formats:

Office Open XML Text (.docx)
Microsoft Word 97–2003 (.doc)
Rich Text Format (.rtf)
Text Encoded (.txt)
HTML Document (.html and .htm)

Microsoft Word 2007–2013 XML (.docx)
Microsoft Word 2003 XML (.xml)
Text (.txt)
Unified Office Format text (.uot, .uof)
DocBook (.xml)

Encryption support within the Microsoft Word 97/2000/XP filter allows password protected Microsoft Word documents to be saved.

 Note

> The .rtf format is a common format for transferring text files between applications, but you are likely to experience loss of formatting and images. For this reason, other formats should be used.

Saving spreadsheet files

In addition to OpenDocument formats (.ods and .ots), Calc can save in these formats:

Office Open XML Spreadsheet (.xlsx)
Microsoft Excel 2007–2013 XML (.xlsx)
Microsoft Excel 97–2003 (.xls and .xlw)
Microsoft Excel 97–2003 Template (.xlt)
Microsoft Excel 2003 XML (.xml)
HTML Document (Calc) (.html and .htm)

Data Interchange Format (.dif)
dBase (.dbf)
SYLK (.slk)
Text CSV (.csv and .txt)
Unified Office Format spreadsheet (.uos)

Saving presentations

In addition to OpenDocument formats (.odp, .otp, .fodp, and .odg), Impress can save in these formats:

Microsoft PowerPoint 97–2003 (.ppt)
Microsoft PowerPoint 97–2003 Template (.pot)
Microsoft PowerPoint 97–2003 AutoPlay (.pps)
Microsoft PowerPoint 2007–2013 XML (.pptx, .potm)
Microsoft PowerPoint 2007–2013 XML AutoPlay (.ppsx)
Office Open XML Presentation (.pptx, .potm, .ppsx)
Unified Office Format presentation (.uop)

Impress can also export to MacroMedia Flash (.swf) and any of the graphics formats listed for Draw.

Saving drawings

Draw can only save in the OpenDocument Drawing formats (.odg, .otg, and .fodg), the OpenOffice.org 1.x formats (.sxd and .std) and StarDraw format (.sda, .sdd, and .vor).

However, Draw can also export to BMP, EMF, EPS, GIF, JPEG, MET, PBM, PCT, PGM, PNG, PPM, RAS, SVG, SVM, TIFF, WMF, and XPM.

Writer/Web can save in these formats

HTML document (.html and .htm), as HTML 4.0 Transitional
Text and Text Encoded (LibreOffice Writer/Web) (.txt)

Exporting to other formats

Different from the command **Save as**, LibreOffice uses the term "export" to create a new file with another format without leaving the current content and file format. If you cannot find the file type you are looking for under **Save As**, look under **Export** for additional types.

PDF is the well known export format since OpenOffice.org 1.5 and EPUB is a new format for export since LibreOffice 6.0.

LibreOffice can export files to HTML and XHTML. To publish on a Wiki server, export the documents with MediaWiki (.txt) format. In addition, Draw and Impress can export to Adobe Flash (.swf) and a range of image formats.

To export to one of these formats, choose **File > Export**. On the Export dialog, specify a file name for the exported document, then select the desired format in the *File format* list and click the **Export** button.

Lightning Source UK Ltd.
Milton Keynes UK
UKHW010720250520
363803UK00001B/37